The Shi'is of Iraq

The Shi'is of Iraq

WITH A NEW INTRODUCTION BY THE AUTHOR

Yitzhak Nakash

PRINCETON UNIVERSITY PRESS

PRINCETON AND OXFORD

Copyright © 1994 by Princeton University Press
Published by Princeton University Press, 41 William Street,
Princeton, New Jersey 08540
In the United Kingdom: Princeton University Press,
3 Market Place, Woodstock, Oxfordshire OX20 1SY

First paperback edition, 1995

Second paperback edition, with a new introduction, 2003

Library of Congress Control Number 2002115083

ISBN 0-691-11575-3

British Library Cataloging-in-Publication Data is available

This book has been composed in Linotron Sabon

Printed on acid-free paper. ∞

www.pupress.princeton.edu

Printed in the United States of America

3   5   7   9   10   8   6   4   2

To my parents
And to Beth, Neta, and Talya

In his attitude he is an Arab,
a Muslim in his plea,
and by creed he is a Shiʻi.
He strives for the Arab character of Islam,
advocates Islam for Muslim unity,
and he views his Shiʻi creed as a gift.

ʻAli al-Khaqani, *Shuʻaraʼ al-ghari aw al-najafiyyat*,
2d ed., 12 vols. (Qum, 1988), 5:506.

CONTENTS

PREFACE

MY INTEREST in writing on the Shi'is of Iraq grew out of the Iran-Iraq War of 1980–1988, when like other observers I was puzzled by the fierce fighting between Shi'is of Iran and their coreligionists of Iraq, who were said to form the majority of the rank and file of the Iraqi infantry. As I began studying Iranian and Iraqi Shi'ism more closely, I was intrigued by the role of culture and society in shaping different patterns of religious and political development among Shi'is. This book is the result of my attempt to examine these issues in the context of related economic and political factors.

The department of Near Eastern Studies at Princeton University provided me with a home where I pursued the preparation, much of the research, and the writing of both this book as well as the dissertation from which it evolved. I would like to acknowledge the financial assistance which I received from the Center of International Studies and the Council on Regional Studies at Princeton, as well as from ISEF and the American Historical Association. I am indebted to the many gracious librarians and archivists who facilitated my research in institutions in the U.S., Germany, India, and England. I would like to mention in particular the kind hospitality at the University of Köln and the assistance of Werner Diem and Amir Arjomand. My research in New Delhi was greatly aided by the invaluable assistance of R. K. Perty, Director of the National Archives of India, and the efficiency of Ms. M. Kapoor and Mr. J. C. Dabi. Thanks are also due to the Controller, H. M. Stationary Office in England, for permission to quote crown copyright material in the Public Record Office and the India Office in London.

It was a pleasure working with the Princeton University Press staff. Walter H. Lippincott, Director of the Press, was an enthusiastic supporter from the very start, and, together with his assistant Mary Guillemette, saw the work through the various stages of production. My copyeditor Bill Laznovsky polished the rough edges of the book with meticulous care. Other associates at the Press were also unfailingly helpful, doing their best to bring the book to a safe shore in a timely fashion.

A number of people shared with me their intellectual wisdom, thus helping me to formulate my own thinking. I benefited from the sound advice which L. C. Brown, Ulrich Haarmann, Charles Issawi, Joseph Kostiner, Ezra Suleiman, and Avrom Udovitch were always willing to offer. My understanding of Shi'i Islam and Iraqi society and politics improved significantly following informative discussions with Abbas Amanat, Amatzia Baram, Juan Cole, Werner Ende, the late Elie Kedourie, Etan Kohlberg, Meir Litvak, and Peter Sluglett and Marion Farouk-Sluglett. John Waterbury introduced me to major relevant topics in the social sciences and critiqued an early version of the book. Abbas Kelidar also read a draft, giving me more time and advice than I had any right to expect. I owe a particularly deep gratitude to Michael Cook, who read the many drafts of the book and saw the project through completion. This book would have been significantly poorer without his insightful ideas and stimulating thinking.

INTRODUCTION
to the 2003 Paperback Edition

MORE THAN A DECADE after the Gulf War of 1991 America is on the brink of a new war with Iraq. September 11, 2001, has changed the U.S. administration's view of the world, or at least its way of handling it, and prompted President Bush to declare a war against terrorism and against states that harbor terrorism. The collapse of the Taliban regime in Afghanistan has thus redirected the administration's attention toward Iraq—a country that the United States did not entirely defeat in the Gulf War, and which the administration has accused of training members of the al-Qaeda terrorist network.

Iraq's leader, Saddam Husayn, has defied all those who predicted in the wake of the Gulf War that his days in office were numbered. While his Ba'th regime regained much of its prewar coercive domestic power, the Iraqi leader has played a game of chicken with the United States and the international community, intending to get a timetable from the United Nations for ending its weapons inspections and for lifting sanctions against Iraq. I described the early stages of Saddam's reassertion of power in the epilogue to this book, written in October 1993. In the period since then Saddam has further consolidated power and frustrated the attempts of three U.S. administrations to undermine his rule and keep him "boxed in."

In October 1994 Saddam moved Iraqi army units, including the elite Hammurabi division, which had escaped destruction in the Gulf War, toward the Kuwaiti border. This threatening deployment of Iraqi forces prompted President Clinton to dispatch navy and marine units to the Persian Gulf to force the Iraqi leader to withdraw his troops. Although in 1994 Saddam backed down, two years later he again demonstrated his resolve and signaled to his people and to the international community who was boss in Iraq. In late August 1996 Saddam invaded the Kurdish safe haven in northern Iraq established by the United States and its allies after the Gulf War. In one stroke he managed to destroy the infrastructure of an entire C.I.A. operation intended to topple the Iraqi leader. The handful of C.I.A. clandestine officers overseeing this covert operation fled the country. Hundreds of Iraqi opposition members were killed by Saddam's troops, and thousands more were arrested or driven into exile. By the time his troops retreated from the city of Erbil in early September, Saddam had regained substantial influence over an area he had been yearning to recover since the Gulf War. Saddam also succeeded in creating a rift within the allied coalition. Arab governments viewed his excursion to the north as a legitimate Iraqi government attempt to reassert its sovereignty over the Kurdish area. And France, Russia, and China—permanent members of the U.N. Security Council and once important trading partners with Baghdad—indicated that the strict economic sanctions against Iraq should be reviewed.

In subsequent years Saddam acted to isolate the Clinton and Bush administrations, and he managed to drive a wedge between the United States and the international community over the question of how to deal with the Iraqi leader. On several occasions during 1997 and 1998 Saddam broke off cooperation with U.N. weapons inspectors and forced the Clinton administration to rely on Russian and other face-saving solutions so as to avert a serious confrontation. In September 1998, a few months after U.N. Secretary-General Kofi Annan clinched a deal with Saddam allowing the return of weapons inspectors to Iraq, the Iraqi leader refused to permit spot arms checks. Several months later Iraq halted arms monitoring altogether—a move that led to the disbanding of the United Nations Special Commission overseeing the disarmament of Iraq. Emboldened by his success in blocking weapons inspections, Saddam ordered his government in November 1999 to cut off the oil Iraq was allowed to export in exchange for food, sending crude oil prices to a nine-year high of $27 a barrel. The pressure the Iraqi leader put on the international community found embodiment in a U.N. Security Council resolution in mid-November promising Saddam that sanctions against Iraq could be suspended within a year if he resumed cooperation with weapons inspectors. Saddam rejected this proposal. He also rejected a U.N. offer backed by the Clinton administration to allow Iraq to buy more goods with its oil, demanding instead an immediate and unconditional lifting of all sanctions against Iraq.

By the time the Bush administration took office in January 2001, it was clear that U.S. policy toward Iraq, built on sanctions and containment, had failed to undermine Saddam's grip on power. President Clinton inherited an enemy whom his predecessor in the White House had equated with Hitler. But during its eight years in power the Clinton administration vacillated on its policy on Iraq; it let the Iraq issue slip into the middle distance, in part because of the president's fixation on the grand prize of a broader Middle East peace between Israel and its Arab neighbors. Starving Iraq for eleven years has not subverted Saddam Husayn. Striking at his army bases with cruise missiles has not toppled him. Sanctions have slowed his drive to build nuclear, biological, and chemical weapons, but have not stopped it. All this was known to the Bush administration when it took office. Yet it was not until the terrorist attacks of September 11, 2001, that President Bush made Iraq a top priority of U.S. foreign policy.

As these lines were written in November 2002, the president pledged to take action against Saddam Husayn. The administration obtained congressional and senatorial approval authorizing President Bush to use military force against Iraq. On November 8 it led the U.N. Security Council in adopting a resolution giving Iraq a "final opportunity" to surrender its weapons of mass destruction, or face "serious consequences." Iraq was given seven days to accept the resolution and pledge its compliance, and thirty days to produce a full and accurate list of its nuclear, chemical, and biological programs as well as its secret ballistic missile developments. It remains to be seen how Iraq will respond to this resolution, and what course of action the Bush administration will pursue in dealing with Saddam Husayn in the months ahead.

The standoffs between Iraq and the United States in the period since the Gulf War have overshadowed the suffering of ordinary Iraqis, many of whom were reduced to the level of bare subsistence. While Baghdad is rebuilt with glittering new palaces and imposing new statues of Saddam Husayn, elsewhere in the city and in the country there is another story—of children begging wretchedly in the streets for their families, of parents selling their valuables to buy food for their children. The economic collapse of Iraq has gutted the intelligentsia, once one of the most respected in the Arab world. A famous Iraqi playwright, who was forced to work in a kiosk selling cigarettes and soda after the collapse of the entertainment industry, told Youssef Ibrahim of *The New York Times* in 1998: "What matters now is survival. What you do to make money carries no value in itself anymore. Our society and our sense of values have changed." The Iraqi middle class has indeed suffered greatly in the past ten years, and very little is heard of the poor classes, whose members must be in even worse condition. For ordinary Iraqis, sanctions have meant an almost surreal descent into a poverty they believe they do not deserve. A retired office worker told Stephen Kinzer of *The New York Times* in 1999: "First I sold my television, then my car, then my house. Everything that I built up over a lifetime is gone. A bomb can kill you in a second, but sanctions kill you everyday." The people who matter in Iraq today, other than Saddam Husayn, are the buyers and sellers of prohibited goods—the smugglers and business tycoons with connections to Saddam or to one of his two sons, Uday and Qusay.

Many of those Iraqis who have suffered under sanctions are Shi'is, belonging to the community whose history is discussed in this book. Shi'is are a majority of 55 to 60 percent in Iraq, but they have been dominated by a Sunni minority elite since the establishment of modern

Iraq in 1921. The claim of Sunnis to rule Iraq has been backed by the preponderance of Sunnis over Shi'is in the wider Arab world and by the support of Arab Sunni leaders, including the rulers of Saudi Arabia, who have viewed Shi'ism as heresy and have felt more comfortable with Sunni rule next door. In the event of a U.S. war with Iraq, the Shi'is could play a major role in national politics in a new Iraq after the fall of Saddam Husayn.

The Shi'is of Iraq sheds light on a political community marked by its own distinct identity—people who are not necessarily the precursors of a radical Islamic state that would align itself with Iran. This book shows that the Iraqi Shi'is are by and large Arabs, and recent converts to Shi'ism; their conversion took place mainly during the nineteenth century as the bulk of Iraq's Arab nomadic tribes settled down and took up agriculture. These tribesmen, both those who converted to Shi'ism and those who remained Sunni largely because they kept to their desert way of life, still share Arab social codes and cultural attributes. This suggests that behind the power struggle between Arab Sunnis and Shi'is in modern Iraq there exist two sectarian groups that are in fact quite similar. The tension fueling the sectarian problem between Sunnis and Shi'is is thus primarily political rather than ethnic or cultural, and it reflects the competition of the two groups over the right to rule and to define the meaning of nationalism in the country. The book also shows that Iraqi Shi'ism is radically different from its Iranian counterpart, not in its formal doctrine, but in the way it has interacted with politics and the economy. These differences between Iraqi and Iranian Shi'ism help explain why twenty-three years after the Iranian Islamic revolution, the large majority of Iraqi Shi'is have not been swayed by it, and why they have continued to show allegiance to Iraq in spite of their discontent with Saddam Husayn and his Ba'th regime.

I described in the epilogue the Shi'i uprising against Saddam Husayn in the wake of the Gulf War, which was encouraged by the first Bush administration, as well as Saddam's brutal suppression of this uprising after the administration ruled out action to help the rebels. In the period since the uprising Saddam has moved to pacify the Shi'is, and he rebuilt those areas surrounding Shi'i shrines in Najaf and Karbala that his army had destroyed in 1991. Yet at the same time, Saddam continued to check all signs of Shi'i opposition to his rule. The Iraqi leader sanctioned a series of killings of Shi'i clerics in Iraq that culminated in 1999 with the assassination of Iraq's leading Shi'i religious leader, Muhammad Sadiq al-Sadr. Although in 1992 the Iraqi government had acknowledged Sadr's standing as the leading Shi'i cleric, the relationship between Sadr and the government became strained in 1999 after Sadr called upon the government to release imprisoned Shi'i clerics and after he issued a religious ruling calling on Iraqis to attend Friday prayers in mosques instead of watching them on television at home, thereby defying a government ban on large crowds. Sadr's attempt to distance himself from the government, and to establish himself as an independent cleric commanding popular support, was cut short by mysterious gunmen who shot him to death in Najaf.

Scores of Iraqi Shi'is have left their country in the period since the Gulf War, bringing the number of Iraqis who today live in exile to around two million. I met a good number of Iraqi Shi'is, both secularists and observant Muslims, after the translation of *The Shi'is of Iraq* into Arabic in 1996. The enthusiasm that some Shi'is have expressed toward the book, and the ambivalence and reservation of others, echoed an old debate between reformers and conservatives within Shi'i Islam. In this book I discuss aspects of this debate as manifested in the struggle among Shi'is in Najaf during the 1930s over the future of the Shi'i college institution (*madrasa*) in the period following the establishment of nation-states in the Middle East. While the reformers sought to detach Shi'i education from the influence of the past and reshape it in conformity with modern times, the conservatives insisted on preserving the curricula and teaching methods as they had existed in the time of their predecessors. At the turn of the twenty-first century, a similar debate is under way among Shi'is. Its content, however, has larger ramifications for Shi'is than the debate of the 1930s because of the growing dilemmas and pressing needs of a younger generation of Iraqi Shi'is, many of whom live in exile. Today, the debate centers around the question of what Shi'ism should be in the twenty-first century: Should it be a set of fixed religious values, unaffected by time, which cut across national, ethnic, and cultural boundaries, or should it evolve into a flexible identity shaped by the particular circumstances and the environment in which Shi'is live? The suggestion in my book that Shi'ism in Iraq and Iran are different in character has been picked up by participants in the current debate among observant Shi'is—something that I had not anticipated or intended at the time of writing the book.

Like their parents and grandparents in the twentieth century, the younger generation of Iraqi Shi'is continues to search for its identity. A very perceptive Iraqi Shi'i journalist explained to me what was on the mind of young Iraqis, both ordinary people and activists of various political inclinations:

On the one hand, we have the staunch secularists among us—mainly communists and Ba'thists—who deny that there is a sectarian problem or that there is such a thing as a Shi'i identity, stressing that we are all Arabs; on the other, our ulama tell us that Iraq is the cradle of Shi'ism, that Shi'i

Islam is universal, and that our Shi'ism dates back to the time of the Prophet. Your book is immensely important for people like me. The idea that many of us are recent converts to Shi'i Islam, and that Iraqi and Iranian Shi'ism are different in nature, fills a huge gap between those two extreme positions. It throws a new light on our past, and it enables us to approach our history as well as our Iraqi Shi'i origin and identity from an entirely different angle.

I wrote in 1993 in concluding the epilogue that the responsibility for Iraq's future lies mainly with its people. This remains very much true today when the United States and Iraq are on the brink of war. In the event of war, the best-case scenario would be the destruction of the repressive Ba'th regime followed by a U.S. commitment to see through the reconstruction of Iraq as a pluralistic state. The worst-case scenario would be a U.S. attempt to replace Saddam Husayn with a "nice" Sunni general amenable to its interests and to the interests of Iraq's neighboring countries. Such a policy will backfire because the Shi'is would oppose a state in which they are again assigned a marginal political role. The former scenario may not be easy to accomplish, but it is the only one worth trying.

By virtue of their majority position among the population, the Shi'is stand to play the leading role in Iraqi politics. Yet they would need to set aside their grievances regarding the historical injustices done to them by the ruling Sunni minority and to assure the Sunnis that a change of regime in Iraq would not expose them to Shi'i revenge and tyranny. Iraq's Shi'a would need to develop a leadership that could unite observant Shi'is and secularists, rural and urban dwellers, Shi'is living inside Iraq as well as those in exile. The religious Shi'is among them would need to reconcile Western ideas of democracy with Islamic concepts of freedom and justice. Accomplishing these tasks may ultimately enable a Shi'i to emerge as a national leader recognized by the majority of Iraqis. Iraq's Sunnis may not be easily persuaded to relinquish their political hegemony, however. To allay their fears, Iraqis must agree upon a power sharing formula soon after the U.S. liberation of Iraq. Arab Shi'is and Sunnis together form some 75 percent of Iraq's population. As the largest ethnic group, they would need to rethink the relationship between Arabs and Kurds, and to offer the Kurds a pact recognizing their distinct culture and safeguarding their sociopolitical rights within a re-unified Iraq. In return, the Kurds would have to overcome the factionalism that has torn their society apart and forge new links with the Iraqi state.

In a new Iraq, power should not be monopolized by Baghdad, but shared between the central, southern, and northern parts of the country.

Nevertheless, Baghdad should remain the locus of Iraqi national politics. Iraq's foreign and defense policy, and its economic budget and oil fields, should be controlled by the federal government in Baghdad. A good part of the proceeds from oil, however, should be reinvested in the northern and southern regions where oil is found. The United States would need to encourage Iraqis to develop a strong parliamentary system composed of regional assemblies and a national parliament in Baghdad. The latter should serve as a major arena for public debate, and it should be capable of checking the executive's decisions. Seats should be distributed among Iraq's various social and ethnic groups (including Turkomans, Assyrians, Chaldeans, and Arab Christians) in proportion with their size.

The composition of the federal government, like that of the national parliament, should reflect the social fabric of Iraqi society and the majority status of Shi'is within the population. To maintain the credibility of the new government, ministerial posts should be filled by Iraqis who are respected within the country, including members of Iraqi opposition groups in exile. Until such time as Iraqis are ready to elect their national leader, it may be necessary to appoint a triumvirate consisting of, say, a Shi'i president, a Sunni prime minister, and a Kurdish speaker of parliament. Their roles should be clearly defined by the constitution and endorsed by the national parliament. The Iraqi army should be transformed from an institution used to suppress opponents of the regime into a symbol of national unity. To achieve that goal, the United States would need to assist the central government in disarming Kurdish Peshmerga units as well as the Sadr Brigades, composed of Iraqi Shi'i refugees who have fled to Iran over the past twenty years, and who may try to re-enter Iraq as they did in the wake of the Gulf War. To ensure Iraq's stability, the United States would also need to pressure Turkey, Iran, Syria, and Saudi Arabia not to interfere in Iraqi affairs, allowing Iraqis to develop their own vision of a new Iraq.

The prospect of the Shi'is coming to power should not raise the fear that Iraq might be swept away by Islamic radicalism, or that Iran would be able to increase its leverage in the country to a significant extent. On the contrary, for more than a decade Islamic radicalism in the Middle East has been largely shaped by Sunnis, many of whom have been influenced by the Wahhabi-Hanbali school dominant in Saudi Arabia. Although the Iranian revolution has emboldened Arab Shi'is, the Islamic Republic has failed to reshape Arab Shi'ism in its own image. Indeed, a revival of the academic center in Najaf will only generate healthy competition between that city and Qum in Iran for the leadership of the Shi'i world. An Iraq where minority rights are enshrined in the constitution, and respected by the majority, could serve as a model for reducing tension between governments and minority groups elsewhere in the Middle East, including Saudi Arabia and Turkey.

In seeking to rebuild their country, Iraqis would need to establish trust among Iraq's various groups and develop a broad and unifying Iraqi political identity drawing on Iraq's Babylonian past and on the tribal customs and traditions governing Iraqi society. Down the road, there may be a backlash against the wish of the majority to bring decency and tolerance to Iraqi sociopolitical life. It would be the responsibility of the United States to assure Iraqis that their desire for an Iraq that serves its people and does not threaten its neighbors will prevail.

Yitzhak Nakash
November 11, 2002

A NOTE ON TRANSLITERATION

WITH as much consistency as possible, I have used the system of transliteration adopted by the *International Journal of Middle East Studies* for Arabic and Persian. Diacritics have been reduced to a minimum. The plural of Arabic words has been marked by an addition of an "s" to the singular, except in such cases as "ulama," where the plural form has become standard. The article "al-" has been omitted from last names indicating a person's Iranian place of origin, such as Isfahani, Khurasani, or Shirazi.

ABBREVIATIONS

AAS   *Asian and African Studies*
AHR   *The American Historical Review*
AJES   *The American Journal of Economics and Sociology*
AM   *The Atlantic Monthly*
ASQ   *Arab Studies Quarterly*
BHCF   Baghdad High Commission File, The National Archives of
              India, New Delhi
BOUIES   *Bulletin of the Oxford University, Institute of Economics*
              and Statistics
BSMESB   *British Society for Middle Eastern Studies Bulletin*
BSOAS   *Bulletin of the School of Oriental and African Studies*
CO   Colonial Office, The Public Record Office, London
EDCC   *Economic Development and Cultural Change*
FO   Foreign Office, The Public Record Office, London
HR   *History of Religions*
IC   *Islamic Culture*
IJMES   *International Journal of Middle East Studies*
IO   India Office, London
IS   *Iranian Studies*
ISE   *Islamic Shi'ite Encyclopedia* (Beirut)
Isl   *Der Islam*
JNES   *Journal of Near Eastern Studies*
JRCAS   *Journal of the Royal Central Asia Society*
MEJ   *The Middle East Journal*
MES   *Middle Eastern Studies*
MW   *The Moslem (Muslim) World*
NAI   The National Archives of India, New Delhi
PP   *Past and Present*
RAF   The Royal Air Force, The Public Record Office, London
SA   *South Asia*
SH   *Social History*
SI   *Studia Islamica*
USNA   The U.S. National Archives, Washington, D.C.
WI   *Die Welt des Islams*
ZDMG   *Zeitschrift der Deutschen Morgenländischen Gesellschaft*

The Shi'is of Iraq

———————————

TURKEY

Zakhu

SYRIA

Mosul
Irbil

Sulaymaniyya

Tigris

Kirkuk

IRAN

Qasr-i Shirin

Khanaqin

Samarra

Ba'quba

Kazimayn
Falluja
Rarnadi
Baghdad

Rutba

Mahmudiyya

Musayyib
Karbala
Hindiyya
Barraj
Kut

JORDAN

Tuwayrij
Hilla
Hayy
Kumayyit

32°
32°

Kufa
Bahr al-Najaf
Najaf
Diwaniyya
'Amara

Rumaytha

Qal'at Salih

Samawa
Nasiriyya

Suq al-Shuyukh

SAUDI

Basra

IRAQ

0   50   100

miles

ARABIA

NEUTRAL
ZONE

KUWAIT

NEUTRAL
ZONE

Introduction

OUR RECEIVED WISDOM on the nature of modern Shiʻism is derived mainly from the large number of studies on Iranian Shiʻi Islam and society. While shedding important light on Iranian Shiʻism, these studies have also influenced our perception of the nature of Shiʻi Islam in general, which has come to be identified with Iranian culture and social values. The tendency to overlook the unique features of the Arab Shiʻis, especially in so important a country as Iraq, may also be attributed to the very small number of studies dealing with Iraqi Shiʻi society and the shrine cities. Indeed, it is only since the outbreak of the Iran-Iraq War that one can detect a significant effort mainly by Batatu, Kelidar, Luizard, Litvak, and Wiley to characterize the distinct features of Iraqi Shiʻism.[1] But overall, the balance of literature on Shiʻism has tilted toward Iran, leaving important lacunas concerning the process of formation of modern Iraqi Shiʻi society, the distinct cultural and social values of Iraqi Shiʻis, and the different patterns of ritual and organizational form taken by Shiʻi Islam in Iraq and Iran. Consequently, observers of the Middle East have tended not to appreciate the different religious and political development of the Iraqi and the Iranian Shiʻis, and the extent to which the history of the two groups has diverged in the twentieth century.

This book provides a corrective to some of the widely held assumptions regarding the nature of Shiʻi Islam in Iraq, most notably the perception that Iraqi Shiʻi society was formed a long time ago and that Iraqi Shiʻism is patterned after the Iranian model. The study focuses on the Shiʻis of Iraq during a period of major change, beginning with the rise of Najaf and Karbala as the two strongholds of Shiʻism from the mid-eighteenth century and leading up to the collapse of the Iraqi monarchy in 1958. The year 1958 is the cut-off point not only because of the change in regime but also due to the different source material and issues that one can fruitfully explore thereafter. Nonetheless, I will provide keys, as well as an epilogue on

---

[1] Hanna Batatu, "Iraq's Underground Shiʻa Movements: Characteristics, Causes and Prospects," *MEJ* 35 (1981): 578–94; idem, "Shiʻi Organizations in Iraq: al-Daʻwah al-Islamiyah and al-Mujahidin," in *Shiʻism and Social Protest*, ed. Juan Cole and Nikki Keddie (New Haven, 1986), 179–200; Abbas Kelidar, "The Shiʻi Imami Community and Politics in the Arab East," *MES* 19 (1983): 3–16; Pierre-Jean Luizard, *La Formation de l'Irak Contemporain: Le Rôle Politique des Uléma Chiites à la Fin de la Domination Ottomane et au Moment de la Construction de l'Etat Irakien* (Paris, 1991); Meir Litvak, "The Shiʻi Ulama of Najaf and Karbala, 1791–1904: A Socio-Political Analysis" (Ph.D. diss., Harvard University, 1991); Joyce Wiley, *The Islamic Movement of Iraqi Shiʻas* (Boulder, 1992).

the Gulf War and its aftermath, to elucidate Shi'i aspirations and the position of Shi'i Islam in contemporary Iraq.

The study is concerned with the following major questions: How was modern Iraqi Shi'i society formed and during which period? What was the impact of the rise of the modern state on the status of the Iraqi Shi'i leadership and classes, and on the socioeconomic and political position of the shrine cities vis-à-vis Baghdad? What are the basic political aspirations of the Iraqi Shi'is? What are the fundamental differences between the subjective cultural beliefs and social values of Iraqi and Iranian Shi'is as evident in their rituals and religious practices? In what ways did Iraqi and Iranian Shi'i Islam differ in their organizational forms? What were the consequences of the weakening financial power of the Shi'i religious establishment, and of the decline of its major source of intellectual strength, the madrasa, on the position of the Shi'i ulama and their ability to mobilize people for political action in modern Iraq?

The basic contention of this book is that the Iraqi Shi'is are by and large recent converts to Shi'ism, a result of a development which took place mainly during the nineteenth century as the bulk of Iraq's Arab nomadic tribes settled down and took up agriculture. This development marked the beginning of a process of Shi'i state formation in southern Iraq, which was aborted following the British occupation in 1917 and the subsequent formation of the Iraqi monarchy in 1921. Although it is difficult to define the territorial boundaries and institutions of this Shi'i regional polity, it is possible to see it as a continuum in the evolution of fragmented tribal confederations into a state, and to identify the main stages and features of this process.[2]

The rise of Najaf and Karbala as the two strongholds of Shi'ism in Iraq from the mid-eighteenth century set the stage for this process of Shi'i state formation. The development and expansion of the polity was marked by the settlement of the tribes and their subsequent conversion to Shi'ism during the nineteenth century. The settlement fragmented the old tribal confederations, altered the balance between the nomadic and sedentarized groups, and increased agricultural production and trade in southern Iraq. The conversion of the tribes resulted in the establishment of a more unified religion and a more cohesive value system embracing the urban dwellers in the shrine cities and the tribesmen of their hinterlands. Both the settlement and the conversion of the tribesmen increased the degree of stratification and the power of the ruling hierarchy among the tribes. They led to the appearance of new figures, who fulfilled socioeconomic and religious functions among the tribes, as well as to the formation of a class of Shi'i notables

---

[2] For general background on the evolution of states see Allen Johnson and Timothy Earle, *The Evolution of Human Societies: From Foraging Group to Agrarian State* (Stanford, 1987), esp. 21, 207–11, 246, 269–70, 318–19.

and a Shi'i elite whose members controlled resources. The introduction of Shi'i Islam as a unifying religion was essential to the maintenance of the various classes, ethnic groups, and tribal and urban elements that constituted the new society, as well as to the expansion of the Shi'i polity. Indeed, the increased domination which Najaf and Karbala exerted over their hinterlands was not achieved through conquest, but through the conversion of the sedentarized tribes and the close contacts that marked the relations between the two cities and the tribes.

The defining feature of the Shi'i polity was the massive socioeconomic and religious interaction between the converted tribes and Najaf and Karbala, the nerve centers of the polity. This interaction was essentially a kind of political partnership between the tribal and urban components as well as between ordinary people and the elite of the Shi'i society, which was constantly growing in scale. While the converted tribesmen were expected to refrain from internal disputes and to contribute forces for the protection of the shrine cities, the urban dwellers provided the tribesmen with access to marketing and organized religion. At the top of the hierarchy stood the grand mujtahids, whose function was to supervise this partnership and to control such resources as derived from religious taxes and contributions. The process of Shi'i state formation in southern Iraq came close to maturing early in the twentieth century, when leading mujtahids formulated a theory defining the nature of the state which they had envisaged and laid foundations for their own representation in politics. The attempt of the mujtahids to establish an Islamic government in Iraq did not materialize, however, and the process of Shi'i state formation was aborted following the British occupation and the subsequent formation of a Sunni state in the country.

The distinct features of this case of Shi'i state formation may be appreciated through a comparison to three other prominent cases of religious state formation in the Middle East and North Africa during the late Ottoman period, namely the Wahhabiyya in Arabia (1745–1818, 1823–1880s, and 1902–present), the Mahdiyya in the Sudan (1881–1898), and the Sanusiyya in Libya in the late nineteenth and early twentieth centuries. Although in all four cases the religious leadership sought to use Islamic ideology as a vehicle for unifying the tribes, the Shi'i case differed from certain patterns which characterized the other three. Whereas the Wahhabi, Mahdi, and Sanusi cases involved tribes mainly in the peripheral desert, where central government control was nominal, the process of Shi'i state formation gained momentum only from 1831, after the Ottomans had assumed direct control over Iraq and were attempting to settle the tribes and increase centralization in the country. Moreover, in contrast with the major role which conquests played in the territorial spread of the Wahhabi, Mahdi, and Sanusi states, the expansion of the Shi'i polity was achieved mainly through the peaceful conversion of Iraq's sedentarized and nominally Sunni tribes to Shiʻism.[3]

The second major contention of this book is that the diverging development of Shiʻi Islam in Iraq and Iran in the twentieth century reflected the essentially different characters of Shiʻi religion and society in the two countries. The contrasts between Iraqi and Iranian Shiʻism are borne out in the differing patterns of ritual and organizational form of Shiʻi Islam in Iraq and Iran, which in turn were reinforced by the rise of the modern state. This study shows that the unique moral and cultural values of Iraqi Shiʻi and Iranian societies were built into their rituals and religious practices. It illustrates the fact that Iraqi and Iranian Shiʻi Islam have differed greatly in their organizational form, a phenomenon which helps explain why the Shiʻi ulama of Iraq did not emerge as a powerful player in national politics, and were unable to mobilize large numbers of people for political action.

Iran's population by and large became Shiʻi by the eighteenth century following the establishment of the Safavid state in 1501. Since then Shiʻi Islam has been the state religion in Iran (save for a short period after the Sunni Afghan occupation of Isfahan in 1722), and on the whole the state supported the Shiʻi religion and the ulama well into the twentieth century. Moreover, religious life in modern Iran has been rooted in the daily activity of ordinary Iranian Shiʻi believers, most notably the bazaaris. Indeed, students of Iranian Shiʻism have pointed out that it was religion which for centuries held Iranian society together, and that the pressures and sanctions to behave in proper Shiʻi Islamic fashion stemmed largely from Iranian public opinion. Thus, the active involvement of ordinary Iranians in shaping religious activity and belief suggests that Shiʻism in modern Iran might be seen as a system of socioeconomic and religious values, which rather than being imposed on social reality, arose from within it.[4]

In contrast with these characteristics of Iranian Shiʻism, there exists at the core of Shiʻism in Iraq a society whose strong Arab tribal value system was encapsulated by Shiʻi religion, not permeated by it. Unlike the state-sponsored conversion of the Iranian population to Shiʻism, the process by which Iraqi Shiʻi society was formed reflected the frontier nature of Iraq, the rise of Najaf and Karbala as the two strongholds of Shiʻism in a country

---

[3] For the Wahhabi, Mahdi, and Sanusi cases see Philip Khoury and Joseph Kostiner, eds., *Tribes and State Formation in the Middle East* (Berkeley, 1990), 12.

[4] Ann Lambton, "Social Change in Persia in the Nineteenth Century," *AAS* 15 (1981): 139; Nikki Keddie, "The Roots of the Ulama's Power in Modern Iran," *SI* 29 (1969): 48; idem, "Can Revolutions be Predicted; Can their Causes be Understood?" *Contention* 1 (1992): 169; Michael Fischer, *Iran: From Religious Dispute to Revolution* (Cambridge, Mass., 1980), 31; Joanna de Groot, "Mullas and Merchants: The Basis of Religious Politics in Nineteenth Century Iran," *Mashriq* 2 (1983): 20.

which was a Sunni Ottoman possession, and the relatively recent conversion of Iraq's settled tribes to Shi'ism. Against the Persian ethnic origin of the large majority of Iranians, the Iraqi Shi'is on the whole have been distinguished by their Arab tribal attributes and moral values, which were evident in their rituals and endured long after the establishment of modern Iraq. And in contrast with the close interaction between the bazaaris and the ulama in Iran, the Shi'i mercantile classes in Iraq were on the whole unwilling to channel funds into the support of religious institutions and causes.

The rise of the modern state reinforced the differences between Shi'i Islam in Iran and Iraq in the twentieth century. In Iran, the centralization and modernization programs of Reza Shah and his son, Muhammad Reza Shah, lessened the power of the clergy but did not decisively subvert it. By contrast, the formation of modern Iraq as a Sunni-dominated state dealt a severe blow to the position of Shi'i Islam in the country. Iraq's Sunni rulers succeeded in eradicating much of the power traditionally held by the Shi'i religious establishment based in such shrine cities as Najaf and Karbala. The Iraqi government undermined the two cities' position as desert market-towns, and curtailed the Shi'i clergy's income from charities, the pilgrimage, and the corpse traffic (the practice of Shi'is in transporting their dead for burial in holy cemeteries in the shrine cities). It hindered the position of Shi'i institutions of higher learning as many of Najaf's madrasas lost their economic independence and came under government control. The establishment of modern Iraq also pulled many Arab Shi'is toward Baghdad, and the Iraqi state emerged as the major focus of identity for Shi'is. The policies of successive Sunni Iraqi governments, supported by Iran's Pahlavi rulers, reduced the ties between Shi'is in Iraq and Iran, and accelerated the decline of Shi'i financial and intellectual institutions in Iraq. A different type of Shi'i Islam developed in Iraq as compared to its Iranian counterpart. Consequently, Iraqi and Iranian Shi'is were pulled further apart in the twentieth century.

While there is no need to sketch here a table of contents, a word on structure is in order. This book is divided into four parts. The two chapters which constitute the first part examine the abortive process of Shi'i state formation which took place in southern Iraq, as well as the nature of the state which the mujtahids envisaged. In the first chapter I will trace the rise of Najaf and Karbala as the strongholds of Shi'i Islam in Iraq, and the conversion of many of Iraq's tribes to Shi'ism mainly during the nineteenth century. In the second chapter I will show how the Shi'i mujtahids developed a political theory which provided a mode for their representation in state affairs, and illustrate the power of the Shi'i clergy in mobilizing people for political action, which culminated in the 1920 revolt.

The second part is also composed of two chapters, dealing respectively with the rise of the modern state and the search of the Iraqi Shi'is for political representation and influence in the state. My task in the first chapter is to show that the policies of successive Sunni Iraqi governments split the pre-monarchic Shi'i elite, reduced the position of Najaf and Karbala vis-à-vis Baghdad, and dealt a blow to the position of Persians in the country. In the second chapter I will examine the nature of Shi'i political demands as well as the activities which Shi'is pursued to influence government decision-making. I will show that the nature of their demands reflected the search of Shi'is for integration, as well as a position of power, in the state.

The third part contains three chapters. One underlying theme in this part is that the development of Shi'i rituals and religious practices in Iraq during the nineteenth century was closely connected to the process of formation of Iraqi Shi'i society. The second theme is that the Arab tribal attributes of Iraqi Shi'i society, as contrasting with the influence of Sufism and elements of martyrdom in Iranian society, were evident in the commemoration of 'Ashura' and the cult of the saints. In demonstrating the different moral and cultural values of Iraqi Shi'i and Iranian societies, I will also assess the impact of the rise of the modern state on the intensity of Shi'i rituals as well as on the pilgrimage and the corpse traffic. I will show that the Iraqi state succeeded in reducing the effectiveness of Shi'i rituals as a political tool, in decreasing contacts between the shrine cities and Iran, and in curtailing the sources of income of the Shi'i clergy as well as of other groups in Najaf and Karbala.

The fourth part of the book includes two chapters. Focusing respectively on Shi'i money and the Shi'i madrasa, these chapters elucidate the different organizational form of Shi'i Islam in Iraq and Iran. One of my major tasks in this part is to demonstrate that the lack of community of interest between the Shi'i bourgeoisie and the religious classes in modern Iraq, which was reinforced by state policies, undermined the position of Shi'i institutions of higher learning in the country as well as the power of the clergy vis-à-vis the government. My second major purpose in this part is to investigate the process by which many of Najaf's madrasas lost their economic independence and power and came under state control. The decline of the Shi'i madrasas of Najaf was a major factor in contributing to the rise of those in Qum in Iran in the twentieth century. I will also examine the implications of the establishment of a new Iraqi Shi'i madrasa in Najaf in 1935, the curriculum of which was approved by the Ministry of Education. These developments not only placed much of Iraqi Shi'i religious education under state control, but enabled the government to cultivate a new generation of Shi'i teachers and religious functionaries loyal to the state.

The Iran-Iraq War of 1980–1988 and the Gulf War of 1991 demonstrated the saliency of the issues that the book addresses. Yet both caught us not fully aware of the distinct nature of Iraqi Shi'i society and the fundamental differences between Iraqi and Iranian Shi'ism. This book is intended to sharpen our understanding of Iraqi society and politics as well as the different manifestations of Shi'ism in the twentieth century.

PART ONE

The Formative Years

Chapter One

THE MAKING OF IRAQI SHI'I SOCIETY

FROM ITS OUTSET, Shi'i Islam was closely associated with Iraq as several of the formative events of Shi'i history took place there. In A.D. 661 'Ali ibn Abi Talib, the fourth caliph and the first Shi'i imam, was assassinated in a mosque in Kufa. 'Ali's son Husayn, who laid claim to the caliphate, was killed with his companions in a battle which took place on the plain of Karbala in 680. Many of the twelve Shi'i imams spent at least part of their lives in Iraq. The four most sacred Shi'i shrine cities, Najaf, Karbala, Kazimayn, and Samarra are in Iraq. Since the early stages of Islamic history, much of Shi'i academic activity took place in such centers in Iraq as Kufa, Hilla, Baghdad, Najaf, and Karbala. And finally, Iraq was also once a territory ruled by Shi'i dynasties, notably, the Buyids (945–1055).

But can all this explain the nature and position of Shi'i Islam in Iraq as we know it at the beginning of the twentieth century? Can it shed light on how the Shi'is came to form the majority of the population? The Shi'is are concentrated mainly in the southern and central regions of Iraq.[1] The rough British census of 1919 put the number of Shi'is at 1,500,000 out of a total of 2,850,000, that is, about 53 percent of the population. These figures were adjusted in 1932, when their number was put at 1,612,533 out of 2,857,077 Iraqis, i.e., around 56 percent.[2] The bulk of Iraq's Shi'i population are Arabs. Persians formed about 5 percent of the Shi'is in the 1919 census, and Indians less than 1 percent; their numbers have fallen since. With few exceptions, the Shi'is of Iraq adhere to Imami Shi'ism, and it is with this segment of the Shi'i population that this study is concerned.

The composition of Shi'i society, as well as the nature and position of Shi'i Islam in Iraq on the eve of the formation of the monarchy, were largely the result of the interaction between major events and trends, and between cities and tribes from the mid-eighteenth century. This interaction marked the beginning of a process of Shi'i state formation in southern Iraq.

---

[1] In this study, the name Iraq refers to the region consisting of the three Ottoman provinces of Mosul, Baghdad, and Basra. The northern region includes the divisions of Erbil, Kirkuk, Mosul, and Sulaymaniyya. The central region includes Baghdad, Diyala, Dulaym, Hilla, Karbala, and Kut. The southern region includes 'Amara, Basra, Diwaniyya, and Muntafiq. Whereas the Najd part of the Basra province was excluded after World War I, the mountains and the Kurdish region were added during the 1920s to form the modern state of Iraq.

[2] 1919 Census by Religion, FO 371/4152/175918; Religious Statistics for Iraq, 1 August 1932, FO 406/70.

IRAQ THE FRONTIER

In what sense was Iraq a frontier? It was not just a matter of the distance and isolation which this term brings to mind. For five centuries following the breakdown of the 'Abbasid State in 1258, Iraq did not have a government strong enough to restore its former extensive irrigation systems, or to subdue the Arab tribal confederations that took possession of desolate countryside which had lost its urban focus. Moreover, the development of Iraq between the sixteenth and twentieth centuries had been marked by two other major features. The first was the slow and long drawn-out process of Ottoman conquest, domination, and settlement of the tribal population. The second was the position of the country, and particularly the shrine cities, as a cultural-religious contact zone between the Sunni Ottoman Empire and Shi'i Safavid, and later Qajar, Iran. Thus, Iraq became a region of extensive warfare as the country contained resources which both the Ottomans and the Iranians were anxious to control.

The emergence of Safavid Shi'i Iran in 1501 coincided with the consolidation of the Sunni Ottoman Empire and the subsequent attempts of Selim I (1512–1520) and Suleyman I (1520–1566) to establish their state as a world empire. This created a new reality in Iraq, which became a battle zone between two rival powers. With the outbreak of conflicts in the sixteenth and seventeenth centuries between the Ottomans and the Safavids, the Ottoman Sultan and the Safavid Shah each referred to himself as the sovereign of Islam. The conflict between them was expressed in terms of Shi'i-Sunni strife, and polemics raged between the two sides.[3] Although Iraq became an Ottoman territory following the occupation of Baghdad in late 1533, Ottoman rule of the country until the nineteenth century was often nominal and incomplete, because of Iraq's remoteness from the center of power in Istanbul and Iranian pressures on the country, which included two periods of occupation in 1508–1533 and 1622–1638. These pressures were reinforced by the claim of the Safavids, and their eventual successors the Qajars (1794–1925), that the Shah should be the sole protector of Shi'i interests in Iraq, at the core of which were the shrine cities of Najaf, Karbala, Kazimayn, and Samarra. Until the formation of the Iraqi monarchy in 1921, Ottoman-Iranian rivalry for political, religious, and socioeconomic control turned Iraq into a frontier zone, influencing the composition of Shi'i society and the organization of Shi'i Islam in the country.

The frontier nature of Iraq, and the position of the shrine cities as a magnet which attracted Shi'i believers, help explain the motivation of Persians and Indians in migrating to the country. At the turn of the sixteenth

---

[3] Ann Lambton, *State and Government in Medieval Islam* (Oxford, 1981), 212–13.

century, Iraq's Shi'i society was by and large Arab. The rise of Safavid Iran
exposed Iraq's population to Persian Shi'i influences. Shi'i Persian merchants first came to Iraq during the two periods of Safavid occupation of
the country, appropriating a good share of the commerce of Baghdad.[4]
Following the first occupation, the Kammuna family, which had held the
influential position of *naqib al-ashraf* (head of the descendants of the
Prophet) in Baghdad, became connected to the Shah's court in Iran, and
was gradually Persianized.[5] Early in the seventeenth century, there were
still no Persians in Basra, the population of which was composed mainly of
Arabs and some Turks.[6] At that time there were a few thousand Persians in
such cities as Karbala, Najaf, Kazimayn, and Baghdad. Many of them,
however, escaped to Iran following the second Ottoman occupation of
Baghdad in 1638, which had resulted in the killing of some 1,700 Persians.[7] The Persian colony in seventeenth-century Iraq was composed
mostly of merchants and other individuals who came to the country in
search of economic opportunities. There was no significant number of
Persian students and ulama in Iraq at that time since the main Shi'i academic centers were in Iran.

It was only from the eighteenth century that Persian ulama and students
arrived in Iraq on a massive scale. The Sunni-Afghan capture of Isfahan in
1722, and the attempts of Nadir Shah to promote Sunni-Shi'i rapprochement and to expropriate many of the endowments supporting the Shi'i
clergy in Iran, displaced hundreds of families of ulama, many of whom fled
to Iraq during the period 1722–1763. The center of Shi'i scholarship
shifted from Iran to Iraq, first to Karbala and then to Najaf. At that time,
the Persian language gained much ground in Karbala, Najaf, Baghdad, and
Basra.[8] For three years, Basra was under Zand control after Karim Khan
Zand, the ruler of southwestern Iran, occupied the city in 1776; he introduced Shi'i-style prayers and Shi'i Friday-sermons, and struck coins bear-

---

[4] Stephen Longrigg, *Four Centuries of Modern Iraq* (Oxford, 1925, Beirut reprint, 1968),
19, 57.

[5] 'Abbas al-'Azzawi, *Ta'rikh al-'iraq bayna ihtilalayn*, 8 vols. (Baghdad, 1935–1956),
3:315, 342, 354–56.

[6] Pedro Teixeira, *The Travels of Pedro Teixeira*, trans. William Sinclair (London, 1802),
27–30.

[7] 'Azzawi, *Ta'rikh*, 4:229, 234–35; Teixeira, *Travels*, 51.

[8] Rasul al-Kirkukli, *Dawhat al-wuzara' fi ta'rikh waqa'i' baghdad al-zawra'* (Beirut and
Baghdad, n.d.), 52–63; Muhsin al-Amin, *Ma'adin al-jawahir wa-nuzhat al-khawatir*, 2 vols.
(Beirut, 1981), 2:22–25; 'Azzawi, *Ta'rikh*, 5:269–70, 272, 308; Juan Cole, "Shi'i Clerics in
Iraq and Iran, 1722–1780: The Akhbari-Usuli Conflict Reconsidered," *IS* 18 (1985): 5, 26;
Said Amir Arjomand, *The Shadow of God and the Hidden Imam: Religion, Political Order,
and Societal Change in Shi'ite Iran from the beginning to 1890*, 2d ed. (Chicago, 1987), 215–
17; Hamid Algar, *Religion and State in Iran, 1758–1906: The Role of the Ulama in the Qajar
Period* (Berkeley, 1969), 30, 33.

ing the names of the twelve imams.[9] The Persian ulama who migrated to
Iraq took advantage of the instability in the country, which was caused by
the rise of the Mamluks in 1747 and the subsequent indirect Ottoman rule
of Iraq that lasted until 1831. In Karbala and Najaf, the Persian religious
families managed to overshadow the Arab ulama and succeeded in dominating religious circles. The struggle between the traditionalist Akhbari
and the rationalist Usuli ulama over the methodology of Shi'i law ended
with the latter's victory. Many of the Usulis were the Persian ulama who
had arrived in Iraq between 1722 and 1763, and they rose to prominence
within the Shi'i religious establishment in Iraq following their victory.[10] By
the mid-nineteenth century, the Persian ulama in Iraq already controlled
most of the Shi'i charitable funds and the madrasas, thereby gaining great
power in their dealings with both the Ottoman and the Qajar governments,
as well as with the local population.

Indians began to settle in the shrine cities from the late eighteenth century. By the twentieth century their number in Karbala and Najaf alone
had reached some five thousand. The rise of the Shi'i state of Awadh
(Oudh) in north India from 1722 proved lucrative for the shrine cities
because of the financial remittances made by Awadh officials and other
individuals for mujtahids in these cities.[11] Part of the Indian money was set
aside for Indian pilgrims, many of whom opted to remain in the shrine
cities in search of a livelihood or in pursuit of religious studies. The massive
influx of Indians to the shrine cities took place only from the 1860s, after
the British annexation of the Kingdom of Awadh and the Indian Mutiny. At
that time, several rich members of the royal family of the Nawwabs of
Awadh arrived in the shrine cities with their followers. They distributed
large sums of money to the poor and made endowments for public works.
This attracted more Indians to the shrine cities, who could enjoy the life of
comparative ease assured under the patronage of the wealthy Nawwabs. It
was then a relatively easy matter for Indians to earn their living in the
shrine cities, and those unable to work could depend on charity for their
daily bread. From the late nineteenth century, however, the munificence of
the wealthy settlers was greatly diminished and the proportion of paupers
among the Indians in Iraq increased. Whereas the first generation of Indian
noblemen of Awadh or Delhi who settled in the shrine cities had been rich,
the second were only moderately well-off. Owing to the termination of
pensions and allowances, the third generation were already poor people.
Moreover, when in 1903 the British abolished the special "Indian fund,"

[9] 'Azzawi, Ta'rikh, 6:61, 79–81; John Perry, Karim Khan Zand: A History of Iran, 1747–
1779 (Chicago, 1979), 192.

[10] Cole, "Shi'i Clerics," 20, 22, 26.

[11] Juan Cole, "'Indian Money' and the Shi'i Shrine Cities of Iraq, 1786–1850," MES 22
(1986): 461–80.

which relied on Oudh Bequest money (see chapter 8), and from which Indians in the shrine cities had benefited since around 1860, the welfare of Indians further declined and Karbala was reported to be "a sink of Indian pauperism." In subsequent years, it became an increasingly difficult matter to distinguish who were and who were not Indians among the ethnic elements in the shrine cities.[12]

Much more than the Indian settlers, it was the Persian colony in Iraq that emerged in the nineteenth century as the most active and influential component among the population of the shrine cities. These eighty thousand Persians estimated to be in Iraq in 1919 (perhaps even more if one considers the many cases of mixed marriages) enjoyed the status of Iranian subjects, over whom Iranian consular officers held extra-territorial jurisdiction. The status of Persians in the country was a major cause of strained Ottoman-Qajar relations even after their privileges were officially confirmed in 1875. An agreement between the two states recognized the status of Iranian consuls and consular dragomans in the Ottoman Empire as including the same privileges enjoyed by their European counterparts. The exclusive authority of the Iranian consuls over Iranian subjects in matters of civil and criminal law, and succession was affirmed by the 1875 agreement. While Iranian subjects were declared amenable to the jurisdiction of Ottoman courts in cases of violation of the law, as well as in mixed civil and commercial cases, certain powers of assistance and protection in the proceedings were reserved to the Iranian consular representatives. The agreement also established the exemption of Iranian subjects from taxes to which Ottoman subjects were liable. Although it was laid down that all provisions relating to Iranian subjects in the Ottoman Empire should equally apply to Ottoman subjects in Iran, Iranians were the main beneficiaries of the agreement.[13]

The Ottoman willingness to accord the Persian community in Iraq such a unique status reflected Istanbul's incomplete control of the country and its attempt to avoid a possible war with Iran over the issue of the status of Persians in Iraq. Indeed, while it may be argued that in the nineteenth century Iran was not capable of posing a direct military threat to Istanbul, the Qajar shahs did exert enough power on the regional level to extract capitulations for their subjects in Iraq. The granting of privileges to Persians also reflected Istanbul's attempt to placate Shi'is in Iraq in the face of both the expansionist policy of Muhammad 'Ali of Egypt as demonstrated by his son's occupation of Syria (1831–1841) and the growing European penetration into Iraq in the nineteenth century. Their privileged status,

[12] Lorimer to McMahon, Baghdad, 11 August 1911, FO 195/2368/690–34; Report of the Protector of British Indian pilgrims, 1929, CO 730/159/2.

[13] J. G. Lorimer, *Gazetteer of the Persian Gulf, 'Oman and Central Arabia*, 2 vols. in 5 pts. (Calcutta, 1908–15), 1,1B:1425.

relative importance, and large numbers among the population of the shrine cities gave the Persians an advantage over the Arab Shi'i population of Iraq, enabling them to retain their vested economic interests and strong socio-religious links with their families and coreligionists in Iran. The Persian ulama, students, and merchants had a great impact on the religious life and economy of the shrine cities, most notably Karbala. They were also to be found in significant numbers in Baghdad, Basra, and Tuwayrij. Their socioeconomic and religious position was further bolstered by Ottoman-Qajar agreements which facilitated the influx of pilgrims, and regulated the corpse traffic from Iran to the shrine cities.

The privileged status of the Persians as derived from their protection by the Iranian government, and their control of resources in Iraq, made it difficult for the Ottomans to exercise effective control over Najaf and Karbala, which emerged as the two strongholds of Shi'i Islam in Iraq.

The Shrine Cities

Shi'i believers attach high religious esteem to the holy cities of Najaf, Karbala, Kazimayn, and Samarra, the development of which between the sixteenth and twentieth centuries was shaped by the desire of the Ottoman and the Iranian states to dominate Shi'i affairs in Iraq.

The most prominent of these shrine cities was Najaf, which by the early twentieth century exercised an enormous religious and political influence far beyond the limits of Iraq. Located about 120 miles south of Baghdad, it escaped effective government control throughout much of the Ottoman period. Its semi-autonomous status, and self-image as the great nerve center of the world, found embodiment in its portrayal by both Shi'is and Western writers as the "heart of the world," a "world within a city," and the "receiver of all the news of the world." [14] The city had at least nineteen functioning religious schools at the turn of the twentieth century. It was often the seat of the leading Shi'i mujtahid of the day, who would receive large contributions from Shi'i followers around the Muslim world. Attracting many Shi'i pilgrims, Najaf contains the holy shrine of 'Ali ibn Abi Talib. The city's large cemetery (Wadi al-Salam) has been considered the holiest and most highly sought-after place for burial among Shi'i believers.

Like many other religious centers in the world, Najaf's fortunes changed greatly over the years. The lack of a regular water supply, and its vulnerability to repeated raids by the Arab tribes, were two of Najaf's most acute problems throughout its pre-nineteenth-century history. Following

[14] Agha Najafi Quchani, *Siyahat-i sharq ya zindeginama va-safarnama-yi agha najafi quchani* (Mashhad, 1972), 581; 'Abd al-Rasul al-Sharifi, "Shay' 'an al-najaf aw 'alam fi madina," *al-'Irfan* 35 (1948): 1150–52; Great Britain, Administration Reports for 1918, Najaf, CO 696/1; Thomas Lyell, *The Ins and Outs of Mesopotamia* (London, 1923), 21–22.

the Safavid occupation in 1508, Shah Isma'il I ordered the cleaning of the city's old water canal, which had silted up. His successor Shah Tahmasp, who visited Najaf around 1527, ordered the construction of another canal to bring water from Hilla to Najaf.[15] These projects, however, did not solve Najaf's water problem. In the late sixteenth century very few pilgrims visited Najaf because of water shortages in the city, the pious canal-works having silted up and become almost dry.[16] The desperate condition of Najaf at that time is evident from a petition sent probably by one of the city's dwellers to the Ottoman governor Sinan Pasha, who, in turn, submitted it to Sultan Murad III (d. 1594). The unidentified petitioner complained that the city was subject to repeated attacks by the tribes, and that it suffered from a great shortage of water. Its lack of security and regular water supply forced people to abandon it. Thus, whereas in the past there had been three thousand inhabited houses in the city, in the late sixteenth century there remained only thirty. Those who did stay included the Friday prayer sermon-deliverer, the prayer leader, the attendants and servants of the shrine, as well as a few other individuals. As may be gathered from the governor's dispatch to the Sultan, the petitioner seems to have appealed for the construction of a canal to bring water from the Euphrates to Najaf, and for the repair of the city's wall.[17]

The Portuguese traveler Pedro Teixeira, who visited Najaf in 1604, noted that the city was almost in ruins since the death in 1576 of Shah Tahmasp, who was said to have favored the city. The aqueduct built by Sultan Selim II (d. 1574) was clogged and needed repeated cleaning. The barely five hundred dwellers in Najaf at that time relied for their water supply mainly on some wells inside the city.[18] Although a new canal from Hilla to Najaf was built by Shah 'Abbas I around 1623, it too dried up after a while.[19] During the term of the Ottoman governor Ibrahim Pasha (1681–1683) a canal was constructed to bring water to nearby Kufa, but it did not reach Najaf. Indeed, the latter city could not rely for its regular water supply on any major canal until sometime after 1803, when the construction of the Hindiyya canal was completed.[20] This development was facilitated by the relative improvement in Ottoman-Iranian relations following their last war in 1821–1823, which ended with the first treaty of Erzurum. The Hindiyya gave a great push to the socioeconomic welfare of Najaf; it provided the water needed to sustain massive numbers of pilgrims and helped the city's

15 'Azzawi, Ta'rikh, 3:337; Yusuf Karkush al-Hilli, Ta'rikh al-hilla, 2 vols. (Najaf, 1965), 1:119.

16 Longrigg, Four Centuries, 34; Hilli, Ta'rikh, 1:119.

17 Ya'qub Sarkis, Mabahith 'iraqiyya, 3 vols. (Baghdad, 1948–1981), 2:58–60.

18 Teixeira, Travels, 48.

19 Hilli, Ta'rikh, 1:119.

20 Sarkis, Mabahith 'iraqiyya, 2:60–63.

mujtahids to establish Najaf as the major Shi'i academic center from the 1840s at the expense of Karbala, which decreased in importance. As will be seen later in this chapter, the Hindiyya also had a great impact on the socioeconomic and religious contacts between Najaf and the surrounding tribes, thereby accelerating their conversion to Shi'ism.

Although Najaf's almost entirely Shi'i population was estimated to be only about thirty thousand early in the twentieth century, the periodic influx of pilgrims often more than doubled this figure. The bulk of the city's permanent population was composed of Arabs; Persians formed only a third of the population at that time.[21] Najaf's position on the edge of the desert explains the very strong Arab tribal influences on the city. These features of Najaf found embodiment in the fact that important Arab families of ulama in the city traced their descent to neighboring tribes. Thus, the Kashif al-Ghita family stemmed from the Al 'Ali section of the Bani Malik tribe of the Muntafiq confederation.[22] Moreover, until 1918 Najaf was under the influence of two Arab factions: the Zuqurt and the Shumurt. Najafis traced their formation to the first decade of the nineteenth century, when under the leadership of the mujtahid Shaykh Ja'far Kashif al-Ghita (d. 1812), warriors were recruited from among the city's dwellers to protect Najaf against the Wahhabi attacks. In subsequent years, the two factions managed to dominate Najafi life and they also cooperated with important families in the city. Thus, whereas the Zuqurt was allied with the Kashif al-Ghita family, the Shumurt was associated with the Milalis, who held the position of custodian of 'Ali's shrine from early in the sixteenth century until around 1840.[23] The two factions' bid for power within the city culminated during World War I, when in April 1915 the Zuqurt and the Shumurt expelled the Ottomans from Najaf and divided the control of its four quarters among themselves. Whereas Sayyid Mahdi, Hajji 'Atiyya, and Kazim Subbi of the Zuqurt ruled the Huwayyish, the 'Amara, and the Buraq quarters, respectively, Hajji Sa'd of the Shumurt administered the Mishraq quarter.[24] The four shaykhs enjoyed this position until May 1918, when their power was broken by the British.

[21] Lorimer, *Gazetteer*, 2B:1310–11.

[22] 'Abbas al-'Azzawi, *'Asha'ir al-'iraq*, 4 vols. (Baghdad, 1937–1956), 4:142; Mahdi al-Qazwini, *Ansab al-qaba'il al-'iraqiyya* (Najaf, 1956/7), 99n.

[23] Ja'far al-Mahbuba, *Madi al-najaf wa-hadiruha*, 3 vols. (Najaf, 1955–1958), 1:330–34; Muhammad Hasan al-Najafi, *Jawahir al-kalam fi sharh shara'i' al-islam*, 6th ed., 42 vols. (Najaf, 1958), 1:11; Ja'far al-Khalili, *Mawsu'at al-'atabat al-muqaddasa, qism al-najaf*, 10 vols. (Baghdad and Beirut, 1965–1970), 1:230–31; 'Ali al-Khaqani, *Shu'ara' al-ghari aw al-najafiyyat*, 2d ed., 12 vols. (Qum, 1988), 2:115–26; Meir Litvak, "The Shi'i Ulama of Najaf and Karbala, 1791–1904: A Socio-Political Analysis" (Ph.D. diss., Harvard University, 1991), 112–16.

[24] Administration Reports, 1918, Najaf, CO 696/1.

The strong tribal character of Najaf at that time is evident from the content of the constitution of the Buraq quarter (appendix 1), compiled after the four shaykhs had taken control of the administration of the city in 1915. The traditional loyalty of tribesmen to their tribe and shaykh was transformed in Najaf into a strong loyalty of the Buraq dwellers to their quarter and to its head Kazim Subbi. Moreover, the alliance of blood which united the quarter dwellers, the stress on honor, and the repeated reference to blood-money as the element to be used in conflict resolution, demonstrated the great extent to which Najafi civic spirit was dominated by tribal codes as late as the twentieth century.

In contrast to Najaf's strong Arab character, Karbala's ethnic composition and culture were marked by the city's very large Persian community. At the turn of the twentieth century, Karbala's almost entirely Shi'i population was estimated to be fifty thousand, of whom Persians constituted at least 75 percent, the Arabs forming less than a quarter.[25] Karbala is situated about fifty-five miles south of Baghdad. Western visitors remarked that it did not in any way present the appearance of an Arab city; its architecture and bazaars reflected Persian influences.[26] Karbala contains the shrines of Husayn, son of 'Ali and the third Shi'i imam, and of 'Abbas, Husayn's half-brother. Husayn is known among Shi'i believers as the prince of martyrs (*sayyid al-shuhada'*) because he was killed in his challenge to the accession of Mu'awiya's son Yazid to the caliphate. Together with 'Abbas and a few other followers, Husayn died in the battle which took place on the plain of Karbala in 680. The battle and the heroic stand of Husayn and his small group became the most important event in Shi'i history and mythology. The martyrdom of Husayn was most fervently celebrated by Shi'is, and Karbala emerged as the focus of devotion, particularly for Persian Shi'i believers. Traditions attach blessing to its water and soil, and promise rewards to the believers to be gained from their pilgrimage to the city and from burial in its cemetery (Wadi al-Iman), which stands only second in sanctity to that of Najaf.

Karbala seems to have enjoyed a relatively better water supply than Najaf; its date groves are said to have been irrigated from the Euphrates already in the fourteenth century. Following the Ottoman occupation of 1533, Sultan Suleyman I ordered the construction of the Husayniyya canal to bring water to Karbala. Described as a great engineering achievement, the Husayniyya separated from the Euphrates at Musayyib and flowed to Karbala, where it was divided into two branches.[27] Years of neglect, however, resulted in a shortage of water in the city, and like Najaf, Karbala was

---

[25] Lorimer, *Gazetteer*, 2A:976.

[26] Ibid., 977; British Consulate, Baghdad, 22 February 1943, FO 624/33/537.

[27] 'Azzawi, *Ta'rikh*, 4:36–37; Lorimer, *Gazetteer*, 2A:751–53.

also reported to be almost completely abandoned by pilgrims in the late sixteenth century.[28] It was probably only after a dam was built at the head of the Husayniyya canal by Hasan Pasha, the Ottoman governor of Iraq (1704–1723), that Karbala enjoyed a steady water supply. These developments help explain why Karbala (and not Najaf) emerged first as the most important Shi'i center of study around 1737, replacing Isfahan, which had declined following the Afghan occupation of the city and the subsequent migration of Persian ulama to Iraq. Karbala's welfare increased further as Hasan Pasha built and repaired khans along the route from Baghdad to Karbala, thus improving the conditions for pilgrimage to the city.[29]

During much of the Mamluk period, Karbala's administration was in the hands of Mamluk-appointed Sunnis from Baghdad, who also controlled the shrines and the collection of taxes in the city. Yet because of their weak military power, the Mamluks tolerated such Shi'i practices as the cursing and disavowal of the first three caliphs, which was prevalent in Karbala early in the nineteenth century, fearing that an attempt to abolish them would result in an Iranian reprisal. As Mamluk rule grew weaker from the 1820s, local gangs gradually succeeded in assuming actual control of the city, co-opting its landowners and merchant families. The Arab gang leaders allied themselves with Karbala's ulama. The name of the Ottoman Sultan was not mentioned in Friday prayers, and the city began to function, according to British reports, as a "self-governing semi-alien republic." This alarmed the Ottomans, who resumed direct rule over Iraq in 1831 and sought to increase centralization in the country. Karbala's resistance to Ottoman attempts to bring it under direct control eventually led to its occupation in 1843 by the governor Najib Pasha.[30]

The Ottoman occupation of the city had three major consequences on the relative positions of Karbala and Najaf. First, while the suppression of Karbala ended this city's semi-autonomous position, Najaf escaped a similar fate since it submitted peacefully to Najib Pasha, who had proceeded from Karbala to Najaf to reassert Ottoman authority there; Najaf thus retained its socioeconomic and political position, which remained almost intact until the twentieth century. Second, the occupation of Karbala helped Najaf to emerge as the leading Shi'i center of learning from the 1840s as many students left Karbala and moved to Najaf, which also became the preferred seat of the majority of the grand Shi'i mujtahids. Third, following the news that reached Iran of the bloody occupation of

[28] Longrigg, *Four Centuries*, 34.

[29] 'Azzawi, *Ta'rikh*, 5:210.

[30] Litvak, "Shi'i Ulama," 107, 124–26; Juan Cole and Moojan Momen, "Mafia, Mob and Shiism in Iraq: The Rebellion of Ottoman Karbala, 1824–1843," *PP* 112 (1986): 115–16, 122, 124, 126, 135–37; Lorimer, *Gazetteer*, 1,1B:1349; 'Abd al-'Aziz Nawwar, *Ta'rikh al-'iraq al-hadith* (Cairo, 1968), 92.

Karbala, the Qajars exerted effective pressures on the Ottoman government to grant immunities to Persians in Iraq. Thus, although the Ottoman occupation of Karbala led to the breaking of the power of the Arab gangs, paradoxically Persian influence in the city increased and by the turn of the twentieth century Persians dominated most of the socioeconomic and religious activity in Karbala. Whereas the Arab shaykhs of the Zuqurt and the Shumurt continued to influence Najafi life, Karbala's administration came under growing Persian influence. The strong links of Karbala with Iran as late as the twentieth century were evident in the high status of the Persianized Kammuna family, which practically controlled the city's affairs. The family was led by the two brothers Muhammad 'Ali and Fakhr al-Din, whose grandmother was said to be a daughter of Fath 'Ali Shah. They held the positions of the custodian of Husayn's shrine and the city's mayoralty, respectively, before their power was broken by the British in 1917.[31]

If Najaf and Karbala were the strongholds of Shi'i Islam in Iraq, this cannot be said of Kazimayn and Samarra since the commanding factors in the development of these latter two cities were Kazimayn's proximity to Sunni Baghdad and Samarra's almost entirely Sunni population. Kazimayn's importance stems from its shrine, which contains the tombs of Musa al-Kazim, the seventh imam, and of his grandson Muhammad al-Jawad, the ninth imam. The extensive repairs to the shrine, which had been begun by Shah Isma'il I and completed by Sultan Suleyman I, are yet another example of the benefits that accrued to the shrine cities from Ottoman-Iranian rivalry in their desire to dominate Shi'i affairs in Iraq.[32] Situated only three miles northwest of Baghdad, the town's population was estimated in the early twentieth century to be eight thousand, of whom seven thousand were Shi'is. Arabs formed the bulk of the city's Muslim population; the number of Persians did not exceed one thousand. Kazimayn's strong orientation toward Baghdad was reinforced in 1870 when the city became connected with the capital by a horse tramway. The Ottomans thus enjoyed a greater control of the city than of Najaf or Karbala.[33] As will be shown in chapter 2, Kazimayn's proximity to Baghdad facilitated a good deal of sociopolitical and religious contacts between Sunnis and Shi'is in Iraq, culminating in the events that preceded the formation of the monarchy.

Samarra contains the tombs of the tenth and eleventh imams, 'Ali al-Hadi and his son Hasan al-'Askari. It is also believed to be the place of birth of Muhammad al-Mahdi, the twelfth imam, who allegedly disappeared and is expected to return as the Mahdi. Located sixty-six miles north of

---

[31] Review of the Civil Administration of Iraq, 1914–1918, FO 371/4148/34799.

[32] 'Azzawi, Ta'rikh, 4:34–35; Sarkis, Mabahith 'iraqiyya, 3:155–59.

[33] Lorimer, Gazetteer, 2A:967–68; Review of the Civil Administration of Iraq, 1914–1918, FO 371/4148/34799.

Baghdad, Samarra's population was around 8,500 early in the twentieth century. Its inhabitants had been almost entirely Sunnis before the great mujtahid Muhammad Hasan Shirazi moved to the city from Najaf in 1875. Shirazi's move revived Samarra, which had experienced decline followed by insignificance after it ceased to be the 'Abbasid capital in the late ninth century.[34] The move of a leading Shi'i mujtahid to the city alarmed the Ottomans, who were faced with the sudden spread of Shi'ism to the area north of Baghdad. Indeed, the flow of funds, and Shi'i students and pilgrims to the city, which was followed by the observance of Shi'i rituals in public, exposed Samarra's population to growing Shi'i influences and challenged Sunni dominance in the city and its surroundings. The Ottoman fear of a growing Shi'i presence in this part of Iraq must have also been fed by Shirazi's involvement in the affairs which led to the Tobacco Revolt in Iran in 1891–92.[35]

From the late nineteenth century, Ottoman officials and Sunni ulama both in Iraq and Istanbul made repeated appeals to Istanbul to check the spread of Shi'ism in Iraq. Thus, for example, Husayn Husnu Efendi, a former Shaykh al-Islam, stressed the crucial role of the Sunni madrasas in Baghdad and urged the government to send competent ulama to Iraq to reverse the impact of the Shi'i ulama on the population.[36] The Ottomans established two new madrasas in Samarra, the first of which (al-Madrasa al-'Ilmiyya al-Sunniyya) was opened in 1898 and was placed under a shaykh of a Sufi order, Muhammad Sa'id al-Naqshbandi. It was intended to improve the level of Sunni education in Samarra, and to initiate preaching activities in order to check the function of Shirazi's madrasa as a base for Shi'i propagation both in the city and its surroundings. The Ottomans also appointed a Sunni as the custodian of the Shi'i shrine, thereby improving their control of Shi'i affairs in Samarra.[37] Samarra greatly decreased in importance following Shirazi's death in 1895. Within a year after his death, most of his leading disciples left Samarra and settled mainly in Najaf, which reasserted its superior position as the most important Shi'i academic center. The move of Shirazi's disciple and important mujtahid Mirza

[34] Dhabihallah al-Mahallati, Ma'athir al-kubara' fi ta'rikh samarra', 3 vols. (Najaf and Tehran, 1948–1949), 2:43–45, 52–55; Yunus Ibrahim al-Samarra'i, Ta'rikh madinat samarra', 3 vols. (Baghdad, 1968–1973), 3:89; Khalili, Mawsu'at al-'atabat al-muqaddasa, qism samarra', 8:175.

[35] 'Ali al-Wardi, Lamahat ijtima'iyya min ta'rikh al-'iraq al-hadith, 6 vols. (Baghdad, 1969–1978), 3:90–97; Agha Buzurg Tihrani, Hadiyat al-razi ila al-imam al-mujaddid al-shirazi, Persian trans. (Qum, 1984), esp. 58–59, 223–24, 251–74.

[36] Selim Deringil, "The Struggle against Shi'ism in Hamidian Iraq: A Study in Ottoman Counter-Propaganda," WI 30 (1990): 50.

[37] Samarra'i, Ta'rikh madinat samarra', 2:180–83; "Madha yura' al-yawm fi samarra'," Lughat al-'Arab 1 (1911): 142; Review of the Civil Administration of Iraq, 1914–1918, FO 371/4148/34799; Summary of Events in Turkish Iraq, October 1910, FO 195/2341/989–60.

Muhammad Taqi Shirazi from Samarra to Karbala in 1917 sealed Samarra's decline and the city lost whatever potential it had to become a Shi'i stronghold within Iraq.

Yet, the overall Ottoman inability to check the power of Najaf and Karbala enabled these two cities to emerge as the bases of Shi'i propagation in Iraq from the late eighteenth century. This had a great impact on the very large number of Arab tribes in central and southern Iraq that came under the influence of Najaf and Karbala.

THE CONVERSION OF THE TRIBES TO SHI'ISM

There is no evidence that would suggest that the Shi'is were ever close to forming the majority of the population in Iraq before the nineteenth or even the twentieth century. Although conversion to Shi'ism took place in Iraq throughout Shi'i history, it was confined mainly to cities, where only a small fraction of the country's population lived. Occasionally, some Arab tribes were also converted to Shi'ism like the Bani Sulama, the Tayy, and the Sudan in the marshes near Khuzistan during the Musha'sha' Arab Shi'i dynasty of the fifteenth to sixteenth centuries.[38] It was only following the massive conversion of the bulk of Iraq's nominally Sunni Arab tribes to Shi'ism mainly during the nineteenth century that the share of the Shi'is grew to its 1919 and 1932 estimates of 53 and 56 percent of the population, respectively. How can we account for this relatively late conversion and its magnitude? What was its impact on the religious identity of the tribesmen? Can we really make a clear-cut distinction between the social and moral values of Sunni and Shi'i Arab tribesmen in Iraq on the eve of the formation of the monarchy? It is with these questions that the remaining discussion will be concerned.

Arab tribes formed the bulk of the population of southern and central Iraq during the Ottoman period, the nomads alone constituting as much as half the population in the south as late as 1867.[39] Until the nineteenth century Iraq's tribes were organized in loose confederations, each acting as a sort of a political and self-governing unit established in response to threats by other tribal constellations. Led by paramount shaykhs, these confederations fought over land and trade routes.[40] Periodic government expeditions against the tribes reinforced the group spirit of the confederations, thus further distinguishing each one from the other. The oldest tribal confederations in southern and central Iraq during the Ottoman period

---

[38] *Encyclopaedia of Islam*, 2d ed. s.v. "Musha'sha'."

[39] M. S. Hasan, "Growth and Structure of Iraq's Population, 1867–1947," *BOUIES* 20 (1958): 344.

[40] Robert Fernea, *Shaykh and Effendi: Changing Patterns Among the El Shabana of Southern Iraq* (Cambridge, Mass., 1970), 25.

were the Muntafiq, the Zubayd, the Dulaym, the 'Ubayd, the Khaz'al, the
Bani Lam, the Al Bu Muhammad, the Rabi'a, and the Ka'b. The tribes that
constituted these confederations were composed of camel breeders, sheep
breeders, cultivators, and buffalo-breeding marsh dwellers. These divisions, however, were not always clear-cut and there was often a fusion
between the different groups.[41]

Many of Iraq's tribes migrated to the country from Arabia, thus retaining great similarities in their virtues and moral values with Arabian tribes.
Said to have arrived in Iraq early in Islamic history, most of the Muntafiq
tribes are traced to the old 'Adnani tribes of Arabia although some claim
lineage to Qahtani and Himyari tribes as well.[42] The Zubayd migrated
from Arabia to Iraq sometime after the Muslim occupation of the country
in 634 A.D., and are traced to Qahtani tribes.[43] Two other confederations,
the Dulaym and the Al Bu Muhammad, were formed from the Zubayd, the
latter in the late seventeenth century.[44] The Rabi'a are also said to have
arrived in Iraq around the period of the Muslim occupation, and to have
ties with some of the old tribes of Arabia. The Ka'b claim lineage to the
Rabi'a.[45] The 'Ubayd are traced to Himyari tribes and probably arrived in
Iraq early in Islamic history.[46] The Khaz'al and the Bani Lam are considered two of the oldest known Tayy tribes in Iraq, and are said to have
arrived there around the fourteenth century.[47] Iraq's tribal population
increased in the eighteenth and nineteenth centuries. Sections of the Shammar, notably, the Shammar Tuqa and the Sa'ih, migrated from Ha'il to Iraq
early in the eighteenth century.[48] Another significant addition to the country's tribal population was the migration of large sections of the Bani
Tamim from Najd to Iraq around 1737.[49] As will be seen below, Iraq's
tribal map took its final shape only in the nineteenth century following the
migration from Arabia between 1791 and 1805 of other sections of the
Shammar (the Jarba) and the 'Anaza confederations, as well as the Zafir
tribe, because of Wahhabi pressures. Many of Iraq's Arab tribes claimed
lineage to these confederations, and it is from them that the bulk of Iraq's
Shi'i population was drawn from the late eighteenth century.

[41] Hanna Batatu, *The Old Social Classes and the Revolutionary Movements of Iraq*, 2d ed.
(Princeton, N.J., 1982), 68.
[42] 'Azzawi, *'Asha'ir*, 4:11, 28.
[43] Ibid., 3:30.
[44] Ibid., 61, 105; Longrigg, *Four Centuries*, 80; Lorimer, *Gazetteer*, 2A:456.
[45] 'Azzawi, *'Asha'ir*, 4:162, 181.
[46] Ibrahim al-Haydari, *Kitab 'unwan al-majd fi bayan ahwal baghdad wa al-basra wa-najd* (Baghdad, n.d.), 105.
[47] 'Azzawi, *'Asha'ir*, 3:211–12, 245; Nawwar, *Ta'rikh*, 154.
[48] 'Azzawi, *'Asha'ir*, 1:233–34 and 3:203.
[49] 'Ali al-Wardi, *Dirasa fi tabi'at al-mujtama' al-'iraqi* (Baghdad, 1965), 147; 'Azzawi,
'Asha'ir, 4:217.

In 1869 the prominent Baghdadi Sunni *'alim* Ibrahim al-Haydari listed those tribes which had "recently" been converted to Shi'ism. With the exception of the Khaz'al and the Ka'b (including its Khazraj section), which according to Haydari were converted in the early and mid-eighteenth century, respectively, all the other tribes in his list were converted just before or during the nineteenth century. The Zubayd, the Bani Lam, and the Al Bu Muhammad were the main converted confederations in Haydari's list. In addition, it included large sections of the Rabi'a (including the Dafafi'a, the Bani 'Amir and the Ju'ayfir), the Bani Tamim (including their largest section in Iraq, the Bani Sa'd), the Shammar Tuqa, the Dawwar, and the Sawakin. Also present in Haydari's list were the many tribes along the Hindiyya canal, and the five tribes of Diwaniyya (Aqra', Budayyir, 'Afak, Jubur, and Jaliha) that relied for their water supply on the Daghara canal.[50] Haydari's assertion that the Zubayd confederation was converted just before or early in the nineteenth century is supported by the account of the Iraqi Mamluk historian 'Uthman Ibn Sanad al-Basri (d. 1834). The twentieth-century Baghdadi Sunni *'alim* 'Abdallah Mahmud Shukri al-Alusi also acknowledged the conversion of the Zubayd, as well as sections of the Shammar and the Bani Tamim, just before or during the nineteenth century.[51] To Haydari's list one should also add the great confederation of the Muntafiq, which, with the exception of its shaykhs of the Sa'dun family who remained Sunni, was converted to Shi'ism almost in its entirety in the nineteenth century.[52] In many cases the conversion was not complete, and thus by the formation of the monarchy many tribes had been cut along sectarian lines.

It is perhaps not surprising that large sections of the Shammar, the Zafir, and the Bani Tamim, which arrived in Iraq in the eighteenth century, were converted during the subsequent century. What is striking, however, is that the bulk of Iraq's old confederations, the Muntafiq, the Zubayd, the Du-laym, the Al Bu Muhammad, the Khaz'al, the Bani Lam, the Rabi'a, and the Ka'b, were converted to Shi'ism only from the late eighteenth century and not beforehand. Several major developments accounted for this rapid and relatively late conversion of the tribes. At the core of this process were the Wahhabi attacks on Najaf and Karbala, the emergence of the latter two cities as Iraq's major desert market-towns, the change in the water flow of

[50] Haydari, *'Unwan al-majd*, 110–15, 118.

[51] 'Uthman Ibn Sanad al-Basri al-Wa'ili, *Mukhtasar kitab matali' al-su'ud bi-tayyib akhbar al-wali da'ud*, ed. Amin al-Hilwani (Cairo, 1951/2), 169; 'Abdallah Mahmud Shukri [al-Alusi], "Di'ayat al-rafd wa al-khurafat wa al-tafriq bayn al-muslimin," *al-Manar* 29 (1928): 440.

[52] Lorimer, *Gazetteer*, 2B:1273; Great Britain, Naval Intelligence Division, Geographical Handbook Series, *Iraq and the Persian Gulf*, September 1944, 379–80; Great Britain, Office of the Civil Commissioner, *The Arab of Mesopotamia*, Basra, 1917, 6.

the Euphrates, and most important, the Ottoman policy of tribal settlement beginning in 1831. The transition of the tribes from nomadic life to agricultural activity disrupted tribal order and created a major crisis among the tribesmen, forcing them to reconstruct their identity and relocate themselves on the socioreligious map of their surrounding environment. The conversion was facilitated by the proliferation of *sayyids* (descendants of the Prophet), who soothed the fragmentation of Iraq's tribal system. The scale of the conversion changed according to region as the factors mentioned above had a varying degree of influence on the marshes, the central and southern Euphrates, and the Tigris area.

The rise of the Wahhabis helps explain the drive of ulama in Najaf and Karbala to convert Iraq's tribes to Shi'ism. By 1775, Ibn Sa'ud was a power in Arabia, and his conquest of Hasa in 1795 enabled him to expand his influence beyond the confines of Najd. The Wahhabi pressures pushed the Zafir, parts of the 'Anaza and the Harb (including the Jubur), and the Shammar Jarba to Iraq. The Mamluks encouraged the strong Shammar Jarba to remain in Iraq, seeking to turn this tribe against Ibn Sa'ud and also to use it as a leverage against one of Iraq's strongest confederations, the 'Ubayd.[53] The Wahhabis invaded Iraq several times and raided the Muntafiq and the Khaz'al. They put Najaf under siege twice and sacked Karbala in 1801. The large force of tribal levies composed of the Muntafiq, the Zafir, the Shammar, and the Ka'b, which was sent to Hasa by the Mamluk governor Suleyman Pasha, failed to defeat the Wahhabis.[54] It was only in 1811 that the Wahhabi power was reduced by Muhammad 'Ali of Egypt.

The Wahhabi attacks of Najaf and Karbala reinforced the sectarian identity of the Shi'i ulama and increased their motivation to convert the tribes. Unlike Sunni-Shi'i academic polemics, which posed no real physical threat to Shi'i Islam, the sack of Karbala and the attacks of Najaf exposed the vulnerability of the Shi'i ulama in Iraq, lacking as they did a tribal army which could be mobilized against such a threat to the very existence of the two cities. Moreover, the Wahhabi forays coincided with the rise of Najaf and its attempt to vie with Karbala for the position of the leading Shi'i academic center. With the exception of one case when the Shi'i Khaz'al attacked Wahhabi forces in Iraq that were said to be advancing toward Najaf, this confederation was on the whole either too weak to resist the Wahhabis or indifferent to the city's fate. This alarmed ulama in Najaf and its surroundings, and hence they attempted to reinforce Shi'ism among the

[53] 'Azzawi, *'Asha'ir*, 1:137, 140, 144–45, 165, 231, 260, 290, 295–98, 305–6, and 3:203; idem, *Ta'rikh*, 6:163; Nawwar, *Ta'rikh*, 149; Tom Nieuwenhuis, *Politics and Society in Early Modern Iraq* (The Hague, 1982), 123, 125.

[54] J. B. Kelly, *Britain and the Persian Gulf, 1795–1880* (Oxford, 1968), 99–100; Longrigg, *Four Centuries*, 213–14; Mahbuba, *Madi al-najaf*, 1:324–26.

Khaz'al and to establish an army composed of members of this confederation while still under Wahhabi threat.[55]

The Wahhabi attacks sharpened for the Shi'i ulama the ever-menacing
power of tribes in general and the danger which Iraq's nomadic tribes posed
to their sources of income. This threat surfaced again in 1814 during the
rebellion of Iraqi tribes against the government, motivated by the loose
Mamluk control of the area south of Baghdad. The participants in the
rebellion were the Zubayd, the Khaz'al, the tribes of Shamiyya and the
Jezira, together with the Zafir, the Shammar Jarba, and the Rawala. The
threatening moves of the tribes close to Najaf, Karbala, Hilla, and Kazimayn
coincided with one of the major annual Shi'i visitations of the shrine cities.
The forty thousand Iranian pilgrims who were said to be in these cities at that
time were unable to leave until the tribes had retreated in the face of an
expedition sent by the governor.[56] The Wahhabi attacks, and the pressures of
Iraq's tribes on the Shi'i cities, were a major check on the latter's development. This particularly alarmed the Persian ulama who had migrated to Iraq
between 1722 and 1763 and lacked a solid socioeconomic base in the
country. Seen from their point of view, the conversion of the tribes to Shi'ism
was essential to bolstering their position in southern Iraq and maintaining
their independent status vis-à-vis the Sunni government in Baghdad. Moreover, religion was the major resource of the shrine cities, and the main force
moving their economic activity, which relied heavily on charities, pilgrimage, and the corpse traffic from Iran. The nomadic tribes of Iraq were
not inclined to visit the sacred shrines on pilgrimage, nor did they attach any
other religious importance to them.[57] Aware of that, the Shi'i ulama may
have also regarded the conversion of the tribes to Shi'ism as an opportunity
to increase the number of potential local believers, contributors, and pilgrims, who would be engaged in the rituals connected with the pilgrimage to
the shrine cities and seek burial in the cities' holy cemeteries. Thus, the need
to secure the sacred shrine cities and to augment their sources of income by
creating a local economic base helps explain the drive of the Shi'i ulama to
convert the tribes from the late eighteenth century.

The functioning of Najaf and Karbala as desert market-towns and granary centers in Iraq made them an important channel of contact among the
tribes. The annual cycle of the nomadic tribes of Iraq, the Syrian desert,
and Arabia was spun around two seasons. During the rainy season the
tribes pastured in the desert areas whereas between late April and early
October they were to be found close to the rural-cultivated areas searching

[55] Kirkukli, Dawhat al-wuzara', 212; Hamud al-Sa'idi, Dirasat 'an 'asha'ir al-'iraq: al-
Khaza'il (Najaf, 1974), 68; Lorimer, Gazetteer, 1,1B:1286.

[56] Kirkukli, Dawhat al-wuzara', 263–64.

[57] 'Azzawi, 'Asha'ir, 1:398.

for water and food. This coincided with the harvest season of wheat and barley in southern Iraq, which begins in April.[58] Before the mid-nineteenth century, Hilla was a large tribal market and center of exchange, and it may be that it also acted as a center for Shiʻi propagation among the tribes.[59] While Najaf was almost in ruins until the eighteenth century, Karbala had the potential to act in this capacity at that time because of its relatively more fertile hinterland and the repair of the Husayniyya canal. As will become clear from the discussion of water and agriculture, however, the effectiveness of Shiʻi missionary activity among the tribes improved markedly only after the great increase in the cultivated area around Karbala and Najaf from the nineteenth century as a result of the construction of the Hindiyya canal.

The Hindiyya gave a great push to the economic position of Najaf and Karbala, which emerged as Iraq's major desert market-towns. Najaf assumed the role of an emporium of trade for the desert from the nineteenth century when the Shatt al-Hilla river dried up. Iraq's principal rice grounds developed along the Hindiyya, and especially between Tuwayrij and Kufa, and in the districts of Shamiyya and Samawa, close to Najaf.[60] By the twentieth century Najaf already overshadowed Karbala in its importance as a desert market-town. In addition to its setting as a desert market-town for the sale of grain, rice, dates, and cloth, Najaf was a collecting center for wool and skins of sheep and camels. It attracted tribes from Arabia, as well as from the Syrian desert such as those wandering sections of the ʻAnaza. The tribes used to encamp in an area close to the city called al-Minakha, where much of the dealing took place. Karbala catered mainly to the needs of the wandering Shammar and the ʻAmarat, and for the shepherd-breeding Bani Hasan.[61] The greater economic interaction of Najaf and Karbala with the tribes, particularly during the nineteenth century, enabled the emissaries who originated from these two cities to spread Shiʻi Islam among the tribesmen much more effectively than in earlier periods.

The change in the flow of the water of the Euphrates also had its impact on the process of conversion. It has already been pointed out in the previous section that the rise of Karbala and Najaf from the mid-eighteenth century was closely related to their water supply. Najaf in particular had suffered an acute shortage of water, a result of its relative distance from the

[58] ʻAbd al-Jabbar ʻUraym, al-Qabaʼil al-rahhal fi al-ʻiraq (Baghdad, 1965), 23–24; Lorimer, Gazetteer, 2A:793.

[59] Longrigg, Four Centuries, 10; ʻAbdallah al-Nafisi, Dawr al-shiʻa fi tatawwur al-ʻiraq al-siyasi al-hadith (Beirut, 1973), 69.

[60] Lorimer, Gazetteer, 2A:793–94.

[61] Mekki al-Jamil, al-Badw wa al-qabaʼil al-rahhala fi al-ʻiraq (Baghdad, 1956), 246–50; Talib ʻAli al-Sharqi, al-Najaf al-ashraf: ʻadatuha wa-taqaliduha (Najaf, 1987), 47; ʻAzzawi, Taʼrikh, 6:136; Naval Intelligence Division, Iraq and the Persian Gulf, 538, 546; Review of the Civil Administration of Iraq, 1914–1918, FO 371/4148/34799.

Euphrates and the very small number of wells within the city. Years of neglect almost silted up the Husayniyya canal, which brought water to Karbala, and it was only after a dam was built by Hasan Pasha early in the eighteenth century that the city's water supply improved significantly. The cultivated area in the province surrounding Karbala increased, which in turn attracted some tribes to the city's environs. In 1706 Hasan Pasha attacked sections of the Shammar that had migrated to Iraq a few years earlier. While the Shammar Tuqa consequently settled down in the area between the Diyala and Kut al-'Amara, the Mas'ud ended up in the area near Musayyib and Karbala.[62] Yet, far more than the Husayniyya, it was the construction of the Hindiyya canal which resulted in the attraction of a large number of tribes to the area between Najaf and Karbala, transforming the relations between these two cities and the tribes.

Financed by an Rs.500,000 contribution of the Awadh Chief Minister Hasan Reza Khan in the late 1780s, the Hindiyya canal was built to bring water to perpetually dry Najaf. Its construction, which started in the late eighteenth century, was completed sometime after 1803. The flow of water in the canal greatly improved toward the mid-nineteenth century following major reconstructions, also financed by Shi'i Indian money.[63] The Hindiyya not only assured the prosperity of Najaf in the nineteenth century but also caused major hydrologic and ecological changes in southern and central Iraq. The canal left the Euphrates at a point about five miles below Musayyib. By 1860–1865 it had begun to drain the Euphrates of its water, and sometime between 1865 and 1890 the Hindiyya absorbed the bulk of the river's water, thus changing its course. The Hindiyya grew to be a river which ran for about seventy-three miles before it ended in a lake near Najaf (Bahr al-Najaf). The barrage constructed by the Ottomans in 1890 not only failed to restore the former course of the Euphrates but also caused all its water to pour down the Hindiyya from 1903. The construction of the Hindiyya upset the traditional hydrologic balance between the western and eastern sides of the Euphrates. The upper parts of the western side were inundated, making cultivation impossible, and the area near Hilla gradually dried up as the stream of the Shatt al-Hilla river became thin and sluggish. Hilla lost its position as an agricultural and commercial center. In contrast, irrigation along the Hindiyya grew to be extensive and the area around it became well cultivated.[64]

The irrigated areas around Najaf increased further with the construction

<hr/>

[62] 'Azzawi, Ta'rikh, 5:171, 174.

[63] Cole, "'Indian Money'," 463; Sarkis, Mabahith 'iraqiyya, 2:63–64; Litvak, "Shi'i Ulama," 119–20.

[64] William Loftus, Travels and Researches in Chaldea and Susiana (London, 1857), 43–46; Lorimer, Gazetteer, 2A:496–97, 501–2, 719–28; Nieuwenhuis, Politics and Society, 130, 134; Mahbuba, Madi al-najaf, 1:195–96; Hilli, Ta'rikh al-hilla, 1:152.

of three smaller canals in the late nineteenth century, which also brought water to the city. Whereas the first was financed by a contribution from Muhammad Isma'il Khan, the Iranian governor of Kerman, the other two (known as the 'Abd al-Ghani and the Hamidiyya canals) were constructed in 1887/8 and 1893, respectively, by Ottoman officials.[65] The three new canals further improved the flow of water to Najaf. The many tribes in the Khaz'al sphere of influence, like the Bani Malik (and its sections the Bani Hasan, the Bani Zurayyij, the Al 'Ali, the Al Faraj, the 'Awabid, the Humayyidat, the Al Isma'il, and the Al Ibrahim), as well as the Jaliha, the Al Fatla, and the Qurayyit, were forced to abandon the Shatt al-Hilla region, and settled along the Hindiyya.[66] The attraction of many tribes to the increasingly more fertile area along the Hindiyya between Karbala and Najaf exposed the new settlers to the influence of the two cities. More than ever before, Najaf and Karbala were in a position to act as great nerve centers, and to radiate an active religious force to the tribesmen.

Still, as intensive as the activity of the emissaries might have been as a result of both the drive of the Shi'i ulama to convert the tribes as well as the growing contacts between Najaf and Karbala and the tribes, it cannot fully explain the magnitude of the conversion in the nineteenth century, let alone the willingness of the tribes to espouse Shi'ism. This is all the more apparent given the fact that Sunni, Shi'i, and British sources concur that there was almost no trace of Shi'ism among the nomadic camel breeders of Iraq in the early twentieth century, and that it had spread only among the sedentary tribes. Indeed, those tribes that have kept as a rule to the desert way of life remained almost invariably Sunni to this day.[67]

In view of that observation, it seems that the magnitude of the conversion in the nineteenth century can be fully understood only as an unintended result of the new Ottoman policy of tribal settlement. In 1831 the Ottomans resumed direct control of Iraq, the Mamluk period thus coming to an end. Unlike Mamluk efforts to break the tribes by occasional blows without providing an alternative way of life, the new Ottoman governors encouraged the tribesmen to settle down and take up agriculture. The governors' effort reflected Istanbul's desire to settle the tribes so as to increase agricultural production and tax revenue to sustain the Empire's growing involvement in world capitalist economy. Although tribal settlement developed into a clear policy in Iraq only from the term of Midhat Pasha (1869–

[65] Hajji Pirzadeh, *Safarnama-yi hajji pirzadeh*, ed. Hafez Farman-Farmayan, 2 vols. (Tehran, 1963), 1:346–47; Mahbuba, *Madi al-najaf*, 1:200–203; Sarkis, *Mabahith 'iraqiyya*, 2:64–65; Lorimer, *Gazetteer*, 2B:1311.

[66] Sa'idi, *'Asha'ir al-'iraq*, 82, 115–16; Salih Haider, "Land Problems of Iraq" (Ph.D. diss., University of London, 1942), 109–10.

[67] Anon., "al-Bida' wa al-khurafat wa al-taqalid wa al-'adat 'ind al-shi'a: risala min al-bahrayn, *al-Manar* 13 (1910): 307; Wardi, *Dirasa*, 144, 225; Office of the Civil Commissioner, *The Arab of Mesopotamia*, 5.

1872), his Ottoman predecessors had also sought to settle the tribes in their attempts to raise tribal revenue demands. Irrigation of cultivated areas was improved by the construction of new canals like the Jahala, which watered part of the 'Amara and the Zubayr districts. Old canals were cleaned in order to extend the cultivated areas, particularly during the term of Rashid Pasha (1853–1857). Midhat accelerated the process of settlement when he introduced the Ottoman Land Code in 1869, giving taxpayers security of tenure by granting them title deeds (*tapu sanads*) to plots on state domain. Applying this policy first to the Hindiyya district, and to the region between Hilla and Diwaniyya in general, he encouraged the selling of tracts of state land to individual holders and reduced land rent fees, thereby attaching tribesmen to land in central and southern Iraq.[68]

Beginning mainly with Najib Pasha (1842–1849), successive governors took great pains to extend government authority to the rural south. The Ottomans considered settlement the means by which they could "civilize" the nomads, instill the shari'a among them, and force them to settle their disputes in religious courts rather than according to tribal custom.[69] In seeking to settle the tribes and bring them under strict government control, the governors attempted to restructure tribal society. They sought to break the great tribal confederations and to undermine the status of their paramount shaykhs as "lords" who controlled large dominions. In this struggle over taxes, and the control of food and trade routes, the governors attempted to reduce the power of the shaykhs, partly by conferring their position to others. Many of Midhat's predecessors made rigorous demands for tax increases and appointed paramount shaykhs to farm taxes, thereby estranging the relations between the latter and the tribes in their area of influence. The divisions between the various component tribes of the confederations increased, and main sections became virtually independent as the government made each tribe accountable for its own share of the crop.[70]

Whereas early in the nineteenth century the great part of the cultivated area of central and southern Iraq was held under a system of communal tribal ownership, by the end of the century a large part of the land was

[68] 'Azzawi, *Ta'rikh*, 7:245–49; Longrigg, *Four Centuries*, 291, 306; Lorimer, *Gazetteer*, 2A:895–96; Albertine Jwaideh, "Midhat Pasha and the Land System of Lower Iraq," in *St. Antony's Papers: Middle Eastern Affairs* 3, ed. Albert Hourani (London, 1963), 119–20; Marion Farouk-Sluglett and Peter Sluglett, "The Transformation of Land Tenure and Rural Social Structure in Central and Southern Iraq, c. 1870–1958," *IJMES* 15 (1983): 494.

[69] Selim Deringil, "Legitimacy Structures in the Ottoman State: The Reign of Abdülhamid II (1876–1909)," *IJMES* 23 (1991): 347.

[70] 'Azzawi, *'Asha'ir*, 4:113–20; Haider, "Land Problems," 578–80; Longrigg, *Four Centuries*, 289–92; Lorimer, *Gazetteer*, 1,1B:1361, 1366, 1426, 1430; Nieuwenhuis, *Politics and Society*, 132–38; Batatu, *The Old Social Classes*, 75–76; Fernea, *Shaykh and Effendi*, 34.

already registered by the leading families of the tribes in their own names. In granting title deeds to individuals under the Land Code from 1869, the Ottomans further upset the organization of tribal society and the relations between shaykhs and tribesmen. The Code was probably designed to fit conditions in Anatolia and the Balkans, where individual peasant proprietors had actually existed. Since it did not recognize communal ownership of land, the Code stood in conflict with tribal custom under which land was held collectively by all members of the tribe. Fears that their rights might somehow be taken away or that land registration might facilitate conscription deterred individual tribesmen from registering their rights. Many opted instead to pass their title deeds to their shaykhs, to former tax farmers, and even to city merchants in return for cultivation rights and a share of the crop. Unsuccessful in their attempt to create a class of small landowners and taxpayers in Iraq, the Ottomans realized later in the nineteenth century that the new system had resulted in a great loss of revenue and government control over large tracts of cultivated land. They therefore attempted to ban further granting of title deeds after 1881, and sought to repossess the lands that had been granted.[71]

The Ottoman effort to reduce the power of the shaykhs and to repossess land inflamed the tribes of the Hindiyya canal, and the Muntafiq and the Shamiyya regions, leading to a series of rebellions in 1849, 1852, 1863–1866, 1878–1883, and 1899–1905. The revolts involved the Bani Lam, the Khaz'al, the Zubayd, the Dulaym, the Zafir, the 'Afak, and the Al Bu Muhammad. Some of the early revolts reflected the objection of the paramount shaykhs to the Ottoman attempt to break their power. Others signaled the reaction of tribesmen to tax demands, which they could not meet, to government attempts to reclaim title deeds, or to military conscription. And still others reflected the estranged relations between shaykhs and tribesmen.[72] Ottoman officials and ulama in Najaf and Karbala shared a common interest in trying to pacify the tribes. Whereas the former were mostly concerned with increasing tax revenues, the latter desired to secure the pilgrimage, the corpse traffic, and the flow of charities to the shrine cities. Thus, for example, during his first tenure as governor (1852), Namiq Pasha sought the intercession of Shi'i ulama with such tribes as the 'Afak, the Shammar Tuqa, the Khaz'al, the 'Ubayd, the Zafir, and the Dulaym in order to end their revolt, which was probably encouraged by Wadi Bay, the paramount shaykh of the Zubayd, who was the tax

[71] Sluglett, "Land Tenure," 494–95; Jwaideh, "Midhat Pasha," 124.

[72] Lorimer, *Gazetteer*, 1,1B:1358–59, 1361–62, 1366, 1425–27, 1430, 1434, 1505–10; Nieuwenhuis, *Politics and Society*, 135–38; Jwaideh, "Midhat Pasha," 116, 128; Samira Haj, "The Problems of Tribalism: The Case of Nineteenth-Century Iraqi History," *SH* 16 (1991): 55; Sa'idi, *'Asha'ir al-'iraq*, 94.

farmer of the Hindiyya district.[73] Some of these tribal sections were still not Shi'i, and the function of the ulama as mediators between them and the government increased their influence among the tribes.

During the nineteenth century, the bulk of Iraq's tribes settled down and took up agriculture. While the Bani Tamim, sections of the Shammar and the Dafafi'a, and the Bani 'Amir showed a tendency to settle down already during the term of the last Mamluk governor, Da'ud Pasha (1816–1831), tribal settlement gained momentum only after the Ottomans resumed direct control over Iraq.[74] The population estimates for Iraq demonstrate the scope of this process of settlement and its impact on the social composition of southern and central Iraq. Whereas in 1867 the percentage of the nomadic and rural elements of the population of southern Iraq was 50 and 41 percent, by 1905 this changed to 19 and 72 percent, respectively. Similarly, in central Iraq this ratio changed from 23 and 39 percent to 7 and 78 percent, respectively.[75] The establishment of cities in central and southern Iraq in the latter part of the nineteenth century was yet another indication of the changing relations between the desert and the sown in the area. With the exception of Diwaniyya, Suq al-Shuyukh, Zubayr, and Hayy, which were established just before or early in the nineteenth century, no less than twenty cities, including 'Amara and Nasiriyya, were either established or expanded from small villages in the latter part of this century. The increase in the number of cities reflected the breaking of confederations and the increase in tribal settlement.[76]

The transition to agriculture diversified tribal economy and stratified tribal society. The possession of agricultural property altered the balance of political power between the settled and the nomadic tribes. It greatly affected the internal relationships of the settled tribes, in changing the role of the shaykh and widening the gap between the rich and the poor sections. In his capacity as tax farmer or title-deeds holder, the shaykh assumed new responsibilities. He had to maintain order and security in his tribe's territory, to arbitrate in disputes among his tribesmen, to represent the tribe vis-à-vis the government, to organize forced labor and other communal works, and to supervise the distribution of water among the tribal cultivators.[77]

[73] Nawwar, Ta'rikh, 173, 175, 178; Lorimer, Gazetteer, 1B:1366.

[74] Nawwar, Ta'rikh, 141, 156, 158–59; 'Azzawi, Ta'rikh, 6:246, and 7:220; Lady Anne Blunt, Bedouin Tribes of the Euphrates (New York, 1879), 384.

[75] Hasan, "Growth and Structure," 344.

[76] 'Azzawi, Ta'rikh, 7:136, 236–38; Wardi, Dirasa, 162–63; Sarkis, Mabahith 'iraqiyya, 1:264–77, 315–16; Albertine Jwaideh, "Aspects of Land Tenure and Social Change in Lower Iraq during Late Ottoman Times," in Land Tenure and Social Transformation in the Middle East, ed. Tarif Khalidi (Beirut, 1984), 346.

[77] Charles Issawi, The Economic History of the Middle East, 1800–1914 (Chicago, 1966), 172.

On their part, small tribal sections and individual tribesmen became attached to land and grew conscious of its function as a tribal home. Tribal linguistic terms for both the territorial area in which tribes moved with their flocks and herds (*dira*) and for holding (*lazma*) evolved among the settled tribes along the middle Euphrates to convey a sense of holding landed property.[78]

In contrast with nomadic communities, the life of which reflected great mobility and fluidity, the opportunity for continual change of residential area was all but denied to the settled tribesmen. The attachment of individual tribesmen to small pieces of land triggered disputes between tribes and tribesmen over water and land. This, in turn, reinforced the fragmentation of tribal society and diminished group solidarity, particularly in the areas close to cities. Similar developments were observed in other parts of the Middle East where sedentarization of nomadic tribes took place during the nineteenth century. While in Egypt the beginning of the process had preceded that of Iraq by almost half a century, in both countries the process was greatly influenced by the introduction of perennial irrigation based on extensive water canal systems. Like their Iraqi counterparts, Egyptian shaykhs of formerly nomadic and semi-nomadic tribes had also emerged as big landowners, while the tribesmen "were lost among the fellahin."[79] Thus, both in Iraq and in Egypt the common socioeconomic interests of shaykhs and tribesmen grew weaker as they were pulled apart in the process of tribal settlement. Yet, unlike the relatively uncomplicated and completed procedures carried out in Egypt under Muhammad 'Ali and Sa'id, the confused conditions of land registration in Iraq resulted in a larger number of claims of tribes, and individual tribesmen, for land occupancy, cultivation rights, and water supply than in Egypt.[80] Indeed, the case of the 'Afak and the Daghara tribes, which clashed over land and water around 1881, and that of the tribes of Samawa, which quarreled in 1900 over the cultivation of rice, are only two examples of many such disputes among the settled tribes.[81]

Whereas the economy of nomadic tribes relies mainly on camels that are not so much water-dependent, agricultural occupation places a far heavier demand on fresh water supply. Water became the lifeblood of tribal cultivators and a scarce resource for which Iraqi tribes and tribesmen competed to maximize its use and to increase their crop. The physical proximity of fields to water canals was critical. Those near the top of the canals had an

---

[78] Jwaideh, "Land Tenure," 333–35; idem, "Midhat Pasha," 130.

[79] Gabriel Baer, "The Settlement of the Beduins," in his *Studies in the Social History of Modern Egypt* (Chicago, 1969), 6–12, citation on 7.

[80] Jwaideh, "Land Tenure," 338–39; Sir Ernest Dowson, *An Inquiry into Land Tenure and Related Questions* (Letchworth, 1931), 26.

[81] 'Azzawi, *Ta'rikh*, 8:65, 138, 197–98.

immense advantage of access to water over those farther down. In the absence of countervailing custom, social sanction, or physical force, the users near the top of the canal satisfied their own needs first before allowing water to flow on down to their less-fortunate neighbors below. Those near the tail end of the canal thus often received less water, and in a less timely fashion, than those near the top. Thomas Lyell, who served as assistant director of land registration and magistrate in the Baghdad district just after the British occupation of Iraq in 1917, remarked: "Among the tribes, brother will fight against brother over the question of a small canal . . . [and over] the action of one brother in damming up the water so as to divert it on to his land, and not removing the dam at the promised time, thereby depriving the other brother of his rightful share and endangering his crop."[82]

The disorder which followed the fragmentation of tribal structure, and the decline in the political and military power of the shaykhs, help explain the emergence of the *sirkals* (from the Persian word *sarkar*: the head of work) and the *sayyids* among the settled tribes. The origin of both the *sirkals* and the *sayyids* among the tribes of Iraq is obscure and it may very well be that their increase in number and influence, if not initial appearance, was closely tied to the settlement of the tribes and the reconstruction of tribal order. Whereas the *sirkals* essentially assumed a socioeconomic role, the *sayyids* also fulfilled religious and administrative functions within the tribe, thus greatly stimulating the conversion of the tribesmen to Shi'ism.

The *sirkals* proliferated in numbers during the nineteenth century. They were to be found only among the tribal cultivators and had no counterpart among the nomads. They assumed such roles as foremen, headmen, group leaders, or small sectional chiefs. Sometimes they also acted as minor shaykhs or heads of small tribal sections, but more frequently they appeared as spokesmen or representatives of the tribesmen-cultivators. The *sirkals*, whose office became semi-hereditary, superintended the work of a group of cultivators and assigned the work load of each group member. The shaykhs, and those city dwellers who were holders of title deeds, needed the *sirkals* to extract their share of revenue from the tribesmen to whom they had granted their pieces of land for cultivation. The *sirkals* were thus brokers whose main role was to keep the land under cultivation and to collect revenues for the landowner.[83] As will be seen in chapter 3, the status of the *sirkals* vis-à-vis the shaykhs, and their influence within the tribes, increased further following the establishment of the monarchy.

There are no indications that *sayyids*, or any other religious figures, lived

[82] Lyell, *The Ins and Outs of Mesopotamia*, 42.

[83] Jwaideh, "Land Tenure," 343–44, 347, 349; idem, "Midhat Pasha," 130, 132–33; Fariq al-Muzhir Al Fir'awn, *al-Qada' al-'asha'iri* (Baghdad, 1941), 159.

among the nomadic tribes of Iraq. This was also the case with respect to the
nomadic tribes of Arabia, who had not had any religious figures among
them before they accepted the Wahhabi creed.[84] As in modern southern
Arabia and in the Funj Sultanate of the Sudan (1504–1821), the *sayyid*s in
Iraq were associated with settled and semi-settled tribes rather than with
camel breeders.[85] Their absence among nomads was probably due to the
fact that life in the desert invoked puritanism rather than rich religious
rituals and cults of saints.[86] The tribal *sayyid*s abounded particularly in
the settled Shi'i areas of central and southern Iraq. They claimed descent
from 'Ali, the first Shi'i imam, through his wife Fatima al-Zahra, who was
the Prophet's daughter.[87] Among the Shabana marsh tribe, for example,
the *sayyid*s constituted as much as 20 percent of the population even in the
mid-twentieth century.[88] In the marshes, where the tribesmen were rice
cultivators and buffalo breeders, there were few villages that did not boast
at least one family who claimed descent from the Prophet, and there were
also certain small villages which consisted entirely of *sayyid*s.[89] The economic welfare of *sayyid*s varied. While some became wealthy landowners,
the majority were engaged in humble occupations, relying on their claim to
the Shi'i religious tax of one-fifth of the income (the *khums*) incumbent
upon all faithful Shi'is. Among the settled tribes, their claim for a fifth of
the crop was known as "my ancestor's right" (*haqq jaddi*).[90]

The authenticity of the greater number of *sayyid*s in Iraq had not gone
unquestioned. Since membership in this stratum conferred social prestige
and potential material gain, claimants sometimes changed their place of
residence to avoid a thorough examination of their status by the tribesmen.[91] Some *sayyid*s were emissaries who originated from the shrine cities
to propagate Shi'i Islam and opted to settle down among the tribes. Others

[84] John Burckhardt, *Notes on the Bedouins and Wahabys*, 2 vols. (London, 1831), 1:99.

[85] On modern southern Arabia see Patricia Crone, "Tribes Without Saints," Paper Submitted in the Melon Seminar, 19 April 1991, Department of Near Eastern Studies, Princeton
University, esp. 5, 22–23. On the Funj Sultanate see Abdel Ghaffar Ahmed, "Tribal and
Sedentary Elites: A Bridge between Two Communities," in *The Desert and the Sown: Nomads in the Wider Society*, ed. Cynthia Nelson (Berkeley, 1973), 83.

[86] Alois Musil, *The Manners and Customs of the Rwala Bedouins* (New York, 1928),
417–18; Michael Meeker, *Literature and Violence in North Arabia* (Cambridge, 1979), 23–
24; Ernest Gellner, "Flux and Reflux in the Faith of Men," in his *Muslim Society* (Cambridge,
1981), 81–82; Emrys Peters, "The Paucity of Ritual among Middle Eastern Pastoralists," in
Islam in Tribal Societies: From the Atlas to the Indus, ed. Akbar Ahmed and David Hart
(London, 1984), esp. 210.

[87] 'Azzawi, *'Asha'ir*, 4:229.

[88] Fernea, *Shaykh and Effendi*, 95.

[89] Wilfred Thesiger, *The Marsh Arabs* (London, 1964), 67.

[90] Batatu, *The Old Social Classes*, 155–56; Wardi, *Dirasa*, 246.

[91] 'Azzawi, *'Asha'ir*, 4:229; 'Ala' al-Din al-Bayati, *al-Rashidiyya: dirasa antrobolojiyya
ijtima'iyya* (Najaf, 1971), 122; Batatu, *The Old Social Classes*, 74, 153; S. M. Salim, *Marsh*

were wandering holy men, diviners, or soothsayers who arrived in Iraq mainly from Arabia, Syria, and Iran. Thus, the Abu Tabikh family originated in al-Hasa, the Zuwayn migrated to Iraq from Mecca, the Yasari and the 'Abbas from Medina, the Al Magutar from Syria, and the Qazwinis from Iran.[92] Some *sayyids* had most likely been Sunnis before their arrival in Iraq and they accepted Shi'ism after their settlement among the tribes. In two cases, the increase in influence of *sayyids* was also closely associated with the Ottoman attempt to break the confederations and the power of the shaykhs, and with the desire of *sayyids* to acquire landed property. The *sayyids* of 'Amara were said to have arrived there from the Hijaz around 1798, when many of the tribes of the former region were still subordinated to the Muntafiq. During either the first or the second tenure of Namiq Pasha (1852 and 1861–1868) as governor of Iraq, some of them were appointed tax farmers.[93] In the case of the Khaz'al, the Ottomans encouraged extraneous *sayyids* to settle among some of its tribal sections in order to undermine the influence of the paramount shaykhs. Given lands, they attracted tribesmen from various clans to work on their estates, thereby splitting them away from their parent unit.[94] The Ottomans thus acted like the Funj Sultans, who had granted lands to religious figures that settled with their followers among the sedentary tribes in the Sudan, thereby creating an alternative to the tribal leaders.[95] Yet, the use of *sayyids* to split confederations in Iraq seemed to be more the exception than the rule, and for the most part their religious, sociopolitical, and administrative roles in the tribes were intended to soothe the breaking down of tribal society and to restore unity.

The *sayyids* proliferated among those tribes in Iraq whose former social structure had been broken in the process of settlement. The transition of the tribes from nomadism to agriculture created a pressing need for additional mechanisms to cope with the new socioeconomic complexities as well as for saintly services. Tying individual tribesmen to water and small pieces of land, agriculture fragmented the tribal community. The confederations ceased to function as political communities and their large component tribes lost their distinction as collective economic units. The settled tribesmen became more vulnerable than their nomadic counterparts because of their dependency for their livelihood on a crop which could be

---

Dwellers of the Euphrates Delta (London, 1962), 62; Thesiger, Marsh Arabs, 67; George Harris, *Iraq: Its People, Its Society, Its Culture* (New Haven, 1958), 71.

[92] Pierre-Jean Luizard, *La Formation de l'Irak Contemporain: Le Rôle Politique des Uléma Chiites à la Fin de la Domination Ottomane et au Moment de la Construction de l'Etat Irakien* (Paris, 1991), 197–98.

[93] 'Azzawi, 'Asha'ir, 4:249.

[94] Batatu, *The Old Social Classes*, 75.

[95] Ahmed, "Tribal and Sedentary Elites," 85.

easily destroyed. The shaykhs, who had lost much of their former political authority, were asked by the Ottomans to administer economically complex and socially stratified tribal systems, a task for which they were not well equipped. The *sayyids* were thus highly sought after by all members of the settled tribes and became an integral part of the fragmented society. They defused tension within and between tribes, or between tribesmen and non-tribesmen, installing themselves as "traffic lights" in the fragmented system and acting as the "grease in its wheel."

Aware of the decline in their authority and esteem among the tribesmen, the shaykhs needed the *sayyids* to restore order and stability among the fragmented tribal units, for it was the *sayyids* who possessed such eminence as derived from a valued descent group which could compensate for the decline of the influence of the shaykhs. This point is neatly illustrated by the case of shaykh Sattar of the Al 'Ali section of the Bani Hasan tribe. In the late nineteenth century Sattar gave his two daughters in marriage to *sayyids*, Hadi Qazwini and Muhammad Ibrahim Bahr al-'Ulum, who were each members of distinguished Shi'i religious families. It is known that in the latter case Sattar exerted pressures on the Bahr al-'Ulum family to concede to the marriage and he gave his new son-in-law large tracts of land and orchards in the Hindiyya area between Karbala and Tuwayrij. Since he wished to take personal care of his new property, Sayyid Bahr al-'Ulum left Najaf and settled among the tribesmen, to whom he began to teach Islam.[96]

Sayyids often acted as the political agents of the shaykhs, keeping them informed of the affairs within their tribal section. In order to mobilize their tribes either for fighting or for some corporate enterprise, the shaykhs first needed to secure the *sayyids*' support. Once that was achieved, the shaykhs could usually rely on the *sayyids* to convince the various tribal groups of the justice and value of the shaykhs' cause. Moreover, since the shaykhs rarely knew how to conduct their own correspondence, the *sayyids* would also write letters on their behalf, signing them with the impress of the shaykhs' ring.[97] The position of *sayyids* as the shaykhs' confidants, and their function as mediators between alienated groups and in inter-tribal conflicts, increased their influence among the tribesmen. The status of *sayyids* further increased since some functioned as saints, their reputation as holy men being particularly strong among the marsh dwellers of 'Amara. *Sayyids* claimed to possess supernatural powers to cure maladies, cause misfortune, bring blessing, and practice various other magic rites. They

[96] Muhammad Mahdi Bahr al-'Ulum al-Tabataba'i, *Rijal al-sayyid bahr al-'ulum al-ma'ruf bi al-fawa'id al-rijaliyya*, 3 vols. (Najaf, 1965–1966), 1:157–58.

[57] Fulanain, *The Marsh Arab Haji Rikkan* (Philadelphia, 1928), 103–4; Fernea, *Shaykh and Effendi*, 96–97.

gained money on account of this, as well as the respect and veneration of tribesmen, who used to swear oaths in their name. Their high status was evident in the fact that blood money for a *sayyid* was double that of an ordinary person. The *sayyids* gave sanction to weddings, circumcisions, funerals, and other celebrations. Their prayers in times of drought, sickness, or any other crisis were looked upon as the collective prayers of the tribesmen. Usually the only literate men in most groups, they also served as physicians, scribes, and constituted the link to the outside world.[98] Their influence over the tribesmen rendered the *sayyids* a catalyst of conversion and most valuable to the emissaries who came to propagate Shi'i Islam among the tribes.

The intensification of Shi'i propagation from the early nineteenth century is evident in local chronicles. At that time the Shi'i emissaries and preachers were assisted by the relative peaceful conditions in the country and by the loose Mamluk control of the area south of Baghdad. They also benefited from the indifference of the last Mamluk governor, Da'ud Pasha, who apparently was willing to tolerate Shi'i missionary activity.[99] The emissaries took further advantage of the Ottoman reversal in 1831 of the Mamluk policy which had prohibited the public exercise of Shi'i rituals in Iraq. They gained still greater freedom of activity among the tribesmen following the new strategy of Sultan 'Abd al-Hamid II (1876–1909) which called for Islamic unity, and the emphasize of the doctrine of equality by the Young Turks after their 1908 Revolution.

Sunni ulama and Ottoman officials cited 'Abd al-Hamid's strategy as the major factor which enabled the Shi'is to bolster their position in Iraq and send emissaries to the tribes. They pointed to the lack of Ottoman counterpropaganda, and to the very small number of Sunni ulama in Iraq, who were overshadowed by their Shi'i counterparts. It was claimed that the Shi'i emissaries took advantage of the ignorance of the tribesmen, who fell under their influence. So strong was their persuasive power that even some Ottoman soldiers and policemen were converted to Shi'ism, rendering them no longer reliable in the eyes of the government.[100] Proposed solutions to counteract the Shi'i activity included an increase in Sunni education and preaching in Iraq. In 1900 Muhammad Rashid Rida noted the

[98] Wardi, *Dirasa*, 246–48; Salim, *Marsh Dwellers*, 62–63; 'Abd al-Karim al-Nadwani, *Ta'rikh al-'amara wa-'asha'iriha* (Baghdad, 1961), 22–24; Lorimer, *Gazetteer*, 2A:790; Harris, *Iraq*, 60, 70–71.

[99] Kirkukli, *Dawhat al-wuzara'*, 278–79; Ibn Sanad, *Matali' al-su'ud*, 169. See also Longrigg, *Four Centuries*, 250.

[100] Ibn Sanad, *Matali' al-su'ud*, 169; Haydari, *'Unwan al-majd*, 111, 112; Anon., "Kalimat 'an al-'iraq wa-ahlihi li-'alim ghayur 'ala al-dawla wa-madhhab ahl al-sunna," *al-Manar* 11 (1908): 46; "al-Bida' wa al-khurafat," 307; Deringil, "The Struggle Against Shi'ism," 49, 54.

intention of the Ottoman government to send ulama to the districts of Basra, the Muntafiq, and Karbala to educate the tribes.[101] Those five Sunni ulama who were sent to Iraq in 1905 to organize Ottoman education and to counter Shi'i propaganda failed to reverse the trend. Besides their very small number, they lacked the support of local officials, and were not highly motivated because they did not receive their salaries regularly. Thus, in 1907 the Baghdadi *'alim* Ahmad Shakir al-Alusi reiterated the need for trustworthy Sunni ulama in Iraq, and proposed to institute "mobile madrasas" consisting of ulama who would travel among the tribes to instill Sunni Islam among them.[102]

The Ottomans failed to curtail the activity of the Shi'i emissaries not only because of the insufficient measures that they had taken toward that end or because of their lack of a social base in Iraq. They failed in large part because of the swiftness and intensity of the conversion particularly during the second half of the nineteenth century. Indeed, the development of the Bani Hukayyim (of the Zubayd), the Shibil (of the Khaz'al), the Al Fatla and their section the Daghara (of the Dulaym), the Bani Hasan (of the Bani Malik), and the 'Afak show the increasing settlement of their shepherd sections close to Najaf and Karbala, and their conversion to Shi'ism, in the latter part of the nineteenth century.[103] The magnitude of the conversion was not fully appreciated outside Iraq before the late nineteenth century, and in the absence of detailed population estimates that distinguished between Sunnis and Shi'is, some Ottoman officials still considered the Shi'is a minority of only 40 percent of the population. As may be gathered from Selim Deringil's findings in the Ottoman archives, repeated references to the spread of Shi'ism in Iraq were made mainly during the late 1890s and early 1900s.[104] These references must have been stimulated by Shirazi's move from Najaf to Samarra in 1875 and his subsequent involvement in the affairs which led to the Iranian Tobacco Revolt of 1891–92. While the scant number of references during the Mamluk period may be attributed to the infrequent reports of the governors to Istanbul, it cannot explain the very few, if any, references after 1831, when the Ottomans resumed direct rule over Iraq. Part of the explanation has to do with the fact that the Ottomans did not grasp the implications of the transition of the tribes from nomadism to sedentary life in Iraq, and were not fully aware of the magnitude of the conversion until late in the nineteenth century.

British officials were also dazed by the scope of the conversion, which continued as late as the twentieth century. It was noted in 1917 that the process was still going on vigorously, and that there were examples of

[101] "Bab al-akhbar," *al-Manar* 2 (1900): 687.
[102] Deringil, "The Struggle Against Shi'ism," 52, 55.
[103] Stephen Longrigg, *Iraq, 1900 to 1950* (Oxford, 1953), 25.
[104] Deringil, "The Struggle Against Shi'ism," 49, 50.

conversion even among the Sa'dun family, who claimed descent from the *Sharif* of Mecca and whose members served as paramount shaykhs of the Muntafiq.[105]

THE NATURE OF THE CONVERSION

The rapid conversion of Iraq's tribes to Shi'ism was by no means perfect and by the twentieth century Arab tribesmen were still divided along sectarian lines as the conversion cut across confederations and tribes.

Thus, the Shurayyifat of the Muntafiq confederation became Shi'i whereas the Shuhayyim, a constituent of the Bani Humayyid section of the Muntafiq, remained partly Sunni as late as the twentieth century.[106] The Fadagha tribe in the district of Kazimayn was split between Shi'is and Sunnis, and so were the Bani Sa'id of the Muntafiq and the Zubu' of the Shammar, who lived in the districts of Suq al-Shuyukh and Kazimayn, respectively. Whereas the majority of the Bani Tamim became Shi'i, a few of its sections remained Sunni. Likewise, although the Zubayd confederation became almost entirely Shi'i, parts of its Bani 'Ajil and the 'Azza sections remained Sunni early in the twentieth century. The Jubur al-Wawi of the Euphrates valley became Shi'i but the Jubur of the Tigris remained Sunni, both being sections of the Zubayd as well. Still in the Zubayd, the Janabiyyin, who lived near Musayyib, remained mostly Sunni and only some of its branches became Shi'i. The Al Bu Muhammad confederation became almost entirely Shi'i except a few small branches who remained Sunni. The Muhaysin section of the Ka'b that settled upon Shatt al-'Arab chiefly below Basra was also mostly Shi'i, with the exception of parts of Bayt Ghanim, which remained Sunni. The Rabi'a confederation also became almost entirely Shi'i, save for the important Kawwam section that was to be found both near Kut al-'Amara and in the district of Kazimayn.[107] The Shammar and the Dulaym confederations were split along religious lines as well. The Shammar Jarba that migrated to Iraq only in the late eighteenth century and whose tribal domain was in the Jezira in between the Euphrates and Tigris, remained Sunni. The Shammar Tuqa settled down near Karbala early in the eighteenth century and became Shi'i. Some of its branches frequented the Shamiyya and the Najaf districts and their tribesmen were converted to Shi'ism. Similarly, whereas most of the Dulaym confederation, whose domain was north of Baghdad remained Sunni, its Al Fatla branch settled in the Hindiyya district and became Shi'i.[108]

In converting the tribesmen to Shi'ism the emissaries apparently did not

---

[105] Office of the Civil Commissioner, *The Arab of Mesopotamia*, 69–70.
[106] Ibid., 69; Longrigg, *Iraq*, 22.
[107] Lorimer, *Gazetteer*, 2A:777, 779, 780, 785, 788, and 2B:1253, 1254, 1570, 1949.
[108] Ibid., 2B:1748; Batatu, *The Old Social Classes*, 41.

use any specific procedure since conversion to or within Islam did not involve any formal process.[109] It is most likely that the introduction of Shi'i rituals and Islamic law among the settled tribes facilitated the conversion as the tribesmen began sharing the peasants' view of the holy. One may assume that the conversion took place in stages and that at any period of time it entailed anywhere between several individuals and entire tribal sections. It may be that in some cases tribesmen followed their shaykhs. But this is by no means a binding scenario as may be gathered from the case of the Muntafiq confederation. Although the entire tribal sections of this confederation became Shi'i during the nineteenth century, most members of the Sa'dun leading family were still Sunnis on the eve of the British occupation of Iraq. It is possible that in several cases the *sayyids* were the first to accept Shi'ism, and that they were subsequently followed by some or all of the tribal sections among whom they settled.

While some Sunni ulama regarded the conversion of the tribesmen as their defection from the Sunni faith, others viewed the tribesmen as barely Muslims prior to their conversion to Shi'ism. Yet they all perceived the change in the religious status of the tribesmen in Iraq as a conversion. Thus, in referring to the Shi'is and describing the conversion, some Sunni ulama used linguistic variations as derived from the Arabic term *rawafid*.[110] This term conveys clear connotations of "rejection" of and "defection" from Sunni dogma. Moreover, the following remarks made by Muhammad Rashid Rida in a comment to an article published in his *al-Manar* in 1908 even go so far as to suggest that in his eyes the tribesmen had hardly been Muslims before they were converted to Shi'ism, and indeed, to Islam: "If those [Shi'i] emissaries preach [religion] among the [tribesmen], and teach them the Islamic duties, as well as what is permissible and what is prohibited, then, from the point of view of their religion, the current position of the tribesmen is better than their former status."[111]

It may be that in accepting Shi'ism the tribesmen sought to evade conscription. It may also be as in the case of the Muntafiq that the conversion was an act of protest on the part of ordinary tribesmen against the widening gaps between the rich and the poor sections of the confederation, and particularly the transformation of the Sunni Sa'duns from tribal shaykhs into a landed aristocracy with strong urban vested interests. It is possible that the conversion symbolized an anti-government act of protest on the part of the tribesmen. The Ottoman attempts from 1831 to settle the nomadic population, expand agriculture, distribute title deeds to individuals, and increase the collection of taxes in Iraq led to feelings of injustice

---

[109] Richard Bulliet, *Conversion to Islam in the Medieval Period* (Cambridge, Mass., 1979), 33.

[110] See, for example, Alusi, "Di'ayat al-rafd," 440.

[111] "Kalimat 'an al-'iraq," 49.

and opposition among the tribesmen as well as to acts of violence and resistance. Involved as they were in an intense conflict with the government, the tribesmen became receptive to Shi'i Islam since they found the anti-government aspects of Shi'ism and its struggle against oppression and tyranny appealing.[112] But as valid as these reasons may be, they still do not entirely clarify the relation between the radical change which the tribesmen experienced following their transition from nomadic life to agricultural activity and their motivation to espouse Shi'ism.

It is the fragmentation of tribal system, which generated an identity crisis among the settled tribesmen, as well as their need to relocate themselves on the social map of their surrounding environment, that can fully explain the motivation of the tribesmen. The settlement transformed the former way of life of the tribesmen, creating a sense of displacement and alienation among them. As such, the conversion to Shi'ism was a reaction of the tribesmen to the crisis which they experienced following the breaking down of their former socioeconomic and political organization. The conversion was a compensation for the tribesmen's loss of their former way of life and an indication for their pursuit of stability. Moreover, the increase in sedentarization resulted in new socioeconomic contacts between the settled tribesmen and the cities around them, notably, Najaf and Karbala. These contacts sharpened for the tribesmen the issue of their identity, and increased their motivation for social inclusion and mobility. Seen from this point of view, the conversion reflected the attempt of tribesmen, as well as shaykhs, to adjust distances between them and their new neighbors in the Shi'i urban centers. Their conversion to Shi'ism gave the tribesmen a greater religious legitimization, enabling them to consider themselves "better Muslims." In adopting an overt religious behavior they could gain more respect. And in observing Shi'i rituals, like the visitation of the Shi'i holy cities, they could improve their socioeconomic contacts with the urban Shi'i population in southern Iraq. Conversion was thus the vehicle through which the tribesmen attempted to gain a new start and to rearrange their religious complex and social identity.

Nonetheless, the conversion to Shi'ism did not pervade the former social and moral values of the tribesmen. This was evident in the nature of Shi'i rituals and the position of Shi'i Islamic law among the tribesmen, as well as in the relations between Sunni and Shi'i tribes. The Shi'i emissaries promoted the visitation to the tombs of the imams, the cult of Shi'i saints, and the rituals connected with the commemoration of Husayn, the third imam. As will be seen in chapters 5 and 6, the emissaries adjusted Shi'i rituals to conform with Arab ideal attributes of manhood (muruwwa) and Iraqi tribal styles of celebration, notably, the hosa, which included clamorous

---

[112] Luizard, La Formation de L'Irak, 112, 119, 190–91.

receptions, horse riding, and firing weapons in the air. Since the tribesmen always preferred to hear the songs of heroes, the emissaries used Arabic poetry to dramatize the heroic stand of Husayn and his companions in the battle of Karbala. They also highlighted 'Ali's courage, his eloquence of speech, his honesty, and his simple way of life, thereby appealing to tribal values of masculinity, courage, pride, honor, and chivalry. The Shi'i emissaries thus acted in much the same fashion as the Prophet Muhammad, who had adjusted Islamic teaching to the Arab value system in order to facilitate the conversion of the Arab tribes to Islam.

The rituals were supplemented by the introduction of Shi'i law into the tribes by the religious agents (the *mu'min*s). The latter were sent to the settled tribes by the chief mujtahids who resided in Najaf and Karbala. Unlike the *sayyid*s, the *mu'min*s were not members of the tribe. Assumed to be graduates of the madrasa, the *mu'min*s were authorized to settle such matters as marriage, divorce, and inheritance. They were also said to have introduced the practice of temporary marriage (*mut'a*) into the tribes, thus enabling affluent shaykhs and *sayyid*s to contract a large number of marriages. The *mu'min*s conducted religious services and led the mourning ceremonies in commemoration of Husayn. Acting as religious advisors to the shaykhs, they were paid for their services from the communal contributions of tribesmen.[113]

But while Shi'i rituals and Islamic law helped the converted Arab tribesmen to cope better with their more complex daily life, Shi'ism did not preempt the role of genealogy among them, which became even more essential to establishing an individual's identity following the erosion of tribal cohesiveness.[114] Indeed, religious worship (*'ibadat*) among the tribesmen and their daily activities (*mu'amalat*) continued to reflect their former social values. Although the new rituals enriched their cultural life, they did not erode tribal moral values, which continued to function underneath the newly acquired religious identity of the tribesmen. The rituals, which stressed Arab attributes of ideal manhood, provided the tribesmen with new heroes with whom they could identify and in whose names they could swear oaths. The crisis that resulted from the breakdown of tribal organization and lack of political authority encouraged the cult of Shi'i saints, whose images articulated the wish of the tribesmen for authority. Likewise, Shi'i religious law did not permeate tribal legal institutions, which eclipsed Islamic codes in importance. Tribal law and custom varied by tribes, and in spite of the introduction of basic Shi'i Islamic law, there did not develop a unified legal system among the tribes of Iraq. Indeed, the

---

[113] "Bab al-akhbar," 687; Ahmad Fahmi, *Taqrir hawla al-'iraq* (Baghdad, 1926), 49; Bayati, *al-Rashidiyya*, 127–28; Salim, *Marsh Dwellers*, 64.

[114] Muhammad Rida al-Muzaffar, "Hifaz al-qaba'il al-'arabiyya 'ala taqalidiha," in Fir'awn, *al-Qada' al-'asha'iri*, xxxviii.

impact of Shi'i law was confined mainly to marriage and divorce. Many tribes continued to retain their own distinct legal customs, and their socio-economic dealings and customs regarding women continued to reflect tribal codes. Even their methods of conflict resolution remained strongly tribal in nature, clans and tribes continuing to pay blood money collectively well into the twentieth century.[115]

The continuous interaction between Sunni nomads and Shi'i sedentary groups further reinforced the latter's tribal moral values and heritage as well as their Arab identity. Thus, even the old men of the marsh Arabs continued to tell legendary tales of the courage, honor, and generosity of their tribal ancestors, and Iraqi villagers persisted in calling themselves settled nomads, and claimed descent from old fathers and former nomadic tribes well into the twentieth century.[116] The durability of kinship among the settled tribes also found embodiment in the relations between the converted tribes that settled in between the two rivers and the Arab marsh dwellers. The area of settlement of many of the marsh dwellers cut across Iraqi and Iranian territories, and it may be that some of them were converted to Shi'ism as a result of their contacts with Iranians outside Iraqi-Ottoman territory. The tribesmen despised the marsh dwellers because of what they considered the latter's mixed blood, their practice of temporary marriage, and their name *ma'dan* or *al-ma'adi*, which outside the marshes connoted "yokel."[117]

The image of the marsh dwellers as inferiors is illustrated by the case of the Al Bu Muhammad confederation, from which the bulk of 'Amara's tribes were drawn. Early in the twentieth century the Al Bu Muhammad all lived in reed huts. Their area proper was between 'Amara down to 'Uzayyir in Iraq and partly inside Persian Arabistan. Although their principle occupation was buffalo breeding, they were engaged in rice cultivation and fishing as well. In spite of their descent from the Zubayd, they were despised by the neighboring Arab tribes, and it was rumored that they were of Indian or Persian origin. The neighboring tribes refused to give their daughters in marriage to the Al Bu Muhammad and pointed to their intermarriage with Persian tribesmen as proof of their inferiority. It was also said that the shaykhs of the Al Bu Muhammad, and the *sayyids* who lived among them, enjoyed far more latitude than the Koran permitted regarding the number of their wives.[118] The view of the marsh dwellers as

[115] Ja'far al-Khalili, "al-Qada' al-'asha'iri," in Fir'awn, *al-Qada' al-'asha'iri*, xxvi; Muzaffar, "Hifaz al-qaba'il," in Fir'awn, *al-Qada'*, xxxix; Salim, *Marsh Dwellers*, 51; Hanna Batatu, "Iraq's Underground Shi'a Movements: Characteristics, Causes and Prospects," *MEJ* 35 (1981): 585–86.

[116] Wardi, *Dirasa*, 152–53; Salim, *Marsh Dwellers*, 4, 7, 43; Fernea, *Shaykh and Effendi*, 12–13; Thesiger, *The Marsh Arabs*, 93; Harris, *Iraq*, 72.

[117] Doris Adams, *Iraq's People and Resources* (Berkeley, 1958), 23–24.

[118] Lorimer, *Gazetteer*, 2B:1254–55. See also 'Azzawi, *'Asha'ir*, 3:66.

inferiors because of their "Persian connection" and the practice of temporary marriage by their shaykhs and *sayyid*s demonstrates both the strong
Arab identity of Iraq's converted tribesmen as well as their general reluctance to adopt this practice, which was more common in Iran. Indeed, with
the exception of affluent shaykhs and *sayyid*s, who could afford to contract
marriages with several women, temporary marriage did not take root
among the common tribesmen in Iraq.[119]

The massive conversion of the bulk of Iraq's tribes to Shi'ism mainly
during the nineteenth century facilitated the expansion of a Shi'i polity in
southern Iraq. Although in the nineteenth century the nature of the polity
and its institutions were still unclear, by 1908 the Shi'i mujtahids had
already formulated a political theory which defined the form of government in the state which they envisaged.

[119] Muhsin al-Amin, *al-Husun al-mani'a fi radd ma awradahu sahib al-manar fi haqq al-shi'a* (Damascus, 1909), 37; Muhammad Jawad Mughniyya, "al-Mut'a 'ind al-shi'a al-imamiyya," *al-'Irfan* 37 (1950): 1096; "Bab al-akhbar," 687; Fahmi, *Taqrir hawla al-'iraq*, 49. See also Werner Ende, "Ehe auf Zeit (*mut'a*) in der Innerislamischen Diskussion der Gegenwart," *WI* 20 (1980): 17.

Chapter Two

YEARS OF UPHEAVAL

THE GROWING TREND toward activism in Shi'i Islam and the emergence of the mujtahids as a major force in politics between 1908 and 1920 were influenced by the revival of the Usuli legal school, the centralization of the Shi'i leadership, and the impact of the modernist Islamic thinkers. With the establishment of the Usuli school as the authoritative method of Shi'i Imami jurisprudence in the late eighteenth century, the functions of the mujtahid were defined with greater clarity than previously. The Usuli school also prohibited the imitation of deceased authorities, thus encouraging Shi'i believers to emulate a living mujtahid. Moreover, the period from the second half of the nineteenth century experienced an increase in centralization within the Shi'i leadership in Iraq, which subsequently became more politicized than in the past. The concentration of legal and material power in the hands of a few leading mujtahids, who enjoyed a charismatic aura as well as significant mass followings and funding, was facilitated by the introduction of the telegraph in Iraq and Iran in the 1860s. The telegraph lines between the two countries enabled Iranians to maintain regular contact with their mujtahids in Iraq from the 1870s. While the frequent contacts with their laity increased the authoritative status of the mujtahids in Iraq, the latter now came under increasing pressures from their major financial backers in Iran to take part in worldly affairs. The subsequent growing involvement of leading mujtahids in Iranian political affairs was borne out in 1891–92 when Muhammad Hasan Shirazi led an Iranian mass movement against the Tobacco Concession. This episode symbolized the politicization of the Shi'i leadership and contrasted with the relatively quietist attitude and cooperation that marked the relations between the mujtahids in Iraq and the Qajars during much of the nineteenth century. Although by the time of the Iranian Constitutional Revolution the participation of leading mujtahids in Iraq in Iranian national politics had become a norm, the mujtahids still lacked a political theory that would define the form of their representation in state affairs.[1]

---

[1] Hamid Enayat, *Modern Islamic Political Thought* (Austin, 1982), 161, 162, 167–68; 'Abd al-'Aziz Sachedina, *The Just Ruler (al-Sultan al-'Adil) in Shi'ite Islam* (Oxford, 1988), 21, 23; Meir Litvak, "The Shi'i Ulama of Najaf and Karbala, 1791–1904: A Socio-Political Analysis" (Ph.D. diss., Harvard University, 1991), 104, 119, 168, 173, 175, 282; Abbas Amanat, "In Between the Madrasa and the Market Place: The Designation of Clerical Leadership in Modern Shi'ism," in *Authority and Political Culture in Shi'ism*, ed. Said Amir Arjomand (Albany, 1981), 116–17, 122.

The growing political activism in Shi'i Islam was influenced by the ideas of the modernist Islamic thinkers. At the turn of the twentieth century students and ulama in the shrine cities were not unfamiliar with ideas of patriotism toward one's country (*watan*) as distinguished from the Muslim believer's responsibility toward the Islamic nation (*umma*), the importance of Shi'i-Sunni unity in the face of European expansion, and the need to revive Islam and reconcile it with modernity. These ideas had been advocated by Islamic modernist thinkers like Rafi' al-Tahtawi (1801–1873), Jamal al-Din al-Afghani (1838–1897), Muhammad 'Abduh (1849–1905), and Muhammad Rashid Rida (1865–1935). Their ideas were gradually transmitted to the shrine cities and developed a life of their own as students and ulama received them with little or no regard to their authors.[2] Until the Young Turk Constitutional Revolution of 1908, however, Shi'is in Iraq had difficulties in articulating these ideas largely because of the Ottoman ban on publications and political associations.

THE IMPACT OF TWO REVOLUTIONS

The importance of the constitutional period in Iraq was twofold. First, it enabled Shi'i mujtahids to develop a political theory which laid the foundations for their own representation in state affairs, a goal which they would attempt to pursue not only during the Iranian Constitutional Revolution but also in the course of the establishment of the Iraqi monarchy. Second, the constitutional period created the opportunity for Shi'is in Iraq to debate and articulate the ideas advocated by the Islamic modernists, to spread them outside the madrasa, and ultimately to try to implement them in their own country. The growing European pressures and invasions of Iranian and Ottoman territories that intensified from the time of the constitutional period acted as a further catalyst. The European occupation of Muslim lands stimulated religious and political activism and enabled Shi'i mujtahids to emerge as the leaders of Muslim opposition in Iraq.

The Iranian Constitutional Revolution of 1905–1911 provided the mujtahids with a vision of what an Islamic government should be. The work of Muhammad Husayn Na'ini, *Tanbih al-umma wa-tanzih al-milla* (The Awakening of the Islamic Nation and the Purification of the Islamic Creed), was the most famous theoretical and systematic work written by a Shi'i jurist in support of the Iranian Constitution. The importance of Na'ini's work, which was published in Najaf around 1909, lay in its formulation of a political theory which defined government accountability in the eyes of Shi'i mujtahids and set principles for both their resistance to a

---

[2] Albert Hourani, *Arabic Thought in the Liberal Age*, 2d ed. (Cambridge, 1984), 78–79, 80, 82, 115–19, 128, 140–51, 228–31; Enayat, *Islamic Political Thought*, xi, 41, 47.

ruler and their own representation in state affairs without impairing the shariʻa.[3]

In the course of the Iranian Revolution, the prominent mujtahids Muhammad Kazim Khurasani and ʻAbdallah Mazandarani explained that their two major aims in supporting the constitution were the protection of religion and the overthrow of Muzaffar al-Din Shah, whom they considered an un-Islamic ruler. In the minds of the mujtahids, constitutionalism connoted Islamic law. While they accepted the necessity of a monarchy headed by a king (the Shah), the mujtahids argued that the king could be removed from the throne if he became "careless and lascivious." On 5 August 1906 Muzaffar al-Din Shah was forced to sign a proclamation convening a Constituent National Assembly. For a while, some of the mujtahids supported the Assembly since they considered it an institution capable of checking the Shah's actions and the process of legislation. Thus, the Second Amendment to the Constitution, which was formulated by the delegates to the Assembly, stipulated that a supreme committee of five mujtahids was to scrutinize the bills introduced into parliament to ensure that no law contradicted the shariʻa.[4]

One might argue that the Iranian Constitutional Revolution was merely an internal Iranian affair, as may be gathered from the frequent references of the Persian mujtahids based in the shrine cities to the "Persian homeland" as well as their consideration of the Ottoman and Persian states as two different political entities. As Iranian subjects residing in Ottoman Iraq, the mujtahids drew their main support from among the Shiʻis in Iran and had strong vested economic interests in that country. In backing the Constitution, the pro-constitutionalist mujtahids acted in part in the interest of their major financiers, the Iranian bazaaris, and fought for a form of government that would secure the bazaaris' as well as their own economic interests.[5] Yet, one cannot dismiss the ramifications of the Iranian Revolution in Iraq. The active involvement of Iranian students and mujtahids residing in Iraq in the Revolution generated a heated debate in the shrine cities, dividing the religious circles into pro- and anti-constitutional camps. Moreover, the attempt of prominent mujtahids, who were based in the shrine cities, to shape political institutions in Iran in the course of the Revolution was in many respects a prelude to the role that they would

[3] Enayat, *Islamic Political Thought*, 167, 169. A detailed analysis of Naʼini's work may be found in Abdul-Hadi Hairi, *Shiʻism and Constitutionalism in Iran* (Leiden, 1977), esp. 161–97. An Arabic translation by Salih al-Jaʻfari appeared in 1930–31: "al-Istibdad wa al-dimuqratiyya," *al-ʻIrfan* 20 (1930): 43–46, 172–80, 432–38; 21 (1931): 45–52, 534–52.

[4] Abdul-Hadi Hairi, "Why Did the *Ulama* Participate in the Persian Constitutional Revolution of 1905–1909?" *WI* 17 (1976–77): 131, 133, 144–49; Sachedina, *The Just Ruler*, 24, 226; Ervand Abrahamian, *Iran Between Two Revolutions*, 2d ed. (Princeton, N.J., 1983), 89–90.

[5] Hairi, "*Ulama*," 148, 150–51.

attempt to play, and the goals that they would seek to achieve, in Iraq during the formative years of the establishment of the monarchy.

The full implications of constitutionalism were felt in Iraq following the restoration of the Turkish Constitution in 1908. The implementation of a series of imperial decrees and laws issued by the Ottoman government between August 1908 and May 1909 had an impact throughout the Empire and transformed urban life in Iraq as well.[6] The new laws created opportunities for education as well as a freedom of publication and political association hitherto unknown in the country. The Young Turk Revolution had a particularly strong impact on those Arab Shi'is who had perceived the Iranian Revolution as an internal Iranian affair and were not swayed by it. In contrast, the period from 1908 enabled Arab Shi'is to become involved in political matters, and to articulate the ideas advocated by the Islamic modernists as well as basic problems of religion and nationality.

The restoration of the Turkish Constitution marked the beginning of Shi'i secular education in Iraq. Public primary schools for boys were opened in Baghdad, Kazimayn, Najaf, and Hilla from 1909. The first Shi'i school in Baghdad, *Maktab al-Taraqqi al-Ja'fari al-'Uthmani*, later known as *al-Madrasa al-Ja'fariyya*, was opened in December 1909. The school was meant to train Shi'is in French and mathematics in order to enable them to assume positions and provide services hitherto fulfilled mainly by Jews. The initiative came from 'Ali Bazirgan—an educated Sunni involved in Shi'i community affairs—and from Ja'far Abu al-Timman, a wealthy Shi'i merchant of Baghdad, who would later emerge as an important national figure in Iraq. They obtained a *fatwa* (legal opinion) sanctioning the school from the mujtahid Muhammad Sa'id al-Habbubi, who acknowledged the importance of providing young Shi'is with modern education. Funding for the school, which was attended by some three hundred students, was donated by Shi'i merchants in Kazimayn and Baghdad. The drive for opening two schools in Najaf, *al-Madrasa al-'Alawiyya* and *al-Madrasa al-Murtadawiyya* in 1909, came from supporters of the Iranian Constitution in that city. They secured the necessary *fatwa* and some financial aid from the mujtahid Kazim Khurasani. English, French, and mathematics were taught in both schools.[7] The importance of the beginning of Shi'i secular education is that it created a nucleus of Shi'is whose education

[6] Stanford Shaw and Ezel Koral Shaw, *History of the Ottoman Empire and Modern Turkey*, 2 vols. (Cambridge, 1976–1977), 2:274–76, 282–86; Bernard Lewis, *The Emergence of Modern Turkey*, 2d ed. (Oxford, 1968), 213, 230–31; 'Abbas al-'Azzawi, *Ta'rikh al-'iraq bayna ihtilalayn*, 8 vols. (Baghdad, 1935–1956), 8:157–58, 160–64; Ghassan Atiyya, *Iraq, 1908–1921: A Socio-Political Study* (Beirut, 1973), 53–64.

[7] 'Ali al-Bazirgan, *al-Waqa'i' al-haqiqiyya fi al-thawra al-'iraqiyya* (Baghdad, 1954), 44–48; 'Abd al-Razzaq 'Abd al-Darraji, *Ja'far abu al-timman wa-dawruhu fi al-haraka al-wataniyya fi al-'iraq* (Baghdad, 1978), 31–37; Yusuf Karkush al-Hilli, *Ta'rikh al-hilla*, 2 vols.

reflected a major departure from the curriculum of the traditional madrasa.

The Young Turk Revolution stimulated literary life and the publication of magazines and books in the shrine cities. By the end of the first decade of the twentieth century, people in the shrine cities were reading journals from Turkey, Iran, Egypt, and India. It was estimated in 1911 that fifty to one hundred newspapers and journals arrived in Najaf every week and were distributed to various libraries in the city. Among the magazines that circulated were *al-Manar*, *al-Muqattam*, *al-Muqtataf*, *al-Hilal*, *al-Muqtabas*, and *al-Habl al-Matin*.[8] One newspaper and two magazines were published in Najaf between 1909 and 1911. These were *Ghari* (in Persian, published in 1909 for a year), *Najaf* (in Persian, published for about a year from 1910), and *al-'Ilm* (in Arabic, published for two years from 1910).[9] *Al-'Ilm* was the first Shi'i Arabic magazine to be published in Iraq and the second in the Shi'i Arab world following *al-'Irfan*, which had appeared in Sidon in 1909. It received the blessing of the important mujtahid Shaykh al-Shari'a Isfahani. According to its editor Hibat al-Din al-Shahrastani, the magazine was issued to spread education, to enlighten the minds of the general public in Najaf, to defend Islam along the lines laid down by the modern Islamic reformers, to point to the consistency of Islamic law with the new sciences, and to establish contacts between Najaf and other parts of the Islamic world.[10] Many of the issues that were treated in *al-'Ilm* set the agenda for discussions in Shi'i magazines that appeared in Iraq following the establishment of the monarchy in 1921, and I will refer to these issues in various parts of this study.

The freedom of expression granted by the Turkish Constitution was followed by publication of books in the shrine cities. Hibat al-Din al-Shahrastani's *al-Hay'a wa al-islam* (Astronomy and Islam) is a good example of the attempts of Shi'is to reconcile Islamic teaching with the new sciences. The book was first published in 1910 and was well received in Egypt. Shahrastani maintained that Islamic teaching did not contradict modern scientific discoveries or theories. He attempted to prove that the Prophet Muhammad had already pointed to the existence of the universe and the relations between the earth, the moon, the stars, and the sun a

---

(Najaf, 1965), 1:160–61; 'Ali al-Wardi, *Lamahat ijtima'iyya min ta'rikh al-'iraq al-hadith*, 6 vols. (Baghdad, 1969–1978), 3:262–65.

[8] Hibat al-Din al-Shahrastani, "Hayat majallat al-'ilm fi al-'am al-awwal," *al-'Ilm* 1 (1911): 6–7 (at end of volume). On the opening of a library of newspapers and magazines in Najaf already around 1905 see Agha Najafi Quchani, *Siyahat-i sharq ya zindeginama va-safarnama-yi agha najafi quchani* (Mashhad, 1972), 460. See also 'Ali al-Khaqani, *Shu'ara' al-ghari aw al-najafiyyat*, 2d ed., 12 vols. (Qum, 1988), 10:85; 'Abd al-Halim al-Rahimi, *Ta'rikh al-haraka al-islamiyya fi al-'iraq: al-judhur al-fikriyya wa al-waqi' al-ta'rikhi, 1900–1924* (Beirut, 1985), 119.

[9] 'Abd al-Razzaq al-Hasani, *Ta'rikh al-sihafa al-'iraqiyya* (Sidon, 1971), 30, 32, 65.

[10] Shahrastani, "Hayat majallat al-'ilm fi al-'am al-awwal," 1–9 (at end of volume).

thousand years earlier than their discovery by European scientists.[11] The
hitherto unknown freedom of publication in Iraq created greater possibilities for exchange of ideas between Shi'is and Sunnis both within and
outside the country. As will be shown below, the increasing contacts and
cooperation between the two groups would manifest themselves in the
period that preceded the establishment of modern Iraq.

The most noticeable effect of the Iranian and the Young Turk Revolutions on Shi'ism in Iraq was the opportunity given to the mujtahids to
develop their self-image as the leaders of Muslim opposition. This image
had begun to take shape during the Iranian Revolution and was sharpened
by the freedom of publication provided under the Turkish Constitution,
which enabled the mujtahids to reach a wider audience both within and
outside Iraq. Na'ini's work, which has already been mentioned in this
chapter, was only one example of these consequences of the constitutional
period. The appearance of his work coincided with other publications in
Najaf that specifically called for Sunni-Shi'i unity and attempted to define
the role of the Shi'i mujtahids as the leaders of Muslim opposition. I will
give two examples of this type of work.

The contents of a book written by Muhammad Husayn Kashif al-Ghita,
who would emerge as one of the most prominent Arab Shi'i mujtahids in
Iraq under the monarchy, demonstrates the search for Shi'i-Sunni unity
and for the ideal Muslim society. First published around 1909, it was
entitled *al-Din wa al-islam aw al-da'wa al-islamiyya* (Religion and Islam or
the Islamic Call). The author lamented the decay of Islam and the divisions
between Muslims. Pointing to the insults hurled at Islam by Europeans, he
argued that the decline of religion was primarily the outcome of the believers' loss of their Muslim identity and the neglect of their religion. He
called for the renewal of Islam and its purification from extremism, super-
stitions, and popular practices. For Kashif al-Ghita, the revival of Islam
could only be accomplished through the combination of education and
action (*al-'ilm wa al-'amal*), and through cooperation between rulers and
ruled. He considered the people of the pen and the sword the foundations
of the Muslim community's power. Their role was to shield the community,
care for its progress, and help the ruler-king in the task of government.
Kashif al-Ghita called upon all Muslims to spare no effort in protecting
their country and nation (*watan* and *umma*) and in maintaining the integrity of their territory and community (*dawla* and *milla*).[12]

[11] Hibat al-Din al-Shahrastani, *al-Hay'a wa al-islam*, 3d ed. (Najaf, 1964/5), esp. 21, 23–
27. See also "Kitab al-hay'a wa al-islam li al-sayyid hibat al-din al-shahrastani," *al-Muqtataf*
38 (1911): 93. Other publications of Shahrastani relevant to his *al-Hay'a wa al-islam* were
"Tasrih al-din bi-kathrat aqmar al-sama'," *al-Muqtataf* 39 (1911): 358–61, and *Jabal qaf*
(Baghdad, 1927).

[12] Muhammad Husayn Kashif al-Ghita, *al-Din wa al-islam aw al-da'wa al-islamiyya*, 2d
ed., 2 pts. (Sidon, 1912/13), 1:2–27.

The reproduction in *al-ʿIlm* of a late nineteenth-century speech attributed to Afghani is a good example of the attempts of mujtahids to develop their image as opposition leaders. Apparently Afghani had accused Nasir al-Din Shah of selling the rights and property of Iran to foreigners and warned that the hurling of insults at Islamic law hindered religion and exposed it to a great danger. Afghani argued that the duty of protecting Islam fell in the first place on the Shiʿi ulama, and he was cited as calling upon them to depose the Shah, to nominate one of his sons as the new king instead, and to install a new government based on Islamic law. The commentary that followed the publication of Afghani's text in *al-ʿIlm* stopped short of suggesting that his speech had served as an unwritten testament which the mujtahids fulfilled through their participation in the Iranian Revolution.[13]

The Iranian and Young Turk Revolutions transformed political life in the shrine cities. Many people took clear stands either for or against constitutionalism and debated the usefulness and implications of a parliamentary system. The resulting turmoil and polarization of opinion of the population were neatly captured by a local poet:

> The world has changed and its evil
> has gone back and forth between excessiveness and negligence
> A person seeking stability has nobody to turn to
> for the people are either supporters or opponents of constitutionalism.[14]

The two Revolutions enabled the Shiʿi mujtahids to articulate their vision of constitutionalism and to develop their image as leaders of Muslim opposition. The growing European challenge gave meaning and immediacy to the need for Muslim unity, enabling the mujtahids to emerge as the leaders of a jihad movement.

MUSLIM UNITY AND THE JIHAD MOVEMENT

European penetration of Iranian and Ottoman territories greatly intensified from the summer of 1908. Russian troops were present in northern Iran to secure Russia's economic interests there. At that time there was a strong fear among mujtahids in the shrine cities that Russia and Britain intended to make further loans to the Shah, which in turn would have increased the influence of those two states on Iran. In the Ottoman Empire, between October 1908 and April 1909, the Committee of Union and Progress lost more territories than Sultan ʿAbd al-Hamid II had been forced to give up since 1882: Austria annexed Bosnia-Herzegovina, Bulgaria proclaimed its independence, and Greece annexed Crete.

---

[13] "Al-Hujja al-baligha aw istinhad al-ʿulamaʾ al-rabbaniyyin," *al-ʿIlm* 1 (1910): 338–56.

[14] Cited by Muhsin al-Amin, *Aʿyan al-shiʿa*, 56 vols. (Beirut, 1960–1963), 7:289.

Faced with an increasing European threat, the Ottomans intensified their calls for Muslim unity. 'Abd al-Hamid's period (1878–1909) was marked by calls for Ottoman-Iranian rapprochement in the late nineteenth century and the beginning of the twentieth century. The Ottomans made repeated appeals for unity and the Sultan emphasized his position as the caliph and the defender of the holy places. The Ottoman drive for Muslim unity culminated in World War I when the Young Turks sought to use Islam as the pillar of their ideology. The use of religion as a unifying force was intended to rely on the Muslim population as the base of support of the Empire while changing many aspects of their lives so as to increase central government control.[15] Ottoman policy toward the Shi'is in Iraq involved overlapping, at times even contradicting, strategies. The Ottomans needed the mujtahids to mobilize Shi'is and therefore distributed munificent largesse in the shrine cities and attempted to reconcile Sunni and Shi'i ulama. Yet, alarmed as they were by the propagation of Shi'ism among the tribes in Iraq and by the involvement of the mujtahids in state affairs in Iran, the Ottomans also sought to reduce the mujtahids' influence and to project their own legitimacy among the Shi'i population in Iraq.[16] Hence, they allowed the appearance of Shi'i magazines and associations, and the opening of Shi'i secular primary schools. At the same time, however, they imposed restrictions on the madrasas and on the Iranian pilgrimage to the shrine cities, and attempted to counter the propagation of Shi'i Islam in Iraq.

Not only were the Ottomans unsuccessful in their attempt to significantly reduce the power of the Shi'i mujtahids in Iraq, but their call for Muslim unity enabled the mujtahids to gain further freedom of action, to increase their contacts with the local population, and to emerge as leaders of political protest within Iraq. In the absence of the Imam, who embodies political authority, there always existed the potential in Imami Shi'ism that well-qualified mujtahids would attempt to assume some of his functions.[17] Thus, as early as 1906 leading Shi'i mujtahids urged all Muslims to develop a system of Islamic economics based on self-sufficiency and called for the opening of Muslim factories to avoid the need to purchase foreign goods. This manifested itself in *fatwa*s which the mujtahids issued following a query addressed to them by Shi'is in India through the *Habl al-Matin*

---

[15] Jacob Landau, *The Politics of Pan-Islam: Ideology and Organization* (Oxford, 1990), 24, 31–32, 34–35, 44–45, 90–91; Stephen Duguid, "The Politics of Unity: Hamidian Policy in Eastern Anatolia," *MES* 9 (1973): 139, 144–45, 151; Selim Deringil, "Legitimacy Structures in the Ottoman State: The Reign of Abdülhamid II (1876–1909)," *IJMES* 23 (1991): 346, 350, 353, 355.

[16] Deringil, "Legitimacy Structures," 347–49; idem, "The Struggle Against Shi'ism in Hamidian Iraq: A Study in Ottoman Counter-Propaganda," *WI* 30 (1990): 48, 51–52, 61.

[17] Sachedina, *The Just Ruler*, 117.

newspaper published in Calcutta. Moreover, from late 1908 prominent mujtahids based in Ottoman Iraq began acting like "heads of state." In October, three of the leading four mujtahids of Najaf—Muhammad Kazim Khurasani, 'Abdallah Mazandarani, and Husayn Mirza Khalil—issued communications to the British, Russian, French, and German consuls in Baghdad to the effect that Iranian concessions to foreigners were void and that future foreign loans to Iran would not be repaid. On several occasions in 1909–1910 they called for the establishment of an Iranian National Loan Fund that would pay off Iran's foreign debts and avert the necessity for raising further loans from Europe.[18]

While urging economic self-sufficiency, the mujtahids also began organizing a defensive jihad movement. The first mujtahid who himself led a defensive jihad had been Shaykh Ja'far Kashif al-Ghita. In assuming the role of the leader of a jihad against the Wahhabis who laid siege to Najaf in 1805, Kashif al-Ghita followed his own judicial decision that a mujtahid, in his capacity as the deputy of the Hidden Imam, can lead a jihad against enemies of Islam.[19] The mujtahids' organization of a jihad movement in Iraq between 1909–1915 was a further demonstration of their growing willingness to assume political authority.

In July 1909 a group of mujtahids led by Khurasani's son initiated a meeting with the British consul in Baghdad at which they threatened to declare a jihad against Russia if the latter did not withdraw its forces from Iran. A direct warning was sent in October 1910 to the Russian consul by Khurasani himself.[20] In December the Shi'i mujtahids issued an urgent call for Muslim unity. It took the form of a *fatwa* phrased in strong ecumenical terms, which claimed to reflect the opinion of the Sunni ulama of Baghdad as well. Its contents read:

> In our judgement, the disagreement among the ulama over the principles of faith, and the split between the different groups of Muslim [society] is the cause of the decline of the Islamic states and of the seizure of most of their lands by foreigners. In order to preserve Muslim unity and defend the shari'a, the *fatwas* of the heads of the Shi'a Ja'fariyya, and those of the respected ulama of the Sunna of Baghdad, have agreed on the necessity to adhere to the reins of Islam . . .

[18] "Translation of an Article in the *Habl al-Matin*," no. 33, 20 April 1906, FO 371/113/28442; Political Diaries of the Baghdad Residency for the Weeks Ending 24 October 1908 and 1 February 1909, FO 195/2275/958–708 and FO 195/2308/104–12; Summary of Events in Turkish Iraq for March, April, and May 1910, FO 195/2338/285-12 and FO 195/2339/285–12.

[19] Sachedina, *The Just Ruler*, 22.

[20] Ramsay to Lowther, Inclosure 1 in No. 346, Baghdad, 28 June 1909, FO 416/41; Memorandum by Consul-General Ramsay, Inclosure 2 in No. 464, Baghdad, 14 July 1909, FO 416/41; Lorimer to Lowther, Baghdad, 6 November 1910, FO 195/2341/975–59.

[Our *fatwas*] have concurred that it is obligatory upon all Muslims to unite in order to defend the Islamic lands and to guard all the Ottoman and Iranian territories against the obstinacy of foreigners and their attacks. We have unanimously agreed to go to any length and explore every possible way in order to protect the Muslim territories. We have confidence in the complete unity of the two eminent Islamic states and in the [efforts] that each one will utilize to protect the independence and the rights of the other.

We have notified all Muslims of our common *fatwas* and agreement or this issue. We have also notified the Iranian community of its need to liv in peace and cooperate in order to preserve the independence of the Ottoman state, to defend its sovereignty, and to protect its frontiers from foreign intervention . . .

We remind all Muslims of the brotherhood by which God has joined the believers. We notify them of their need to avoid and keep away from [anything] that could cause a split [*nifaq*]. We [also call upon] them to take pains in protecting the confidants of the nation, to cooperate with and assist one another, and to express a union of opinion in order to protect the noble Islamic banner and preserve the high position of the eminent Ottoman and Iranian states.[21]

The *fatwa* was signed by Muhammad Kazim Khurasani, 'Abdallah Mazandarani, Shaykh al-Shari'a Isfahani, Isma'il ibn Sadr al-Din al-'Amili, and Muhammad Husayn Mazandarani. The Ottomans probably encouraged the publication of such an important *fatwa*. It was also welcomed in Egypt by Muhammad Rashid Rida, who published it in *al-Manar*. The *fatwa* may have been in part a response of the mujtahids to Sunni criticism that they were not committed to Shi'i-Sunni conciliation and unwilling to put aside traditional polemics and disagreements between the two sects. In his commentary Rida stated that the *fatwa* was the first indication of the willingness of the Shi'i and Sunni religious establishments to promote Islamic unity.[22] While the publication of the *fatwa* reflected Ottoman attempts to use the mujtahids' influence over their constituency in Iran and Iraq to create Shi'i opposition to the European threat to the Empire, its contents signaled the readiness of the mujtahids in Iraq to lead a jihad movement. The commentary that followed the *fatwa*'s publication in *al-'Ilm* was indicative of that. The commentator stated that the Ottoman Empire and Iran were determined to protect their independence and regain their former power. He warned that the continuous intervention of Britain and Russia in Ottoman and Iranian affairs would ultimately lead to the rising of the Muslims of India, Bukhara, and the Caucasus.[23]

---

[21] *Al-'Ilm* 1 (1911): 434–36. With minor changes this *fatwa* was reproduced in *al-'Irfan* 69 (1981): 4–5.

[22] "I'tisam al-fi'atayn al-kabiratayn min al-muslimin," *al-Manar* 14 (1911): 77–78.

[23] *Al-'Ilm* 1 (1911): 436–40.

In October 1911 Italy occupied Tripoli and Bengazi. By the end of the month nearly all the leading Shi'i mujtahids in the shrine cities had signed a *fatwa* which called for a jihad against Italy.[24] Both British and Iraqi accounts concur that the *fatwa* had a strong impact in Iraq. Its announcement was followed by public meetings and demonstrations, the collection of contributions for war against Italy, and the formation of Muslim committees for the defense of Libya. The impact of the *fatwa* was particularly strong in such mixed cities as Kazimayn, Baghdad, and Samarra which served as important contact zones between Shi'is and Sunnis in Iraq. Emotions in Kazimayn ran high and the meetings were attended by Shi'is and Sunnis, and officials of all classes. "A wave of pro-Sunni feeling," the British consul wrote, "seems to have swept over the Shi'ias" of Kazimayn. In a speech, an Arab Shi'i *'alim* compared the Italian invasion to the Crusades and urged unity among all Muslims. On the ninth of October a crowd of people from Kazimayn, led by Shi'i ulama and other dignitaries, marched to Baghdad in procession. The writer of the British report noted, not without surprise, that while the ulama chanted "there is no God but God," the Shi'i common people responded "and Muhammad is the Prophet of God," without completing the usual Shi'i formula "and 'Ali is the friend of God and the heir of the Prophet of God."[25]

The occupation of Libya had a noticeable impact on the Arab Shi'i population in the urban centers of Iraq, reinforcing their ethnic identity. This development also found expression in the Shi'i political poetry of the day. The following three examples are extracts from poems by Muhammad Rida al-Shabibi (d. 1966), 'Ali al-Sharqi (d. 1964), and 'Abd al-Muttalib al-Hilli (d. 1920), respectively:

> [Libyan] face bears the Arab lineaments and their hand
> is clearly marked with the sign of the best place of birth.

> Oh Arabs, do not exempt yourselves from [the duty of] war
> and do not trade your pride for comfort.

> You [the West] have disregarded that we are by birth
> Arabs and that damage cannot be inflicted upon us.[26]

The strong ethnic identity of Arab Shi'is in Iraq as expressed in the first decade of the twentieth century should come as no surprise to us. The

---

[24] For its contents see Summary of Events in Turkish Iraq for October 1911, Annex A, FO 195/2369/912–42.

[25] Summary of Events in Turkish Iraq for October 1911, FO 195/2369/912–42. See also Rahimi, *Ta'rikh*, 151–52; Wamidh Nadhmi, "Shi'at al-'iraq wa-qadiyat al-qawmiyya al-'arabiyya: al-dawr al-ta'rikhi qubayl al-istiqlal," *al-Mustaqbal al-'Arabi* 41 (1982): 80–82.

[26] Muhammad Mahdi al-Basir, *Nahdat al-'iraq al-adabiyya fi al-qarn al-tasi' 'ashara* (Baghdad, 1946), 344; 'Ali al-Khaqani, *Shu'ara' al-hilla aw al-babiliyyat*, 5 vols. (Baghdad, 1951–1953), 3:230; Nadhmi, "Shi'at al-'iraq," 80–81, 91–93.

historical role of the Arabs in preserving Islam had been praised by Islamic reformers from the late nineteenth century. At that time, Hilla was experiencing a literary revival which allowed Arab Shi'is in Iraq to reconfirm the position of the Arabic language as a major attribute distinguishing Arabs from Turks and Persians. This found expression in late nineteenth-century Shi'i poetry when Radi Qazwini (d. 1870) wrote:

> Why should Tabriz be a shelter for eloquent Arabic
> and who are the Turks as compared with the Arabs of Iraq?[27]

The important role of Arabic in preserving Islam was emphasized also by Muhammad Husayn Kashif al-Ghita in his *al-Din wa al-Islam* to which I had referred earlier in this chapter. This might have been one of the reasons for the decision of the Ottoman authorities in Iraq to destroy all copies of the book.[28]

In October–November 1911 Russian and British troops occupied parts of northern and southern Iran. The most significant development at that time was the concurrence of all the mujtahids of the shrine cities over the urgent need to defend Islam. Hence, Kazim Yazdi, who enjoyed a large following among the Shi'i Arab tribes, put aside his deep disagreements with the pro-constitutionalist mujtahids and issued a *fatwa* calling upon Muslims to sacrifice their lives in order to expel the Italian as well as the Anglo-Russian troops from Tripoli and Iran, respectively.[29] The mujtahids' call for a jihad incited the local population, particularly as it was rumored that Khurasani himself intended to lead the warriors to Iran. Tribal shaykhs agreed to contribute arms, volunteers were recruited, and all other necessary arrangements for the journey were completed. Khurasani's unexpected death on the eve of departure, however, led to the cancellation of the expedition.[30]

The jihad movement which the mujtahids had attempted to organize materialized in World War I. On 6 November 1914 the first British units landed in southern Iraq and Basra was occupied on the 23d. With British forces in Iraqi territory, the European challenge to Islam could not be more alarming from the point of view of the mujtahids since it posed a direct threat to their own status and influence within the country. According to British accounts, by January 1915 a jihad had been preached in every mosque in Iraq. Emissaries from the shrine cities were sent to the tribes urging them to fight the British in the name of Islam. The effect was ostensi-

---

[27] Khaqani, *Shu'ara' al-hilla*, 3:198–203; Nadhmi, "Shi'at al-'iraq," 88, 92.

[28] Kashif al-Ghita, *al-Din wa al-islam*, 2:110–13, 121, 124–27; Khaqani, *Shu'ara' al-ghari*, 8:112.

[29] For its contents see Hairi, *Shi'ism*, 118.

[30] Quchani, *Siyahat-i sharq*, 479–82; Ruhaymi, *Ta'rikh*, 151; Wardi, *Lamahat*, 3:123–25.

bly great on the Shi'i tribes of the Euphrates among whom a great number of *sayyids* lived. By virtue of their status as mediators and venerated figures, the *sayyids* were extremely important in mobilizing tribesmen for the jihad.[31] Some eighteen thousand volunteers were said to be recruited from among the Shi'i Arab population of the Euphrates and placed under Turkish command. The warriors were led by prominent Shi'i religious figures, among whom were Shaykh al-Shari'a Isfahani, Mahdi al-Khalisi, Muhammad Sa'id al-Habbubi, Mustafa al-Kashani, Mahdi al-Haydari, and Muhsin al-Hakim.[32]

From a military point of view the jihad failed, and the British occupation of Iraq was completed in 1918. Yet, the occupation itself could not fill the power vacuum created by the end of Ottoman rule in Iraq. The British were only beginning to consolidate their control of the country in 1918, at a time when the political future of Iraq was still very unclear. Into this vacuum of power stepped the Shi'i mujtahids. The active role played by the mujtahids during the constitutional period, and their emergence as the leaders of a jihad movement in Iraq between 1908 and 1915, enabled them to mobilize the local population. Subsequent events would demonstrate the full might of the mujtahids as well as their greater activism and freedom of action in comparison with the Sunni ulama of Iraq.

THE 1919 PLEBISCITE

With the entry of the United States into World War I, and the publication of President Wilson's fourteen points, long-established assumptions of British imperial policy had to be reconciled with new global requirements. In Iraq it was necessary to adapt the existing machinery derived from Indian administrative models to an indirect rule under an Arab facade that would still assure British strategic and commercial interests in the Persian Gulf leading to India, as well as Britain's growing interests in the country's oil resources.[33] When Baghdad fell in 1917, the Sharifians had asked that Iraq be within the administrative province of Sharif Husayn. While presenting memoranda and making appeals to London, they also launched a well-organized propaganda campaign in Iraq which called for Arab independence. The secret society al-'Ahd, which was controlled by ex-Ottoman

[31] Arnold Wilson, *Loyalties: Mesopotamia, 1914–1917* (London, 1930), 22; Great Britain, Office of the Civil Commissioner, *The Arab of Mesopotamia*, Basra, 1917, 86–87.

[32] Ja'far al-Mahbuba, *Madi al-najaf wa-hadiruha*, 3 vols. (Najaf, 1955–1958), 1:340–41; 'Abdallah al-Nafisi, *Dawr al-shi'a fi tatawwur al-'iraq al-siyasi al-hadith* (Beirut, 1973), 86–87. See also Werner Ende, "Iraq in World War I: The Turks, the Germans and the Shi'ite Mujtahids' Call for Jihad," in *Proceedings of the Ninth Congress of the Union Européenne des Arabisants et Islamisants*, ed. Rudolph Peters (Leiden, 1981), 57–71.

[33] Peter Sluglett, *Britain in Iraq, 1914–1932* (London, 1976), 14; Elie Kedourie, *England and the Middle East* (London, 1956), 176.

officers, had Shi'i sympathizers in Iraq, notably Muhammad Rida al-Shabibi, as well as branches in Baghdad and Basra.[34] Al-'Ahd's Shi'i sympathizers would facilitate contacts between the Sharifians and the mujtahids between 1919 and 1920.

Against the growing interest of British officials in London to the idea of installing a son of Sharif Husayn as ruler of parts of Iraq, Arnold Wilson, the Acting Civil Commissioner, suggested in November 1918 to hold a plebiscite to ascertain the opinion of "educated" men in the country. In advocating a plebiscite, Wilson hoped to discredit any proposal supporting the Sharifian cause. The plebiscite consisted of three questions: (1) Do you favor a single Arab state under British tutelage stretching from the northern boundary of Mosul Wilayat to the Persian Gulf? (2) In this event, do you consider that a titular Arab head (Amir) should be placed over this new state? (3) In that case, whom would you prefer as Amir?[35]

The conduct of the plebiscite, which was authorized by the British government, did not prove judicious for it was followed by further turmoil in Iraq, culminating in the 1920 revolt. The answers received after long delays and against the background of pressures from conflicting interest groups revealed a lack of unified opinion among the various segments of Iraq's population. The Shi'i answers, as included in the group of opinions sent to London, highlighted the different motivations of tribal shaykhs, merchants, and urban notables, as well as the mujtahids who participated in the plebiscite. The conflicting aspirations of groups and individuals were at times noticeable even among members of the same family.

As Wilson had hoped, the majority of tribal shaykhs, holders of administrative positions, and the commercial classes expressed an opinion in favor of continued British control.[36] In doing so, both Shi'i and Sunni members of these groups demonstrated that economic factors and the desire to maintain their own welfare, which improved following the British occupation of Iraq, played dominant roles in shaping their opinions.

In Najaf, Sayyid Hadi al-Rafi'i, the *naqib al-ashraf* (head of the descendants of the Prophet), managed to organize a petition bearing twenty-one signatures of the city's notables and merchants asking for direct British rule.[37] There was also a group of six mujtahids in Najaf who were willing

[34] Kedourie, *England*, 179–83; Wamidh Nadhmi, *al-Judhur al-siyasiyya wa al-fikriyya wa al-ijtima'iyya li al-haraka al-qawmiyya al-'arabiyya (al-istiqlaliyya) fi al-'iraq* (Beirut, 1984), 133, 171n.

[35] Kedourie, *England*, 183–84; Philip Ireland, *Iraq: A Study in Political Development* (New York, 1938, reprint, 1970), 161.

[36] For the opinions of the various segments of Iraq's population see *Self Determination in Iraq, 1919*, FO 248/1250.

[37] This petition was said to have been later counteracted by another one signed by opponents of British rule: Wardi, *Lamahat*, 5,1:72.

to support British administration of Iraq's affairs until the country proved ready for self-rule. Their only condition was that the British would assure the free practice of Islam in Iraq and preserve the status of the mujtahids. The existence of such a group in Najaf demonstrated a degree of British influence in the shrine cities through their control of charitable funds of Indian origin and nomination of mujtahids to distribute these funds (see chapter 8). Among this group of mujtahids there were three Indians who were British subjects: Sayyid Hashim al-Hindi al-Najafi, Mahmud al-Hindi al-Najafi, and Muhammad Mahdi Kashmiri, all of whom were considered by British officials as pro-British. There was one mujtahid of Persian origin, Ja'far Bahr al-'Ulum, who was also considered pro-British. Two Arab mujtahids completed the group, Hasan ibn Sahib al-Jawahiri, who was of Arab origin and held Iranian nationality, and 'Ali ibn Muhammad Rida Kashif al-Ghita. The latter was head of the Kashif al-Ghita family and was closely connected to Kazim Yazdi, the most prominent mujtahid of the day, who himself refused to participate in the plebiscite. 'Ali was openly pro-British and was considered to have great influence among the Shi'i Arab tribes.[38]

In Kazimayn, the mayor Sayyid Ja'far al-'Utayfa, who was himself one of the city's most important merchants, succeeded in preparing a petition signed by some forty notables composed of merchants, heads of the city's quarters, some Indian mujtahids, and tribal shaykhs. It called for British rule in Iraq under Sir Percy Cox, at that time the British minister in Iran.[39] In the district of Karbala, important notables, merchants, and tribal shaykhs also expressed a similar opinion, thus throwing their weight against the position of the city's leading mujtahid, Mirza Muhammad Taqi Shirazi, who, as will be shown shortly, adopted a radically different view. A wish for a continuation of British rule was also expressed in predominantly Sunni Samarra and in the mixed city of Basra.[40]

In contrast with the desire of Arab Shi'i merchants, notables, tribal shaykhs, and even some mujtahids for the continuation of British rule, important Najafi mujtahids and other figures in the city expressed a wish for an independent state extending from Mosul in the north to the Persian Gulf in the south. They stated: "Since the majority of the people of Iraq are Arabs, and as every person favors the people of his race with whom he is

[38] *Self Determination*, FO 248/1250. The evaluations of these mujtahids' political positions is given in Prominent Personalities in Najaf and Shamiyya, Appendix 3, Great Britain, Administration Reports for 1918, Najaf, CO 696/1; Special Service Officer, Baghdad, 2 July 1926, Air 23/379.

[39] *Self Determination*, FO 248/1250; Wardi, *Lamahat*, 5,1:78–79.

[40] *Self Determination*, FO 248/1250; Weekly Summaries, Baghdad, 25 January and 20 September 1919, FO 248/1252; Wardi, *Lamahat*, 5,1:86–87.

united by [ties of] religion, language, values, and customs, we consider it appropriate that this new kingdom will be placed under the rule of an Arab Amir." Among the signatories were Shaykh al-Shari'a Isfahani, 'Abd al-Karim al-Jaza'iri, Jawad ibn Sahib al-Jawahiri, and Mahdi Kashif al-Ghita.[41] This opinion was reiterated about two weeks later by important Shi'i tribal shaykhs, reflecting mounting Sharifian pressures and propaganda in Najaf and its surroundings. Indeed, one of the signatories was the literary figure Muhammad Rida al-Shabibi, who maintained contacts with supporters of the Sharifians in Baghdad and acted as a link between the capital and mujtahids in Najaf. It is also interesting to note that the position of Mahdi Kashif al-Ghita and Jawad ibn Sahib al-Jawahiri differed from that which had been expressed by other members of their families, 'Ali Kashif al-Ghita and Hasan ibn Sahib al-Jawahiri, who supported the idea of the British administration of Iraq.

As much as Wilson might have disliked this pro-Sharifian Najafi opinion, the most alarming development from his, and indeed the British, point of view was a new petition formulated in Karbala under the influence of the pro-constitutionalist mujtahid Mirza Muhammad Taqi Shirazi, who was second in importance only to Kazim Yazdi of Najaf. Dated 19 January 1919 and signed by prominent mujtahids, sayyids, and other religious functionaries in Karbala, it read:

> We the people of Karbala . . . have decided to seek the protection of the Arab-Islamic banner and we have selected one of the sons of Sharif Husayn to be an Amir over us bound by an assembly elected by the people of Iraq [to] enact the rules approved by the clergymen of this nation and [to administer] its affairs.[42]

All the major principles advocated by the pro-constitutionalist mujtahids during the Iranian Revolution were incorporated into this petition: a king whose acts are supervised by a national assembly and a political system that would enable the mujtahids to dominate state affairs. It is said that when this petition was submitted to the British official in charge he refused to accept it on the ground that it did not meet the deadline set for submission of opinions on self-determination.[43] This petition was not included among the group sent to London. And one British report even went so far as to suggest that "in the end, Karbala had the distinction of being prac-

---

[41] This opinion was dated 9 Rabi' al-Awwal 1337/January 1919: Self Determination, FO 248/1250.

[42] The text was dated 15 Rabi' al-Awwal 1337. A reproduction of it may be found in 'Abd al-Razzaq al-Wahhab, Karbala' fi al-ta'rikh (Baghdad, 1935), 48–51. Nafisi gives 15 Shawwal 1137/August 1919 as the date in which this petition was compiled but he does not provide a reference: Dawr al-shi'a, 209.

[43] Wahhab, Karbala', 53; Wardi, Lamahat, 5,1:67.

tically the only place of importance in Iraq which expressed no opinion on a question which has excited the keenest interest throughout the length and breadth of the country."[44]

The effect of the Karbala petition was amplified in late January 1919 when Shirazi issued a *fatwa* forbidding the selection of other than a Muslim ruler.[45] This had an immediate impact on Baghdad and Kazimayn, where two new petitions were compiled. Kazimayn's stated: "We opt for a new Arabic Islamic state whose Muslim king would be one of the sons of . . . Sharif Husayn, bound by a national assembly." Bearing the signatures of forty-five Shi'i and Sunni ulama as well as other prominent figures in Baghdad, the petition of that city stated: "We, the representatives of Islam from among the Shi'i and Sunni population of Baghdad and its suburbs . . . have opted for . . . an Arab state ruled by an Arab Muslim king, one of the sons of . . . the Sharif Husayn, bound by a national legislative assembly based in Baghdad, the capital of Iraq."[46] The opinions expressed in these two cities demonstrated the ability of the Shi'i religious establishment to stimulate religious and political feelings among the Sunni ulama and population of Baghdad. This would clearly manifest itself in the 1920 revolt.

The plebiscite exposed a lack of community of interest between the Arab Shi'i tribal shaykhs and merchants, and the predominantly Persian mujtahids. Yet it resulted in two important developments, which, in 1919–1920, overshadowed the conflict of interests of various groups within Iraqi Shi'i as well as Sunni society. The first was the emergence of the prominent mujtahid Shirazi as a power capable of influencing Shi'i and Sunni public opinion. The second development was the willingness of the mujtahids and the Sharifians to cooperate against the continuation of British rule. Despite their fundamentally different aspirations, the mujtahids and the Sharifians agreed to work together under a vague formula which called for an "Arab-Islamic state ruled by an Arab Amir bound by a legislative assembly." Each side interpreted it according to its own vision. Whereas some of the prominent mujtahids led by Shirazi hoped that this formula would enable them to oversee the legislative process and the affairs of Iraq once British control of the country was removed, the Sharifians considered this formula an opening for their own effective rule of Iraq through the nomination of one

---

[44] Administrative Report of Political Officer, Hilla, Regarding Karbala and Status of Mujtahids, 5 April 1920, FO 371/5074/5285.

[45] Weekly Summary, Baghdad, 25 January 1919, FO 248/1252; Wahhab, *Karbala'*, 44–47.

[46] The petitions of Kazimayn and Baghdad are dated, respectively, 5 and 19 Rabi' al-Thani 1337/February 1919: *Self Determination*, FO 248/1250. The two prominent mujtahids, Shirazi and Isfahani, expressed a similar wish in their letter to President Wilson dated 12 Jumada al-'Ula 1337/March 1919. For its contents see Muhammad 'Ali Kamal al-Din, *Thawrat al-'ishrin fi dhikraha al-khamsin* (Baghdad, 1970), 182.

of the sons of Sharif Husayn as king. Since both sides had to rely on one another to maximize anti-British opposition in the country, the mujtahids and the Sharifians put aside their different aspirations for the time being. The alliance between the two groups would prove effective in mobilizing Shi'is and Sunnis for political action.

THE 1920 REVOLT

The 1920 revolt has been the subject of much discussion and debate among students of modern Iraqi history. The debates and different interpretations have focused mainly on the nature of the revolt as well as on the role and motivations of the different groups, tribes, and cities that took part in it. Yet despite the different interpretations, agreement exists over the major role of the Shi'i ulama in inciting the tribes to revolt.[47] In dealing with the revolt, I will focus on the following questions: What were the motivations of the mujtahids in calling for a revolt? Did all segments of Shi'i society share the goals of the mujtahids? By what means was Shi'i-Sunni unity achieved in the mixed cities of Kazimayn and Baghdad?

Within the Shi'i religious leadership, Mirza Muhammad Taqi Shirazi emerged as the leading mujtahid following the death of Kazim Yazdi on 29 April 1919. Shirazi was greatly assisted by his son Muhammad Rida, and together the two set the agenda of the Shi'i religious establishment in the period leading up to the revolt. The decision of the mujtahids to sanction the revolt was greatly influenced by British policies in Iran and Iraq, which posed a danger to the socioeconomic status of the mujtahids of the shrine cities. They perceived the growing British influence in Iranian political and economic affairs as a threat to their own welfare, which relied heavily on contributions from Iran. In April 1919 the details of a proposed Anglo-Iranian agreement became public. Britain promised to loan Iran £2 million and to assist in the construction of railroads, revision of tariffs, and collection of war compensation from third parties. In return, Britain was to gain a monopoly over the supply of arms, military training, and administrative advisers. Alarmed by Britain's growing influence in Iran, the three prominent mujtahids, Shirazi, Isfahani, and Isma'il Sadr, sent a letter to the Iranian Premier. They wrote that the proposed treaty eliminated Iran's

---

[47] See, for example, Wardi, *Lamahat*, 5,1:345; 'Abdallah al-Fayyad, *al-Thawra al-'iraqiyya al-kubra sanat 1920* (Baghdad, 1963), 235; Nafisi, *Dawr al-shi'a*, 148; Nadhmi, *al-Judhur al-siyasiyya*, esp. 126; Anon., *al-Haraka al-islamiyya fi al-'iraq* (Beirut, 1985), 42; Elie Kedourie, *The Chatham House Version and Other Middle Eastern Studies* (London, 1970), 249–50; idem, *England*, 190; Amal Vinogradov, "The 1920 Revolt in Iraq Reconsidered: The Role of Tribes in National Politics," *IJMES* 3 (1972): 124; Pierre-Jean Luizard, *La Formation de l'Irak Contemporain: Le Rôle Politique des Uléma Chiites à la Fin de la Domination Ottomane et au Moment de la Construction de l'Etat Irakien* (Paris, 1991), 403–13.

independence and urged the Premier not to sign it.[48] Although the treaty was signed in August, members of the Iranian Majlis refused to ratify it, in part because of pressures from the mujtahids.

British presence in Iraq increased the fear of the mujtahids as well as that of the *sayyids*. From an early stage of the occupation, the British sought to regulate the flow of Iranian charities as well as the pilgrimage and the corpse traffic to the shrine cities. Were the British to succeed in controlling these sources of income, the mujtahids stood to lose much of their independence and influence among the local population. The British occupation also posed a grave challenge to the status of the *sayyids* who resided among the Shi'i tribes, and whose income was derived largely from the contributions of tribesmen. British administrative skills and organizational power, which were greater than those of the *sayyids*, threatened to erode the latter's image and influence among the tribesmen.[49] The Arab *sayyids* and the Persian mujtahids thus had a common interest in inciting the tribes to revolt so as to preserve their own eminent position among their Shi'i constituency in Iraq.

The religious factor also played a major role in the decision of the mujtahids to call for a revolt. Their religious motivations were already evident in their leadership of the jihad movement of 1909–1915. From their seat in the shrine cities, the mujtahids regarded the occupation of Muslim Iraq by Christian infidels as a sign of the collapse of Islamic civilization. The propaganda from Karbala described the occupation of Palestine by Allenby's forces as the latest and most threatening crusade ever waged against Islam. All Muslims were called to take arms against the attempts of Christian states to demolish the pillars of the Islamic religion in Syria, Palestine, and Iraq.[50] In Najaf, Shaykh al-Shari'a Isfahani, by now second in importance only to Shirazi, called in a speech at the Hindi mosque for an Islamic union in order to drive away all heretics from the Islamic territories.[51] The strong religious motivations of the mujtahids may be gathered from a leaflet distributed among the tribes by Shirazi's son:

> As everybody knows, the position of the Muslims at this period of time has reached great difficulty and gravity. The most knowledgeable ulama, and the tribes who express readiness, can no longer keep silent against this and they [should] make every conceivable sacrifice for the sake of this religious rising and for the incumbent Islamic movement. It is obligatory for all Muslims at

[48] Wardi, *Lamahat*, 5,1:110–11.

[49] Hanna Batatu, *The Old Social Classes and the Revolutionary Movements in Iraq*, 2d ed. (Princeton, N.J., 1982), 172.

[50] Ahmad al-Katib, *Tajrubat al-thawra al-islamiyya fi al-'iraq* (Beirut, 1981), 12, 20–21, 24; Nafisi, *Dawr al-shi'a*, 138.

[51] Mesopotamia Police, Abstracts of Intelligence, Baghdad, 10 July 1920, IO L/P&S 10/839.

this time to perform the duty of defending the distinguished religion, to guard the holy shrines from the stain of the infidels, and to protect their pure confidants from the assaults of infidelity.[52]

The aim of the mujtahids in calling for a revolt was to establish an Islamic government in Iraq free from foreign control. The mujtahids had expressed a desire for an Islamic government already in the 1919 plebiscite, and they reiterated it in the period that immediately preceded the revolt when there were reports that an agreement was reached in Najaf between several Shi'i tribal shaykhs and ulama to institute "a theocratic government built up on one of the fundamental principles of the Shi'ah doctrine."[53] Indeed, Shirazi sought to implement "a constitutional system and to establish a national assembly" in Iraq according to the principles that had been advocated by the pro-constitutionalist mujtahids during the Iranian Revolution.[54]

The motivations of the mujtahids were not shared by the majority of Shi'is, many of whom were exposed to strong Sharifian propaganda. The Sharifians did not emphasize the struggle between Muslims and Christians and stressed instead their plans for Arab independence and the rights of Iraqis for self-rule along the lines of the Syrian model.[55] When Faysal's name was still being mentioned as the proposed king of Syria, the name of his brother 'Abdallah was floating in Iraq. Thus, throughout 1919–1920 two conflicting movements, each calling for Iraq's independence, were at work and a fusion was created between Sharifian and Shi'i symbols. This also manifested itself in the Shi'i poetry of the day as may be gathered from the following extract of a poem by Muhammad Baqir al-Hilli, said to be recited often in public meetings in Najaf before the revolt:

> Long live 'Abdallah for he is to our people
> a king and his father the Sharif an imam.[56]

The details of the San Remo resolutions giving Britain a mandate over Iraq reached the country early in May 1920. Both the Sharifians and the mujtahids now gave the highest priority to achieving unity between Shi'is and Sunnis. Anti-mandate activity was coordinated in Najaf, Karbala, Kazimayn, and Baghdad. The members of a secret society, the *Haras al-Istiqlal*, which had been established in Baghdad in late 1919 and had

---

[52] An undated dispatch cited by 'Abd al-Razzaq al-Hasani, *al-'Iraq fi dawray al-ihtilal wa al-intidab* (Sidon, 1935), 112.

[53] Administrative Report of the Muntafiq Division, 1920, CO 696/3.

[54] Katib, *Tajrubat al-thawra*, 45–47, and esp. 265. See also Civil Commissioner, Baghdad, 5 August 1920, FO 371/5228/9849; Nafisi, *Dawr al-shi'a*, 142, 148.

[55] Nafisi, ibid., 138; Arnold Wilson, *Mesopotamia, 1917–1920: A Clash of Loyalties* (London, 1931), 251; Kedourie, *England*, 183.

[56] Wardi, *Lamahat*, 5,1:190.

branches in Kazimayn, Najaf, and Hilla, played an extremely important role in pushing for unity among Shi'is and Sunnis.[57] Some of the most prominent Shi'i figures who encouraged Muslim unity were Sayyid Muhammad al-Sadr, Sayyid Hadi Zuwayn, Muhammad Mahdi al-Basir, Muhammad Baqir al-Shabibi, and Ja'far Abu al-Timman. The latter two acted respectively as links between Karbala and Najaf and Baghdad, thus coordinating anti-mandate activity between these three cities.[58]

In order to create a common denominator that would help mobilize Arab Sunnis and Shi'is, the speeches and writings of members of the two groups emphasized the disgrace of Arab honor, a symbol to which Arabs in Iraq could relate well and which had no connection to their sectarian identity. The political poetry of the day invoked strong anti-British sentiments and feelings of deep humiliation as caused by the declaration of the mandate. The following extracts from a poem by the Sunni poet Muhammad Habib al-'Ubaydi (d. 1963) is a good example of both the feelings that Arab Shi'is and Sunnis shared and the symbols which appealed to the two groups:

> Set the fire O you noble Iraqis
> and wash the shame with flowing blood
> O you the people of Iraq, you are not slaves
> to adorn your necks with collars
> O you the people of Iraq, you are not prisoners
> to submit your shoulders to the chains
> O you the people of Iraq, you are not women
> whose weapon is the tears that flow from the depth of the eye
> O you the people of Iraq, you are not orphans
> to seek guardianship [a mandate] for Iraq
> You shall no longer enjoy the water of the Tigris
> if you are content with humiliation and oppression.[59]

Professional Shi'i preachers and sermon leaders, notably Sayyid Salih al-Hilli and Mahdi al-Basir, provoked Islamic and anti-British feelings in the cities and among the tribes. The excitement of the population in such mixed cities as Baghdad and Kazimayn culminated in the religious ceremonies during the holy month of Ramadan, which fell that year between 19 May and 18 June. In an effort to transform the religious spirit of Ramadan into political fervor, Shi'i lamentations (ta'ziyas) in commemoration of imam Husayn were incorporated into the religious ceremonies of that year.

[57] For its political program see Mahdi al-Basir, Ta'rikh al-qadiyya al-'iraqiyya, 2 vols. (Baghdad, 1924), 1:136–37.

[58] Wardi, Lamahat, 5,1:97–98; Nafisi, Dawr al-shi'a, 126; 'Abd al-Darraji, Ja'far abu al-timman, 82–85.

[59] Ibrahim al-Wa'ili, Thawrat al-'ishrin fi al-shi'r al-'iraqi (Baghdad, 1968), 37.

Sunni celebrations of the Prophet's birthday (the *mawlid*) and Shi'i lamentations were organized by members of the *Haras al-Istiqlal* and held together in private homes and mosques. Addressing thousands of Shi'is and Sunnis in the mosques, preachers and poets from among the two communities emphasized the need for union under the banner of Islam.[60] The following extract from another poem of 'Ubaydi was said to be most effective in reducing sectarian barriers, leading Shi'is to believe that the long-awaited Sunni-Shi'i reconciliation had finally been reached:

> Do not talk of a Ja'fari or Hanafi
> do not talk of a Shafi'i or Zaydi
> For the shari'a of Muhammad has united us
> and it rejects the Western mandate.[61]

Police informants were dazed by the scope of the ceremonies in Baghdad and Kazimayn, and the writer of one of the police reports went as far as to suggest that such a phenomenon had never before occurred in Islam. From the police reports it is clear that the main object of the ceremonies was to reach the lower classes and incite them to take an interest in political affairs. This aim seems to have been successfully achieved. In late May it was reported that "political matters are now discussed everywhere and by everyone and with little reserve." The Shi'is and Sunnis, it was reported, "have gained confidence by this union whether imaginary or real."[62] British political maneuvering and deterrent measures, including the outlawing of the *Haras al-Istiqlal* and the expulsion from Iraq of some of its members as well as Shirazi's son Muhammad, proved ineffective in stopping the momentum created by the celebrations. In his memoirs Arnold Wilson wrote: "The fervent appeals which were made to religion and patriotism, and to the Amir 'Abdallah, urging him to hasten the advent of his holy kingdom, roused extreme enthusiasm." Wilson concluded that in light of subsequent events it was a grave error of judgement on his part to allow the ceremonies to continue.[63]

Seeking to maximize the effect of the ceremonies in Baghdad and Kazimayn, and to generate a similar momentum throughout Iraq, Shirazi published a dispatch in the midst of Ramadan. It was distributed in various parts of Iraq and read in public meetings:

[60] Mesopotamian Police, Abstract of Intelligence, Baghdad, 22 May 1920, FO 371/5076/8448; Wardi, *Lamahat*, 5,1:172–76, 188–93, and 5,2:31.

[61] Wa'ili, *Thawrat al-'ishrin*, 41; Wardi, *Lamahat*, 5,1:193–94; Ra'uf al-Wa'iz, *al-Ittijahat al-wataniyya fi al-shi'r al-'iraqi al-hadith, 1914–1941* (Baghdad, 1974), 100.

[62] Mesopotamian Police, Abstract of Intelligence, Baghdad, 22 and 29 May, 5 June 1920, FO 371/5076/8448, FO 371/5076/8611, and FO 371/5076/8864.

[63] Wilson, *Mesopotamia*, 253.

Your brethren in Baghdad and Kazimayn have agreed to hold meetings and to attend peaceful demonstrations . . . It is obligatory upon you and upon all Muslims to conform with your brethren in this noble principle. Beware of violating peace [and] of disagreements and quarrels amongst you for this will inflict damage upon your goals and [will result in] the loss of your rights; the time for their attainment by you has now come.[64]

Shirazi's dispatch was followed by the intensification of the call for a jihad among the tribes of the central Euphrates carried by Shi'i emissaries from Karbala and Najaf. Only a very small number of the big tribal shaykhs responded to the call to revolt, the overwhelming majority still preferring continued British rule as expressed in the plebiscite.[65] The change in the position of some paramount shaykhs was largely a result of temporarily effective pressures by Shi'i ulama rather than a reflection of their desire for an Islamic government in Iraq. Thus, for example, when in May 1920 a strong anti-British propaganda offensive was waged among the Hindiyya tribes, the paramount shaykh of the Bani Hasan, 'Umran al-Hajj Sa'dun, reported the matter to the local political officer and strongly advised him to take action against the ringleaders at Karbala. Later the same month all the Hindiyya shaykhs were summoned to Karbala and called upon to sign a petition to the effect that they desired a purely Arab government, free of foreign interference. In the face of the pressures applied, 'Umran felt that he might as well throw in his lot with the Karbala ulama, and the other shaykhs followed his example.[66] The decision of individual tribesmen and small tribal shaykhs to join the revolt reflected their protest against British policy of rebuilding and solidifying the power of the paramount shaykhs, which had been in decline prior to the occupation. Their resentment of British tribal policy helps to explain the motivation of the tribesmen in agreeing to revolt.[67]

The first shot signaling the 1920 revolt was fired on 30 June at Rumaytha in Diwaniyya province. Just a few days before Shirazi's death on 13 August, an important *fatwa* attributed to him drew other tribes to join the revolt: "It is obligatory upon the Iraqis to demand their rights . . . and they are allowed to use force and arms if the British refuse to accept their demands."[68] Around the middle of August, Shaykh al-Shari'a Isfahani

[64] The dispatch is dated 9/10 Ramadan 1338. For its contents see Hasani, al-'Iraq, 97–98.

[65] Batatu, The Old Social Classes, 82, 84.

[66] "Brief Note on the Activities of the Anti-Government Party at Karbala," 14 July 1920, FO 371/5078/10653.

[67] Batatu, The Old Social Classes, 88; Wardi, Lamahat, 5,1:24–25.

[68] 'Abd al-Razzaq Hasani, al-Thawra al-'iraqiyya al-kubra (Sidon, 1952), 99. The *fatwa* was not dated and various accounts suggest different dates between the end of June and the beginning of August.

was recognized as the most prominent mujtahid. Najaf now assumed the leading role in the revolt, attempting to maintain its momentum among the tribes of the lower Euphrates.[69] Only in October were the British able to subdue the tribes and regain control over the central and lower Euphrates—the backbone of the revolt.

The result of the revolt was far from serving the goals of the Shiʿi mujtahids. The brief alliance between the mujtahids and the Sharifians came to an end. The mujtahids' plan to oust the British and to dominate the affairs of Iraq had misfired. "Later generations of Iraq [Sunni] politicians," wrote one British official in summarizing the revolt, "may appreciate the gratitude they owe the British for saving them from [Shiʿi] Najaf."[70] The British machinery, now headed by Sir Percy Cox following the recall of Wilson, was preparing the ground for the accession of Faysal as the King of Iraq.

In the course of the 1919 plebiscite and the period leading up to the 1920 revolt, the mujtahids pushed for a political system in Iraq, which, had they been successful in accomplishing their goal, would have enabled them to dominate the politics of the new state from its inception. By the time of the establishment of the Iraqi monarchy, the power of Shiʿi Islam had reached its peak. The Shiʿi religious establishment could compete with any government in Iraq over the influence and mobilization of the local population. The existence of such a highly autonomous and politically active religious establishment posed a danger to the authority of the nascent Iraqi state. Successive Sunni governments would therefore seek to eradicate the power of Shiʿi mujtahids and institutions in the country, and to reduce the links between Najaf and Karbala and Iran.

[69] For dispatches sent from Isfahani to the tribes to increase their motivation see Wardi, *Lamahat*, 5,2:77–78.

[70] Administration Report of the Muntafiq Division, 1920, CO 696/3.

PART TWO

The State and the Shi'is

Chapter Three

EXERCISING SOCIAL CONTROL

THE ESTABLISHMENT of modern Iraq created new realities. The country ceased to be the frontier between the Sunni Ottoman Empire and Shi'i Iran which it had been for centuries, and Pan-Arabism became the major nationalist ideology in the new state. In August 1921 the British installed Faysal as king and a government was formed. Iraq was a British Mandate until October 1932 when it gained its independence from Britain. The latter, however, retained influence in the country throughout the next twenty-six years until the 1958 Revolution. Internal politics were dominated by the British, the Sunni ex-Ottoman officers, and by the royal family (the Sharifians) in the palace. While many aspects of Iraqi political life under the monarchy reflected the different motivations of these three groups, they shared a degree of common interest in their attempt to undermine the position of Shi'i Islam in Iraq. The state's effort to curb Shi'i Islam continued after the collapse of the monarchy in 1958, culminating under the Ba'th when the government acted to monopolize all aspects of public life in Iraq.

CONTAINING THE MUJTAHIDS

The conflict between the Shi'i mujtahids and Iraq's Sunni politicians in the early 1920s stemmed from the clash between the process of Shi'i state formation, which had begun in the mid-eighteenth century, and the establishment of the Iraqi monarchy. This conflict manifested itself in the struggle between the two groups over the nature of government as well as the control of the Shi'i population in the new state. With the collapse of the 1920 revolt, the authority of the mujtahids in Iraq sustained a serious blow. Noting that the great majority of the mujtahids were Iranian subjects whose political outlook was "colored" by events in Iran, the British insisted that from an Iraqi national point of view clerical intervention should be avoided in dealing with the revolt. The British refused to allow the leading mujtahid Shaykh al-Shari'a Isfahani to negotiate the terms of submission of the insurgent Shi'i tribes so as to check the influence of the mujtahids among the tribes of the Samawa and the Rumaytha districts. In rejecting the claim of ulama and tribal shaykhs that Isfahani was the representative of Shi'i public opinion, the British prevented any mujtahid from exercising the power of an *Imperium in Imperio*.[1]

The inability of the mujtahids to agree on one leading mujtahid following the death of Shaykh al-Shari'a Isfahani in December 1920 further hindered the power of the Shi'i religious establishment in Iraq. Although from the nineteenth century the Shi'i religious leadership in Iraq had become more centralized than in previous periods, a formal Shi'i religious hierarchy was not established and there did not develop any clear mechanism for the selection or appointment of the supreme mujtahid. Thus, like in the period following the death of the great mujtahid Murtada al-Ansari (1864), a struggle for the Shi'i religious leadership erupted again in Najaf in the twentieth century. While several mujtahids, notably, Abu al-Hasan Isfahani, Muhammad Husayn Na'ini, and Muhammad Firuzabadi laid claim to the leadership, for several years none of them was able to assert himself as the premier mujtahid.

The lack of one recognized grand mujtahid who would act as the supreme Shi'i authority, and the growing gaps between the Arab tribesmen and the Persian mujtahids, improved the position of the less senior Arab mujtahids in Iraq. Some of the Arab mujtahids originally descended from Arab tribes in Iraq (most notably 'Ali Kashif al-Ghita and his son Ahmad, who are traced to the Muntafiq confederation), and they attempted to use their tribal connection to enhance their own status both among the population and within the Shi'i religious hierarchy. The tribes of the middle Euphrates accused the Persian mujtahids of battening on the wealth of Iraq and leading the people astray during the revolt. Hints were thrown that they might suitably return to Iran and leave the guidance of Arab Shi'is to the Arab mujtahids. Given this mood of the tribesmen, it was perhaps not quite surprising that even Sayyid 'Ali Yazdi, son of the former grand mujtahid Kazim Yazdi, whose rank as compared with the other three Persian mujtahids was not high, could draw on the esteem that his father had once enjoyed to increase his own influence among the tribes. His position was enhanced by his frequent declarations that in spite of his Iranian background he considered himself an Arab and an Iraqi. 'Ali subsequently assumed the position of a premier mujtahid in the estimation of the Hilla and the Shamiyya tribes.[2] As will be seen later in this chapter and elsewhere in the book, these challenges to the position of the senior Persian mujtahids would intensify in subsequent years.

Defeated in their attempt to oust the British through the revolt, and

[1] Intelligence Reports nos. 1 and 2, 15 and 30 November 1920, FO 371/6349/1011 and FO 371/6349/2172.

[2] Intelligence Reports nos. 4, 6, 8, and 12, 31 December 1920, 31 January, 1 March, and 1 May 1921, FO 371/6348/2904; FO 371/6350/3824; FO 371/6350/4506; FO 371/6351/6351.

divided over the issue of the religious leadership, the mujtahids had little choice but to accept the nomination of Faysal as king of Iraq. They found it hard to disqualify Faysal since they themselves had asked for a son of Sharif Husayn as king of Iraq during the 1919 plebiscite. From their point of view, there were perhaps some advantages to be gained from the nomination of a son of the Sharif as king of Iraq. Aware of the hostilities between the Sharifians and the Sa'ud family of the Hijaz, which espoused the Wahhabi creed, the mujtahids hoped that Faysal would defend Shi'i Islam in Iraq against possible future Wahhabi attacks in the form of the Ikhwan of Ibn Sa'ud.[3] Also, Faysal apparently assured some senior mujtahids that he had come to Iraq to save it from the British, thus leading them to hope that with the King's help they would manage to oust the British. Nonetheless, the mujtahids' support of Faysal was conditional, as may be gathered from the position of Shaykh Mahdi al-Khalisi and Sayyid Muhammad al-Sadr, the two leading mujtahids of Kazimayn. Although Faysal managed to gain a pledge of allegiance from Khalisi, the latter set a condition that the King's rule should be free of foreign interference and that Faysal would agree to be bound by a parliament. Sadr was even said to demand Faysal's rejection of the proposed British Mandate as a condition for his pledge of allegiance to the King.[4] In giving conditional support to Faysal, the mujtahids hoped to prevent the establishment of a strong government in Iraq and to influence national politics.

Faysal was nevertheless alarmed by the power of the Shi'i mujtahids and sought to eradicate it. In December 1921 the King had a conversation with Sir Percy Loraine, the newly appointed British minister to Iran who had stopped in Baghdad *en route* to Tehran. The two discussed the Iranian government's inability to convene a parliament to ratify the 1919 Anglo-Iranian Agreement and its eventual cancelation by the new government of Sayyid Ziya in February 1921. In evaluating the main factors behind this act, Faysal pointed to the role of the Persian mujtahids in the shrine cities in Iraq. The King, reported Loraine, "strongly expressed the opinion that until the influence of the ulama was broken, no satisfactory progress could be made in Persian affairs."[5] When Faysal pointed to the influence of the mujtahids over Iranian affairs in his conversation with Loraine, he no doubt had in mind their role in leading the 1920 revolt in Iraq as well as their refusal to give him an unconditional pledge of support. As his rule in Iraq was to prove, Faysal's strongest political virtue was his ability to

[3] Muhammad 'Ali Shams al-Din, *al-Islah al-hadi: nazra fi fikr wa-suluk al-mujtahid al-sayyid muhsin al-amin al-'amili* (Beirut, 1985), 152.

[4] 'Ali al-Wardi, *Lamahat ijtima'iyya min ta'rikh al-'iraq al-hadith*, 6 vols. (Baghdad, 1969–1978), 6:107–10, 114.

[5] Loraine to the Marquess Curzon of Kedlestone, Baghdad, 11 December 1921, FO 371/7802/414.

control the country by balancing the different groups and moderating their conflicting interests. The existence of a strong opposition force to his rule on the part of the mujtahids was something that the King could not tolerate. Indeed, a few weeks after his talk with Loraine, Faysal was reported to be especially anxious to weaken the influence of the Persian mujtahids, whom he considered disloyal to the Iraqi state.[6] It was not long before such an opportunity presented itself.

Between December 1921 and August 1922 discussions on an Anglo-Iraqi treaty took place in Baghdad. There was to be a main treaty defining the shape of Anglo-Iraqi relations, and subsidiary agreements dealing with military and financial matters and with the number and duties of the British officials to be employed by the Iraqi government. The treaty was initially intended to last twenty years. Although it was signed by the government in October 1922, it still had to be ratified by the Constituent Assembly, the elections for which were scheduled for 1923. The discussions of the treaty and the preparations for the elections to the Assembly coincided with the Ikhwan's attack on Shi'i tribes in Iraq, as well as with Turkish propaganda which called for Arab autonomy under Turkish authority.

In March 1922 the Ikhwan of Ibn Sa'ud raided Iraq, attacking some of the Muntafiq tribes and killing several hundred tribesmen. People worried that this was only a prelude to a wider attack of the Ikhwan on the country, and the mujtahids portrayed it as a move instigated by the British to weaken Iraq. Asserting that the Iraqi government was unable to protect the tribes from the Ikhwan, the mujtahids sought to seize the opportunity to bolster their own position in the country. Led by Abu al-Hasan Isfahani, Husayn Na'ini, and Mahdi al-Khalisi, the mujtahids decided to hold a conference in Karbala on the occasion of the Shi'i annual visitation to the tomb of imam Husayn on 15 Sha'ban (18 April 1922) to consider measures for the defense of Iraq against the Ikhwan. British officials warned that the real object of the mujtahids in proposing the conference was to secure a pledge of obedience by the tribal shaykhs and to protest against the Mandate. They feared that if a tribal force was to be recruited against the Ikhwan the mujtahids would ultimately use it for agitation within Iraq.

On 1 April Khalisi issued invitations to Sunni and Shi'i tribal leaders to assemble at Karbala on 13 April, five days before the actual date of the visitation. The mujtahids also invited the Sunni ulama of Baghdad and King Faysal. While a delegation of Sunni ulama arrived at Karbala, it did not include such an important figure as Mahmud Shukri al-Alusi, who refused to sanction counterattacks against the Ikhwan. And although Faysal had initially promised to attend the conference on 14 April, he did

---

[6] Intelligence Reports nos. 2 and 3, 15 January and 1 February 1922, CO 730/19/10792.

not show up because of pressures from Sir Percy Cox. The upshot of the Karbala conference was the compilation of a petition which called for the recruiting and arming of a tribal force to be placed under the command of Faysal to fight the Ikhwan.[7] The attempt of the mujtahids to use the Karbala conference to create anti-Mandate agitation failed largely because of the refusal of the big tribal shaykhs to side with the mujtahids, a decision which I will explain later in this chapter when dealing with the tribal shaykhs.

Having failed to organize an anti-British movement through the Karbala conference, Isfahani, Na'ini, and Khalisi now focused their opposition on the proposed Anglo-Iraqi treaty and the elections. From the mujtahids' point of view, Faysal had broken his promise to them to free Iraq from British control and the King was now identified by some mujtahids as a British "agent." Faysal's failure to attend the Karbala conference was taken by the mujtahids as a proof of his increasing reliance on the British. They feared that through the King the British would be able to further bolster their position in the country and to undermine the status of the mujtahids. The mujtahids also worried about a political process that would enable the laity to elect representatives for parliament. This carried the danger that the mujtahids' representatives would not be elected as the British and the Iraqi government were likely to exercise pressures on the voters to choose their own candidates. Indeed, the mujtahids considered the elections a "death penalty for the Islamic nation" and were said to view them as capable of reducing their position within the Iraqi state to a level similar to that of the Vatican in Italy.[8]

On 20 October 1922 the Minister of Interior 'Abd al-Muhsin al-Sa'dun instructed the provincial governors to begin preparing for the elections to the Constituent Assembly for which only males over twenty-one years old were eligible to vote. With Faysal's approval the governors were also instructed to discreetly urge the voters to select only those candidates who were likely to ratify the proposed Anglo-Iraqi agreement.[9] By 5 November, Khalisi, Isfahani, and Na'ini issued *fatwas* declaring the participation of all Muslims in the elections unlawful. Some of these *fatwas* threatened that those who disobeyed the mujtahids' verdict would be excommunicated. One of Khalisi's *fatwas* read: "We have passed judgement against the elections. Whoever takes part in them is fighting God, the Prophet, and the

---

[7] Wardi, *Lamahat*, 6:140–49; Intelligence Reports nos. 8 and 9, 15 April and 1 May 1922, CO 730/21/21724 and CO 730/21/24559.

[8] Anon., *al-Haraka al-islamiyya fi al-'iraq* (Beirut, 1985), 47; 'Abdallah al-Nafisi, *Dawr al-shi'a fi tatawwur al-'iraq al-siyasi al-hadith* (Beirut, 1973), 178–79; Ahmad al-Katib, *Tajrubat al-thawra al-islamiyya fi al-'iraq* (Beirut, 1981), 76, 78.

[9] M. M. al-Adhami, "The Elections for the Constituent Assembly in Iraq, 1922–1924," in *The Integration of Modern Iraq*, ed. Abbas Kelidar (London, 1979), 18.

Imams, and will not be buried in Muslim cemeteries." Another *fatwa*, by Isfahani, contained a threat that any Muslim who participated in the elections would be deprived of his wife, would be prohibited from entering the public bath, and would be ostracized by all other Muslims.[10] It was consequently reported from Karbala and Ba'quba that the local election committee had tendered its resignation.

For almost nine months it was impossible to prepare for the elections in the Karbala province and in other areas of Iraq as the Shi'i population followed the *fatwa*s of the mujtahids. Even Sunnis as far away as Mosul were influenced by the *fatwa*s, probably because of people's fear that the registers of the elections might be used for conscription. The stalemate was reinforced by the fact that at that time the big tribal shaykhs resented the limited number of seats assigned to them in the Constituent Assembly. Since under the electoral law only twenty seats were allotted to the tribes of the total of one hundred, the shaykhs probably feared that they would be overwhelmed by townsmen in the Assembly. They therefore sought to use the mujtahids' *fatwa*s to exert pressures on the King and the government to increase their own share among the constituents.[11]

The mujtahids attempted to use the stalemate to weaken Faysal and the government, and to incite the population to revolt again. They were encouraged by the resignation of Lloyd George's coalition government in November and the news from Britain that the new British government was considering the possibility of evacuating Iraq. The mujtahids also benefited from the fact that at that time the British still had not secured Mosul for Iraq and there was thus a possibility of a war between Britain and Turkey. The latter country deployed troops along Iraq's northern frontier while Turkish propaganda portrayed the British as infidels and called for Arab self-rule under Turkish authority.[12] In Karbala a local *sayyid* was reportedly urging the population to prepare a petition for Mustafa Kemal, inviting him to take over Iraq. In Kazimayn *fatwa*s were posted in the mosques forbidding the defense of Iraq against the Turks. Notices signed by "the servants of Islam" were posted in the mosques of Najaf as well, and at least one clearly called for a revolt:

> O chiefs who defend the religion of the lord of [the] Apostles! O Muslims who inhabit this country! O persons who live on this chaste land! Where is the Islamic and patriotic zeal? Where is he who follows the example of his ancestors, and endeavors to raise higher the banner of Islam? Brothers, look for the

[10] Iraq Police, Abstract of Intelligence, 10 November 1922, NAI, BHCF, file 23/15/1, vol. 1; Wardi, *Lamahat*, 6:202–3; Anon., *al-Imam al-sayyid abu al-hasan* (Najaf, 1946/7), 47.

[11] Intelligence Report no. 6, 15 March 1923, FO 371/9009/3679; Adhami, "Elections," 20, 22.

[12] Peter Sluglett, *Britain in Iraq, 1914–1932* (London, 1976), 78–79; Wardi, *Lamahat*, 6:211, 213.

occasion and awaken from your sleep, demand your legitimate rights, your complete independence and full liberty from the usurpers.[13]

By June 1923 the ban which the mujtahids imposed on the elections had begun to lose its impact in Baghdad, Basra, the Muntafiq, 'Amara, Kut, Diwaniyya, and Diyala. The position of Faysal and the government had somewhat improved because of the withdrawal of Turkish forces from the north and the decrease in Turkish propaganda in Iraq, and thanks to Britain's proposal to reduce the period of the Anglo-Iraqi agreement from twenty years to four. The mujtahids therefore had to issue new *fatwa*s to reinforce the impact of their previous ones. At that time there were even rumors that the mujtahids were considering issuing a *fatwa* against Faysal and the lawfulness of the Iraqi government as it was then constituted.[14]

The particularly furious anti-election campaign of Mahdi al-Khalisi as well as of his three sons and nephew involved a direct attack on Faysal, and challenged the King's attempt to assert his rule in Iraq. Mahdi al-Khalisi declared his pledge of allegiance to Faysal void since the King had broken his promise to oppose the British presence in Iraq. One of Khalisi's sons, Muhammad, who had fled from Iraq to Iran in August 1922 because of his role in leading anti-British agitation, published several statements in the latter country demanding among other things the immediate abrogation of the Mandate and the formation of an Iraqi national cabinet. One statement also accused the King of betraying the Iraqi people and selling Iraq to the British. Faysal's approval of the Anglo-Iraqi treaty was described as an insult to Islamic law since article 12 of the proposed treaty allowed missionary activity in Iraq. Copies of the statement arrived in Iraq soon after its publication in Tehran.[15]

Faysal now became determined to break the power of the leading mujtahids by forcing them to leave the country. This action was considered by the King at least as early as April 1923. It was also advocated by the new Sunni Prime Minister 'Abd al-Muhsin al-Sa'dun, who had replaced the aging *naqib* in November 1922 and perceived the Persian mujtahids as aliens in Iraq. By June it was evident that British officials in the country also considered this move, more than any other measure, as likely to provide an opportunity to carry out the elections for the Constituent Assembly. Aware

[13] Iraq Police, Abstract of Intelligence 23, 19 August 1922, NAI, BHCF, file 7/15/3. See also Intelligence Reports nos. 1, 6, and 8, 1 January, 15 March and 15 April 1923, FO 371/9009/1190; FO 371/9009/3679; FO 371 9009/4743.

[14] Wardi, *Lamahat*, 6:215; Intelligence Reports nos. 11 and 12, 1 and 13 June 1923, FO 371/9009/6469 and FO 371/9009/7388.

[15] Muhammad Mahdi Kubba, *Mudhakkirati fi samim al-ahdath, 1917–1958* (Beirut, 1965), 26–27; The British Residency, Baghdad, 27 January 1923, FO 371/9003/2112; Intelligence Report no. 19, 1 October 1922, CO 730/25/52603; Intelligence Report no. 3, 1 February 1923, FO 371/9009/2341.

of the fact that the bulk of the mujtahids were Iranian nationals, the government introduced an amendment to the existing Law of Immigration on 9 June 1923 permitting the deportation of foreigners who were found engaging in anti-government activity. Articles were also published in Baghdad's newspaper, *al-'Asima*, calling for measures against "those aliens who did not belong in Iraq." The government thus began to prepare public opinion for its intended action.[16]

On 21 June, a nephew of Mahdi al-Khalisi was arrested while attempting to post a copy of an anti-election *fatwa* on the gate of the Kazimayn mosque. That same evening two sons of Khalisi were also arrested on the ground that they had attempted to force the release of Khalisi's nephew. On the 23d, Mahdi al-Khalisi ordered the closing of the bazaars in Kazimayn and Baghdad. The government acted swiftly. On the night of the 25th, Mahdi al-Khalisi was arrested, an act which the King had endorsed. The next day, Khalisi, his sons, and his nephew, all being Arabs who had taken Iranian nationality during the Ottoman period to avoid conscription, were deported to 'Aden under the new provision of Iraq's Immigration Law. In an injudicious act of protest on their part, and much to the relief of the government, the nine most prominent Persian mujtahids of the shrine cities, including Na'ini and Isfahani, left Iraq for Iran on 2 July and settled in Qum. In October they were joined by Mahdi al-Khalisi, who had completed a pilgrimage to Mecca following his deportation to 'Aden.[17]

In Iran a disagreement broke out between Khalisi and the other mujtahids. Following his arrival in Iran, Khalisi was said to have issued a *fatwa* in which he ruled that a portion of the fifth, which was set aside by Shi'i believers for general religious services as well as for the *sayyid*s, should now be paid to the Iranian government to enable it to strengthen its armed forces. Khalisi also advocated that the endowment revenue of the shrines of Kazimayn and Mashhad should be set aside for that purpose too. Khalisi's *fatwa*, which may have been intended in part for the consumption of the Iranian government, was rejected by the other mujtahids since its implementation would have meant a blow to their own sources of income and those of the shrines. Na'ini even stated that Khalisi had apparently the intention of acting contrary to the tenets of Islam.[18] This disagreement enabled the mujtahids to disassociate themselves from Khalisi and to seek to negotiate the terms of their return to Iraq without him.

[16] Intelligence Reports nos. 8, 9, and 13, 15 April, 1 May, and 21 June 1923, FO 371/9009/4743; FO 371/9009/5237; FO 371/9009/7388; Wardi, *Lamahat*, 6:218.

[17] Intelligence Report no. 14, 5 July 1923, FO 371/9009/7681; Iraq, Administration Report for the Year April 1923–December 1924, CO 730/73/15758; Wardi, *Lamahat*, 6:221–33.

[18] Intelligence Report no. 22, 15 November 1923, FO 371/9010/11793; External Intelligence Report no. 32, 20 March 1924, CO 730/58/15340; Intelligence Report no. 3, 7 February 1924, FO 371/10097/1616; Wardi, *Lamahat*, 6:249.

The mujtahids were anxious to return to Najaf to preserve the eminent position of that city and to avoid a loss of esteem among their followers in Iraq. Their stay in Qum had created some tensions between them and the leading cleric there, 'Abd al-Karim Ha'iri, who was just beginning to establish his own position and madrasa in that city. Ha'iri did not fully identify publicly with the position of the Najafi mujtahids and did not lead a mass movement in their favor as they had probably expected him to do. While there are no indications that Ha'iri himself sought to undermine the position of the Najafi mujtahids, some other Iranian ulama did attempt to use this episode to increase both their own power vis-à-vis the Najafi mujtahids as well as the status of Qum as a Shi'i academic center at the expense of Najaf and Karbala.[19] Also, in the Shi'i religious establishment the concept then was that Najaf should be the seat of the leading mujtahid of the day and Na'ini and Isfahani considered themselves strong candidates for that title. In February, Shaykh Jawad al-Jawahiri wrote from Najaf to Na'ini begging him and the other mujtahids to return as they would otherwise lose their position in Iraq, which was rapidly being taken over by other mujtahids. Apparently Firuzabadi, who remained in Najaf, was making preparations for his own recognition as the premier mujtahid.[20] Moreover, the mujtahids possessed houses, various other property, and a remunerative distribution of charitable funds in Iraq, and lacked a solid economic base in Qum. Describing themselves as being bankrupt, Na'ini and Isfahani sent letters to their agents in Najaf in January 1924 instructing them to sell property administered by the mujtahids to provide for their expenses in Iran.[21]

After a long period of negotiations aimed at embarrassing the mujtahids and diminishing their esteem among their Shi'i followers, the mujtahids were allowed to return to Iraq on 22 April 1924. By that time Khalisi had died of apoplexy, the elections for the Assembly had been completed, and the Anglo-Iraqi treaty had been ratified.[22]

Khalisi's deportation and the departure of the leading mujtahids to Iran had far-reaching consequences on Iraqi Shi'i society, the relation between religion and state in Iraq, and the position of Shi'i Islam in Iraq and Iran. Kinahan Cornwallis, the British adviser to the Iraqi Ministry of Interior,

[19] Abdul-Hadi Hairi, *Shi'ism and Constitutionalism in Iran* (Leiden, 1977), 138; Mohammad Faghfoory, "The Ulama-State Relations in Iran: 1921–1941," *IJMES* 19 (1987): 418.

[20] Intelligence Report no. 5, 6 March 1924, FO 371/10097/2498; Wardi, *Lamahat*, 6:247.

[21] Report to Special Officer 1, 24 January 1924, Air 23/453.

[22] The main documents covering the negotiations and conditions for the mujtahids' return are: British High Commissioner for Iraq to the Secretary of State for the Colonies, 13 February 1924, FO 371/10147/1519; Iraq, Ministry of the Interior, Baghdad, 23 April 1924, Air 23/453; Intelligence Report no. 9, 1 May 1924, CO 730/59/22547; Persia, Annual Report 1924, FO 416/112. See also Wardi, *Lamahat*, 6:261.

wrote to Henry Dobbs, the new High Commissioner, that the action taken
against Khalisi was of "historical importance" since it dealt Persian influence in Iraq "a staggering blow" and "showed the people for the first time
that they have a government which can act forcibly and effectively on its
own initiative."[23] Dobbs himself wrote: "Present is unique opportunity
through which the shia holy cities can be purged of predominance of
Persian influence which has been exercised for year[s] to [the] detriment of
true Arab interests with the object of prolonging anarchy . . . amongst the
tribes. There might never be recurrence of so favorable an opportunity."[24]

The uncommitted attitude of large segments of Shi'i society to the cause
of the Persian mujtahids signaled the latters' diminishing power as well as
the widening gap between them and the laity in Iraq. The Shi'i Arab
populations of Baghdad and Basra were the quickest to demonstrate their
readiness to work with the King and the government as they considered it
the best way to improve their socioeconomic position in the state. A delegation of Baghdad's leading Shi'i personalities presented a manifesto to
Faysal in December 1923. Its contents stated the signatories' conviction
that the Shi'i community had been in error in opposing the treaty and
proposed a radical change of policy toward the state. In the Euphrates,
'Amara, and Nasiriyya, the departure of the Persian mujtahids created only
little excitement among the Arab population. The Shi'i tribes evinced no
eagerness to take precipitate action on behalf of the mujtahids, and
throughout Iraq the government commanded increased respect on account
of its firm stand against the mujtahids.[25]

The departure of the leading mujtahids exacerbated the vacuum of
power in the Shi'i religious hierarchy in Iraq, which had been created by the
lack of one recognized premier mujtahid following the death of Shaykh al-
Shari'a Isfahani. The government used the intense competition that
erupted between Arab and Persian mujtahids for the leadership to decrease
the power of the Shi'i clergy in Iraq. Even before the mujtahids' departure,
many of the relatively low-ranking Arab mujtahids, most notably 'Ali Kashif al-Ghita and his son Ahmad, though afraid of coming out openly in
defiance of the Persian mujtahids, had privately told their followers that
they did not support the ban on the elections. Following the departure of
the mujtahids, it was alleged in Iran that the British bribed several leading
mujtahids in Iraq, notably Firuzabadi, "to corrupt the Arab clergy" so that
the elections would be declared lawful.[26] In quietly supporting the elec-

[23] Cornwallis to Dobbs, Baghdad, 18 July 1923, FO 371/9047/8907.

[24] Cited by Sluglett, *Britain*, 308.

[25] Intelligence Report no. 23, 1 December 1923, FO 371/9010/12099; Extracts from
Special Administration Interim Report of Principle Events between 5 to 12 July 1923, FO
371/9047/8090; Intelligence Report no. 15, 26 July 1923, FO 371/9009/8559.

[26] Intelligence Report no. 1, 1 January 1923, FO 371/9009/1190; British Military At-
taché, Tehran, no. 32–7, 8 September 1923, NAI, Government of India, Foreign and Political
Department, file 575x.

tions, the Arab mujtahids sought to increase their own influence among the Shi'i population and thus to improve their status within the religious hierarchy. The challenge to the leadership of the more prominent Persian mujtahids continued following the latter's return to Iraq.

In December 1925 a strong struggle was observed within the Shi'i religious establishment, which had split into two camps: the Persian camp led by Isfahani and Na'ini, and the Arab camp led by Ahmad Kashif al-Ghita. The struggle surfaced when an Arab Sayyid, Salih al-Hilli, who was the most famous sermon and *ta'ziya* leader in Iraq in his time, asked Isfahani for funds to build a small gathering place for the mourning of imam Husayn in 'Amara. Isfahani, who around that time issued a *fatwa* forbidding several practices connected with the commemoration of *'Ashura'* (see chapter 5), refused to give money to Hilli, whereupon the latter started censuring Isfahani in his public sermons. Consequently, Isfahani proclaimed it unlawful for Hilli to give sermons and declared him irreligious. In an attempt to increase his own position within the religious hierarchy in Iraq, Ahmad Kashif al-Ghita declared Isfahani's proclamation invalid and allotted a sum of money to Hilli.[27]

This dispute was followed by the propaganda activity of both camps for support among the Shi'i population. The Arab mujtahids were backed by many important tribal shaykhs and landowners in Diwaniyya, who opposed the introduction of a new system for the assessment of rice crops for tax purposes. The shaykhs first appealed to the prominent Persian mujtahids to gain their support against the new system of taxation. The latter rejected their appeal, however, on the ground that the shaykhs had ignored the mujtahids' plight when they left in protest to Iran. Ahmad Kashif al-Ghita also gained the support of the governor of Karbala province, who sought to undermine the position of the Persian mujtahids. Only in April 1926, after the death of Ahmad Kashif al-Ghita, were the Persian mujtahids able to overcome the challenge to their authority, and a temporary reconciliation was reached.[28]

The Arab-Persian struggle surfaced anew in 1932, the government taking an active part in the dispute and supporting the Arab mujtahids. The *casus belli* was again Salih al-Hilli. He was preaching in Shi'i districts, particularly in 'Amara, making remarks calculated to enrage Isfahani and Na'ini. Hilli urged that one-third of the residue of estates of deceased Shi'is which had often been handed over to the leading mujtahids, should be paid instead to the poor, either through religious welfare foundations in their

[27] Air Staff Intelligence, Nasiriyya, 12 December 1925, and Special Service Officer, Baghdad, 31 December 1925, Air 23/379. See also Ja'far al-Khalili, *Hakadha 'araftuhum*, 2 vols. (Baghdad, 1963–1968), 1:108–11, and 2:145–49.

[28] Office of the Administrative Inspector, Diwaniyya, 22, 24, and 30 December 1925, Air 23/379; Special Service Officer, Baghdad, 31 December 1925, Air 23/379; Intelligence Reports nos. 1 and 7, 7 January and 1 April 1926, CO 730/105/1.

neighborhoods, or through himself. Hilli was supported in this campaign by two important Arab mujtahids, Muhammad Husayn Kashif al-Ghita (d. 1954) and Muhammad 'Ali Bahr al-'Ulum (d. 1936). Kashif al-Ghita, who would emerge as the most famous Arab mujtahid under the monarchy, was then vying for a higher position within the Shi'i religious hierarchy and he had been Faysal's choice for Iraq's representative at the Jerusalem Muslim Conference of December 1931. Under the monarchy, Bahr al-'Ulum was appointed a senator; he was said to act as a link between the government in Baghdad and ulama and other social groups in Najaf.[29]

The rise of Arab mujtahids to a relatively high position within the Shi'i religious hierarchy in Iraq was evident both during and after the monarchic period. Iraqi Shi'is sometimes disregarded the lower status of Arab mujtahids in the Shi'i universal hierarchy, emulating those mujtahids (like Muhammad Baqir al-Sadr, d. 1980) whom they felt were of their own and capable of addressing the specific needs of Iraqi Shi'i society. At the same time, however, the government managed to exert a degree of influence over some Arab mujtahids and used them to undermine the position of the Persian mujtahids and to prevent the emergence of a strong Shi'i religious leadership in Iraq. The inability of the Shi'i religious establishment to develop as strong a leadership as it had had at the turn of the twentieth century hindered the contacts between the mujtahids and the laity in modern Iraq. Shi'i ulama have acknowledged this weakness and pointed to the ethnic, linguistic, and cultural gaps between the prominent Persian mujtahids and the Arab masses, and to the mujtahids' inability to produce a link between them and the laity in the form of mid-level Arab ulama.[30] The gaps between the mujtahids and the tribal population were reinforced by the decline in the position of the sayyids. The building up of a state apparatus followed by the introduction of modern education hindered the mystical image of the sayyids and the saintly attributes attached to them by the rural population. The erosion in their power of mediation and influence among the tribesmen was also a result of the intense competition between the sayyids and the mu'mins, who were sent to the tribes by the leading mujtahids to settle such matters as marriage, divorce, and inheritance. By the end of the monarchy, the term sayyid had practically lost its former meaning in Iraq and had come increasingly to mean "mister."[31] The gaps

[29] Special Service Officer, Baghdad, 18 June 1932, Air 23/385; Muhammad Mahdi Bahr al-'Ulum al-Tabataba'i, Rijal al-sayyid bahr al-'ulum al-ma'ruf bi al-fawa'id al-rijaliyya, 3 vols. (Najaf, 1965–1966), 1:160.

[30] Muhammad al-Kazimi al-Qazwini, al-Islam wa-waqi' al-muslim al-mu'asir (Najaf, 1961), 18, 56; al-Lajna al-thaqafiyya li-madrasat al-imam amir al-mu'minin al-'ilmiyya, al-Qadiyya al-'iraqiyya min khilal mawqif al-imam al-shirazi (Mashhad, 1981), 17–18; Katib, Tajrubat al-thawra al-islamiyya, 62.

[31] Hanna Batatu, The Old Social Classes and the Revolutionary Movements in Iraq, 2d ed. (Princeton, N.J., 1982), 209–10. See also Nafisi, Dawr al-shi'a, 77; 'Abd al-Karim al-Nadwani, Ta'rikh al-'amara wa-'asha'iriha (Baghdad, 1961), 25.

between the mujtahids and other segments of Iraqi Shi'i society, to which I will refer in later parts of this book, help explain why the mujtahids in Iraq, in contrast with Iran, failed on the whole to mobilize people for political action against the state in the twentieth century.

Successive Iraqi Sunni governments achieved a clearer separation between religion and state in Iraq than that achieved in Iran, thus preventing the mujtahids from emerging as a major player in Iraqi national politics. In Iran, where there has been for centuries a close interaction between religion and politics, the clergy constituted part of the power elite and ulama were also elected to the Constituent Assembly in the twentieth century. On various occasions under the Iranian monarchy the ulama and the government formed alliances, each side thus seeking to promote its own interests. The influence exercised by the ulama in Iranian national politics, and the need of Iran's monarchs to forge alliances with the clergy, were evident when both Reza Shah and his son Muhammad Reza relied on the ulama to establish and consolidate their own rule in Iran. At times the government also called for, and received, the clergy's backing in dealing with other internal opposition groups in exchange for concessions that led to the growth of religious institutions and to an increase in the ulama's influence in Iranian politics in the twentieth century. Thus, in its attempt to fight communism the Iranian government fostered religion, seeking to placate the ulama and turn them against the Iranian Communist Party (the Tudeh). The anti-Baha'i campaign, which broke out in May–June 1955, demonstrated the willingness of the government to appease the ulama on issues related to the status of minorities and religious freedom in Iran. In return, the government sought to secure the ulama's acquiescence, if not support, against the nationalists, who objected to the amount of oil revenue that the Western Consortium of oil companies proposed to pay to Iran and to Iran's entry into the Baghdad Pact. One consequence of the headway given by the state to the clergy in Iran, as exemplified by the anti-Baha'i campaign, was the growing confidence of the ulama in their ability to influence public policy in the latter part of the twentieth century.[32]

In contrast to Iran, successive Sunni governments in Iraq strove to isolate the Shi'i mujtahids and established clearer boundaries between religion and politics in Iraq. Faysal, who was well aware of the importance of reducing the political power of the mujtahids, used the opportunity of their departure to Iran to work toward that end. Thus, before allowing the leading mujtahids to return to Iraq, the King secured a pledge from them to

[32] Ervand Abrahamian, *Iran Between Two Revolutions*, 2d ed. (Princeton, N.J., 1983), 372–74; Willem Floor, "The Revolutionary Character of the Ulama: Wishful Thinking or Reality?" in *Religion and Politics in Iran: Shi'ism from Quietism to Revolution*, ed. Nikki Keddie (New Haven, 1983), 73, 75, 93; Shahrough Akhavi, *Religion and Politics in Contemporary Iran: Clergy-State Relations in the Pahlavi Period* (Albany, N.Y., 1980), 28, 30, 59, 72, 77, 79–80, 90; Faghfoory, "Ulama-State Relations," 414, 423.

abstain from Iraqi politics in the future. Later generations of Shiʻi ulama noted the success of the monarchy in achieving a separation between religion and state in Iraq.[33] As will be shown in the next chapter in dealing with the 1935 revolt, the Iraqi government was also able to prevent the mujtahids from emerging as a strong power in Iraqi politics under the monarchy. The Sunni state reduced the areas of influence of the Shiʻi mujtahids in Iraq, and its ability to curtail the activity of the Shiʻi clergy was nowhere more evident than in its success in limiting the size of their constituency by stopping the spread of Shiʻism in the country. In 1927 Shiʻi emissaries were arrested near Kirkuk while attempting to convert Turcoman villagers to Imami Shiʻism.[34] There is no evidence that in subsequent years the number of Shiʻis in Iraq increased as a result of the activity of Shiʻi emissaries. In blocking any further spread of Shiʻism in Iraq, the government was able to end the process of conversion which had taken place in the country mainly during the nineteenth century.

The rise of the modern state dealt a blow to the position of the Shiʻi mujtahids in Iraq, which manifested itself in the shift of the religious leadership (the *marjaʻiyya*) from Najaf to Qum following the death of Abu al-Hasan Isfahani in 1946 and the subsequent emergence of Husayn Burujirdi as the grand mujtahid (*marjaʻ al-taqlid*). This development, which I will discuss in greater detail in chapter 9, symbolized the decline of Shiʻi Islam in Iraq and its rise in Iran in the twentieth century.

Managing the Tribal Shaykhs

If the grand mujtahids were one major component of the Shiʻi elite in premonarchic Iraq, the big tribal shaykhs constituted the other important element of this group. The modern state succeeded in splitting the Shiʻi elite. While seeking to undermine the power of the mujtahids, the state offered economic and political incentives to the big shaykhs, who were for the most part Shiʻis, turning them into a player in national politics.

As seen in chapter 1, Ottoman tribal policy in the nineteenth century resulted in the fragmentation of the great tribal confederations in Iraq and diminished the status of their paramount shaykhs. On the eve of the British occupation, Iraq's tribal system was generally enfeebled and the political and military power of the tribal shaykhs was in decline.[35] By contrast, the British bolstered the position of the big tribal shaykhs, whom they considered the best medium through which the countryside could be administered. In return for economic privileges, the shaykhs were expected to keep

---

[33] See, for example, Qazwini, *al-Islam*, 28–30.

[34] Office of the Administrative Inspector, Kirkuk, 21 November 1927, Air 23/432; Ministry of the Interior, Baghdad, 23 November 1927, Air 23/432; Shiʻi Missionaries among the Semi-Pagan Sects, 27 January 1929, Air 23/432.

[35] Batatu, *The Old Social Classes*, 77.

their tribes in order and to assist in regulating the collection of taxes. The shaykhs became dependent on the British and "ruled not by virtue of their own power and authority or the acclamation and loyalty of their tribesmen, but by virtue of the powers conferred to them by the British authorities."[36]

With the establishment of the monarchy, the economic position of the big shaykhs was strengthened by various tax immunities and their political weight was enhanced by their election to parliament. The British used the shaykhs not only to check the King and the government, but also to maintain a balance between one shaykh and another. Although the Sharifians were eager to subordinate the shaykhs to their authority, Faysal and his successors on the throne did not envision their destruction as a group. The Sharifians lacked economic and political bases in the country and needed the shaykhs to improve their own position in Iraq. Moreover, the rise in the period between 1936 and 1941 of army officers drawn from the middle and lower middle classes to a position of political strength threatened the position of both the Sharifians and the shaykhs, fostering an alliance between the two groups which lasted until the collapse of the monarchy in 1958. This alliance found embodiment in two areas: First, the acquisition and ownership of land, which was preserved by laws made with a view to promoting the common economic interests of the two groups; and second, the high number of parliamentary seats allocated to the shaykhs, which culminated in the period of the Regent 'Abd al-Ilah. Thus, whereas the highest percentage of seats allocated to them in 1933 was about 21 percent, this had reached almost 38 percent in September 1954. The Baghdadi politicians were also willing to establish the tribal shaykhs as a landed aristocracy since they too considered them an important component of the power struggles of the different factions in the capital.[37]

The alliance of Iraq's monarchic rulers with the big shaykhs differed from Reza Shah's tribal policy, which was aimed at undermining the power of the tribal chiefs in Iran. During 1927–1929, once he no longer had to rely on the military power of the Bakhtiyaris, Reza Shah broke the upper levels of their tribal organization; he inflamed feuds between various families, shifted the tax burden onto them, and forced their chiefs to sell their lands to local merchants as well as their oil shares to the central government.[38] In contrast with the estranged relations between the Shah and the tribal chiefs in Iran, the monarchy in Iraq built up the big tribal shaykhs as

[36] Marion Farouk-Sluglett and Peter Sluglett, "The Transformation of Land Tenure and Rural Social Structure in Central and Southern Iraq, c. 1870–1958," *IJMES* 15 (1983): 496. See also idem, "Some Reflections on the Sunni/Shi'i Question in Iraq," *BSMESB* 5 (1978): 82.

[37] Batatu, *The Old Social Classes*, 91, 101–3; Elie Kedourie, *The Chatham House Version and Other Middle-Eastern Studies* (London, 1970), 267–68.

[38] Abrahamian, *Iran*, 141–42; Gene Garthwaite, *Khans and Shahs: A Documentary Analysis of the Bakhtiyari in Iran* (Cambridge, 1983), 104, 138–39; Richard Tapper, "Anthropologists, Historians, and Tribespeople on Tribe and State Formation in the Middle

an aristocracy whose welfare was tied to that of the rulers, thereby reducing the possibilities of cooperation between the shaykhs and the mujtahids against the state.

The increase in the economic welfare and political weight of the big tribal shaykhs in Iraq weakened their sectarian identity. While their status as part of the Shi'i elite declined, the shaykhs, together with their Sunni counterparts, emerged as a class in modern Iraq. The state's advocacy of Pan-Arabism further reinforced the ethnic differences between the Arab shaykhs and the predominantly Persian mujtahids. The success of the state in splitting the Shi'i elite and winning the tribal shaykhs to its side was evident on a number of occasions, when the behavior of the shaykhs demonstrated the growing conflict of interest between them and the mujtahids.

The results of the Karbala conference of 1922 following the Ikhwan raid on Iraq demonstrated the different motivations of the mujtahids and the tribal shaykhs. No Sunni shaykh obeyed the summons of the mujtahids to attend the conference and those Shi'i shaykhs who did show up were in no mood to respond to a call for agitation. The majority of the leading Shi'i tribal shaykhs regarded the mujtahids' initiative as intervention in political matters and refused to participate in an anti-British movement similar to that which led to the 1920 revolt. The paramount shaykhs of the Daghara, the Bani Hasan, the Zubayd, and the Jubur organized a countermovement in support of the British. It was backed by the paramount shaykhs of the Khaz'al, the shaykhs of the Hindiyya tribes, and fifty shaykhs from the Shamiyya, Shinafiyya, and the Rumaytha areas. The British were informed that the entire Euphrates was solemnly banded together to resist any interference with the Mandate. In addition, a counterpetition in support of Faysal, the British, and the Prime Minister (at that time still the *naqib* of Baghdad) was prepared at a meeting of tribal shaykhs in Baghdad. The signatories protested against the Karbala conference, and accused the mujtahids of using the incident of the Ikhwan attack on Iraqi tribes for their own benefit.[39]

The split between the tribal shaykhs and the mujtahids manifested itself again following the deportation of Khalisi and the departure of the leading mujtahids to Iran. Before leaving Iraq, Na'ini and Isfahani signed *fatwas* in which they prohibited the participation of the tribesmen in the elections. The letters were handed over to religious students for distribution among the tribes after the mujtahids had reached the border. It is important to

East," in *Tribes and State Formation in the Middle East*, ed. Philip Khoury and Joseph Kostiner (Berkeley, 1990), 69.

[39] For the petition see Intelligence Report no. 9, 1 May 1922, CO 730/21/24559. See also Intelligence Reports nos. 8 and 10, 15 April and 15 May 1922, CO 730/2121724, and CO 730/22/27688; Wardi, *Lamahat*, 6:149–56; 'Abd al-'Aziz al-Qassab, *Min dhikrayati* (Beirut, 1962), 227–28.

note that the *fatwa*s were addressed to both the shaykhs and the *sirkal*s since the mujtahids feared that the shaykhs would oppose any attempt to influence the tribesmen. The mujtahids' fear was well founded since the majority of the shaykhs, as well as some important Arab *sayyid*s, expressed a thorough approval of Faysal's hard-line policy toward the mujtahids.[40]

Faysal succeeded in winning over the tribal shaykhs and detached them from the influence of the mujtahids. While the mujtahids were preparing for their departure, the King was touring some of the Shi'i regions, striving to convince the shaykhs that the Iraqi government was not hostile to their interests. The King also promised the shaykhs to secure an amendment to the Electoral Law so as to provide for a larger representation of tribal shaykhs in the Assembly. Faysal gained the support of the important shaykhs of the Shamiyya region in a meeting in Diwaniyya on 28 June 1923, only two days after the deportation of Khalisi. The shaykhs' support of the King also found expression in letters published by some of them in Iraqi newspapers in condemnation of the mujtahids. The contents of one of these letters, which constituted part of a government-inspired campaign against the mujtahids, reflected the ethnic barriers between the Arab shaykhs and the Persian mujtahids: "These wavering [mujtahids] played around and sought shelter in Arab Iraq . . . . Their intention was to undermine the blessed Arab movement. In doing so, they betrayed the country under the protection of which they have led a life of ease and comfort so as to serve a foreign people [the Persians] who were one of the major causes of the termination of the Arab Empire."[41] The invocation of the memory of the collapse of the 'Abbasid Empire demonstrated how past historical episodes could be used to reinforce enmities between Shi'i Arabs and Persians.

The split between the tribal shaykhs and the mujtahids manifested itself again following the latter's return from Iran. When in September 1926 the mujtahids attempted to secure the signatures of tribal shaykhs on a petition to the government in which they asked for the return of two other mujtahids who were still not allowed to return to Iraq, the shaykhs rejected their request.[42] In subsequent years the gap between the two groups widened, a phenomenon that was noted by Shi'i ulama both during and after

[40] Mahdi al-Basir, *Ta'rikh al-qadiyya al-'iraqiyya*, 2 vols. (Baghdad, 1924), 2:500–502; Special Service Officer, Baghdad, 1 July 1923. I owe the last reference on the mujtahids' *fatwa*s to Peter Sluglett.

[41] King Faysal to Sir Percy Cox, 30 November 1922, NAI, BHCF, 23/15/1, vol. 1; Special Service Officer, Hilla, 2 July 1923, Air 23/453; Intelligence Report no. 14, 5 July 1923, FO 371/9009/7681. For the citation see Wardi, *Lamahat*, 6:233–35.

[42] Special Service Officer, Nasiriyya, 30 September 1924, Air 23/108; Air Staff Intelligence, Nasiriyya, 12 December 1925, Air 23/379; Extracts of Special Service Officer, Baghdad, Report no. I/Bd/35, 11 December 1926, Air 23/379.

the monarchy.[43] Indeed, whatever limited cooperation there existed between the tribal shaykhs and the mujtahids under the monarchy, it mainly
reflected the attempts of the shaykhs to use the mujtahids, as in the 1935
revolt, to enhance their position vis-à-vis the government on issues involving their own economic welfare and their participation in parliament.

The growing diverging interests of the shaykhs and the mujtahids coincided with the diminishing influence of the shaykhs among their own
tribesmen. Under the monarchy, the tribal shaykhs became big landowners
and developed new political and socioeconomic interests, which connected
them to Baghdad. The shaykhs spent the greater part of the year in the
capital than among their tribes or in Najaf and Karbala in the Shi'i south.
Iraq's rulers encouraged the shaykhs to find new ways to make their influence felt in Baghdad. Beside their membership in parliament and the
lower chamber, another sign of the political incorporation of the shaykhs
into the capital was the enrollment of many of them in the Constitutional
Union Party (established in 1949 under Nuri Sa'id, who served fourteen
terms as the Iraqi Premier between 1930 and 1958). Like their counterparts in Syria, the big tribal shaykhs in Iraq were drawn into the orbit of the
capital and they began to forge new socioeconomic relations with city
entrepreneurs.[44]

While the political and socioeconomic status of the big shaykhs was
strengthened under the Iraqi monarchy, they lost much of their remaining
military power and ability to mobilize their tribes against the government
in Baghdad. This was largely the result of the growing gaps between the
shaykhs and their tribesmen as well as effective government control of key
tribal offices, notably, the *sirkal*s. As shown in chapter 1, the appearance of
the *sirkal*s among Iraq's tribes was closely related to the process of tribal
settlement and transition to agriculture during the nineteenth century. In
Ottoman times, the *sirkal*s acted mainly as foremen whose role was to keep
the land under cultivation and to collect revenues for the landowners.
Under the monarchy, the enhanced economic and political position of the
big tribal shaykhs, and their growing vested interests in Baghdad, further
detached the shaykhs from their tribesmen as they did not represent the
agricultural interests of either the cultivators or the *sirkal*s. The *sirkal*s
became the actual shaykhs on the spot. Appointed and backed by the
government, they often had their own guest house and were surrounded by

[43] Anon., *al-Haraka al-islamiyya*, 52–53; Katib, *Tajrubat al-thawra al-islamiyya*, 73.

[44] Roger Owen, "Class and Class Politics in Iraq before 1958: the 'Colonial and Post
Colonial State,'" in *The Iraqi Revolution of 1958: The Old Social Classes Revisited*, ed.
Robert Fernea and Wm. Roger Louis (London, 1991), 159; Batatu, *The Old Social Classes*,
104. On Syria see Philip Khoury, "The Tribal Shaykh, French Tribal Policy, and the Nationalist Movement in Syria between Two World Wars," *MES* 18 (1982): 186–87.

armed followings.[45] Thus, some of the revolts in the rural south in the 1920s and 1930s were less an assertion of Shiʻi tribal independence than a manifestation of the struggle for power between different components of tribal leadership.[46] As the following case demonstrates, the government defused the influence of the big shaykhs over their tribes in part by building up the power of the *sirkal*s.

In the early 1920s, Salim al-Khayun was paramount shaykh of the Chibayish and other tribes that were attached to the Suq al-Shuyukh district. As a member of the Constituent Assembly and a minister-without-portfolio in the interim Iraqi government, Khayun perhaps found it too degrading to obey administrative officers. He carried out a campaign of disobedience, incited neighboring tribes to defy the new government, and refused to pay his land dues. After several warnings, British planes bombed Khayun's guest house and a police-post was established on its site. Khayun was arrested and sentenced to imprisonment, which was later commuted to compulsory residence in Mosul. In 1931 the government granted him 9,151 acres of land near Baghdad and he then moved to his new estate. Following Khayun's arrest, the government established its own direct control over the Chibayish through the *sirkal*s who acted as chiefs and political heads. Under the new system, the *sirkal*s were appointed and removed by the provincial governor. The *sirkal*s undertook to pay government dues and were held responsible for any disobedience among their clans. Recognizing their new power and prestige, and knowing that they stood to lose their lands should they fail to properly administer the clans under their control, the *sirkal*s cooperated with the government, thus ensuring its control of the Chibayish. The loyalty of the *sirkal*s to the government manifested itself during the 1935 revolt, and in the failed attempt of Khayun to return to the Chibayish in 1945, when on both occasions the *sirkal*s supported the government.[47]

In winning over the big tribal shaykhs, the state was able to split the pre-monarchic Shiʻi elite and to reduce the possibilities for cooperation between its two major components, the shaykhs and the mujtahids. The trend whereby the class and ethnic identities of the shaykhs increased at the expense of their sectarian allegiance continued even after the collapse of the monarchy. Their position as players in contemporary Iraqi politics was evident as late as 1991–92, when in the aftermath of the Gulf War Saddam

[45] Batatu, *The Old Social Classes*, 87; idem, "Class Analysis and Iraqi Society," *ASQ* 1 (1979): 230; Marion and Peter Sluglett, "Transformation of Land Tenure," 499; ʻAbd al-Razzaq al-Hasani, "al-Hala al-ijtimaʻiyya fi al-ʻashaʼir al-ʻiraqiyya," *al-ʻIrfan* 30 (1940): 194; Shakir Salim, *Marsh Dwellers of the Euphrates Delta* (London, 1962), 72.

[46] Marion and Peter Sluglett, "Reflections," 82.

[47] Salim, *Marsh Dwellers*, 31–35, 40–41.

Husayn met regularly with Shi'i tribal leaders to gain their legitimacy and support (see epilogue).

BAGHDAD AND THE SHRINE CITIES

While the mixed cities of Kazimayn and Samarra did not give the Ottomans much trouble, Najaf and Karbala were the strongholds of Shi'ism in pre-monarchic Iraq. Their ruling groups enjoyed a level of freedom that could not be tolerated by the new state, which sought to bring the overwhelmingly Shi'i populated south under its authority. On the eve of the British occupation, Najaf and Karbala acted as socioeconomic and politicoreligious centers and hence the relations between Baghdad and these two cities under the monarchy cannot be seen as mere conflicts between center and periphery but as a struggle between different centers over the loyalty and focus of identity of the Shi'is in the new state.

As noted in chapter 1, the influence of the Zuqurt and the Shumurt in Najaf culminated in 1915 when these two tribal factions expelled the Ottomans from the city. The actual control of Najaf's four quarters was divided among four shaykhs, the heads of the Zuqurt and the Shumurt. Before Iraq's occupation was completed, the British permitted the four shaykhs to maintain order in their quarters and they were each paid a monthly allowance. Later, in February 1918, in an attempt to increase control of the city, Captain Marshall was put in charge of Najaf. He took residence in a house just outside the city's walls. Marshall attempted to organize a police force in the city not subject to the authority of the four shaykhs and sought to regulate the payment of municipal taxes. At his suggestion the allowance that had been paid to the four shaykhs was also discontinued.

Faced with a serious threat to their authority, the shaykhs rebelled. On 19 March Marshall was murdered in his residence by a squad sent by Hajji Sa'd and Kazim Subbi, heads of the Shumurt and the Zuqurt, respectively. The rebellion broke out shortly after Najaf had experienced food shortages and leaping prices in the bazaars caused by the city's inability to supply all the needs of the British ally 'Anaza tribe of the Syrian desert, one of whose shaykhs had sent 1,200 camels to Najaf to purchase grain on passes signed by himself. The rebels may have been encouraged by German propaganda and finances. Although the rebellion was also influenced by the Islamic Rebellion Committee, whose members were drawn from among the lesser ulama, the leading mujtahids in the city, notably Kazim Yazdi and Shaykh al-Shari'a Isfahani, did not support it. Najaf was put under siege and its fresh water supply cut off. The blockade was raised only on 4 May 1918 after the rebels had given up, and the rule of the Zuqurt and the Shumurt over Najaf was thus put to an end.[48]

Breaking the power of the Kammuna family in Karbala proved relatively easier. On the eve of the British occupation, the Kammunas were the dominant power in the city, controlling the major posts of importance. The main figures of the family were the two brothers Fakhr al-Din and Muhammad 'Ali Kammuna. When in April 1916 the Ottomans made an effort to subdue the city, Karbala rebelled and drove the Ottomans out. Later that year, before they had completed the occupation of Iraq, the British still experienced a shortage of officers and adequate personnel guards. Hence, the Kammunas were permitted to continue to administer the city's affairs and Muhammad 'Ali was appointed the British agent in Karbala. Soon after, according to British reports, a brisk traffic in supplies to Turkish forces still camping along the Euphrates started from Karbala, in which Fakhri was said to be actively involved. In September 1916, Fakhri was deported to India, Muhammad 'Ali's position was discontinued, and a British officer was nominated in his stead. At this point the family had not yet been completely stripped of all its privileges. Muhammad 'Ali was allowed to hold on to his property, his son still held the post of the custodian of Husayn's shrine, and a brother of Muhammad 'Ali was appointed head of the municipality. The Kammunas' control of the administration of Karbala ended in July 1917 when members of the family were accused of spreading anti-British propaganda. Muhammad 'Ali was also deported to India and the city's administration passed into government hands.[49]

In breaking the semi-autonomous status of Najaf and Karbala following the War, the British helped bring the two cities under effective government control during the monarchy. The decline in the power of the Najafi muj-

[48] For an interesting account of life at Najaf during the blockade see Agha Najafi Quchani, *Siyahat-i sharq ya zindeginama va-safarnama-yi agha najafi quchani* (Mashhad, 1972), 582–610. On the revolt see Ja'far al-Mahbuba, *Madi al-najaf wa-hadiruha*, 3 vols. (Najaf, 1955–1958), 1:344–51; Nafisi, *Dawr al-shi'a*, 54–67; From Civil Commissioner to Foreign Office, Baghdad, 14 April 1918, IO L/P&S 10/667; Review of the Civil Administration of Iraq, 1914–1918, FO 371/4148/34799; Fortnightly Reports, nos. 10, 11, 12, 13, and 14, 9 and 23 April, 8 May and 10 June 1918, FO 371/3397/110227; FO 371/3397/3544; FO 371/3397/165202; Translation of an undated letter from Shaykh al-Shari'a Isfahani to Sayyid Muhammad Behbahani, intercepted on 3 Ramadan 1336/late 1918, FO 248/1207.

[49] Review of the Civil Administration of Iraq, 1914–1918, FO 371/4148/34799; Great Britain, Administration Reports, Karbala District, 1918, CO 696/1; 'Abd al-Razzaq al-Wahhab, *Karbala' fi al-ta'rikh* (Karbala, 1935), 13–22; 'Abd al-Hamid 'Abd al-Majid al-Tuhafi, "Al Tu'ma fi al-ta'rikh," *al-'Irfan* 57 (1979): 453; Muhammad Hasan al-Kilidar Al Tu'ma, "Safahat majhula min ta'rikh karbala': al-fawda fi karbala'," *al-'Irfan* 68 (1980): 63–66; idem, "Safahat majhula min ta'rikh karbala': 'awdat al-atrak," *al-'Irfan* 69 (1981): 77–80.

tahids vis-à-vis the state was reinforced by their lack of armed following as a result of the breakup of the Zuqurt and the Shumurt. With the end of the Kammunas' control of Karbala, the government took measures to enhance the position of the heads of the city's seven quarters (the *mukhtars*). Prior to the British occupation, the *mukhtars* in Karbala had not been paid. By contrast, under British rule each of the city's seven *mukhtars* was paid by the municipality Rs.25 a month. The British thus increased the status of the *mukhtars* in Karbala and turned them into government employees responsible for law and order in their quarters.[50] In subsequent years, religious and administrative posts in both Karbala and Najaf would be held by Iraqi government employees.

Against the decline in the political and socioeconomic power of Najaf and Karbala, Baghdad emerged as the dominant center in the new state. Baghdad's position as the center of economic opportunities in modern Iraq was evident as the capital became the target city for Shi'i migrants. Excessive migration from southern Iraq, mainly to Baghdad, took place in Iraq from the end of the 1920s and continued throughout and after the monarchic period. The push and pull factors for this migration were mainly Iraq's land tenure system, which enabled the shaykhs to register much of the land in their own names while forcing the tribal cultivators into debt, as well as the industrial and political growth of Baghdad, which offered the migrants greater job opportunities than their home territories in the rural south.[51] 'Amara, where the concentration of landed property in the hands of a few landowners was particularly high, led the list of Iraqi provinces that sent migrants to Baghdad and Basra, followed by Karbala and Kut. By 1947, 25, 13, and 12 percent of those persons born in 'Amara, Karbala, and Kut, respectively, were living in other provinces in Iraq, mostly in Baghdad. The preference for the capital by Shi'i migrants was most noticeable in the case of 'Amara: until 1957 about 67 percent of the migrants from that province moved to Baghdad, whereas only 25 percent migrated to Basra.[52]

This migration was a major factor in establishing the Shi'is as the majority group in Baghdad under the monarchy, the other being the exodus of

[50] Administration Reports, Karbala, 1917, CO 696/1.

[51] Report on a Visit to 'Amara, 3 March 1931, C. J. Edmonds Papers, box 7, file 5, St. Antony's College, Oxford University; Report by Wilfrid Thesiger on Tribal Conditions in 'Amara, British Embassy, Baghdad, 5 August 1955, FO 371/115748/1015–11; Marion and Peter Sluglett, "Land Tenure," 499–501; idem, "Reflections," 82–83; Fuad Baali, "Social Factors in Iraqi Rural-Urban Migration," *AJES* 25 (1966): 359; Doris Adams, "Current Population Trends in Iraq," *MEJ* 10 (1956): 158; Atheel al-Jomard, "Internal Migration in Iraq," in Kelidar, *Integration of Modern Iraq*, 116–17.

[52] Doris Phillips, "Rural-to-Urban Migration in Iraq," *EDCC* 7 (1959): 409; Adams, "Population Trends," 158; M. Azeez, "Geographical Aspects of Rural Migration from 'Amara Province Iraq, 1955–1964" (Ph.D. diss., Durham University, 1968), 195.

Jews from Iraq in the late 1940s and early 1950s. Thus, whereas the share of Shiʿis among Baghdad's population was some 20 percent before World War I, by 1958 it had increased to more than 50 percent.[53] The arrival of the Shiʿi migrants to Baghdad had two other major consequences. First, it led to a "ruralization" of some sections of Baghdad, reinforcing the role that clan and tribal affiliation played in the daily life of the capital. Second, life in the capital changed the political and religious outlook of many Shiʿis. A large number of migrants adopted urban clothes, showed a growing tendency to settle their disputes in the state civil courts, and enrolled in "wiping out illiteracy" classes.[54] An erosion of the migrants' religious identity occurred in Baghdad, where Shiʿi religious life was much less intense than in southern Iraq. The growing rate of education among the Shiʿi migrants and their contact with other population groups led many to reexamine their Shiʿi religious practices and to see them in a wider context, where their former validity was less evident. The rise of communism in Iraq also eroded the religious identity of the Shiʿi migrants and their contacts with the mujtahids in Najaf and Karbala as the Iraqi Communist Party gave much attention to the ideological education of the migrants in the 1940s and 1950s.[55]

The migration of Shiʿis from the south also resulted in the population decrease of Najaf and Karbala vis-à-vis Baghdad and in relation to Kazimayn and Samarra. The negative impact which the Shiʿi population shifts had on Najaf and Karbala may be gathered from the changes in the population growth of Iraq and the shrine cities under the monarchy. Between 1935 and 1947 the annual rate of population growth in the central and northern regions of Iraq was as high as 3.7 and 2.2 percent per annum, respectively, whereas their counterpart in the southern region was as low as 1.1 percent per annum. Most of the southern provinces showed a net reduction in population, while all northern provinces showed a net gain at that time.[56] Najaf's population, which in 1918 was around 45,000,

[53] J. G. Lorimer, *Gazetteer of the Persian Gulf, ʿOman and Central Arabia,* 2 vols. in 5 pts. (Calcutta, 1908–15), 2A:201–2; Hanna Batatu, "Iraq's Shiʿa, their Political Role, and the Process of their Integration into Society," in *The Islamic Impulse,* ed. Barbara Stowasser (London, 1987), 206, 209.

[54] ʿAbd al-Razzaq al-Hilali, *al-Hijra min al-rif ila al-mudun fi al-ʿiraq* (Baghdad, 1958), esp. 64–67; Fuad Baali, *Relation of the People to the Land in Southern Iraq* (Gainesville, Florida, 1966), 50; Marion Farouk-Sluglett and Peter Sluglett, "The Historiography of Modern Iraq," *AHR* 96 (1991): 1411; Basil Najar, "The Dynamics of Rural-Urban Migration and Assimilation in Iraq" (Ph.D. diss., Wayne State University, 1976), 116–17.

[55] Hanna Batatu, "Shiʿi Organizations in Iraq: al-Daʿwah al-Islamiyah and al-Mujahidin," in *Shiʿism and Social Protest,* ed. Juan Cole and Nikki Keddie (New Haven, 1986), 188.

[56] M. S. Hasan, "Growth and Structure of Iraq's Population, 1867–1947," *BOUIES* 20 (1958): 339–43; Phillips, "Migration in Iraq," 409.

reached only 57,947 in 1947 and 91,165 in 1957.[57] Karbala's population was estimated in 1908 to be around 50,000. In subsequent years, mainly as a result of diminishing resources, high rates of mortality caused by diseases, lack of development, and migration, its population dropped markedly and was put at only 24,889 in 1928. So serious was the decline of Karbala at that time that it was feared that its very existence was at stake. The censuses of 1947 and 1957 put the town's population at 44,150 and 60,294, respectively.[58]

The relative population decrease of Najaf and Karbala stood in contrast to the population increase of Kazimayn and Samarra, as the rapid development of these latter two cities in modern Iraq was influenced by their proximity to Baghdad. Kazimayn experienced an exceptionally high population growth rate, over 5 percent annually in the years 1947–1957, at a time when Iraq's annual average population growth did not exceed 3 percent. The population of Kazimayn, which became part of greater Baghdad, was estimated in 1917 to be 15,000. The censuses of 1947 and 1957 put the town's population at 62,162 and 127,224, respectively.[59] Samarra also benefited from the migration toward Baghdad; its population, which in 1917 was only about 5,000 people, reached 30,014 and 48,940 in 1947 and 1957, respectively.[60]

The rise of the modern state undermined the political and socioeconomic status of Najaf and Karbala vis-à-vis Baghdad. As the capital emerged as the center of power, Najaf and Karbala found it increasingly difficult to command the focus of identity of the Shi'is in the new state. Shi'i tribesmen dreamed of going to Baghdad.[61] In choosing the capital as their main objective, Shi'i migrants demonstrated their conviction that it was in Baghdad where they were likely to improve their life, not in Najaf or in Karbala. Indeed, neither Najaf nor Karbala could provide the socioeconomic and political opportunities that the capital seemed so capable of offering to Shi'is. Unlike Kazimayn and Samarra, the development of which was influenced by the growth of Baghdad, Najaf and Karbala continued to

[57] Administration Report, 1918, Najaf, CO 691/1; Naval Intelligence Division, *Iraq*, 545; Census of Iraq 1947: *Mudiriyyat al-nufus al-'amma, ihsa' al-sukkan li-sanat 1947*, 3 vols. (Baghdad, 1954), 1:196; Census of Iraq 1957: *Mudiriyyat al-nufus al-'amma, al-majmu'a al-ihsa'iyya li-tasjil 'am 1957*, 1 vol. in 7 pts. (Baghdad, 1961), 1,3:18.

[58] 'Abd al-Razzaq al-Hasani, "Liwa' karbala'," *al-'Irfan* 16 (1928): 498; "Karbala' fi khatar," *Lughat al-'Arab* 4 (1927): 564; Census of Iraq 1947, 1:184; Census of Iraq 1957, 1,3:14.

[59] N. al-Dalwi, *al-Jughrafiya al-ijtima'iyya li-madinat al-kazimiyya al-kubra* (Baghdad, 1975), 87, 62–64, 80–83; Administration Reports of the Baghdad Wilayat, 1917, CO 696/1; Census of Iraq 1947, 1:34; Census of Iraq 1957, 1,1:36.

[60] Administration Reports of the Baghdad Wilayat, 1917, CO 696/1; Census of Iraq 1947, 1:62; Census of Iraq 1957, 1,1:48.

[61] Robert Fernea, "State and Tribe in Southern Iraq: The Struggle for Hegemony before the 1958 Revolution," in Fernea and Louis, *The Iraqi Revolution*, 143.

rely on the pilgrimage, the corpse traffic, and the flow of charities as their main sources of income. Najaf and Karbala did not develop alternative sources of income or industries under the monarchy, and they suffered from lack of government investment. Consequently, unemployment in both cities was rife; its rate in Najaf was estimated to be as high as 50 percent in 1938.[62]

Baghdad reigned supreme over the country. It disposed of a parliament, exercised a monopoly over law-making, and had an army which was capable of checking the tribes. The state thus possessed all the instruments of power necessary to undermine the position of Najaf and Karbala vis-à-vis Baghdad as well as their sources of income. The consequences of government policies toward the pilgrimage, the corpse traffic, and the flow of charities from Iran to Najaf and Karbala will be explored later in this book. Here I will elaborate briefly on the setback to the position of Najaf and Karbala as desert market-towns, a development which greatly diminished their contacts with the tribes in the twentieth century.

As shown in chapter 1, Najaf and Karbala acted in the nineteenth century as emporiums of trade for the desert. Under the monarchy Iraqi and Sa'udi tribes continued to purchase large quantities of rice in both cities. Najaf was still one of the major granary centers in Iraq and overshadowed Karbala in its importance as a desert market-town. The position of the latter city decreased in part because of the rise of Samawa and Zubayr as new granary centers in southern Iraq in the twentieth century. Until 1950 the volume of purchase of Sa'udi tribes in the two cities was apparently not restricted by Iraqi government quotas. In that year the government prohibited the sale of rice to Sa'udi tribes, an act which hindered the welfare of Najaf in particular. Both the city's chamber of commerce and the governor of Karbala province sent letters to the Ministry of Interior, urging it to reverse its decision. In his letter, the governor argued that Najaf's main trade had long been based on its dealings with Sa'udi tribes and that the prohibition of the sale of the rice surplus to these tribes would paralyze local commercial activity and harm merchants in the entire Karbala province. Although in 1951 the government reversed its decision, it now set quotas of 3,000 and 500 tons for Najaf and Karbala, respectively, for their sale of rice to Sa'udi tribes.[63]

This affair not only reveals the extent to which the welfare of Najaf and Karbala depended on their trade with Sa'udi tribes as late as the 1950s, but also the ability of the government to use this dependency to check the two

[62] Ja'far al-Khalili, "Mushkilat al-batala fi al-najaf," al-Hatif 127 (10 July 1938): 3–4.

[63] For the letters see "Shu'un tijariyya wa-iqtisadiyya: raf' al-hazr 'an iktiyal al-hubub min al-najaf," al-Hatif 749 (13 May 1950): 4; "Tasdir al-hubub min al-najaf ila al-badiya," al-Hatif 750 (14 May 1950): 4. See also Mekki al-Jamil, al-Badw wa al-qaba'il al-rahhala fi al-'iraq (Baghdad, 1956), 249–50, 252.

cities. The economy of Najaf and Karbala, which had already suffered greatly from the decline in the pilgrimage, the corpse traffic, and the flow of charities from Iran, now experienced yet another setback as a result of government restrictions of their trade with the tribes. The increase in settlement of Iraqi and Sa'udi tribes in the latter part of the twentieth century probably served to further thwart the welfare of both cities as well as their potential influence over the tribes.

Unlike Kazimayn and Samarra, Najaf and Karbala found it difficult to develop new sources of income and did not become as integrated into the state as the two other cities. The feeling of frustration caused by this lack of integration was particularly painful in Najaf since in that city, as British officials reported in 1943, the majority of the notables were of Arab origin, all classes spoke Arabic, and the Najafis possessed an amount of genuine Iraqi national feeling and were intensely interested in Iraqi national politics.[64]

THE BLOW TO THE STATUS OF PERSIANS

As has been pointed out in chapter 1, the number of Persians in Iraq on the eve of the formation of the monarchy was put by the British census of 1919 at eighty thousand. While their number may have been higher, if one takes into account cases of mixed marriages and families whose members resided in Iraq for several generations, one should not confuse in this category Shi'is of Arab origin who took Iranian nationality to escape conscription during the Ottoman period. In the nineteenth century, the Ottoman-Iranian struggle for resource control in Iraq enabled Iran to gain leverage over the affairs of the shrine cities and resulted in the granting of privileges to Persians in Iraq, who continued to hold their Iranian nationality until the twentieth century. The formation of the modern state of Iraq transformed this reality. Iraq was no longer the frontier to which Iranian nationals could emigrate as easily as in the past. The blow to the status of Persians was reinforced by the policies of the Iraqi government and by Iran's diminishing influence in Iraq.

Even before the establishment of the monarchy, the British sought to reduce Persian influence in Iraq. In 1919, Arnold Wilson, the British Acting Civil Commissioner, noted the very excessive number of Persian consular officers, who were present "in every town and village of any size." He suggested that any unnecessary posts should be allowed to lapse as those officers who were present in Iraq died off or resigned. Persian influence was particularly strong in Karbala. In contrast to the strong Arab character of

---

[64] Report by Vice-Consul Bagley on Najaf and Karbala, Baghdad, 22 February 1943, FO 624/33/537.

Najaf, Persians constituted some 75 percent of Karbala's population on the eve of the British occupation. Particular attention was therefore given by the British to reinforcing the Arab character of Karbala, and Arabic was introduced as the language of administration there.[65]

Following the establishment of the monarchy both British officials and successive Iraqi governments gave much attention to the question of Persians in Iraq. British officials argued that, as with Muslims of Syrian or Turkish nationality living in Iraq, there was no need to accord Persians the privileges and capitulations enjoyed by European nationals under the Anglo-Iraqi agreement. It was asserted that due to the large number of people holding Iranian nationality in Iraq, British judges would not be able to cope with the volume of work involving Persians and that their cases should be transferred to Iraqi courts.[66] The Iraqi government proved particularly anxious to diminish Persian influence in the country. Around May 1922 Iraqi merchants in Iran complained about the lack of any authority that would protect their interests in that country, owing to the refusal of the Iranian government to accept the intervention of British consuls on their behalf. The Iraqi government countered by declaring that it did not recognize the judicial rights of Persian subjects in Iraq and that it would not accept any diplomatic intervention on their behalf.[67]

In order to abolish the privileges and immunities enjoyed by Iranian nationals in Iraq, successive Iraqi governments adopted and implemented a series of laws and regulations. The Iraqi Nationality Law of 1924 had an impact on virtually every person of Persian origin residing in Iraq. Under this law, Persians were automatically considered Iraqi nationals unless they themselves renounced it by a fixed date, which was extended twice until it was set for January 1928. The Iraqi Nationality Law was followed by the introduction in 1927 of a law prohibiting the employment of foreigners in government posts. A law regulating the appointments and promotions of civil as well as religious judges was introduced in 1929. Among other things, it prohibited the appointment of persons who had not acquired Iraqi nationality and did not have a good knowledge of Arabic as judges in the religious courts.[68]

In December 1935 the Iraqi parliament passed a law which prohibited

[65] Political, Baghdad, 24 July 1919, FO 248/1258; Acting Civil Commissioner in Mesopotamia to His Majesty's Minister in Tehran, Baghdad, 29 July 1919, FO 248/1258; Administration Report, Karbala, 1917, CO 696/1.

[66] Cox to Churchill, Baghdad, 13 April 1922, CO 730/21/19161; Dobbs to Devonshire, 5 June 1923, CO 730/40/30811.

[67] Intelligence Reports nos. 10 and 12, 15 May and 15 June 1922, CO 730/22/27688 and CO 730/22/32485.

[68] For these laws see CO, *Reports by Her Majesty's Government to the League of Nations on the Administration of Iraq, 1925–1932*, 1925 Report, 162–65; 1927 Report, 186; 1929 Report, 180–86.

foreign nationals from practicing certain trades and works. It applied to various crafts and professions traditionally fulfilled by Persian residents in the shrine cities. As the Iraqi Prime Minister explained to the British ambassador, while the provisions of the law had to be made general, it was designed to enable the government to "rid the country" of many thousands of Persian residents who were "a constant source of trouble." This law was intended to reinforce the implementation of the Iraqi nationality Law and to "oblige countless Persians established in Iraq . . . to become Iraqis or quit." The law was also aimed at increasing the number of Iraqi craftsmen at the expense of Persians.[69] Finally, Holy Shrine Regulations 25 of 1948 and 42 of 1950 had a direct impact on Persian functionaries and servants at the shrines. The administration of the shrines was given to the Director General of *Awqaf* and it was stipulated that all servants of the shrines should be Iraqi nationals subject to the *Awqaf* Directorate. The Holy Shrine Regulations also defined the role and authority of the custodians and servants of the shrines, and fixed their salaries.[70] Laws and regulations concerning the status of Persians in Iraq as well as employees in the shrines were reiterated and supplemented by successive Iraqi governments after 1958.

The formation of modern Iraq posed a challenge to Iran's position in the Persian Gulf as well as to its economic interests in the region. The establishment of Iraqi Railways and the opening of the road from the western frontier to Hamadan sometime before 1921 were paralleled by the virtual closing of Iran's traditional northern trade routes. The result was the diversion of most of the export and transit-trade of northern and western Iran toward Baghdad and Basra and an increase in Iran's commercial interests in Iraq. By keeping the question of the status of Persians in Iraq alive, the Iranian government sought to maintain its leverage in that country and to stir Iraqi internal affairs. Indeed, Iran attempted to weaken Iraq and was anxious to see any attempts to create a national army in Iraq frustrated.[71]

Not only did those Iranian aspirations not materialize, but the mandatory period proved to be of critical importance in reducing Iran's influence in Iraq. Following the establishment of the Iraqi monarchy, Iran held to the position that there was no legal basis to justify its recognition of the new state. At the same time, the Iranian government maintained that as far as Iranian nationals in Iraq were concerned, the old system of reciprocal capitulations as it had existed in Ottoman times should remain in force.

[69] British Embassy, Baghdad, 16 November, and 10 and 15 December 1935, FO 371/18956/7028; FO 371/18956/7206; FO 371/18956/7273.

[70] *The Iraqi Gazetteer (al-Waqa'i' al-'iraqiyya)*, Baghdad, 26 March 1950 and 21 October 1951.

[71] A Note on Iraqi-Persian Relations and the Situation in Khuzistan, 14 March 1928, FO 371/13021/1391; Persia, Annual Report, 1922, FO 416/112.

But since Iran did not recognize Iraq, Iraqis in Iran were declared subject to local laws. In 1924 Iran linked the issue of its recognition of Iraq to the extension of some special judicial rights and immunities to its nationals in Iraq as enjoyed by certain European and U.S. nationals under the Anglo-Iraqi Judicial Agreement of 1924. The Iranian government also insisted on three other conditions for its recognition of Iraq. First, the exemption of its nationals from military service in Iraq. Second, estates of Iranian nationals who died in Iraq were to be administered by Iranian consuls in that country. Third, in civil and criminal cases, Iranian nationals should be tried by the special court for the trial of European or American nationals. In March 1928 the Iranian government retreated from the position that its nationals in Iraq should be granted the full benefits of the Anglo-Iraqi Judicial Agreement. It suggested that civil and criminal cases in which its nationals were involved should be examined in the first instance in local courts composed of members of the Shi'i sect. The Iranian government still insisted, however, that appeals from such cases should be heard by the special courts that existed for foreign nationals.[72]

On several occasions following the introduction of the Iraqi Nationality Law of 1924 Iran claimed that its nationals in Iraq had no time to grasp the full implications of the law, which, the Iranian government asserted, would turn thousands of Persians into Iraqi nationals. Until the January 1928 deadline set for Iranians to renounce their Iraqi nationality, the government and the parliament in Iran invested much effort in explaining the implications of the law to Persians in Iraq and trying to deter them from accepting Iraqi nationality. At that time, the Iranian government also alleged that census operations of Iraqi officials compelled Persians to register as Iraqis in the census register, to take part in Iraqi national elections, and to accept Iraqi passports or alternatively to leave Iraq.[73]

The Iranian government sought to gain leverage over Iraq by also claiming the right to act as the protector of the Shi'i shrines in Iraq, these being "the holy places of Persia." As early as 1920 the Iranian Foreign Minister asked the British government to authorize the Shah to appoint leading officials to the shrines of Najaf and Karbala. This claim may have been

[72] Persia, Annual Report, 1925, FO 416/112; Relations Between Persia and Iraq, A Memorandum, Persia, 4 June 1928, CO 730/136/2; Note by Secretary of State for the Colonies of his Conversation with Timourtash, 30 July 1928, IO L/P&S 10/1229; Cushendun to Parr, London, 26 September, 1928, IO L/P&S 10/1229; Clive to Dobbs, Tehran, 30 December 1928, CO 730/132/5.

[73] Memorandum on the Persian Complaints against Iraq, Persia, 13 September 1927, FO 371/12274/3908; Alleged ill-treatment of Persians in Iraq, London, 20 February 1928, FO 371/13021/856; Dobbs to Muhsin al-Sa'dun, 23 February 1928, FO 371/13021/1669; Census among the Muhaysin in Iraq, London, 8 March 1928, FO 371/13021/1238; Relations between Persia and Iraq, a memorandum, Persia, 4 June 1928, CO 730/136/2; Report to the League of Nations on the Administration of Iraq, 1928, 39.

motivated by the fact that during World War I Russia and Great Britain contemplated the idea of granting Iran the right to administer the religious affairs of the shrine cities after the War.[74] In 1925 the Iranian government linked its recognition of Iraq to the issue of the protection of the shrines. While it agreed that Iraq would protect the shrines and the endowments bequeathed to them, Iran insisted that Iraq should not interfere with the administration of the shrines without the distinct and collective approval of the mujtahids. Iran was not willing to easily give up its involvement in the administration of the shrines and made several complaints alleging mal-treatment of Persian servants in the shrines. In July 1928, for example, the Iranian government asserted that nine servants in the shrine of 'Ali at Najaf had been asked to adopt Iraqi nationality. Since the nine refused to give up their Iranian nationality, they were forced to leave their work.[75]

Yet the time factor, and overall British support of Iraq, were against Iran, which consequently had to adopt a more pragmatic stand. On 14 December 1927 a new Anglo-Iraqi treaty was signed setting the termination of the Mandate to 1932. Iran recognized that it would be more difficult to deal with independent Iraq once British influence was reduced and hence sought some *modus vivendi* with Iraq before the end of the Mandate.[76] The Iranian government began pursuing a new strategy. In December 1928 the Court Minister Timourtash revealed to the British minister in Iran that his government had a firm intention of attracting back to Iran as many of its nationals in Iraq as possible. He explained that since Iran was underpopu-lated, it could not afford to lose any of its nationals. An emergency bill was passed by the Iranian parliament, allocating a sum of 100,000 krans for expenditure in Iraq in 1928 to carry out a census of the Persian population and to provide them with Iranian passports. It was consequently reported in 1929 that a large number of Persians had returned to Iran and settled in Khuzistan.[77]

The number of Persians in Iraq decreased markedly already under the monarchy, a development which was most noticeable in Karbala. Whereas early in the twentieth century Persians constituted some 75 percent of the city's population, by 1957 their percentage had decreased sharply to 12

[74] From Secretary of State to Civil Commissioner, Baghdad, 26 March 1920, FO 371/5071/2565; Persia, Annual Report, 1926, FO 416/112; Government of India, Foreign and Political Department, Proceedings 315–352, June 1916, NAI, Sec. War-June-315–352.

[75] Recognition of Iraq by Persia, Tehran, 17 April 1925, FO 371/10833/2322; Parr to Dobbs, Tehran, 26 July 1928, FO 371/13022/4370.

[76] Persia, Annual Report, 1927, FO 416/113.

[77] Intelligence Summary no. 19 for the period ending 17 September 1927, Tehran, FO 416/81; Clive to Chamberlain, Gulhek, 22 September 1927, FO 371/12274/4030; Clive to Chamberlain, Tehran, 22 December 1928, FO 416/84; Intelligence Summary no. 3 for the week ending 3 February 1929, FO 416/84.

percent.[78] Persians had either accepted Iraqi nationality or left the country, while Arab Shi'is occupied positions that had been formerly held by Persians. The blow to the position of Persians, and to the fabric of Shi'i culture and society, in Iraq continued after the collapse of the monarchy. It culminated under the Ba'th, when on several occasions the government deported thousands of Shi'is accused of being of Iranian origin.

HUMAN DILEMMAS

The formation of modern Iraq caused major human dilemmas and forced Shi'is in the country to assess their national identity and to make hard decisions as to their future in the new state. Following the death of Shaykh al-Shari'a Isfahani in December 1920, Firuz Mirza Nusrat al-Dawla, the Iranian Foreign Minister, attended a mourning ceremony in the house of the mujtahid Hasan al-Sadr at Kazimayn. Noting that they were all Persians, Firuz asked several mujtahids who attended the ceremony why they took such an active interest in the future of Iraq. The mujtahids replied that they had lived in Iraq for many years and felt themselves to be bound up with its destiny.[79] Their reply was indicative of the position of many Persians in Iraq on the eve of the formation of the monarchy. While they continued to maintain political and socioeconomic ties with Iran, Persians also developed strong vested interests in Iraq. The complexity of the issue, and its impact on Arab Shi'is as well, may be gathered from the following few examples.

The case of the Mazandarani family of Karbala illustrates the intertwined religious, economic, and political interests of Persian mujtahids in Iraq and Iran. Zayn al-'Abidin Mazandarani (d. 1892) migrated from Iran to Iraq around 1835. He settled in Karbala and gained a considerable reputation as a mujtahid. His son Muhammad also became a mujtahid and was an Oudh Bequest distributor in Karbala. Part of his income was thus drawn from Indian money, to which he was entitled only as long as he resided in Karbala. The Mazandaranis were also involved in Iranian affairs and politics. Muhammad's younger brother, Ahmad, who was known as Shaykh al-'Iraqayn, had a son, Zayn al-'Abidin Rahnama, who was at one point a deputy in the Iranian parliament.[80]

An affair connected with the purchase and ownership of land demonstrates the difficult position of the Mazandarani family as well as that of

[78] Census of 1957, 1,3:75. See also "Karbala' fi al-ta'rikh al-hadith," al-'Irfan 24 (1934): 513.

[79] Intelligence Report no. 4, 31 December 1920, FO 371/6348/2904.

[80] Muhsin al-Amin, A'yan al-shi'a, 56 vols. (Beirut, 1960–1963), 33:339–40; Intelligence Report no. 20, 18 October 1923, FO 371/9010/10814.

other urban dwellers of Persian origin living in Iraq. On 18 June 1926, Ahmad Mazandarani sent a written complaint to Henry Dobbs, the British High Commissioner. Mazandarani raised the issue of ownership of several shares of land in the Kharbutliyya garden, situated in the 'Abbasiyya quarter at Karbala. He claimed that he was the administrator of the garden and that he also owned a third of it. He wrote that his son, Sadr al-Din, had legally purchased an additional two shares of the garden. Mazandarani complained that his son, after having his papers confirmed by the governor of Karbala, applied to the Ministry of Interior to register the shares in his name, but his application was turned down on the ground that he was not an Iraqi. The query raised by the High Commissioner revealed the policy adopted by the Iraqi government toward the ownership of land in Iraq by Persians. The letter of reply sent from the Ministry of Interior to the High Commissioner on 6 August 1926 stated:

> On 25th May 1926, one Sadr al-Din applied to the *mutasarrif* [governor] of Karbala for the registration in his name of two shares in the Kharbutliyya garden which is divided into sixty-six shares. As the applicant is a Persian national the case was referred to the Ministry for approval, through the Director of Tapu. In June . . . the Prime Minister, who was at that time Acting Minister of the Interior, ordered that the case should pend until the objections against complying with the applicant's request had been dealt with. . . . The general question of alienation of immovable properties to Persians in Karbala has been repeatedly raised by the successive *mutasarrif*s of that [province] . . . during the past five years. They have pointed out that in Karbala Persians own more property than do Iraqis, and that unrestricted permission to their purchases will eventually result in the registration of all properties in Karbala in the name of Persians. The present policy is to discourage the alienation of agricultural lands or gardens to Persians, particularly in the [province] of Karbala, and the Council of Ministers has recently rejected cases of alienation of gardens in Karbala and Diwaniyah to Persian subjects.[81]

The formation of an Arab state in Iraq posed a sharp dilemma for the Shi'i mujtahids, something which was borne out in the question of Iran's recognition of Iraq. Certain sections of the Iranian ulama exerted strong pressures on their government not to recognize Iraq under the British Mandate. In 1925 a prominent mulla (probably Shaykh Husayn Yazdi, who had close contacts with the government), published in the press a declaration in which he suggested that until Iraq gained independence it should be looked after by "her old nurse, Turkey and her mother, Per-

---

[81] Notables and Personalities: Shaykh al-'Iraqayn, NAI, BHCF, file 27/420.

sia."[82] The declaration was signed by "Ayatollah Yazdi" to create the impression that it was written by no less than the prominent mujtahid of Qum 'Abd al-Karim Ha'iri Yazdi. In contrast to this position of some Iranian ulama, Na'ini and Isfahani were said to have taken a complete opposite stand. In January 1927, Mahmud Khurasani, a son and grandson of previous mujtahids of Khurasan, met with the British minister in Tehran. He told the minister that he had recently visited Iraq and that following his return to Iran, he received a letter from Na'ini and Isfahani, pressing him to work in Tehran for Iran's recognition of Iraq.[83]

This episode demonstrates the growing conflict of interests of ulama in Iraq and Iran in the twentieth century. Whereas the objection of Iranian ulama to Iran's recognition of Iraq may have been influenced by their attempt to build up an Iranian city like Qum as a major Shi'i academic center, the position of Na'ini and Isfahani reflected their own economic considerations as well as motivation to preserve Najaf as the leading academic center. Throughout the 1920s the limitations imposed by the Iranian government on the pilgrimage, the corpse traffic, and the flow of charities from Iran to Iraq hindered the welfare of the shrine cities. The gradual diversion of charities to Qum helped increase its importance and a growing number of Iranian students began pursuing their studies there instead of going to Najaf. Iran's recognition of Iraq, Na'ini and Isfahani probably hoped, would renew the pilgrimage, the corpse traffic, and the flow of charities, as well as the influx of Iranian students to Iraq, thus maintaining Najaf's academic standing and preventing the Shi'i religious leadership from shifting from Iraq to Iran.

The rise of the modern state sharpened national identities. The nomination of the mujtahid Hibat al-Din al-Shahrastani as Minister of Education in September 1921 is a good example of the need of Persian domiciled residents of Iraq who accepted government positions to reconsider their national status. Indeed, in order to qualify for this position, Shahrastani had to formally testify to his intention to become an Iraqi as soon as this could be officially regulated.[84]

The problem of nationality was also posed to some of Iraq's Shi'i Arab tribes, who were attached to land that was cut by Iraqi and Iranian boundaries. In the nineteenth century, the Muhaysin and the Ka'b tribes cultivated land on both sides of the Shatt al-'Arab. Before World War I, these tribes owed direct allegiance to the shaykh of Muhammara and as such were recognized as Persian subjects and were exempted from military ser-

[82] Intelligence Summary no. 8 for the week ending 21 February 1925, FO 416/76; Persia, Annual Report, 1925, FO 416/112.
[83] Enclosure in Tehran despatch no. 18 of 12 January 1927, FO 371/12273/528.
[84] Intelligence Report no. 22, 1 October 1921, FO 371/6353/11914.

vice in the Ottoman army. Shortly before 1927, the Iraqi government ruled that Iranian nationals were not eligible to own land in Iraq. Faced with the real possibility of losing their land, the two tribes opted for Iraqi certificates of nationality.[85]

The question of the national identity and loyalty of the Iraqi Shi'is to the state will become clearer in the next chapter in dealing with their political aspirations.

[85] Iraqi-Persian relations and the situation in Khuzistan, 14 March 1928, FO 371/13021/1391; Report to the League of Nations on the Administration of Iraq, 1928, 39–40. See also 'Abbas al-'Azzawi, 'Asha'ir al-'iraq, 4 vols. (Baghdad, 1937–1956), 4:184–85.

Chapter Four

THE SEARCH FOR POLITICAL REPRESENTATION

IN THIS CHAPTER I will attempt to explain the basic political aspirations of the Iraqi Shi'is as well as the nature of the tension between Shi'is and successive Sunni governments in modern Iraq. I will be primarily concerned with the following two questions: To what extent did loyalty to the Iraqi state on the part of the Shi'is override their sectarian allegiance as well as their discontent with the Sunni government? What political channels were open to the Iraqi Shi'is and what activities did they pursue to gain power sharing and to influence government decision-making?

RECOGNIZING THE STATE

In the period beginning with the deportation of Mahdi al-Khalisi in 1923 and leading up to the 1935 revolt, the Shi'is made their first bid to locate themselves on the political map of the new state. The Shi'is had been alarmed by the consequences of the mujtahids' ban on Shi'i participation in the elections to the Constituent Assembly, which led to an increase in Sunni control of the state machinery. In contrast to their former attitude of abstaining from playing an active role in the political process, the Shi'is now attempted to increase the scope of their participation and power of influence in Iraqi politics. They demanded representation in the government and the civil service in proportion to their numerical weight among the population, and struggled over the nature of education in the state school system as well as the definition of Arab and Iraqi nationalism. Although in the early years of the monarchy the Shi'is had difficulties in articulating their aspirations, by 1927 they had already acquired a degree of blocking power in the state and had begun pushing systematically to attain their political goals.

The Shi'i pursuit of government employment became a major factor in feeding the tension between Shi'is and Sunnis under the monarchy. Iraq's Sunni rulers usually included only one token Shi'i minister in the governments of the 1920s and were reluctant to appoint Shi'is in the administration and the civil service. Thus, for example, in 1921 not a single Shi'i was included in the lists of candidates for the five positions of provincial governors and there was only one Shi'i among the nine candidates for district officers.[1] Throughout the 1920s the Shi'is held only a small share of the

---

[1] Intelligence Report no. 5, 15 January 1921, FO 371/6350/3116.

important government positions. In 1930 it was estimated that whereas the Kurds, who constituted 17 percent of the population, held 22 percent of the high-ranking government posts, the Shi'is, who formed the majority of the population, held only 15 percent.[2] During the first decade of the monarchy the Shi'is were also not well represented in teaching positions in the state school system, the bulk of which were filled by Syrians as well as other Sunni graduates of the Ottoman school system. Clearly, the Shi'is experienced difficulties in penetrating the Sunni network of patronage in the state machinery. Their frustrations surfaced as early as 1924 when 'Abd al-Razzaq al-Hasani (the well-known chronicler of political events under the monarchy and a fervent supporter of Arabism as the framework of identity in Iraq) warned in an article entitled "The Shi'i Majority in Iraq" that government discrimination against the Shi'is would harm the attempt to forge national unity in the country.[3]

The very small number of Shi'is employed in the Iraqi civil service in the 1920s was not only a result of government policies and existing patterns of patronage, but also a reflection of the reluctance of Shi'is to accept government positions. The question of the lawfulness of accepting office under an illegitimate ruler was an old problem in the Shi'i legal system.[4] Shi'i ulama traditionally considered Sunni governments illegitimate, and very few Shi'is were employed by the Ottoman government. As part of their opposition to the British presence in Iraq and the Iraqi government as it was constituted in the early 1920s, the mujtahids declared a ban on accepting government office. Thus, in March 1920 Mirza Muhammad Taqi Shirazi issued a *fatwa* pronouncing all service under British rule unlawful. In 1921 Mahdi al-Khalisi too banned acceptance of government office, considering it as an act of cooperation with the infidels.[5] The ban issued by the mujtahids, which remained in force until 1927, evoked a heated debate within the Shi'i community regarding the morality of becoming a government functionary and the implications of holding state office. While Shi'is viewed government positions as a channel for gaining social mobility and political influence in the new state, many refused to accept the positions offered to them for fear that they would be boycotted by their community

---

[2] Conversation between the U.S. Consul and King Faysal's Assistant Private Secretary, Dispatch from Sloan, 28 January 1930, USNA, 890G.00/127.

[3] 'Abd al-Razzaq al-Hasani, "al-Akthariya al-shi'iyya fi al-'iraq," al-'Irfan 10 (1924): 1015–17.

[4] For a discussion of this issue see Wilferd Madelung, "A Treatise of the Sharif al-Murtada on the Legality of Working for the Government (mas'ala fi al-'amal ma'a al-sultan)," BSOAS 43 (1980): 18–31.

[5] 'Abdallah al-Nafisi, Dawr al-shi'a fi tatawwur al-'iraq al-siyasi al-hadith (Beirut, 1973), 133–34; 'Ali al-Wardi, Lamahat ijtima'iyya min ta'rikh al-'iraq al-hadith, 6 vols. (Baghdad, 1969–1978), 6:43–44.

and face excommunication.[6] The ban also sharpened the difficult dilemma of those educated and ambitious Iraqi Shi'is who did accept government office, thinking that they could make it in a secular world while cutting their ties with the mujtahids. When attempting to build their career, many felt estranged from their mujtahids and at the same time rejected by their Sunni counterparts. Their dilemma was how to reconcile their claim for equal opportunity, mobility, and power sharing in a Sunni-dominated state, without recourse to the leadership of the Shi'i mujtahids.

The desire to gain access to the state school system and to shape the nature of Iraqi secular education also became a burning issue for Shi'is. At the time of the establishment of the monarchy there were only a few Shi'is who had received secular education, mainly graduates of the *Madrasa al-Ja'fariyya* in Baghdad, which was opened in 1909. The number of Shi'is who attended the Iraqi government school system in the early 1920s was low. The mujtahids waged a campaign against secular education and discouraged parents from sending their children to the state schools.[7] Although in the 1920s the position of the Minister of Education was almost exclusively reserved for Shi'is to discredit the mujtahids' campaign, the Shi'i ministers were overshadowed by Sati' al-Husri, who acted as Director General of Education between 1923 and 1927. In his memoirs Husri described the Shi'i ministers as ignorant and backward. Thus, for example, he depicted Muhammad Rida al-Shabibi, who was one of Iraq's leading literary figures, as a person whose knowledge of modern ideas was eclectic and as incapable of understanding the new directions in education. Husri was particularly pejorative about 'Abd al-Husayn al-Chalabi (who served eight times as Minister of Education between 1922 and 1935), designating him as the "clown of Iraqi governments."[8]

There were deep cultural and philosophical divides between Husri, the graduate of the secular Mülkiye Mektebi in Istanbul, and those Iraqi Shi'is who received their formative education in the madrasa. The Shi'is resented Husri, whom they perceived as an outsider in Iraq. They disliked his educational philosophy and his nationalist ideology, which ignored the strong tribal attributes of Iraqi Shi'i society, and opposed his advocacy of allegiance to national over regional bonds. The tensions between Husri and the Shi'is also reflected their resentment of the stereotype of the "ignorant and fanatic Shi'i" which gained ground among Iraq's Sunni politicians and administrators in the 1920s. The Shi'is were annoyed by the insufficient resources allocated for education in the Shi'i provinces, and by the small

---

[6] 'Ali al-Wardi, *Dirasa fi tabi'at al-mujtama' al-'iraqi* (Baghdad, 1965), 344–45.

[7] Ibid., 346.

[8] Sati' al-Husri, *Mudhakkirati fi al-'iraq, 1921–1941*, 2 vols. (Beirut, 1967–1968), 1:277, 433.

number of Shi'is included in the delegations of Iraqi students sent abroad for study. They protested against Husri's opposition to opening a secondary school in Najaf and a teacher training college in Hilla, as well as against his decision to abolish the Directorate of Education in the middle Euphrates in 1925.[9]

The major dispute between Husri and his Shi'i opponents centered around the nature of education in the state school system. Whereas Husri advocated a centralized system controlled from Baghdad, the Shi'is preferred a decentralized form of education; they considered it essential for both meeting the specific needs of Iraq's overwhelming rural population and providing equal opportunity in education. The conflicts over this issue surfaced on a number of occasions. In 1921 King Faysal proposed the establishment of a school for children of tribal shaykhs. Hibat al-Din al-Shahrastani, who was then the Minister of Education, adopted the idea enthusiastically. He prepared a curriculum which stressed the study of Arabic, religion, and agriculture as well as extramural activities aimed at preserving the tribal heritage of the students. Husri strongly objected to the school, for it was not in line with his program of centralized national education in Iraq, and he managed to persuade Faysal to drop the idea.[10] The disagreements between Shi'is and Husri over educational policies were nowhere more apparent than in Husri's clash with Muhammad Fadil al-Jamali, one of his main Shi'i opponents. Jamali was among the first Shi'is to attend the Teacher Higher Training College in Baghdad. He was later sent by the Iraqi government to study at the American University in Beirut. Between 1929 and 1932 Jamali studied at Teachers College at Columbia University, writing his Ph.D. dissertation on bedouin education. Jamali may have instigated the visit of the Monroe Commission, which examined Iraq's education system. He wrote the section on bedouin education in the committee's report, criticizing Husri's policies and recommending decentralization of Iraq's education as well as concentration on rural and tribal areas.[11] Jamali, as will be seen later in this chapter, played a major role in expanding state education in the Shi'i areas after Husri had ceased to play an effective role in shaping Iraq's educational system.

The struggle over the definition of Arab and Iraqi nationalism had been a

[9] 'Abd al-Karim al-Uzri, *Ta'rikh fi dhikrayat al-'iraq, 1930–1958* (Beirut, 1982), 18, 25, 27–31; Hasan al-'Alawi, *al-Ta'thirat al-turkiyya fi al-mashru' al-qawmi al-'arabi fi al-'iraq* (London, 1988), 169; idem, *al-Shi'a wa al-dawla al-qawmiyya fi al-'iraq* (Paris, 1989), 256–57, 286–87; Husri, *Mudhakkirati*, 1:80; William Cleveland, *The Making of an Arab Nationalist: Ottomanism and Arabism in the Life and Thought of Sati' al-Husri* (Princeton, N.J., 1971), 65, 67–69.

[10] Husri, *Mudhakkirati*, 1:147–55.

[11] Reeva Simon, *Iraq Between the Two World Wars: The Creation and Implementation of a Nationalist Ideology* (New York, 1986), 85, 88–90.

major source of tension between Shi'is and successive Sunni governments. While Iraq's rulers adopted Pan-Arabism as their main nationalist ideology, they repeatedly questioned the loyalty and ethnic origin of the Shi'is. Beginning with Husri, who may be regarded as the founder of Pan-Arabism in Iraq, the proponents of this ideology emphasized the fame of the Arab empire and expressed a desire to restore its glory. Under the rubric of *shu'ubiyya*, they presented Shi'ism as a subversive heresy motivated primarily by Persian hatred for the Arabs, and stressed the Persian threat to the idea of Arab nationalism. Much of Shi'i frustration over this issue stemmed from the fact that Iraq's Sunni rulers were able to tie the issue of *shu'ubiyya* to Shi'i protests against their discrimination by the government and to present Shi'i grievances as acts which promoted sectarianism (*ta'ifiyya*) in the state. In doing so, the Sunni politicians were able to place the Shi'is on the defensive.[12]

The Iraqi Shi'is were for the most part Arabs of recent tribal origin. While they acknowledged the existence of religious ties between them and their coreligionists in Iran, the Iraqi Shi'is argued that these ties did not extend to the political level and had no bearing on their own national identity. The Shi'is felt that the propagation of Pan-Arabism excluded the majority of Iraq's tribal population and included only the ruling Sunni urban minority. They resented the government's narrow definition of Arab nationalism as well as the need to prove their Arab origin to Sunni politicians and administrators, who, like Husri, were ex-Ottoman officials. On various occasions Shi'is argued that they were the "indigenous sons of the country" and that, for centuries, it was Iraq and its tribes that preserved the true spirit of Arabism. The Shi'is were annoyed by Husri's accusation that there were groups in Najaf that did not sufficiently resist Turkey's attempt to annex Mosul early in the 1920s. They were offended by the fact that Iraq's nationalist program of education did not make use of the 1920 revolt as a symbol for the success of Shi'i-Sunni unity in leading to the establishment of the Iraqi state.[13] The Shi'is directed their main anger against the Baghdad Sunni politicians with whom they had cooperated during the revolt. Some also expressed their disillusion with the outcome of the revolt, as the following extract of a poem composed in 1926 by 'Ali al-Sharqi demonstrates:

[12] 'Abbas Kelidar, "The Shii Imami Community and Politics in the Arab East," *MES* 19 (1983): 12; 'Alawi, *al-Shi'a*, 159–63, 235–38, 242–44, 248; idem, *al-Ta'thirat al-turkiyya*, 142–44, 156–57.

[13] 'Arabi, "al-Shi'a fi biladihim: 'ibar wa-'izat li-katib siyasi kabir min aqtab al-shi'a fi al-'iraq," *al-'Irfan* 20 (1930): 564; Ibn al-Rafidayn, "al-Shi'a fi al-'iraq," *al-'Irfan* 22 (1931): 435; 'Ali al-Sharqi, "Lawhat al-qawmiyya al-'arabiyya fi al-'iraq," *al-'Irfan* 26 (1936): 773. See also 'Abd al-Karim al-Uzri, *Mushkilat al-hukm fi al-'iraq* (London, 1991), 231, 260; 'Alawi, *al-Shi'a*, 240–47, 252–53, 258.

> Woe to a revolt which was followed
> by the rebels' regret
> Woe to a unity which has collapsed
> because of the greed for spoils
> [A unity which] had been the wreath of glory
> and was snatched by a surprising assault.[14]

Shi'i frustrations over Sunni attempts to dispute their Arab origin and loyalty to the Iraqi state surfaced in 1927 and 1933 following the publication of two books which Shi'is considered highly offensive. Early in 1927 Anis al-Nusuli, a Syrian teacher in Baghdad's main secondary school, published a book entitled *al-Dawla al-umawiyya fi al-sha'm* (The Umayyad State in Syria). The author glorified the Umayyads, whom Shi'is hold responsible for both challenging imam 'Ali's authority when caliph and persecuting later Shi'i imams. In June 1933 a Sunni by the name of 'Abd al-Razzaq al-Hassan published his *al-'Uruba fi al-mizan* (Arabism on the Scales). The author criticized the Shi'is for their alleged Persian orientation, and their inability to reconcile their sectarian loyalties with the large framework of Arab nationalism. Both books caused far-reaching indignation in Shi'i circles, and the publication of Nusuli's book also led to outrage against the government's policy of recruiting Syrians to teach in Iraq's schools.[15] In subsequent years, Iraqi governments continued to encourage publications that called for Pan-Arabism, thereby discrediting the calls of Shi'i mujtahids for Islamic unity and portraying this activity as a danger to Arab nationalism.[16]

The attempts of King Faysal and Iraq's Sunni politicians to establish a regular army posed yet another challenge to the Shi'is. Iraq's rulers were painfully aware that the kingdom depended for its existence on British goodwill and arms. To leading Sunni politicians like Ja'far al-'Askari, Nuri Sa'id, Yasin al-Hashimi, and Rashid 'Ali al-Gaylani, conscription symbolized the ultimate commitment of Iraq's various communities to the Iraqi state. They wanted an army as a symbol and as a defender of national

[14] 'Ali al-Sharqi, *'Awatif wa-'awasif* (Baghdad, 1953), 171.

[15] For details see 'Abd al-Razzaq al-Hasani, *Ta'rikh al-wizarat al-'iraqiyya*, 2d and 3d eds., 10 vols. (Sidon, 1953–1965), 2:84–85; Husri, *Mudhakkirati*, 1:557–69; Uzri, *Mushkilat al-hukm*, 215–30; Special Service Officer, Extract from Report no. I/Bd/39, 2 February 1927, Air 23/379; Extracts from a Letter from Mr. Oglivie-Forbes to Sir Francis Humphrys, 6 June 1933, FO 371/16923/3245.

[16] See, for example, Mahmud al-Mallah, *al-Ara' al-sariha li-bina' qawmiyya sahiha* (Baghdad, n.d.); idem, *al-Wahda al-islamiyya bayn al-akhdh wa al-radd* (Baghdad, 1951); idem, *Ta'rikhuna al-qawmi bayn al-salb wa al-'ijab* (Baghdad, 1956); Muhammad al-Khalisi, *al-'Uruba fi dar al-bawar fa-hal min munqidh: muqayasa bayn al-ghabir wa al-hadir wa-nazra ila al-mustaqbal* (Mashhad, n.d.).

integrity, as well as a bulwark for their own authority.[17] In March 1927 a draft of the National Defense Act was passed by the government, and in May a conscription bill was sent to parliament for approval. Shiʿi politicians, tribal shaykhs, and mujtahids objected to the bill and attempted to form a united front. The Minister of Education Sayyid ʿAbd al-Mahdi resigned in protest, and Shiʿi deputies in parliament met almost daily in Baghdad to coordinate opposition to the bill. They sent letters to the mujtahids of Najaf and to tribal shaykhs in the Euphrates urging them to oppose the bill. At the end of June a meeting of Shiʿi leaders took place in Najaf and the participants agreed to work against the bill through the Nahdah party, which Shiʿis led by Amin al-Charchafchi had revived in 1924.[18]

Shiʿi opposition to the bill did not derive from lack of a nationalist spirit or disloyalty to the Iraqi state, but from their view of conscription as a symbol for Sunni domination and a means for increasing the central authority of Baghdad. Shiʿi memory of conscription during the Ottoman period was not a pleasant one as conscripts were committed to long military service and tribal shaykhs had to pay heavy taxes to secure the exemption of their tribesmen. The shaykhs perceived the bill as aimed at obstructing their authority among their tribesmen and opposed it on the ground that the tribesmen would be the only group of the population to be recruited into the army. Moreover, the Shiʿis greatly resented the fact that whereas the rank and file of the army units that existed in the 1920s were composed mainly of tribal elements, there were hardly any Shiʿis among the officers, who were for the most part ex-Ottomans and ex-Sharifians.[19]

Shiʿi leaders sought to use the conscription bill not only for demonstrating their blocking power in the state, but also as a bargaining chip to gain greater representation in the government. Thus, in 1927 some Arab mujtahids announced their willingness to support the bill provided that Shiʿis would gain an increase in government appointments. In an article published in al-ʿAlam al-ʿArabi in July, Muhammad Baqir al-Shabibi (who was at that time a deputy of the Muntafiq province to parliament) wrote that Shiʿi opposition to the bill would remain in force as long as Iraq's leaders refused to accept the "demands of the people." This theme was echoed in September when the writer of an article published in the Nahdah party newspaper explained that the party would continue to resist conscription as long as political conditions in Iraq remained unchanged. In objecting to

[17] Mohammad Tarbush, *The Role of the Military in Politics: A Case Study of Iraq to 1941* (London, 1982), 86–87; Paul Hemphill, "The Formation of the Iraqi Army, 1921–1933," in *The Integration of Modern Iraq*, ed. Abbas Kelidar (London, 1979), 90.
[18] A Note on the Political Situation to 27th September 1927, CO 730/123/10.
[19] Tarbush, *The Role of the Military*, 78–79, 87; Simon, *Iraq*, 118–19.

the bill, Shi'i leaders hoped to cause a political crisis, which would force the government to resign on account of its failure to pass the bill through parliament. Their intention was to make a point of Shi'i oppositional power and to demand that at least three positions be reserved for Shi'is in the next government.[20] The government avoided a political crisis in 1927 by withdrawing the bill from parliament. In 1932, Faysal again failed to win the support of the Shi'i tribal shaykhs and the mujtahids to a conscription bill. It was not until 1934 that the Iraqi government was able to pass a National Service Law, which went into effect in June the following year. The Shi'is could not sustain an effective opposition in blocking the establishment of a regular army since their attitude toward this institution became a litmus test for their national commitment as Iraqis.

In their effort to gain access to power, Shi'is radically changed their attitude toward the British, whom they considered capable of ending Sunni domination in the state. As early as July 1923 Shi'is began expressing the opinion that it would be far preferable for them to return to the days of complete British rule than to be under the control of a Sunni administration. At that time there were also rumors that Shi'i leaders were considering the submission of petitions to the High Commissioner asking the British government to resume direct rule over Iraq.[21] The reversal of Shi'i anti-British policy was not confined to politicians alone and was shared by some of the Arab mujtahids as well, most notably Mahdi al-Khalisi. In his will he apparently expressed a preference for direct British control instead of the Iraqi government as it had been constituted after his deportation to Iran.[22] Moreover, during the 1920s Shi'i leaders also sided with the British in opposition to the government's attempt to establish a regular army. In adopting the British position over the issue of conscription, the Shi'is hoped to gain British support for their demand for power sharing with the Sunnis.

The Shi'i attempt to draw the British into resuming direct control over Iraq was evident following an incident which took place at the shrine of Kazimayn on 10 July 1927. That day coincided with the tenth of Muharram, on which Shi'i observance of 'Ashura' in commemoration of the martyrdom of imam Husayn reaches its climax. When processions of flagellants passed through the courtyard of the shrine, a clash occurred between Shi'i civilians and police and army forces. Several civilians and soldiers were killed in the riots that followed and over a hundred were injured. While Shi'is alleged that the Iraqi government deliberately engi-

[20] Husayn Jamil, *al-Afkar al-siyasiyya li al-ahzab al-'iraqiyya fi 'ahd al-intidab, 1922–1932* (Baghdad, 1985), 27; Hasani, *Ta'rikh al-wizarat*, 2:100; Intelligence Reports nos. 11 and 12, 26 May and 9 June 1927, FO 371/12264/2556 and FO 371/12264/2870.

[21] Special Service Officer, Hilla, 2 July 1923, Air 23/453.

[22] Special Service Officer, 14 May 1925, Air 23/379.

neered the incident to start trouble, officers of the Iraqi army claimed that the Shiʻis provoked disturbances to compel the British to step in and pressure the government to respond to Shiʻi demands for a greater share of power.[23] In his analysis of the Kazimayn incident the Acting High Commissioner B. Bourdillon stopped short of suggesting that it was precipitated by actions taken by the Iraqi Premier Jaʻfar al-ʻAskari. Bourdillon reported that several weeks before the incident there were strong rumors that the Sunnis intend to stir up strife during Muharram to get the Shiʻis into trouble and thus prevent them from obtaining British support of their political demands. At that time, Shiʻi leaders impressed upon Bourdillon that they were willing to obey any order of the British government. They stressed that their opposition to the Iraqi government was not motivated by anti-British feelings, but by a determination to avoid being dominated by a Sunni government. A leading Shiʻi said to Bourdillon: "We know we are uneducated and so cannot at present take our proper share in the public services. What we want is British control, to save us from Sunni domination, until our sons are educated; then we, who are the real majority, will take our proper place in the government of our country and shall not want British control, but merely advice as you are giving it now."[24]

Although following the riots in Kazimayn the Shiʻis worked with a determination and fixity of purpose that compelled surprise and admiration from British officials, their attempt to draw the British into resuming direct rule over Iraq did not succeed. Shiʻi preachers came from Najaf and Karbala to villages in the lower Euphrates and advised their listeners to agitate for the return of a pure British administration. Some Shiʻi leaders also sought to send a deputation to Bourdillon to ask for the restoration of executive powers to British advisory officers, but they refrained from doing so only at his own advice. The British had no intention of resuming direct control over Iraq or altering the balance of power between Sunnis and Shiʻis. They refused to become directly involved in the disputes between the two groups and sought only to avert political complications in order to maintain their position of influence in the country.[25]

The Shiʻi effort to articulate and push for their political demands found embodiment in the protest movement which developed after the riots of 1927. The movement included Shiʻi Baghdadi figures like Amin al-Charchafchi and Sayyid Muhammad al-Sadr. The inner circle in Najaf

[23] Acting High Commissioner for Iraq to the Secretary of State for the Colonies, 14 July 1927, FO 371/12274/3135.

[24] Acting High Commissioner for Iraq to the Secretary of State for the Colonies, 15 July 1927, FO 371/12274/3505.

[25] Acting High Commissioner for Iraq to the Secretary of State for the Colonies, 25 July 1927, FO 371/12274/3315; Special Service Officer, Basra Reprint no. I/824, 3 September 1927, Air 23/432.

consisted of Hamid Khan, 'Ali al-Sharqi, Muhammad Husayn Kashif al-Ghita, Hadi Kashif al-Ghita, Muhammad Bahr al-'Ulum, Shaykh Jawad al-Jawahiri, Muhammad Jawad al-Jaza'iri, and 'Abd al-Karim al-Jaza'iri. Between the 12th and 14th of September, Shi'i politicians and mujtahids held meetings in Najaf. Although there were calls to appeal to the High Commissioner Henry Dobbs for a change of government, and failing that, for a division of the country and the formation of a Shi'i government in the Shi'i areas, the majority of participants rejected the latter idea. One important outcome of these meetings was the decision of the mujtahids to withdraw their ban on Shi'i employment in government service. This act reflected the attempt of the Arab mujtahids, notably Muhammad Husayn Kashif al-Ghita, to emerge from their retirement from political affairs and to act independently of the grand Persian mujtahids so as to establish themselves as the leaders of the Shi'i community in Iraq. The participants accepted several major resolutions, among them: the allocation of half of the ministerial positions in every government to Shi'is, and the other half to Arab Sunnis, Christians, and Jews; equality in the appointment of government officials; and the holding of new parliamentary elections free of government interference and under the supervision of British inspectors.[26]

Yet the Shi'is experienced difficulties in pushing for these demands because of the lack of one leader acknowledged by the Shi'i community as well as the absence of a strong political party capable of generating mass opposition against the government. Although Hamid Khan and 'Ali al-Sharqi worked hard to bring the various elements of Shi'i society together, an important Baghdadi figure like Ja'far Abu al-Timman did not join the movement. He had disagreements with the mujtahids, and viewed the ban which they had imposed between 1920 and 1927 on accepting government office as an act which impeded Shi'i advance in the state. Abu al-Timman, who in 1928 reestablished the Nationalist party, was also unwilling to adopt a pro-British attitude or to use the conscription bill as a leverage against the government. There were disagreements between Charchafchi and Sadr as well. The latter despaired of obtaining British support and criticized Charchafchi for leaning toward the British. Sadr, who was appointed President of the Iraqi senate in 1929, began advocating that the Shi'is should obtain their rights through parliament. The Nahdah party attracted only a small number of Shi'is and failed to emerge as a major oppositional force. In October 1927 the government banned the Nahdah's newspaper. Although the newspaper reappeared between February 1928 and July 1930, the party itself stopped functioning a short time after Charchafchi's failure to be reelected to parliament.[27]

[26] A Note on the Political Situation to 27th September 1927, CO 730/123/10; Intelligence Report no. 21, 13 October 1927, FO 371/12265/4540; Special Service Officer, 19 December 1927, Air 23/432.

[27] Intelligence Reports nos. 22 and 19, 27 October 1927 and 12 September 1928, FO

Nonetheless, Shi'i discontent over their inadequate representation in the government and the civil service showed no signs of diminishing, and only intensified as the mandatory period drew to an end and Iraq prepared for its independence and admission to the League of Nations in October 1932. The Shi'is were alarmed by the prospects of an increase in Sunni dominance once Iraq gained independence and British influence in the country decreased. Their apprehensions may be gathered from the report of Alexander Sloan, head of the U.S. Legation in Iraq, who wrote that some Shi'i tribes began considering themselves as a minority in Iraq, and that certain Shi'i committees issued proclamations demanding to know what type of protection the Shi'is could look for following Iraq's admission to the League of Nations.[28] In numerous articles published in the Shi'i Lebanese journal al-'Irfan Shi'is protested against their exclusion from the government and the civil service. Some alleged that the government was following a program aimed at containing the Shi'is and depriving them of their rights.[29]

The Shi'i effort to articulate their demands was evident in the petition submitted in early 1932 to foreign representatives in Iraq. The authors had difficulties in printing the petition in Iraq and could not publish it there because of warnings which the police had issued to the presses. The petition appeared in al-'Irfan. Although in some respects its contents represented a partisan exaggeration, both British and U.S. officials considered the petition as reflecting the general mood of Iraqi Shi'i society. The document was signed by "The Executive Committee of the Shi'is in Iraq." Its authors demanded proportionate power sharing between the Shi'is and the other sects in Iraq; an increase in the number of Shi'is included in the delegations of students sent abroad; investment of government resources in the Shi'i areas and the allocation of lands from the public domain to Shi'i cultivators; proportionate distribution of waqf revenues among Shi'i and Sunni religious institutions; and freedom of expression. The petitioners also demanded the conduct of a plebiscite under the supervision of the League of Nations to ascertain Shi'i grievances. Although the petition caused a sensation among Iraq's Sunni politicians, on the whole the Shi'i demands went unanswered.[30]

371/12265/4765 and FO 371/13027/4712; Iraq Police, Abstract of Intelligence no. 53, 31 December 1927, NAI, file 7/15/3; Special Service Officer, Diwaniyya Report for the Period between 15 and 26 May 1930, Air 23/432; Iraq Police, Abstracts of Intelligence, 5 and 26 August 1933, Air 23/589; Jamil, al-Afkar al-siyasiyya, 29.

[28] Sloan to the Secretary of State, 9 February 1932, USNA, 890G.00/177.

[29] See, for example, 'Arabi, "al-Shi'a fi biladihim, al-'Irfan 20 (1930): 564–66, and 21 (1931), 75–76; Anon., "Idtihad al-shi'a fi al-'iraq," al-'Irfan 21 (1931): 442; Ibn al-Rafidayn, "al-Shi'a fi al-'iraq," al-'Irfan 22 (1931): 13, 434, 438–40.

[30] For the Arabic version see "Sawt min al-'iraq," al-'Irfan 23 (1932): 14–16. For an English translation see Sloan to Secretary of State, 11 February 1932, USNA, 890G.00/179.

What had begun in 1927 as a Shiʻi drive to gain a greater share of power through constitutional means and reliance on British support developed by 1933 into a protest movement which reflected the willingness of Shiʻis to use violence in order to obtain their demands. Shiʻis in Iraq began identifying the Sunni government as a "government of occupation" and stated their desire to "rise and wrest their rights from the Sunnis." Shiʻi discontent grew following the publication of the British census in late 1932, which confirmed their claim to be the majority of the population in Iraq. Shiʻi unrest further increased after the publication of Hassan's book in June 1933 and King Faysal's death the following September. The King's death was a major factor in leading to the rapid deterioration of Shiʻi relations with the Sunni government and the subsequent appeal of the tribal shaykhs to the Arab mujtahids to lead a Shiʻi opposition movement against the government. Throughout his rule in Iraq, Faysal had acted as a safety valve. During his periodic visits to the Euphrates region, the King presented himself as a staunch advocate of the Shiʻi cause. He was always extremely careful to stress the importance of unity and the need to avoid sectarian disputes which would hamper the progress of the country as a whole. During these visits Faysal was most meticulous in his observance of tribal customs and was equally careful to avoid offending Shiʻi feelings. The King always left behind him a general impression among the Shiʻi tribal community that better times were about to come soon. He stressed that, provided no attempt was made to force the issue, the question of adequate Shiʻi representation in the government and the administration was merely a matter of patience and implicit trust in the King. Following Faysal's death, Shiʻi leaders concluded that the possibility of obtaining Shiʻi demands through constitutional methods was very remote and that some form of direct action would have to be taken.[31]

The 1935 Revolt

In September 1934 the government of ʻAli Jawdat al-Ayyubi dissolved the parliament. In the new elections which were held in December, the government did not include some paramount Shiʻi tribal shaykhs in the list of candidates, and they consequently lost their seats in parliament to other shaykhs and *sirkal*s. The government also gave a large proportion of the

---

See also Sloan to Secretary of State, 4 May 1932, USNA, 890G.00/193; Shiʻa Activities, Report no. I/Bd/28, 14 March 1932, Air 23/385.

[31] Al-Najafi, "Idtihad al-shiʻa fi al-ʻiraq," *al-ʻIrfan* 24 (1934): 315; Iraq Police, Abstract of Intelligence, 17 June 1933, Air 23/589; Extract from RAF Monthly Intelligence Summary for September 1933, FO 371/16923/6677; Khabenshue to Secretary of State, 26 September 1933, USNA, 890G.00/277.

fifteen seats allocated for the Shi'i tribal provinces of Diwaniyya and the Muntafiq to Sunni townsmen from Baghdad and elsewhere who did not represent the tribal interests of the two provinces.[32] The exclusion from parliament of 'Abd al-Wahid al-Hajj Sikkar, the powerful shaykh of the Al Fatla tribe in the Diwaniyya province, was an injudicious act on the part of the government. As he wished to see the fall of Ayyubi's government, Sikkar allied himself with the Ikha party and the Sunni opposition group, which included Rashid 'Ali al-Gaylani, Yasin al-Hashimi, Hikmat Sulayman, and Naji al-Suwaydi.

Throughout January 1935 the opposition encouraged anti-government demonstrations in Shi'i tribal areas. Sikkar was the mouthpiece of the Ikha party in the middle Euphrates. Knowing that he would gain a limited backing if he merely appealed for a change of government, Sikkar presented himself as the advocate of Shi'i rights. While he managed to win the support of about half of the tribal shaykhs of the middle Euphrates, a large group of Shi'i shaykhs (some of whom had been elected to parliament) remained loyal to the government. The tensions between the two groups of rival shaykhs strained the relations between the Shi'i tribes of the middle Euphrates as the tribesmen began to take up arms and performed their war dances. Unable to cope with the growing tribal unrest, Ayyubi's government resigned late in February. Although King Ghazi invited the leaders of the Ikha party to form a government, they declined because of his refusal to dissolve the parliament elected under Ayyubi's government. The King then turned to Jamil al-Midfa'i, who formed a new government early in March. The change of government did not appease the Ikha leaders, who did not join Midfa'i's government, nor did it pacify Sikkar and his group of shaykhs. On the contrary, the Baghdadi opposition intensified its anti-government propaganda in the Shi'i areas and tribal defiance in the middle Euphrates increased. Under the threat of a tribal uprising, Midfa'i's government resigned on 15 March after only two weeks in office. The King now sent for Yasin al-Hashimi, who formed a new government on his own terms in which Gaylani acted as the Minister of Interior.

In encouraging Shi'i tribal unrest in order to topple the governments of Ayyubi and Midfa'i, Gaylani and his counterparts in the opposition set in motion forces which they could not easily control. The Ikha leaders attempted to widen the front of their attacks on Ayyubi's government by bringing into the struggle the Arab mujtahids of Najaf, most notably Muhammad Kashif al-Ghita, 'Abd al-Karim al-Jaza'iri, and Jawad al-Jawahiri. On 9 January the group of tribal shaykhs led by Sikkar appealed to Kashif al-Ghita for consultations regarding the sociopolitical conditions

---

[32] Hasani, *Ta'rikh al-wizarat*, 4:31–33; A. D. Macdonald, "The Political Developments in Iraq Leading up to the Rising in the Spring of 1935," *JRCAS* 23 (1936): 27–28.

of the Shi'i community. After meeting the mujtahid in his home in Najaf, the shaykhs traveled on the 14th to Baghdad. They delivered a petition to the King protesting against the inadequate representation of Shi'is in politics and the civil service. This development alarmed the anti-Sikkar shaykhs, who did not wish to see Sikkar emerging as the self-constituted leader of the Shi'i movement. The anti-Sikkar shaykhs were also afraid that in rejecting the demands for improving Shi'i conditions, they could lose their tribesmen's loyalty. Therefore, in their turn, the anti-Sikkar shaykhs appealed to Kashif al-Ghita as well, asking for his guidance and notifying him of their willingness to resign their seats in parliament.[33]

The appeal of the two groups of rival shaykhs to Kashif al-Ghita led to a shift in the source of inspiration of tribal unrest from Sunni politicians in Baghdad to the Arab Shi'i mujtahids in Najaf. The mujtahids were by no means disposed to take sides in a struggle between two groups of Sunni politicians and instead sought to use the tribal unrest to force the Shi'i demands on the government. In this the mujtahids were assisted by a group of Shi'i lawyers from Baghdad, most notably Dhiban al-Ghaban, Muhammad 'Abd al-Husayn, and Amin al-Charchafchi. The mujtahids took advantage of the fact that the anti-Sikkar shaykhs did not trust the new government of Yasin al-Hashimi and perceived Gaylani as too committed to Sikkar's group.

On 23 March, the Baghdadi lawyers met with Kashif al-Ghita in Najaf. They formulated a manifesto listing twelve demands, many of them resembling those which the Shi'is had expressed in 1927 and 1932. The authors demanded Shi'i participation in government, parliament, and the civil service in accordance with their share among the population; new elections to parliament free of government interference; the teaching of Shi'i jurisprudence in the law school; an inclusion of a Shi'i member in all sections of the court of succession; freedom of the press; distribution of *waqf* revenues among all Islamic institutions; the establishment of an agricultural bank; the cancellation of land rents and water rates as well as changes in various other forms of taxation in the rural south; the replacement of civil servants of objectionable character as well as a decrease in the salaries and pensions of high-ranking officials and officers; and government investment in health and education in the Shi'i areas.[34] British officials considered most of these demands reasonable and to a large extent justified.

In formulating this manifesto, the Shi'i Baghdadi lawyers and the Arab mujtahids sought to unite the two groups of rival shaykhs in order to

[33] Hasani, *Ta'rikh al-wizarat*, 4:46–49; Humphrys to Simon, 17 January 1935, FO 371/18945/623; RAF Intelligence Report, 20 February 1935, FO 371/18949/1198.

[34] For the Arabic text see Hasani, *Ta'rikh al-wizarat*, 4:84–86. For English translations see Enclosure in Kerr to Simon, 28 March 1935, FO 371/18945/2295; Enclosure in Khabenshue to Secretary of State, 4 April 1935, USNA, 890G.00/326.

pressure the government to yield to Shiʻi demands. While the anti-Sikkar shaykhs signed the manifesto in an attempt to rob Sikkar of the initiative and oblige him to come over to their side as a suppliant follower, Sikkar and some of the tribal shaykhs associated with him refused to sign it, asserting that it would lead to sectarian strife. Calculating that they had gained the support of the majority of Shiʻi tribal shaykhs, the mujtahids submitted the manifesto to the government of Yasin al-Hashimi sometime after its establishment. In an effort to increase pressures on the government, Kashif al-Ghita also issued a *fatwa* late in March in which he appealed to all Shiʻis to sever their connections with political parties. The mujtahid called on the government to begin negotiations over Shiʻi demands, and authorized action according to the circumstances.[35] The appeals of the mujtahids to the government went unanswered.

Tribal unrest continued to spread throughout April in spite of the government's attempts to appease the anti-Sikkar shaykhs. The Prime Minister sought to pacify the tribes of the middle Euphrates by giving the anti-Sikkar shaykhs assurances that in the forthcoming elections they would be given as many seats as they had had in the last parliament. In an attempt to demonstrate its impartiality, the government also suspended the Ikha party in which Hashimi and Gaylani played a prominent role. Nonetheless, the anti-Sikkar shaykhs remained profoundly mistrustful of Gaylani, and tribal defiance toward the government increased as many of the anti-Sikkar shaykhs gave binding promises to Kashif al-Ghita to support the mujtahids in the struggle for the Shiʻi cause.[36] Events were moving fast toward a trial of strength between the government and the tribes of the middle Euphrates.

On 6 May police officials arrested Ahmad Asadallah, a Shiʻi *ʻalim* and follower of Kashif al-Ghita who was inciting the tribes of Rumaytha against the government. That evening, the Abu Hasan, the Bani Zurayyij, and the Zawalim tribes revolted, tearing up the railway line on both sides of the town of Rumaytha. The government declared martial law, and on the 11th Iraqi planes began bombing the villages of the insurgent tribes in the Diwaniyya province. Subsequently, the four leading Arab mujtahids of Najaf sent a letter to the King asking the government to end its military operations against the tribes and to begin negotiations with the mujtahids. Once again, the mujtahids' call to the government went unanswered. On the 13th the government exiled the Shiʻi lawyers Dhiban al-Ghaban and Amin al-Charchafchi from Baghdad to Kirkuk, charging that the two were in contact with some of the rebelling shaykhs. That same day the Muntafiq

---

[35] Hasani, *Ta'rikh al-wizarat*, 4:88–89; Macdonald, "The Political Developments in Iraq," 32; Enclosure in Kerr to Simon, FO 371/18945/2295.

[36] Hasani, *Ta'rikh al-wizarat*, 4:94; Enclosure in Kerr to Simon, 2 April 1935, FO 371/18945/2455; Kerr to Simon, 15 May 1935, FO 371/18953/3287.

tribes of Suq al-Shuyukh and Nasiriyya revolted as well. These tribes joined
the revolt a short while after their shaykhs had traveled to Najaf to sign the
manifesto of Shi'i demands and pledged to unite in rising against the
government of Yasin al-Hashimi. During the night of the 15th, the rebels
cut the railway line between Basra and Nasiriyya and occupied the town of
Suq al-Shuyukh.[37]

The government was alarmed by the danger that the revolt might spread
from Diwaniyya and Nasiriyya to Hilla province and cut off army forces in
the middle Euphrates from Baghdad. It therefore signaled its willingness to
negotiate with Kashif al-Ghita over Shi'i demands through Muhsin al-
Shallash, a wealthy merchant of Najaf who had been at one point a Minister
of Finance. At the same time, the government acted to divide the rebelling
tribes. While the Defense Minister Ja'far al-'Askari met the shaykhs of the
Muntafiq tribes in an attempt to persuade them to agree to a truce, government forces continued their operations against the tribes of Rumaytha and
suppressed their revolt on 21 May. The end of the revolt in Rumaytha left
the government free to deal with the Muntafiq tribes and the mujtahids.
Salih Jabir, the Shi'i governor of Karbala province, met with Kashif al-
Ghita and persuaded him to send an exhortation to the Muntafiq tribes to
refrain from all fighting. Once it reestablished control over Rumaytha,
Nasiriyya, and Suq al-Shuyukh, the government no longer had an interest
in pursuing negotiations with Kashif al-Ghita. Although Yasin al-Hashimi
was generally sympathetic to the idea of increasing Shi'i participation in
government and public service, he resented the attempt of Shi'is to force
their demands on the government and objected to recognizing the mujtahids as the representatives of the Shi'i community in political affairs.[38]

The 1935 revolt demonstrated how violence had developed to be a part
of the political game in Iraq from the mid-1930s. Violence had become not
only a tool in the hands of the government for exercising political control,
but a vehicle to which people resorted in an attempt to influence government policies. The revolt also uncovered a lack of a community of interest
among various segments of Iraqi Shi'i society as well as the absence of a
strong Shi'i political leader who could systematically represent and defend
the interests of his community in Baghdad. The Shi'i merchants, as well as
politicians like Ja'far Abu al-Timman and Muhammad Rida al-Shabibi,
did not support the revolt; they were reluctant to flaunt their sectarian
identity and objected to the attempt to force Shi'i demands on the govern-

[37] Hasani, Ta'rikh al-wizarat, 4:95–97, 102, 106, 107; Kerr to Simon, FO
371/18953/3287.
[38] Hasani, Ta'rikh al-wizarat, 4:110–13; Kerr to Simon, 22 May 1935, FO
371/18953/3433; Khabenshue to Secretary of State, 4 April 1935, USNA, 890G.00/326. See
also Salih Jabir's letter to Rashid 'Ali al-Gaylani, 22 May 1935, cited in Uzri, Mushkilat al-
hukm, 78.

ment. Although the Arab mujtahids attempted to assert themselves as political leaders, they failed to gain government's recognition and the position of Kashif al-Ghita in Najaf was shaken after the revolt as some Shi'i groups resented his approval of the use of violence. The Shi'i tribal shaykhs were the only group to benefit from the revolt. In the second half of the 1930s the government increased the representation of tribal shaykhs in parliament, thus fostering the class identity of the shaykhs.[39]

THE BID FOR POWER

The struggle for power between Shi'is and Sunnis intensified in the 1940s and 1950s following the great increase in the number of young educated Shi'is who were equipped to compete with Sunnis for positions in the government and the civil service. The relations between the two groups reflected growing Shi'i frustrations with their inability to achieve parity with the Sunnis as well as Sunni apprehensions of being swamped by the Shi'i majority.

By the mid-1930s the Shi'is had already come close to dominating the Ministry of Education, a development which reflected the growing political clout of Shi'is within the state as well as their ability to shape government policy. In 1927 Shi'i opposition to Husri was such that he had to resign his position as Director General of Education. Although in 1931 Husri was appointed Inspector General of Education, he resigned after only three months in office. From then until his exile from Iraq in 1941, Husri held the post of Director of Antiquities. The removal of Husri from a position of influence in the Ministry of Education paved the way for Shi'is to push for the expansion of state education in the rural areas beginning with the 1933–34 academic year. The two main Shi'i figures in the Ministry of Education who were responsible for this radical change in government policy toward education were 'Abd al-Karim al-Uzri and Muhammad Fadil al-Jamali. While Uzri acted as the secretary of the Ministry between 1931 and 1934, Jamali was general advisor to the Ministry from 1932 to 1934, Director General of Education between 1934 and 1935, Inspector General from 1935 to 1937, and Director General of Public Instruction between 1937 and 1943. Uzri and Jamali were assisted by the fact that the position of the Minister of Education in Iraq in those years still remained almost exclusively reserved for Shi'is.

Jamali acted to decentralize Iraq's educational system, thereby increasing Shi'i access to secular education. In 1934 he established directorates of education in each province in Iraq and encouraged the directors to intro-

[39] Iraq Police, 15 June 1935, Air 23/590; Tribal Situation in Lower and Middle Euphrates Areas, 5 July 1939, FO 371/23202/5963; Uzri, *Mushkilat al-hukm*, 65–66, 83; 'Alawi, *al-Shi'ia*, 316.

duce reforms in the schools under their jurisdiction according to the specific social needs of their province. As Director General, Jamali controlled educational policies and the curriculum, and was responsible for the increase in the number of Shi'is in the student missions sent abroad. Jamali facilitated the admission of Shi'is to the teachers' training institutions as well as to the Teachers' Higher Training College in Baghdad. He established government schools in the rural areas, including a secondary school in Najaf which was staffed by graduates of the American University in Beirut and the Teachers' Higher Training College. It was estimated that between 1930 and 1945 the number of pupils in Iraq at the elementary level more than tripled, and that the number at the secondary level increased sixfold in the corresponding period. Much of this increase took place in the Shi'i areas.[40]

The great increase in the number of educated Shi'is in Iraq reflected the radical change in mentality and attitude toward secular education which took place in the Shi'i community under the monarchy. In May 1944 officials of the U.S. Legation in Iraq led by Loy Henderson visited Najaf and Karbala. Henderson reported that the government schools in the Shi'i areas were overcrowded. He noted that Shi'i religious and political leaders understood the need to change the practices and outlook of their followers, and that they were clamoring for the establishment of additional schools for the benefit of Shi'i children. Henderson was impressed by the commitment of the older generation of Shi'is to increasing the level and quality of education of their youth. He remarked that Shi'i parents pushed their children to prepare themselves for government positions by assiduous study, and that they were anxious to send them abroad to acquire further education. A member of the Literary Society in Najaf revealed to Henderson the vision which many of the older Shi'is shared:

> The time has come when we should apply our intellect and our energy to improving the lot of our people; to raising their education qualifications, and to assisting them to benefit from the scientific knowledge of the advanced countries in the West. We realize that we personally cannot hope to be scientists, economists, or political scientists in the Western sense. Nevertheless, we hope that by our efforts we shall make it possible for those coming behind us to partake of the fruits of Western civilization.[41]

Although by 1945 there were already a significant number of educated Shi'is in Iraq capable of competing with the Sunnis over government positions, the Shi'is were still barred from access to key positions in the state.

---

[40] Uzri, *Dhikrayat*, 25–34, 36–62; Phebe Marr, "The Development of a Nationalist Ideology in Iraq, 1920–1941," *MW* 75 (1985): 98–100; Simon, *Iraq*, 93–94.

[41] "The Shia Sect and the Position of the Shias in Iraq," Henderson to Secretary of State, 15 July 1944, USNA, 890G.00/7–1544.

The Shi'is resented the political reality in Iraq during the interwar period whereby the complex interests of their community were represented by one or two Shi'i ministers in government and a block of tribal shaykhs in parliament. Their frustrations surfaced once again following the second British occupation of Iraq in May 1941. On a number of occasions Shi'is in the south and in Baghdad approached British officials and expressed their desire for an increase in Shi'i representation in government, as well as in British influence in Iraq. Thus, for example, Sayyid Muhammad al-Sadr, the President of the senate, met in September with C. J. Edmonds, the British adviser to the Iraqi Ministry of Interior. While Sadr wanted to learn what the British intentions were concerning the administration of Iraq, he also told Edmonds that among the Shi'is there was a deep feeling of dissatisfaction with the political system whereby a small group of Sunni politicians enjoyed a virtual monopoly of high and effective office. Sadr explained that the Shi'is resented the system because the leaders of Iraq were not "sons of the soil at all but the descendants of foreigners with no real love for Iraq in their veins."[42] In the years immediately after World War II Shi'i deputies in parliament also protested against the government's policy in admitting only a few Shi'is to the military and the police academies, as well as against the very small number of Shi'i officers in the army and on the police force.[43]

The Sunni politicians responded to Shi'i pressures for a greater share of power in the state by gradually increasing the number of Shi'is in the government, the senate, and the administration. Yet at the same time, Iraq's rulers expanded the size of the government and the bureaucracy, thus insuring Sunni control of the state machinery. The changes in the distribution of ministerial positions during the monarchic period illustrate this point. Of the total of 645 positions of ministers under the monarchy, the Shi'is held 182, ranging from 21 in the 1920s to 76 in the 1950s. Although Shi'i representation in government doubled from 18 percent in the 1920s to 36 in the 1950s, the Shi'is still constituted less than half of the ministers and much of the power continued to rest with the Sunni ministers, who occupied most of the key positions.[44] Likewise, while in the 1940s and 1950s the Sunnis no longer enjoyed a monopoly in the administration, they were able to retain their dominance by greatly expanding the size of the bureaucracy. A Sunni politician explained this policy to the British ambas-

[42] Letter from C. J. Edmonds to Sir Kinahan Cornwallis, 2 September 1941, reproduced in Elie Kedourie, "The Shiite Issue in Iraqi Politics, 1941," *MES* 24 (1988): 497–99. See also Report from 'Amara for the Period Ending 28 August 1941, FO 838/1; Report from 'Amara for the Period Ending 23 January 1943, FO 838/2.

[43] Uzri, *Dhikrayat*, 237–43; idem, *Mushkilat al-hukm*, 30, 136.

[44] Ayad al-Qazzaz, "Power Elite in Iraq, 1920–1958: A Study of the Cabinet," *MW* 61 (1971): 277–78.

sador Henry Mack, saying that whenever the need for a new official post arose, two had to be created, one for a Sunni and the other for a Shi'i.[45]

Whatever increase there was in Shi'i representation in the 1940s and 1950s, it did not end Sunni control of the state's key political institutions. This was nowhere more apparent than in the case of Salih Jabir, the first Shi'i to become Prime Minister in Iraq. Jabir was born in 1900 to a poor family in Nasiriyya. He developed close tribal connections through marriage with the daughter of the paramount shaykh of the Al Bu Sultan of the Hilla district. A lawyer by profession, Jabir served a few times as deputy to parliament and was also the provincial governor of Karbala and Basra. In 1933 and 1936 Jabir held ministerial positions in education and justice, respectively, and in 1941 he was the first Shi'i to be nominated Minister of Interior. Jabir built his career in government with the backing of Nuri Sa'id, who was Iraq's most influential politician in the 1940s and 1950s. It was on account of the support of a Sunni politician of the magnitude of Sa'id that Jabir was appointed Prime Minister in March 1947. Jabir advocated cooperation between Britain and Iraq, and his appointment reflected the perception of Sunni politicians that he would be the right man to deal with the difficult task of revising the Anglo-Iraqi treaty of 1930.

Yet the advent to power of an able Shi'i politician who embodied the political aspirations of the young generation of educated Shi'is caused a reaction among Sunnis. Sunni politicians in Baghdad accused Jabir of hiring too many foreign experts in order to satisfy Britain, and voiced their resentment toward his appointment of Shi'is to government positions. Jabir's nomination to the Premiership also alarmed the Sunnis in Basra, who were outnumbered by the Shi'is, and considered this new development as likely to increase Shi'i power in the state. Although the Portsmouth treaty which Jabir negotiated constituted an improvement of the 1930 treaty, it was repudiated by violent protests (known as the *wathba*) in Baghdad as soon as the news of its signature reached the capital in January 1948. In the face of very strong opposition to the treaty, as well as demonstrations by Sunni students whose main slogan was "down with the *rafidi*" (a derogative term meaning a Shi'i), Jabir resigned on 27 January. Subsequently, Shi'is in 'Amara and Basra were incensed by what they termed a Sunni plot against the Shi'i Premier, while the leading Sunni families in the latter city expressed their relief at Jabir's resignation. Although members of these families had previously informed the Regent that they considered the proposed treaty to be fair, many changed their mind following the demonstrations in Baghdad and declared that the treaty did not realize Iraqi national aims at all. Seeking to avoid laying too much stress on the part

---

[45] Mack to Bevin, 13 December 1950, FO 371/82408/1016–35. See also Henderson to Secretary of State, 15 July 1944, USNA, 890G.00/7–1544.

which Sunni-Shi'i rivalry had played in Jabir's fall, the Baghdad Sunni politicians appointed Sayyid Muhammad al-Sadr as Jabir's successor.[46]

Following the overthrow of Salih Jabir's government, a move to which Nuri Sa'id had given his consent, Jabir set to work to assert himself as a national leader independent of Sa'id's patronage. Between January and November 1949 a government led by Sa'id was in power. While Jabir was not included in the government, he remained a key political figure since he enjoyed the backing of a large number of Shi'i deputies from tribal areas in the middle Euphrates. In May U.S. officials reported that Jabir and the Shi'i deputies were considering withdrawing their support from Sa'id. The officials cited the spread of strong rumors about this possibility as one of the factors for the general feeling in Iraq that Sa'id's position had weakened, as well as an indication that Jabir might attempt to bring down Sa'id in order to succeed him as Prime Minister.[47]

Although after the downfall of Sa'id's government Jabir did not become Prime Minister, he continued to exercise influence in Iraqi politics. Between February and September 1950 Jabir acted as the Minister of Interior in the government of Tawfiq al-Suwaydi at a time at which five of the twelve ministers were Shi'is. Jabir and Sa'id vied for the control of Suwaydi's government and its policies. While Sa'id remained outside the government, he retained influence in it because of his intimate association with the Regent and the fact that five ministers belonged to his Constitutional Union Party. Yet Jabir eventually managed to dominate the government from his strategic position as Minister of the Interior. The fact that Shi'is held the important portfolios of interior, finance, and economics alarmed the Sunni politicians since it threatened to upset the balance of power in Iraq. The Sunni fears increased because of Shi'i efforts to cement their control of the Ministry of Education. Under the direction of the Shi'i Minister Sa'd 'Umar there was a drive to oust Sunnis from the remaining dominant positions which they still held in that Ministry. The Sunni Director of Higher Education was dismissed and his position abolished. The secretary of the Ministry, who acted as a liaison between the Ministry and the provincial directors of education, was dismissed as well. The Sunni politicians regarded these moves as part of the Shi'i effort to intensify their drive for greater political and administrative power, and they accused Jabir

---

[46] Tawfiq al-Suwaydi, *Mudhakkirati: nisf qarn min ta'rikh al-'iraq wa al-qadiya al-'arabiyya* (Beirut, 1969), 457–58; From American Consulate in Basra to Secretary of State, 9 December 1947, 8 January 1948, and 17 February 1948, USNA, 890G.00/12–947, 890G.00/1–2848, and 890G.00/2–1748; Mack to Bevin, 13 December 1950, FO 371/82408/1016–35; Majid Khadduri, *Independent Iraq, 1932–1958* (Oxford, 1960), 261–70; Kelidar, "The Shi'i Imami Community," 15.

[47] From American Embassy, Baghdad, to the Secretary of State, 16 May 1949, USNA, 890G.00/5–1649.

and the Foreign Minister Muhammad Fadil al-Jamali of giving their support to the Minister of Education in pursuing these anti-Sunni moves.[48]

Jabir's adoption of an overt pro-Shi'i attitude, and his increasing reliance on Shi'i support, led the Sunni ministers to accuse him of favoritism toward the Shi'i community. Jabir attempted to appeal to the Shi'i tribes in carrying out plans for progressive taxation and land reform, much to the dissatisfaction of the Sharifians and the Sunni urban landlord politicians. His attempts to undermine Sa'id's position in Iraqi politics further alienated the Sunni politicians. Sa'id's supporters in the government complained that Jabir and the Finance Minister 'Abd al-Karim al-Uzri were making "too many" Shi'i appointments to high office. There was also a reaction against Jabir among the older Sunni politicians, such as Jamil al-Midfa'i and 'Ali Jawdat al-Ayyubi, who considered Jabir as an "upstart, semi-educated Shia."[49] Clearly, the Sunni politicians were alarmed by the attempts of Shi'is to change the rules of the game in Iraq by recruiting their coreligionists to key positions in the state.

The rivalry between Jabir and Sa'id continued after the fall of Suwaydi's government. It caused repercussions not only in Baghdad but in the south as well, particularly in the provinces of 'Amara and the Muntafiq. While in late 1950 Shi'is in 'Amara expressed only a vague discontent against the Sunni politicians, which they had no intention of acting upon, by March 1951 the tensions between Shi'is and Sunnis had increased significantly. The Shi'is were annoyed by certain actions of the Baghdad Sunni politicians and regarded the removal of several Shi'i officials from their positions in 'Amara as a plan calculated to remove all Shi'is from government office in the province. Some Shi'is, who until 1951 had expressed their support of Sa'id and considered him a stronger and more effective leader than Jabir, warned that in case of a serious Shi'i-Sunni breach they would not be able to put their Shi'i identity aside.[50]

The struggle between Nuri Sa'id and Salih Jabir took a more elaborated form as the latter attempted to expand his power base by establishing his own political party early in 1951. Jabir was bitter over the fact that Sa'id had let him face the consequences of the ill-fated Portsmouth treaty alone. He sought to capitalize on the growing enmity between Shi'is and Sunnis, and to position his Popular Socialist Party as an alternative to the Constitu-

[48] From American Embassy, Baghdad, to the State Department, 18 May 1950, USNA, 787.00/5/850.

[49] Suwaydi, *Mudhakkirati*, 506–08; From American Embassy, Baghdad, to the State Department, 3 April 1950 and 10 June 1950, USNA, 787.D00/4–350 and 787.00/6–1050.

[50] Mack to Attlee, 25 September 1950, FO 371/82408/1016–28; From British Embassy in Baghdad to Consulate in 'Amara, 31 October 1950, FO 838/9; From British Consulate in 'Amara to Embassy in Baghdad, 10 December 1950 and 30 March 1951, FO 838/9 and FO 838/13. See also Elie Kedourie, "Anti-Shiism in Iraq under the Monarchy," *MES* 24 (1988): 249–50.

tional Union Party of Nuri Sa'id. Moreover, when Sa'id established his party late in 1949, Jabir apparently agreed that some of his Shi'i followers among the tribal deputies to parliament would join Sa'id's party. Yet, by late 1950 Jabir's followers found their membership in Sa'id's party of political advantage to them and they began shifting their personal allegiance from Jabir to Sa'id. Jabir was alarmed by the fluid identities of the Shi'i tribal deputies and considered their shift of allegiance to Sa'id as a threat to his own position. It was against this background that Jabir established his own party, acting against the advice of Jamali and Uzri. Although Jabir included several Sunnis in the national executive of the party, he relied predominantly on Shi'i support in the middle Euphrates. The party was reported to be particularly strong in the provinces of Basra, the Muntafiq, Diwaniyya, and Karbala. While it included a large group of wealthy Shi'i landowners, Jabir also attracted young Shi'is and members of the petite bourgeoisie by advocating agrarian reforms, as well as state sponsorship of agricultural and industrial development. A young Shi'i with close personal contacts to the party leaders told the U.S. political officer in Iraq that the main purpose of the Popular Socialist Party was to create a balance in Iraqi politics, which would enable Jabir to form his own government whenever a government led by Sa'id was forced to step down.[51]

Jabir attempted to achieve this balance by blocking Sa'id from controlling a majority in parliament. One of the major demands of the Popular Socialist Party since its establishment was the direct election of deputies to parliament. On various occasions in 1952 Jabir and his supporters criticized the Iraqi electoral law and the making up of official lists of candidates to parliament. They argued that direct elections free of government interference would be the first step toward improving political life in Iraq. In the light of strong pressures and disturbances in Baghdad, the Regent and Nuri Sa'id decided to call in the army. In November the Regent nominated the army chief of staff as Prime Minister. The new Premier imposed martial law and dissolved all political parties, but he also promised to change the electoral law, to conduct free and direct elections to parliament, and to lift martial law during the elections.[52] The elections took place in January 1953. In spite of its promises for free and direct elections, the government exercised tight control of the polls. Of the 135 seats available, 77 were set

[51] Reviews of Political Developments and Political Attitudes in Iraq, 9 January and 14 July 1950, USNA, 890G.00/12–3049 and 787.00/7–1450; From American Embassy, Baghdad, to the State Department, 23 April 1951, 18 June 1951, and 21 August 1952, USNA, 787.00/4–2351, 787.00/6–1851, and 787.00/8–2152. See also Uzri, *Dhikrayat*, 386–91; idem, *Mushkilat al-hukm*, 140.

[52] From American Embassy, Baghdad, to the State Department, 12 March, 24 July, and 5 November 1952, USNA, 787.00/3–1252, 787.00/7–2452, and 787.00/11–552; From American Embassy, Baghdad, to the State Department, 27 January 1953, USNA, 787.00/1–2753.

aside for deputies of the various political parties while the remaining 58 were to be filled by elected deputies. Jabir learned that the palace proposed to allot him only a few seats in comparison with the 70 which Sa'id's supporters were to gain. Faced with the blunt interference of Sa'id and the palace in the elections, Jabir found himself unable to influence the election of his own candidates. Jabir decided to boycott the elections, but he did not object later that a few of his supporters be nominated to parliament. The elections ended in a sweeping victory for Sa'id, who could rely on ninety votes in the new parliament compared to the six or so of Jabir's block.[53]

Salih Jabir's attempt to challenge Nuri Sa'id's authority resulted in a blow not only to his own political position, but to the aspirations of the younger generation of Shi'is as well. Sa'id was able to demonstrate his political power as well as his ability to influence the elections in his favor. The affairs surrounding the conduct of the elections also illustrated that the Regent was unwilling to allow a Shi'i leader to emerge as an alternative to Sa'id. Jabir's boycott of the elections caused resentment among Shi'i politicians, leading Jamali and Uzri to deplore the boycott. The results of the elections frustrated those young educated Shi'is who had looked to Jabir for leadership and were disappointed by his failure to realize their socioeconomic and political aspirations. Jabir was not included in any of the governments which were formed in Iraq following the elections of 1953. His declining political career ended in 1957 when he collapsed from a heart attack while criticizing Nuri Sa'id in a speech in the senate.

The Radical Options

The growing frustrations of the younger generation of Shi'is with their exclusion from the political process help explain the massive adherence of Shi'is to communism, particularly in the late 1940s and during the 1950s, as well as the revival of Shi'i Islamic ideology in Iraq in the 1960s and 1970s.

Although the roots of communist activity in Iraq can be traced to the late 1920s, communism became a factor in sociopolitical life mainly in the last two decades of the monarchy. The Iraqi Communist Party (ICP) drew its followers in the 1940s and 1950s primarily from Baghdad, as well as from the provinces of the Muntafiq, 'Amara, Hilla, and Basra. It also had concentrations of supporters in Najaf and Nasiriyya. The Shi'is constituted the majority of the rank and file of the ICP and dominated the organizations of

---

[53] Troutbeck to Eden, 10, 17, and 24 January 1953, FO 371/98777/1016–4, FO 371/98777/1016–8, and FO 371/98777/1016–10; Troutbeck to Churchill, 1 June 1953, FO 371/98777/1016–29.

the party. Their share within the high levels of the party apparatus grew from about 21 to 47 percent in the period between 1949 and 1955.[54]

The massive Shiʻi attraction to communism in the 1950s in particular reflected the search of Shiʻis for a political framework which would enable them to play a role in Iraqi national politics. While the growing socio-economic gaps within Iraqi society, the exodus of the Jews from Iraq, and the influx of a large number of migrants from the rural south to Baghdad were important factors contributing to the increase in the role that Shiʻis played in the ICP, it is the younger generation of educated Shiʻis that merits special attention here. The increase in Shiʻi adherence to communism in the 1950s may have been influenced by the downfall of Salih Jabir. Many of the young educated Shiʻi supporters of the ICP were the product of the expansion of state education in the Shiʻi areas in the 1930s, a policy for which Jamali was mainly responsible. These Shiʻis were impatient to occupy positions of influence in the country, to which they felt entitled because of their numerical superiority and advanced education. The increase in the appeal of communism to Shiʻis not only symbolized their opposition to the authority or actions of any one particular government, but to the entire order of Iraqi society and politics. Those Shiʻis who had been barred from access to power and therefore felt deprived of the opportunity for mobility in the state viewed communism as a vehicle through which they could effect change. Indeed, the massive adherence of young Shiʻis to the ICP did not reflect so much their propensity to communism, as it did their search for political participation and social influence, and their attempt to bring about a new political order in Iraq.[55]

The appeal of communism to the Shiʻis was closely related to the failure of Pan-Arabism to act as a unifying framework in Iraq. After a period of decline, Pan-Arabism had been revived in the early 1940s following the arrival in Iraq of Hajj Amin al-Husayni (the former mufti of Jerusalem) and the rise of Rashid ʻAli al-Gaylani to power. To the majority of Shiʻis, Pan-Arabism had little to offer, for the proponents of this ideology were mainly Sunni urban politicians whose interests differed from those of the Shiʻis. By contrast, communism was much more appealing to Shiʻis because of its stress on equality among the country's various classes and ethnic groups, as well as the solutions needed in order to change the socioeconomic and political realities in Iraq. Moreover, the strong opposition which the ICP

---

[54] Hanna Batatu, *The Old Social Classes and the Revolutionary Movements of Iraq*, 2d ed. (Princeton, N.J., 1982), 406, 465, 512, 649–50, 699, 704, 998.

[55] "La-qad ana an yashtarik al-shabab al-muthaqqaf fi al-hukm," *al-Hatif* 569 (9 October, 1949), 1; Troutbeck to Bevin, 13 December 1950, FO 371/82408/1016–35; Troutbeck to Churchill, 22 June 1953, FO 371/98777/1016–32; Batatu, *The Old Social Classes*, 469–70, 476–77; Sami Zubaida, *Islam, the People, and the State* (London, 1989), 94.

voiced both under the monarchy and after 1958 to the idea of including Iraq in a confederation of Arab states reflected the feelings of its large Shiʻi constituency. The majority of Shiʻis perceived the possibility that Iraq would be included in a confederation of Arab states (like the proposed Fertile Crescent Union of 1949–1950 and the United Arab Republic of Egypt and Syria in 1958 and the early 1960s) as a threat to their position in the country. Absorbed as they were in the task of winning political equality with the Sunnis, the Shiʻis feared that if Iraq became a part of an Arab confederation they would cease to be the majority of the population and recede once again into the status of a politically marginal sectarian group. The Shiʻi fear of the consequences of the application of Pan-Arabism, as well as their desire to influence Iraqi national politics, were thus important factors in the massive adherence of the Shiʻis to the ICP.[56]

If communism was one major vehicle through which Shiʻis sought to effect a radical political change in Iraq, Islam was another. The revival of Islamic ideology may be traced to the last years of the monarchy. In its early stages the movement reflected both the fear of the Shiʻi ulama of the impact of communism on the young generation of Shiʻis, whose attraction to the ICP symbolized their rebellion against the authority of their mujtahids, as well as government attempts to foster religion in order to curtail communism. On a number of occasions beginning in 1945 Shiʻi officials and mujtahids, notably Muhammad al-Husayn Kashif al-Ghita and ʻAbd al-Karim al-Zanjani, warned against the spread of communism in Iraq. The mujtahids pointed to the strong measures taken by the Pahlavis in Iran against communism and called upon the government to pursue similar tough policies in Iraq. In newspaper interviews and meetings with British officials, they urged the government and the British to cooperate with the mujtahids, to enhance the power of Najaf and Karbala, to revive religious studies and the pilgrimage to the shrine cities, and to invest in the Shiʻi south so as to combat communism in Iraq. British officials considered their meetings with the mujtahids important, and under their recommendation the mujtahid Muhammad al-Khalisi, a fervent anti-communist, was allowed to return to Iraq from his exile in Iran in order to preach against communism in his native city Kazimayn.[57]

[56] Situation in Iraq, Memorandum by Sir Kinahan Cornwallis, 26 April 1943, FO 371/35010/2755; Troutbeck to Bevin, 13 December 1950, FO 371/82408/1016–35; From Basra to Foreign Office, 8 January 1959, FO 371/140900/1015–13. See also Batatu, *The Old Social Classes*, 480, 815–18, 832; Albert Hourani, *Minorities in the Arab World* (Oxford, 1947, N.Y. reprint, 1982), 94–95; Sami Zubaida, "Community, Class, and Minorities in Iraqi Politics," in *The Iraqi Revolution of 1958: The Old Social Classes Revisited*, ed. Robert Fernea and Wm. Roger Louis (London, 1991), 199.

[57] Edmonds to Cornwallis, Baghdad, 20 January 1945, FO 624/72/323; "al-Imam kashif al-ghita' yu'lin ma yasirruhu wa-ma yasu'uhu, *al-Hatif* 463 (4 July 1947): 1; "Hadith li-samahat al-imam al-mujtahid al-akbar kashif al-ghita'," *al-Hatif* 839 (2 September 1950): 1;

Shi'i mujtahids began identifying communism with the government in Iraq only after the 14 July 1958 Revolution, which brought 'Abd al-Karim Qasim to power. An army officer, Qasim lacked a strong political power base and as the Prime Minister he relied mainly on mass popular support. Already during his first months in office Qasim found the ICP a useful political ally in resisting the pressures which Ba'thists in Iraq and Syria as well as Egypt's President Gamal 'Abd al-Nasir exerted on him to join the United Arab Republic. As the communists made their political support indispensable to Qasim, their influence in the country increased. By 1959, the Iraqi press and radio were largely dominated by communist propaganda, student groups were heavily penetrated, the streets could at short notice be filled by their well-disciplined cohorts, and important sections of several ministries were directly or indirectly dominated by them. Through their influence of Qasim's personal staff, the communists could also partially control access to the Premier. These developments produced a strong reaction from several segments of Iraqi society, including the Shi'i religious community.[58] By 1960 a significant anti-communist movement had already developed in Najaf, Karbala, and Hilla, with the grand mujtahid Muhsin al-Hakim sanctioning some of its activities. Exhortations to Muslims appeared in the non-communist press usually signed by *Jama'at al-'Ulama' fi al-Najaf al-Ashraf* (The Association of Najaf Ulama), some of whose members would form the nucleus of the Shi'i radical organization *al-Da'wa al-Islamiyya* (The Islamic Call). On 15 October 1960, *al-Fayha*, a Hilla weekly, published a memorandum signed by the Islamic Party, which included both Sunnis and Shi'is. Mounting a furious attack on the government for giving way to the communists, the writers identified Qasim as solely responsible for the policy of patronizing the movement in Iraq. Muhsin al-Hakim not only supported the memorandum, but himself issued a *fatwa* attacking communism by name and asserting that it was incompatible with Islam. The tension between the Shi'i mujtahids and the government was further fueled by the introduction of the Personal Status Law of December 1959, which applied to both Shi'is and Sunnis and accorded women equal rights with men in matters of intestate succession. The mujtahids regarded the law as an alarming indication of the power of communism in Iraq, and as a government measure aimed at further diminishing their influence over their Shi'i followers.[59]

Muhammad al-Husayn Kashif al-Ghita, *Muhawarat al-imam al-muslih kashif al-ghita' al-shaykh muhammad al-husayn ma'a al-safirayn al-baritani wa al-amiriki fi baghdad*, 4th ed. (Najaf, 1954), 8–10, 21–22; cf. Troutbeck to Eden, Baghdad, 16 October 1953, FO 371/104666/1016–57. See also Joyce Wiley, *The Islamic Movement of Iraqi Shi'as* (Boulder, 1992), 24.

[58] Annual Report for 1958, FO 371/140896/1011/1.

[59] British Embassy, Baghdad, 15 January 1959 and 18 October 1960, FO 371/140902/1015/19 and FO 371/149845/1015/126; Uriel Dann, *Iraq Under Qassem: A*

It was in the period of instability between the revolution of 1958 and the Ba'th second seizure of power in 1968 that Islam began attracting lay Shi'is in significant numbers, encroaching on communist influence in Iraq. Shi'is became disillusioned and bitter with the outcome of the revolution. The hopes of young educated Shi'is that the revolution and their adherence to communism would bring about a new political order and a change in the distribution of power did not materialize, and many continued to experience difficulties in finding government positions. The growing appeal of Islamic ideology to Shi'is was facilitated by the struggle for power between communists and Ba'thists, which further divided Iraqi society in the 1960s and diminished the power of communism in Iraq. The gradual decline of communism was evident in the fact that the Shi'i Thawra slums of Baghdad (known today as Madinat Saddam), where the ICP had derived much of its strength in the 1950s and early 1960s, became major sources of support of the *Da'wa* in the latter part of the 1960s and during the 1970s, and the Shi'i Islamic organization also attracted students and members of the intelligentsia.[60] Islam thus began filling the ideological and sociopolitical vacuum created by the decline of communism in Iraq.

The success of Islamic ideology in gaining ground among Shi'is was also closely connected to the failure of the Ba'th in generating mass appeal among them. One of the most distinctive features of Ba'thism was its advocacy of Pan-Arab ideology. Ba'thi proposals for Arab unity were unattractive to the majority of Shi'is, who identified Pan-Arabism with Sunnism and instead espoused Iraqi nationalism as their primary framework of identification. The only major exception was the group around Fu'ad al-Rikabi, the Shi'i founder of the Ba'th party in Iraq in 1952. Yet Rikabi recruited supporters mainly among his family and friends, and when he left the Ba'th in 1959 many of them left with him. By 1968 Sunni dominance had risen sharply within the Ba'th highest institutions. This process continued in subsequent years when the Republican Guard was composed almost entirely of Sunnis and the Iraqi core elite became mainly Sunni-Takriti. Although Shi'is did join the various institutions of the Ba'th after it had established itself in power in the 1970s, their participation mainly reflected a search for individual mobility as well as party co-optation and fear. Indeed, the rise of the Ba'th to power in Iraq did not lead to any real power sharing since the key state positions came under tight Sunni-Takriti control.[61]

Political History, 1958–1963 (New York, 1969), 144–45, 246–47, 300–303; "Ma'a al-sayyid muhsin al-hakim fi al-kufa," *al-'Irfan* 48 (1961): 728.

[60] Uzri, *Mushkilat al-hukm*, 182; Batatu, *The Old Social Classes*, esp. 831, 864, 942, 993, 1067; idem, "Shi'i Organizations in Iraq: al-Da'wah al-Islamiyah and al-Mujahidin," in *Shi'ism and Social Protest*, ed. Juan Cole and Nikki Keddie (New Haven, 1986), 184; John Devlin, *The Ba'th Party: A History from its Origins to 1966* (Stanford, 1976), 122, 125.

[61] Samir al-Khalil, *Republic of Fear: The Inside Story of Saddam's Iraq* (Berkeley, 1989,

As the Ba'th acted to control all aspects of public life, it further polarized Iraqi society, leading a growing number of lay Shi'is to consider Islamic ideology as a vehicle for political change which might succeed where communism had failed. While joining the *Da'wa*, Shi'is demonstrated a clear preference for a leadership in the organization composed of Iraqis of Arab origin and they took pride in Muhammad Baqir al-Sadr, whom they felt was one of their own. Sadr had a charismatic aura and was the most prominent intellectual figure among the Shi'i radical ulama of post monarchic Iraq. It is said that sometime in the 1960s he became the *Da'wa*'s head and later on its supreme jurisconsult (*faqih al-hizb*). Sadr began establishing his reputation with his works *Falsafatuna* (Our Philosophy) and *Iqtisaduna* (Our Economic System), which appeared in 1959 and 1961, respectively, and attempted to provide counter-arguments to the political and economic currents of the day. When thousands of Shi'is were expelled from Iraq to Iran in the late 1970s on account of their alleged "Persian connection," the focus of Sadr's discussions and sermons changed and his main concern became the Sunnization of the governing elite in Iraq. The surge in Islamic radicalism symbolized the response of Shi'is to the assault of the Sunni Ba'thi elite on their very identity as Iraqis. While the affairs surrounding the 1978–79 Iranian Revolution served as a major catalyst for stimulating Iraqi Shi'i anti-Ba'thi and anti-Saddam Husayn sentiments, it is doubtful whether there existed a genuine "Islamic revolutionary frame of mind" among the Iraqi Shi'i masses, let alone the socioeconomic infrastructure necessary for carrying out an Islamic revolution. Moreover, the concept of the jurist rule (*wilayat al-faqih*) as developed by Ruhallah Khumayni did not gain ground among the large majority of Iraqi Shi'i laymen affiliated with the *Da'wa*.[62] Also, members of the organization expressed allegiance to an Iraqi entity throughout the 1970s and 1980s, and did not support the idea that Iraq and Iran would merge.[63] The power of the *Da'wa* in Iraq was largely broken following the Ba'th massive campaign

---

N.Y. reprint, 1990), 212–16; Marion Farouk-Sluglett and Peter Sluglett, *Iraq Since 1958: From Revolution to Dictatorship* (London, 1987), 194–95, 197; Batatu, *The Old Social Classes*, 1078–79; Chibli Mallat, "Iraq," in *The Politics of Islamic Revivalism*, ed. Shireen Hunter (Bloomington, 1988), 72–73; cf. Amatzia Baram, "The Ruling Political Elite in Ba'thi Iraq, 1968–1986: The Changing Features of a Collective Profile," *IJMES* 21 (1989): 447–93.

[62] In this respect, we are still in need of a systematic study comparing the writings of Muhammad Baqir al-Sadr, particularly his *Mujtama'una* (Our Society) and *al-Islam yaqud al-hayat* (Islam Governs Life), with Khumayni's formulation of the jurist rule.

[63] Batatu, "al-Da'wah," 199; T. M. Aziz, "The Role of Muhammad Baqir al-Sadr in Shi'i Political Activism in Iraq from 1958 to 1980," *IJMES* 25 (1993): 209, 210, 218–19; Mallat, "Iraq," 75; Slugletts, *Iraq*, 196; Amatzia Baram, "The Radical Shi'ite Opposition Movements in Iraq," in *Religious Radicalism and Politics in the Middle East*, ed. Emmanuel Sivan and Menachem Friedman (New York, 1990), 95, 104; idem, "From Radicalism to Radical Pragmatism: The Shi'ite Fundamentalist Opposition Movements of Iraq," in *Islamic Fundamentalisms and the Gulf Crisis*, ed. James Piscatori (Chicago, 1991), 35–36.

against the organization, culminating in April 1980 in the execution of Sadr, the symbol of Shiʻi opposition to Saddam's Iraq.

The establishment of modern Iraq posed major dilemmas to the Shiʻis and sharpened the problem of their identity. The nature of their demands both under the monarchy and after 1958 reflected the search of Shiʻis for integration as well as power sharing with the Sunnis through increased influence in the government and the bureaucracy as well as the military. Unlike the Kurds, who constituted a distinct ethnic and national group, the large majority of Shiʻis were Arabs and their primary identity came to be Iraqi. Although at times they flaunted their sectarian identity, the Iraqi Shiʻis did not go so far as to advocate self-rule or a merger between Iraq and Iran, and instead stressed their Arab origins and attempted to accommodate their dual identity within the framework of the Iraqi state. This point was perhaps nowhere more apparent than in the Iran-Iraq War of 1980–1988 when Iraqi Shiʻis, who constituted the large majority of the rank and file of the infantry, demonstrated that their loyalty to the state overrode their sectarian allegiance and discontent with the Sunni Baʻthi government.

The strong Arab attributes of the Iraqi Shiʻis will become evident in the next two chapters in dealing with their rituals and cult of the saints.

PART THREE

The Transformation of Rituals and Religious Practices

Chapter Five

THE COMMEMORATION OF 'ASHURA'

In January 661, 'Ali ibn Abi Talib, the fourth caliph, was assassinated. Subsequently Mu'awiya ibn Abi Sufyan, the governor of Syria, managed to secure the caliphate for himself. He procured the abdication of 'Ali's son Hasan, perhaps by promising him that the caliphate would revert to Hasan after Mu'awiya's death. Hasan died eight years later, poisoned, it is rumored, by his own wife at the instigation of Mu'awiya. Mu'awiya died in 680 but prior to his death, he had arranged for his son Yazid to succeed him. Husayn, Hasan's younger brother, who no longer felt bound by Hasan's agreement with Mu'awiya, now decided to advance his claim to the caliphate.

Accompanied by a small party of companions as well as by his women-folk and children, Husayn set out from Mecca to Kufa, the people of which had urged him to come to them to lead the opposition against Yazid. He set out despite the fact that later on he had also received warnings that 'Ubaydallah ibn Ziyad, the governor of Basra, who was loyal to Yazid, had been able to take control of Kufa and kill Husayn's emissary to that city. Before reaching Kufa, Husayn and his party were intercepted by a military force that had been sent by Ibn Ziyad. Subsequently, Husayn and his party proceeded away from Kufa, reaching the plain of Karbala on the second day of the month of Muharram of the year 61 of the Hijra (2 October 680).

The following day, a force of several thousand men sent by Ibn Ziyad surrounded Husayn's camp and cut it off from any fresh water supply. The commander of the force, 'Umar ibn Sa'd, was instructed to prevent Husayn from leaving that place unless he had pledged loyalty to Yazid. Several days of negotiations elapsed before Ibn Ziyad sent new instructions to Ibn Sa'd. He ordered the latter to demand Husayn's unconditional submission or, failing that, to kill him and his followers. The battle took place on the tenth day of Muharram, which came to be known as 'Ashura'. With the exception of the women and his young child 'Ali Zayn al-'Abidin, who were taken captive, Husayn and all his other companions died on that day. The captives, along with Husayn's head, were sent to Yazid in Damascus. The women and the child were later released and allowed to travel to Medina.[1]

---

[1] For details see Mahmoud Ayoub, *Redemptive Suffering in Islam. A Study of the Devotional Aspects of 'Ashura' in Twelver Shi'ism* (The Hague, 1978), 93–120; Moojan Momen, *An Introduction to Shi'i Islam* (New Haven, 1985), 25–31.

rituals

Perhaps no other single event in Islamic history has played so central a role in shaping Shi'i identity as the martyrdom of Husayn and his companions at Karbala. The evocation of the affairs connected with the Karbala episode was left in Shi'ism for the rituals of remembrance that developed around the annual commemoration of 'Ashura'. Over a period of twelve centuries there developed five major rituals around the battle of Karbala. These rituals include the memorial services, the representation of the battle of Karbala in the form of a play, the flagellation, the public mourning processions, and the visitation of Husayn's tomb particularly on the occasions of the tenth day of 'Ashura' and the fortieth day after the battle.[2] The Muharram observances assumed many forms, reflecting the diverse cultures and ethnic groups among which they developed. The particular form of the commemoration of 'Ashura' in Iraq is the concern of this chapter.

THE NATURE OF THE MUHARRAM OBSERVANCES

In contrast with Iran, where the Muharram rites were observed in public from the sixteenth century, Shi'i sources maintain that before the Ottomans resumed direct control of Iraq in 1831 the Mamluks prohibited the commemoration of 'Ashura' in the country. The Mamluk prohibition probably affected the mixed cities of Baghdad, Basra, Kazimayn, and Samarra in particular where government control was more effective. As a result, the memorial services (*majalis al-ta'ziya*) were held in underground cellars inside private houses.[3] While I do not have any data about Karbala, it seems that in Najaf the services were also observed on a very limited scale before the nineteenth century. The first known person to widely promote and establish the services in Najaf during Ottoman rule was said to be Shaykh Nassar ibn Ahmad al-'Abbasi (d. around 1824/5). Apparently he seized the opportunity of the Ottoman-Iranian peace treaty signed in 1823, announcing the sponsorship of memorial services in his home. In subsequent years, this practice gained impetus as many other people, both in Najaf and elsewhere, followed 'Abbasi's example.[4]

The development of the Muharram observances in Iraq coincided with the spread of Shi'ism in the country during the nineteenth century, thus greatly stimulating the process of conversion of the tribes. The Ottoman

---

[2] Yitzhak Nakash, "An Attempt to Trace the Origin of the Rituals of 'Ashura'," *WI* 33 (1993): 161–81.

[3] On Kazimayn see Agha Buzurg Tihrani, *Tabaqat a'lam al-shi'a*, 5 vols. (Najaf and Beirut, 1954–1971), 2:170. On Baghdad see 'Ali al-Wardi, *Lamahat ijtima'iyya min ta'rikh al-'iraq al-hadith*, 6 vols. (Baghdad, 1969–1978), 2:110–11.

[4] Agha Buzurg Tihrani, *al-Dhari'a ila tasanif al-shi'a*, 26 vols. (Tehran and Najaf, 1936–1986), 9,1:32; 'Ali al-Khaqani, *Shu'ara' al-ghari aw al-najafiyyat*, 2d ed., 12 vols. (Qum, 1988), 12:324; Ja'far al-Mahbuba, *Madi al-najaf wa-hadiruha*, 3 vols. (Najaf, 1955–1958), 3:479.

governor 'Ali Rida (1831–1842) not only permitted the conduct of the memorial services, but attended at least one of them in 1832. The Ottoman permission for the Muharram rites also led to the spread of the public processions in Iraq, the first of which was said to have taken place in Kazimayn after 1831 and to have been initiated by Shaykh Baqir ibn al-Shaykh Asadallah. In permitting the Muharram rites, the Ottomans probably intended to placate the Shi'is in Iraq in the face of the expansionist policies of Muhammad 'Ali of Egypt. Later in Ottoman rule, some officials and Sunni ulama in Iraq, notably Midhat Pasha and Ahmad Shakir al-Alusi, sought to restrict and even abolish the Muharram rites.[5] These attempts were unsuccessful, however, and Shi'i emissaries in Iraq were able to promote the Muharram rites almost uninterruptedly among the tribes until the rise of the modern state.

The memorial services were closely connected with the narration of the events of Karbala (the *rawza-khwani*, known also in Iraq as *qraya*, a colloquial form of *qira'a*). Visiting Najaf and Karbala during 1887, the Iranian sufi 'alim Pirzadeh described the various forms of the *rawza-khwani* in both cities. From his account it is clear that by that time the services were not confined to houses alone but were also held in mosques, religious schools, and the shrines themselves. The nature of the recitations, and the language used by the leader of the sermon (the *rawza-khwan*, known in Iraq also as the *mu'min*) differed, being a reflection of the specific ethnic composition, geographical origin, and the class attributes of the participating audience. Thus, groups of pilgrims from Na'in, Azarbayjan, and India each conducted its own service according to the custom observed in their home country, exhibiting various degrees of religious piety.[6]

The poetry used in the recitations reflected the moral values and ethnic attributes of the various Shi'i communities. The majority of Iraq's Shi'i population were Arabs of nomadic origin and only recent converts to Shi'i Islam. The attributes of ideal manhood of the Arabs (*muruwwa*), that is, masculinity, courage, pride, honor, and chivalry, played a dominant role in shaping their moral values and worldview. The strong Arab tribal character of Shi'i society in Iraq was evident in two major genres in Iraqi colloquial poetry, the *abudhiyya* and the *hosa*. Whereas the first genre was used among the tribesmen mainly to describe excellence and prestige, the latter was commonly used on occasions of grief, as well as in tribal ceremonies and wars as a means for emphasizing glory and generating enthusiasm. It was only natural that these two genres were also used extensively in the

---

[5] Wardi, *Lamahat*, 2:110–11; 'Abbas al-'Azzawi, *Ta'rikh al-'iraq bayna ihtilalayn*, 8 vols. (Baghdad, 1935–1956), 7:239; Selim Deringil, "The Struggle against Shi'ism in Hamidian Iraq: A Study in Ottoman Counter-Propaganda," *WI* 30 (1990): 52, 59.

[6] Hajji Pirzadeh, *Safarnama-yi hajji pirzadeh*, ed. Hafez Farman-Farmayan, 2 vols. (Tehran, 1963), 1:350–52.

Iraqi Shi'i poetry that developed around the theme of the battle of
Karbala.[7]

The strong Arab tribal character of Iraqi Shi'i society found embodiment
in the image of 'Abbas, son of the imam 'Ali and Husayn's half-brother, as
portrayed in the Arabic texts, poetry, and plays that narrated and reenacted
the affairs of 'Ashura'. Early Shi'i accounts of the battle (tenth and thirteenth centuries) mention 'Abbas very briefly. They relate that 'Abbas was
one of Husayn's companions in the battle and that he was killed while
attempting to bring water from the Euphrates to his brother. Abu al-Faraj
al-Isfahani (d. 967) also adds that 'Abbas was a handsome man, and that he
rode a noble horse and carried Husayn's banner.[8] By contrast, in nine-
teenth- and twentieth-century Arab Shi'i accounts of the battle, the character of 'Abbas is well developed and he emerges as a central figure in the
battle. It is related that the imam 'Ali desired a son who would excel in
horse racing. He therefore took a bedouin woman from the tribe of
Kilab whose father was considered the bravest man and best rider among
all the Arab tribes. His son, 'Abbas, did indeed excel in horse racing, and
possessed the ideal attributes of chivalry and heroism. 'Abbas loved his
brother Husayn and defended him in the battle of Karbala. When Husayn
urged his family members and followers to flee before it was too late,
'Abbas answered him: "We shall not do that, for how can we live after your
death?"[9]

The Arabic texts and poetry of the memorial services emphasized the
strong physical attributes of 'Abbas, comparing him to a fearless lion.
Indeed, he is not presented as a symbol of religious piety, but rather as the
protector of Husayn, the Hashimite family, and religion. The audience is
not only told that 'Abbas rode a noble horse and carried the banner of
Husayn, but also that on account of his stature, his tall legs would leave a
mark on the ground even when he was riding his horse. In the battle of
Karbala, 'Abbas demonstrated his courage by taking upon himself the
dangerous mission of breaking the siege of Husayn's camp and bringing
water to his thirsty brother, and to the women and children. 'Abbas was

[7] 'Ali al-Khaqani, *Funun al-adab al-sha'bi*, 8 vols. (Baghdad, 1962–1968), 1:7, 55, and
2:38–39. See also Anatoly Kovalenko, "Le Martyre de Husayn dans la Poésie Populaire
d'Iraq" (Ph.D. diss., Université de Genève, 1979), 170, 174.

[8] Ahmad ibn A'tham al-Kufi, *Kitab al-futuh*, 8 vols. (Beirut, 1986), 3:129; Abu al-Faraj al-
Isfahani, *Maqatil al-talibiyyin*, 2d ed. (Tehran, 1970), 84–85; Muhammad ibn Ja'far ibn
Nima al-Hilli, *Muthir al-ahzan* (Najaf, 1950), 53–54; Radi al-Din 'Ali ibn Musa ibn Ta'us, *al-
Luhuf fi qatla al-tufur* (Tehran, 1904), 77–78, 103–4. 'Abbas is also mentioned briefly in the
account provided by the Sunni historian al-Tabari (d. 923): Abu Ja'far Muhammad ibn Jarir
al-Tabari, *Ta'rikh al-tabari*, 11 vols. (Cairo, 1960–1963), 5:412.

[9] 'Abd al-Razzaq al-Musawi al-Muqarram, *al-'Abbas ibn al-imam amir al-mu'minin 'ali
ibn abi talib* (Najaf, n.d.), 69; Muhsin al-Amin, *A'yan al-shi'a*, 56 vols. (Beirut, 1960–1963),
37:75–80.

attacked by several warriors but he managed to scatter them "like a wolf dispersing a flock of sheep." Although he was later ambushed and his right hand cut off, he continued to fight bravely. Holding the sword in his left hand, he faced his attackers chanting:

> By God, even though you cut off my right hand
> I shall forever defend my religion
> And I shall [protect] an absolutely true imam [Husayn]
> the grandson of the righteous and trustworthy Prophet.

'Abbas was finally overcome by his attackers, and, this, the audience is told, signaled the turning point in the battle. Learning of the death of 'Abbas, Husayn is described as saying: "Now my back has been broken and my strength has diminished."[10]

As the memorial services spread in Iraq in the nineteenth century, families and individuals began sponsoring them. This act was not only intended to express the religious piety of the host but also to allow him to gain esteem and higher social status.[11] Studying the Shi'i tribe al-Shabana and the rural community of Daghara in southern Iraq between 1956 and 1958, the Ferneas observed that individuals sponsored recitations as a sign of status and in fulfillment of a vow. The holy month of Ramadan, and the period in the Islamic calendar between Muharram up to the 20th of Safar, were especially favored for holding the sessions. The length of the sessions depended on the host and the amount of money he could afford to spend toward that end. The shaykh of al-Shabana, for example, used to engage the services of a reader for an entire month. The women of government officials also used to host recitations for the women of the community. This occasion afforded women a unique opportunity to assemble together and to attend a social event that extended beyond their immediate neighborhood.[12]

The recitations highlighted the important role of the *rawza-khwan* as a medium for the reenactment of the battle of Karbala. Pirzadeh described the impact of the *rawza-khwan* on an audience in Najaf. He wrote that the

[10] See the poetry of the Iraqi Shi'i *rawza-khwan* Salih al-Hilli in 'Ali al-Khaqani, *Shu'ara' al-hilla aw al-babiliyyat*, 5 vols. (Baghdad, 1951–1953), 3:181–82, 190–92. See also Muqarram, *al-'Abbas*, 162–63; Sharif al-Jawahiri, *Muthir al-ahzan fi ahwal al-a'imma al-ithna 'ashara* (Najaf, 1966), 83–84; Husayn al-Bahrani, *al-Fawadih al-husayniyya wa al-qawadih al-bayyiniyya*, 2d ed. (Najaf, n.d.), 319–20; Muhsin al-Amin, *al-Majalis al-saniyya fi manaqib wa-masa'ib al-'itra al-nabawiyya*, 5 vols. (Damascus, 1954), 1:138–44; 'Abd al-Rida Kashif al-Ghita, *al-Anwar al-husayniyya wa al-sha'a'ir al-islamiyya*, 2 pts. (Bombay, 1927/8), 2:62–65.

[11] Wardi, *Lamahat*, 2:111.

[12] Robert Fernea, *Shaykh and Effendi: Changing Patterns of Authority among the El Shabana of Southern Iraq* (Cambridge, Mass., 1970), 70–71; Elizabeth Fernea, *Guests of the Sheik*, 2d ed. (New York, 1969), 113.

narrator, much like a preacher, would use moving language to bring his audience to tears and to transform their state of mind.[13] Particularly in Najaf and Karbala, the profession of *rawza-khwani* provided social esteem and income for many low-ranked ulama whose livelihood depended on the number of sermons they delivered. Indeed, even in the twentieth century it was still quite common practice for ulama and *sayyids* from the two cities to perform as narrators during the month of Ramadan and the first ten days of Muharram in villages, and in the houses of shaykhs and other people who could afford to pay for this service.[14] Some ulama were more highly sought after and paid accordingly, the criteria being their command of Arabic rhetoric and the intensity with which they coerced the mourners into weeping.

The representation of the battle of Karbala in the form of a play (the *shabih*) was transmitted from Iran to the shrine cities in Iraq. Relying on local informants, the writer of a British report on the Muharram observances in Kazimayn indicated that this ritual was introduced into that city in the late eighteenth century.[15] The permission given in 1831 by the governor 'Ali Rida to hold the memorial services, and the arrival of large numbers of Iranian pilgrims at the shrine cities, probably helped the spread of the play in Iraq. Najafis maintain that during the nineteenth century the *shabih* was performed in the courtyards of mosques in front of the city's notables and *sayyids*. At times, even some Ottoman soldiers who were based in the city participated in the play.[16]

There were fundamental differences in the scope, the metaphors, and the theatrical forms of the play in Iraq as compared with its Iranian counterpart. The dialogues in the Iraqi play were minimal, and it is doubtful whether any textual format was ever developed, let alone published. Among the rural and tribal communities the play often took the form of a carnival. The impact on the audience was achieved largely through the emphasis laid on the use of live metaphors, the movement of the characters, and the participation of a large number of players drawn from the local population. In contrast to Iraq, the texts and theatrical dimensions of the play in Iran were highly developed. The *shabih* in Iran reached its zenith during the Qajar period (1794–1925). Under royal patronage the straightforward form of the *shabih* gave way to a more theatrical form, the *ta'ziya* play, which was enacted on stage. The play evolved into a complex melodrama, particularly in Tehran and in other large cities in Iran. It stopped

[13] Pirzadeh, *Safarnama*, 1:331, 336–37.

[14] Extract from Special Service Officer, Basra, Report no. 484/6, 16 April 1925, Air 23/379; 'Ali al-Wardi, *Wu"az al-salatin* (Baghdad, 1954), 71; 'Ala al-din Jasim al-Bayati, *al-Rashidiyya: dirasa antrobolojiyya ijtima'iyya* (Najaf, 1971), 124–25.

[15] Intelligence Report no. 21, 15 September 1921, FO 371/6353/11315.

[16] Talib 'Ali al-Sharqi, *al-Najaf al-ashraf: 'adatuha wa-taqaliduha* (Najaf, 1978), 234.

short of becoming an Iranian national theater early in the twentieth century.[17]

Elizabeth Fernea described the *shabih* held in the Shi'i village of Sufra in southern Iraq. The occasion drew many people from the neighboring villages and tribal settlements. The play took place in an open field, with as many as sixty costumed players riding horses taking part. The players were divided into two groups representing the camps of Husayn and Ibn Sa'd. The audience was also involved in the reenactment of the battle. Men and women cheered the forces of Husayn and hissed those of Ibn Sa'd. The play culminated in the passing of rifles from the audience to the players, who would then shoot bullets over each other's heads.[18] Another description of a *shabih* in a mixed village in southern Iraq illustrates how the strong physical attributes of 'Abbas were exhibited in the play. Mahmud al-Durra, a Sunni who served as the chief of staff of the Iraqi army for some time from late 1938, described in his memoirs the play as celebrated in al-Bughayla al-Nu'maniyya. As a child in that village, he was particularly impressed by the figure of 'Abbas, who was "chopping off the heads of his Umayyad opponents, exhibiting rare fearlessness and bravery."[19]

It is evident both from Fernea's and Durra's descriptions that the moral values and cultural attributes of the tribesmen were built into the play itself. Fernea's description in particular shows the transformation of a traditional tribal *hosa* into a type of a *shabih*. The *hosa* was the most common form of celebration among the Arab tribes of southern Iraq. It consisted of clamorous receptions on occasions of weddings, circumcisions, and holidays, and was also intended to signal death and to announce war.[20] The fusion between the *shabih* and the *hosa* following the conversion of the tribesmen, is an indication that Shi'ism did not fully permeate Iraqi tribal values and social practices.

As may be gathered from the text published by Lewis Pelly in 1879, the image of 'Abbas in the Iranian play differed greatly from the one attached to him in Iraq. Whereas the Iraqi play (very much like the texts of the memorial services) stressed his attributes of ideal manhood, the scene in the Iranian play where 'Abbas is described asking for Husayn's permission to bring water portrays him as a man seeking martyrdom. Full of emotion, 'Abbas begs Husayn to permit him to go, saying that against the suffering of the children he is melting away from sorrow. He adds: "Be kind enough to permit me to be offered for thee! It is customary for friends to be sacrificed

[17] Farrokh Gaffary, "Evolution of Rituals and Theater in Iran," *IS* 17 (1984): 371.

[18] Elizabeth Fernea, *Guests*, 203–4, 206.

[19] Mahmud al-Durra, *Hayat 'iraqi min wara' al-bawwaba al-sawda'* (Cairo, 1976), 23–24.

[20] For details on the *hosa* see Bayati, *al-Rashidiyya*, 106n; 'Abbas al-'Azzawi, *'Asha'ir al-'iraq*, 4 vols. (Baghdad, 1937–1956), 3:72.

for their beloved ones!" 'Abbas later on reveals his goal to his slave: "O faithful slave, I intend to set out at once for a journey to Paradise. That is what I seriously have at heart."[21]

While face-slapping was a traditional symbol for expressing personal grief and pain in Arab societies, the practice of flagellation was not observed in the shrine cities before the nineteenth century. The flagellation included the use of swords and knives for head-cutting (*tatbir*), chain-flagellation (*zinjil*), as well as harsh breast-beating. The Iraqi Shi'i mujtahid Muhammad Mahdi Qazwini is cited by Werner Ende as claiming around 1927 that the use of iron was initiated "about a century ago" by people not well versed in the rules of the Shari'a.[22] Also, Iraqi Shi'i advocates of flagellation do not seem to be able to point to any unambiguous reference to the practice in the works of pre-nineteenth-century mujtahids. The first clear mention is a reference to Shaykh Khidr ibn Shallal Al Khuddam al-'Afkawi al-Najafi (d. 1839/40). In a work entitled *Abwab al-jinan wa-basha'ir al-ridwan* (The Gates to Paradise and the Good Omens for Delight), Ibn Shallal is cited by 'Abd al-Rida Kashif al-Ghita as writing: "It is permissible to flagellate for [Husayn's] sake and to mourn his death in any manner even if [the flagellant] knows that he would die on account of it. . . . Many people consider life less valuable than money, which the [Shi'i] religious creed, on account of its own needs, ordered people to spend excessively for [Husayn's] commemoration and for his visitation."[23] Ibn Shallal, it should be noted, is described by Shi'i biographers as a "pious ascetic." According to Agha Buzurg Tihrani, Ibn Shallal related that he wrote *Abwab al-jinan* (probably around 1826/7) in a pen which he had received in a dream from the imam 'Ali. Ibn Shallal himself also recounted that this work was not in line with what was the accepted norm at that time.[24]

A distinction should be made between the various forms and symbolic meanings of flagellation in Iraq, the different ethnic and group attributes of the participants, and the type of reward sought by the flagellants. Cutting the head with a sword or a knife constituted the most violent form of flagellation. Its scope, however, was limited, and the number of participants in this act was usually small. Thus, a British report on 'Ashura' in Najaf in 1919 mentions a party of only one hundred engaged in cutting their heads.[25]

[21] For the full scene see Colonel Sir Lewis Pelly, *The Miracle Play of Hasan and Husayn*, 2 vols. (London, 1879), 1:250–69. The citations are on 255, 257.

[22] Werner Ende, "The Flagellations of Muharram and the Shi'ite 'Ulama'," *Isl* 55 (1978): 27–28.

[23] 'Abd al-Rida Kashif al-Ghita, *al-Anwar al-husayniyya*, 2:71.

[24] Tihrani, *al-Dhari'a ila tasanif al-shi'a*, 1:74–75. See also Mahbuba, *Madi al-najaf*, 2:264–65.

[25] Great Britain, Administration Report of the Shamiyya Division, 1919, CO 696/2.

The practice of head-cutting was transmitted to the shrine cites in the nineteenth century by Shi'is of Turkish origin and was confined in Iraq mainly to Shi'i Turks and Persians. Najafi oral history relates that head-cutting was not observed in Karbala and Najaf before the mid-nineteenth century. It was first practiced in Iraq by Shi'i pilgrims from the Caucasus, Azarbayjan, or Tabriz. These pilgrims, who were probably Qizilbash, arrived in Karbala equipped with their personal weapons, notably the swords (*qamat*), which they used for head-cutting. It is also said that while Najafis began observing head-cutting sometime in the 1850s, the organizers and participants in this activity were drawn mainly from among the Turkish and Persian residents of the town.[26] From British, Shi'i, and Sunni descriptions of this ritual it seems that Arabs did not take part in it, the participants being a group of Shi'i extremists of Turco-Iranian origin. Thus, Thomas Lyell, who served for some time as a British officer in Najaf, wrote that "in Najaf, which is full of Persians, this ceremony is largely confined to them, more particularly to the Turcoman tribe." The Iraqi Shi'i poet Kazim al-Dujayli identified the head-cutters as dervishes, and Mahmud al-Durra identified them as reckless fedayeen, Iranians or Kurdish groups from the mountains of Pusht-i kuh.[27]

Both Lyell and Dujayli provide close descriptions of this ritual of head-cutting in Najaf and Karbala, respectively. Lyell recorded in detail the preparations for the ritual. During the first ten days of '*Ashura*', the participants would adopt every conceivable device for working themselves up to a pitch of frenzy, tenderly nursing their swords and vying with each other in sharpening them. On the ninth of Muharram, yards of new white linen or cotton would be brought, and made up into long robes which extended down to the feet. It was the custom in the shrine cities to approach government officials for money to purchase this material. Having procured their white garments, the Turcomans would pass the whole night in the coffee-shops, eating vast quantities of dates and drinking large quantities of tea, which raised their blood pressure. The next morning, they would gather at 'Ali's shrine in anticipation for the ritual itself.[28]

Dujayli described the head-cutters as the "lovers of Husayn," who sought to sacrifice themselves for him in order to gain a reward or a blessing from the imam. On the tenth of Muharram, the would-be martyrs dressed themselves in white cloths, which symbolized the shrouds of a corpse. Their heads shaved so that nothing could diminish the effectiveness of the blades, each took a sword and they all headed toward Husayn's

---

[26] Sharqi, *al-Najaf al-ashraf*, 220–23.

[27] Thomas Lyell, *The Ins and Outs of Mesopotamia* (London, 1923), 67; Kazim al-Dujayli, "'Ashura' fi al-najaf wa-karbala'," *Lughat al-'Arab* 2 (1913): 287; Durra, *Hayat 'iraqi*, 24.

[28] Lyell, *Ins and Outs*, 67–69.

shrine. Inside, a reenactment of the battle would take place in front of a large audience. At the moment of climax, the flagellants would respond to a signal and start beating their heads with the edge of their swords. They would then exit from the shrine and march in a procession through the streets of the city. The crowd would excite the flagellants and some Arabs would shoot in the air. This would incite the flagellants further and their beating would accelerate. Some would consequently faint and collapse, others would die. This death was considered most rewarding by the flagellants and even by some of the city dwellers. Some women would seek a piece of the blood-stained garment of the martyr, considering it a relic possessing a sort of blessing. Several attempts by the Ottoman government to put an end to this violent practice in Karbala were not successful because of the strong objection of the flagellants themselves. It was only in 1899, after their leader Muhammad 'Ali Tabrizi left Karbala, that government officials were able to confine the use of swords to the camp of the flagellants, providing them with fake swords to be used later in the shrine and in the streets of the city.[29]

That the observance of harsh breast-beating and chain-flagellation only came to Iraq in the nineteenth century may be gathered from several pieces of information. Shi'is assert that Shaykh Baqir ibn Shaykh Asadallah al-Dizfuli (d. 1839/40) was the first to introduce breast-beating at the shrine of Kazimayn.[30] Najafi oral history relates that the practice of chain-flagellation was introduced into the city in 1919 by the British governor of Najaf, who had served beforehand in Kermanshah and observed the practice there. It is also said that chain-flagellation took place initially in the Mishraq quarter and that the first such procession paraded in Najaf in 1919, mourning the death of the grand mujtahid Kazim Yazdi.[31] If this assertion is true, the British act was probably intended to modify the Muharram rituals and to reduce violence in substituting the practice of head-cutting with chain-flagellation.

While chain-flagellation and breast-beating were more widespread in Iraq than head-cutting, they were not observed by all major segments of the Shi'i Arab population. These acts were part of the public processions (known in Iraq as al-mawakib al-husayniyya, and mawakib al-'aza' or al-subaya) held during the first ten days of Muharram in the villages, towns, and shrine cities. In the rural area around Daghara, Robert Fernea observed that men and boys participated in the mourning procession of the tenth of Muharram. Stripped to the waist, they marched in procession, chanting and beating themselves rhythmically with lengths of chain and leather whips. The tribesmen of the Shabana, however, did not participate

[29] Dujayli, "'Ashura'," 286–95.
[30] Tihrani, A'lam al-shi'a, 2:170; Wardi, Lamahat, 2:111.
[31] Sharqi, al-Najaf al-ashraf, 239–40.

in these processions. While the shaykh of the tribe took pride in sponsoring the memorial services, he would not support the flagellation since this practice was not considered to be in line with proper tribal activity and moral values.[32]

In Iraq, men used the flagellation to exhibit their masculinity, a point which both Iraqi Sunnis and Shi'is have stressed. In Bughayla, Durra recounted, the majority of the men would march in procession, slapping their bare breasts with their hands. Following them was another group of villagers, their black gallabiyyas covering only the lower part of their bodies. Using iron chains, the men of this group would beat their bare backs in a rhythm set by their leader. The rhythm of the self-flagellation accelerated as the excitement of the crowd and the cries of the women grew louder. The flagellants would then look at the women who stood on the roofs of the houses, and, proudly, they would display the harsh marks left on their bodies. The Iraqi Shi'i sociologist 'Ali al-Wardi also pointed to the role of flagellation in flaunting a man's masculinity in Iraq. A man participating in a procession of flagellation would feel lofty and proud for doing so, knowing that he was being noticed by the crowd. This exhibition of machismo increased whenever he could feel that he was being watched by women. Their crying would drive the man to feel as if he was a victorious conqueror leading a great army. The function of the flagellation in flaunting a man's masculinity, Wardi argued, was an important factor in preserving the vitality of the processions in Iraq in the twentieth century.[33] The use of self-flagellation to exhibit machismo has also been noted in India and Lebanon. Relating his own experience as a young Shi'i mourner in Bombay, Mohammed Fazel wrote: "The constant thrashing that our breasts received turned them red . . . . No mourner talked openly about the stigmata, which attracted many secretive, envious glances."[34] In Nabatiyya, the need to exhibit machismo was also considered important and young men would use the flagellation to attract attention.[35]

The different ethnic identities of the Shi'i population and their attitude toward the government surfaced during the public processions in Iraq. The processions as celebrated in Kazimayn demonstrated the difference between Persians and Arabs. In the Ottoman period, the Persian participants used to perform before the Iranian consul-general, thereby stressing their Persian identity and strong communal sense. The Arabs, in contrast, used to act before the custodian of the shrine, who was a government nominee. The fundamental difference in the attitude of the Persian and Arab participants to the legitimacy of the Iraqi monarchy surfaced as early as 1921. In

[32] Robert Fernea, *Shaykh*, 71–72.
[33] Durra, *Hayat 'iraqi*, 23; Wardi, *Lamahat*, 2:111.
[34] Mohammed Fazel, "The Politics of Passions: Growing Up Shia," *IS* 21 (1988): 47.
[35] Hafiz Adib al-Zayn, "'Ashura' fi al-nabatiyya," *al-'Irfan* 62 (1974): 134.

that year King Faysal attended the processions of 10 Muharram in Kazimayn. It is reported that Sayyid Muhammad al-Sadr wished to alter the
occasion and oblige both the Arab and the Persian teams to perform before
the King. While the Arabs did so, the Persians refused to acknowledge the
King's authority, insisting on acting only in front of the Iranian consul-
general's box.[36]

For the most part, however, the public processions served to confirm the
existing social order rather than to deny it. The processions reflected the
various aspects of life and the structure of Shi'i communities in different
localities in Iraq. This ritual was a kind of symbolic language which com-
municated various coded messages. It articulated the relationship between
the different components of society, marked the religious status of learned
families and sayyids, and ranked tribal shaykhs, notables, and ordinary
people according to their relative socioeconomic position within the community. The mourning processions in Najaf, for example, were also known
as the "processions of the crafts" (mawakib al-asnaf). Members of the
various professions in the city, as well as the religious students, the servants
in the shrine, and the sayyids, used to parade in groups, each formed
according to the unique class and professional affiliations of the participants.[37] Leading religious, tribal, and other elite families often sponsored
the processions in their community. In doing so, they not only sought to
gain social esteem, but to preserve their status and authority within the
community. This function of the Muharram rites in reinforcing class, communal, and guild identity has also been observed in southern Lebanon and
in various locations in India.[38]

The great procession in Karbala on the 20th of Safar (ziyarat al-arba'in,
marking the fortieth day after the battle of Karbala) acted as the meeting
point of the various Shi'i classes as well as urban and rural communities in
Iraq. This occasion, which in the nineteenth century attracted many new
tribal converts to the city, was intended to increase Shi'i communal solidarity in Iraq. It also helped maintain the socioeconomic contacts between
Karbala and its hinterland as well as the city's status as the focus of devotion for the Shi'i believers. These functions are discussed in the next chapter, which deals with the Shi'i visitation of the shrine cities. Here, I will
point to the importance of the procession of the 20th of Safar in concluding
the annual commemoration of 'Ashura'. This event enabled various classes

---

[36] Intelligence Report no. 21, 15 September 1921, FO 371/6353.

[37] Sharqi, al-Najaf al-ashraf, 217.

[38] Emrys Peters, "A Muslim Passion Play: Key to a Lebanese Village," AM 198 (1956):
178–79; idem, "Aspects of Rank and Status among Muslims in a Lebanese Village," in
Mediterranean Countrymen, ed. Julian Pitt-Rivers (Paris, 1963), 197–99; Michael Gilsenan,
Recognizing Islam: An Anthropologist's Introduction (London, 1982), 62, 69; Mrs. Meer
Hasan 'Ali, Observations on the Mussalmauns of India (Oxford, 1917), 53; David Pinault,
The Shiites: Ritual and Popular Piety in a Muslim Community (New York, 1992), 83–114.

and communities to reassert their status and relative importance within the general fabric of Iraqi Shi'i society.

The participants in the local processions would practice in advance for the great procession in Karbala. The expenses of each team were usually assumed by a sponsor (sahib al-'aza'). He would buy such special cloth and equipment as might be needed, and would contribute money to send the team to the great procession in Karbala. The cloth and equipment were stored every year, being the property of the sponsoring individual or family.[39] The number of teams sent from each location varied—usually a number of villages would form one team to be represented in Karbala. An important city like Najaf would send several teams that represented the various quarters and classes of the city. Each team was headed by a leader, who carried the banner of his village, city, or quarter. As may be gathered from a description of the procession in Karbala in 1920, the occasion resembled a huge carnival:

> Parties from the principal towns both in the immediate neighborhood and on the upper Tigris, went in procession through town, each vying with [the] other in representing the tragic occurrence which is the purpose of the festival to recall to memory. . . . The concourse formed by the people of Najaf, which had been patiently awaited for some time, made its appearance at last. . . . This party was so magnificent, that the spectators forgot those which had preceded it. It consisted, as usual, of a party of Arab horsemen, followed by a large number of camels, carrying household utensils and some characters representing the family of Husayn, who were taken prisoners and who are said to have arrived from Damascus on some such occasion. . . . This was followed by a great party from among the following classes: first the sayyids, secondly the theologians and religious luminaries, and thirdly the leading merchants and notables. . . . Then arrived the chest beaters and the chain beaters, who formed some twenty parties of over a hundred persons each. [The Najafis] were the last of the various groups, and consisted of some six or seven thousand people.[40]

The great procession in Karbala fostered the various identities of regional groups and classes, and marked the relative importance of Shi'i communities and cities in Iraq. The sponsoring of a procession enabled individuals and families to highlight their status outside their locality; their wealth could be calculated by the amount of money they spent on the cloth and equipment. The status of cities was reflected in the number of participants and the classes represented. In the case of city quarters, the head of

---

[39] Robert Fernea, Shaykh, 71. See also Talib 'Ali al-Sharqi, 'Ayn al-tamr (Najaf, 1969), 148.

[40] Extract from Administrative Report of Political Officer, Hilla, Regarding Karbala and Status of Mujtahids, 5 April 1920, FO 371/5074/5285.

the team, who was the *mukhtar* or his nominee, could use the occasion to exhibit his position over rival quarter leaders. The residents of one quarter could equally use this occasion to affirm their superiority over residents of the other quarters, thereby demonstrating their strong quarter identity.[41]

The Muharram observances reflected the various ethnic and cultural attributes of Shi'is in Iraq, representing a total social order as well as the motivations of the laity. Leading Shi'i mujtahids and religious families were divided, however, over the legality and usefulness of the rituals of *'Ashura'* as practiced by the laity. This split between individuals and groups resulted in a heated controversy among Shi'is in the twentieth century, reinforced by the rise of the modern state.

THE MUJTAHIDS AND THE MUHARRAM OBSERVANCES

Around 1926 Sayyid Abu al-Hasan Isfahani in Najaf and Sayyid Muham-mad Mahdi Qazwini in Basra issued legal opinions against the flagellation and other Muharram rituals. A similar position was also taken by Muhsin al-Amin, the head of the Shi'i community in Damascus. The debate that ensued following the responses of rival mujtahids had strong repercussions throughout the Shi'i world, and was described by the Iraqi Shi'i writer Ja'far al-Khalili as the great strife among Shi'is.[42]

The debate highlighted the importance of the Muharram observances in reinforcing the socioeconomic status of mujtahids, families, and religious functionaries within Shi'i society. The attempt of the leading mujtahids in Iraq, notably Isfahani, Muhammad Husayn Na'ini, and Ahmad (and later on Muhammad Husayn) Kashif al-Ghita, to use the debate in order to improve their own position within the religious hierarchy manifested itself in the struggle over the leadership in the 1920s. The implications of this struggle on the position of the Shi'i religious hierarchy in Iraq as well as the relations between religion and state in Iraq were discussed in chapter 3 in dealing with the rise of the state. Many ulama and *sayyids* who took part in the debate in Iraq had a vested economic interest in maintaining the Muharram rituals. The livelihood of the *rawza-khwans*, as has been seen, was closely connected to the memorial services and the Muharram ser-mons. The public processions attracted a very large number of visitors to the shrine cities. Indeed, the occasion of the visitation, as the next chapter

[41] See Wardi's discussion of the rivalry between Najaf and Kazimayn as it surfaced in the great procession of Karbala in 1929: 'Ali al-Wardi, *Dirasa fi tabi'at al-mujtama' al-'iraqi* (Baghdad, 1965), 190–91.

[42] For details see Ende, "Flagellations," 21–25; Ja'far al-Khalili, *Hakadha 'araftuhum*, 2 vols. (Baghdad, 1963–1968), 2:20, and 1:205–14; idem, "Bayn al-ifrat wa al-tafrit," *al-Hatif* 24 (27 March 1936), 1.

demonstrates, provided an important source of income for various religious functionaries in these cities.

The debate also reflected the efforts of the mujtahids to protect Shi'i identity, and their own leverage over the lay population in the face of two challenges: the revival of the Wahhabi movement under 'Abd al-'Aziz ibn Sa'ud, and the rise of the modern state in Iraq. It will be remembered that the Wahhabi attacks on Najaf and Karbala early in the nineteenth century had been an important factor in driving the Shi'i ulama to intensify the conversion of the tribes of Iraq, thereby seeking to shore up the position of Shi'ism in that country. Although the Wahhabi power was destroyed in 1818 by Egypt's governor Muhammad 'Ali, Wahhabism reemerged in 1902 under Ibn Sa'ud, who created the Ikhwan. In 1922 the Ikhwan raided southern Iraq, attacking several of the Muntafiq tribes. In 1925 they took Mecca and Medina, destroying important Shi'i tombs in the latter city. The formation of the Sunni monarchy in Iraq in 1921 posed yet another challenge to the position of Shi'ism, since both the British and the Iraqi government sought to reduce the power of the clergy by eradicating the effectiveness of the Muharram observances as a political instrument. These challenges were further reinforced by the strong role that popular influences played in shaping the nature of the Muharram rituals. Against this, the dilemma of the mujtahids was what type of Muharram rituals should be allowed in order to preserve Shi'i identity as well as their own influence over the laity.

The usefulness of weeping in reinforcing Shi'i identity was widely recognized by the mujtahids. Muhsin al-Amin, however, criticized the excessive wailing and acts of face-slapping.[43] The advocates of these practices argued that they were part of the religious symbolism of the Shi'i creed. Weeping and face-slapping, wrote one member of the Kashif al-Ghita family, are among the most sacred acts and secrets of the community; they recall Husayn's memory and enhance religious solidarity.[44]

The use of Traditions of disputed authority and melodies in the memorial services, in addition to the musical instruments used in the processions, posed another problem. Many narrators used Traditions of disputed authority and chanted melodies in their sermons, thereby seeking to attract a following and to increase their impact on their audience. Paralleled by the playing of drums, cymbals, and trumpets in the processions, this created a Shi'i folklore around the episodes of the battle of Karbala; it was based, Amin argued, on hagiographical imagination, and manifested itself in unlawful acts of commemoration.[45] Against this, 'Abd al-Husayn al-Hilli

---

[43] Muhsin al-Amin, *Risalat al-tanzih li-a'mal al-shabih* (Sidon, 1928/9), 4, 30.

[44] 'Abd al-Rida Kashif al-Ghita, *al-Anwar al-husayniyya*, 1:14, 30, 36, 38.

[45] Amin, *Risalat al-tanzih*, 5, 8, 12–14, 22, 23–24.

argued that the *rawza-khwan*s were only the narrators of Traditions, not their inventors or fabricators. While they used weak Traditions too, their purpose was only to recall Husayn's suffering and to have an impact on the audience. The use of sad melodies was also considered vital for reviving the episodes of Karbala and for creating a mood of sorrow among the participants in the memorial services. Musical instruments were needed in order to mark this occasion of sorrow, to organize the mourning processions, and to stimulate the participants.[46]

The debate over the *shabih* touched on the issues of female intimacy and male-female interaction. At times mourning women would be seen unveiled in public on the occasion of *'Ashura'*. Men would ride horses or camels, assuming the role of the women who were taken captive in the battle of Karbala. They would also wear black robes when playing the role of Husayn's womenfolk, who were believed to have traveled from Damascus to Medina after their release. Moreover, the reenactment of the battle by professional actors always carried the risk that they themselves would become the object of popular admiration at the expense of the characters they were intended to recall. The supporters of the ritual maintained that if the only purpose of the *shabih* was to encourage weeping and reinforce Shi'i identity and belief among the laity, then casting actors in the roles of the characters in the Karbala episode, and the disguising of men as women, were permissible.[47]

The practice of flagellation generated heated discussion, since this ritual led at times to the loss of human life. Amin considered the shedding of blood in Husayn's memory unlawful, citing the damage that it caused to the flagellants. He pointed to the late introduction of this practice into Imami-Shi'ism, stressing that the grand mujtahid Muhammad Hasan Shirazi (d. 1895) prohibited it. He argued that only ignorant laymen observed this ritual, imposing their will on ulama who were too weak to prevent the spread of the practice.[48] By contrast, the advocates distinguished between a light injury and a permanent one. They permitted all forms of flagellation provided that they did not cause permanent injury to the flagellant, or lead to his death. Hilli drew an interesting analogy, comparing flagellation to the experience of fasting in Ramadan and the pilgrimage to Mecca, two

[46] 'Abd al-Husayn al-Hilli, *al-Naqd al-nazih li-risalat al-tanzih* (Najaf, 1928/9), 11–12, 15, 35, 126, 136. For the permission to use musical instruments in the mourning processions see also Muhammad Husayn Kashif al-Ghita, *al-Ayat al-bayyinat fi qam' al-bida' wa al-dalalat* (Najaf, 1926/7), 19–20. The permission given by Na'ini may be found in Ibrahim al-Musawi al-Zanjani, *'Aqa'id al-imamiyya al-ithna 'ashariyya*, 2d ed., 3 vols. (Beirut, 1973–1977), 1:291.

[47] Hilli, *al-Naqd al-nazih*, 53, 143–44, 146; Muhammad Husayn Kashif al-Ghita, *al-Ayat al-bayyinat*, 10. See also Na'ini's permission in Zanjani, *'Aqa'id*, 1:290–91.

[48] Amin, *Risalat al-tanzih*, 14–15, 19, 21, 22–23, 25, 27–28.

principles of faith in Islam which can cause some temporary difficulty or harm to those who observed them.[49]

The advocates of the *shabih*, the public processions, and the flagellation sought to use these rituals to preserve the vitality of the symbol of Husayn and to propagate the Shi'i cause. Members of the Kashif al-Ghita family were particularly zealous in defending these rituals. 'Abd al-Rida argued that the open observances of these rituals was vital to recall the major event of Shi'i history. These rituals reminded the world of the great sin committed against Husayn at Karbala. They bolstered the position of Shi'ism in the face of challenges like those posed by the Wahhabis. These rituals, he stressed, constituted the most effective vehicle for propagating Shi'ism among the tribes and other people in non-Muslim territories. Both 'Abd al-Rida and Muhammad Husayn Kashif al-Ghita warned against the restriction of these rituals or their confinement to private houses. The former stressed that the full impact of these rituals could be achieved only if they were observed with vehemence in the open. The latter described them as the greatest symbols of Shi'ism and as vital for its existence. Their restriction, he warned, would lead to the disappearance of Shi'i Islam altogether.[50]

The fear of Muhammad Husayn Kashif al-Ghita that unless fully implemented the rituals of 'Ashura' might lose their impact on the laity was not unfounded, for with the rise of the modern state in Iraq, the intensity of the Muharram rites, and their effectiveness as a political instrument, was greatly diminished.

THE STATE AND 'ASHURA'

During Muharram emotions and religious fervor ran high. The occasion would highlight Shi'i grievances, and the processions could be transformed by ulama into anti-government protests. Successive Sunni governments sought to control, and even abolish, the public processions; this was considered essential for the establishment of the state's authority and to break down sectarian boundaries in Iraq. The government first sought to detach the mixed cities of Baghdad, Kazimayn, Samarra, and Basra from the influence of Najaf and Karbala.

During the monarchy, Kazimayn grew to be a suburb of greater Baghdad

[49] Hilli, *al-Naqd al-nazih*, 39, 43, 53, 63–64, 70–71, 86–88, 116; Muhammad Husayn Kashif al-Ghita, *al-Ayat al-bayyinat*, 9, 17–19. For Na'ini's permission see Zanjani, *'Aqa'id*, 1:290.

[50] 'Abd al-Rida Kashif al-Ghita, *al-Anwar al-husayniyya*, 2:7–8, 16, 42–51, 84–90; Muhammad Husayn Kashif al-Ghita, *al-Ayat al-bayyinat*, 5–6, 20–22. See also Na'ini's similar, although somewhat less zealous, position in Zanjani, *'Aqa'id*, 1:290.

and, in the case of the Muharram ceremonies, was treated like the capital. The public ceremonies were held under tight police control, which reduced the level of religious fervor that could be exhibited in the city. Indeed, it was reported in 1932 that the Kazimayn rites were not well attended, since the prospect of performing the *shabih* in the presence of large numbers of armed policemen persuaded many Shiʻis to go to Karbala instead. In 1935 the government sought to discourage the Shiʻis of Kazimayn from participating in the great procession of the 20th of Safar in Karbala; the local police accordingly informed the organizers of the Muharram observances that the collection of money for the great procession was strictly prohibited.[51] Restrictions were also imposed on the processions in Basra, as well as on the practice of flagellation which by the 1950s was largely confined to private houses and performed on license of the police. The British had economic interests vested in that city, Iraq's gateway to the Persian Gulf and India, and took great pains to reduce any threat to the stability of Basra. This was in line with British policy toward the Muharram processions in Bombay, India's commercial hub. In the latter city, the British also restricted the processions, seeking to modify their format and to abolish the violent rites connected with them.[52]

In seeking to reduce the effectiveness of the Muharram observances as a political instrument, the Iraqi government faced a relatively easier task than its Iranian counterpart. The decisive action of Iraq's rulers against the Muharram rites was part of their effort to retain Sunni predominance in the state. Against the Sunni character of the government in Iraq, Shiʻi Islam was the state religion in Iran. While at times the Pahlavis prohibited the violent aspects of the Muharram rites, on other occasions they sought to gain legitimacy among Shiʻis and to bolster their own position in Iran by bestowing their patronage over these rites. Thus, until 1955 Muhammad Reza Shah gave annual donations to groups of breast-beaters in Qum. And although the Pahlavi state devalued the representation of the battle of Karbala, the court attempted to patronize the play in the late 1970s and transform it into a type of Iranian folklore.[53]

While the Sunni character of the government in Iraq may explain the particularly strong motivation of Iraq's rulers in seeking to reduce the effectiveness of the Muharram rites, it cannot by itself account for their

[51] Special Service Officer, Baghdad, 18 May 1932, Air 23/383; Iraq Police, Political Gazette, 11 May 1935, Air 23/590.

[52] Extracts from Administration Report on Basra Liwa for July 1931, Air 23/107; Monthly Political Review for Basra, August 1955, USNA, 787.00/9–655; Jim Masselos, "Change and Custom in the Format of the Bombay Mohurrum during the Nineteenth and Twentieth Centuries," *SA* 7 (1982): 51, 53, 55.

[53] Michael Fischer, *Iran: From Religious Dispute to Revolution* (Cambridge, Mass., 1980), 133–34.

overall success when compared with Iran's Pahlavi rulers. It is the centrality of the Muharram rites in shaping the nature of Iranian daily life, and the
unique organization of Shi'i Islam in the Iranian urban setting—two key
elements which are absent in Iraq—that elucidate the success of the Iraqi
government. In Iran, far more than in Iraq, the expression of collective
sorrow for the death of Husayn transcended the time boundaries of the
Muharram rituals. By the Qajar period, wrote the Iranian historian Kasravi, "Iranians became preoccupied with various observances and ceremonies of Husayn's death, dedicating half of their life to that end."[54] Residing
in rural Iran between 1959 and 1962, the anthropologist Brian Spooner
observed that the entire month of Muharram is a "season of mourning"
and that it is "the ordinary man, who makes the occasion live." Spooner
was also impressed by the fact that "the overriding religious importance of
Muharram in the mind of the ordinary believer, is proved again and again
by the intensity with which it is observed from year to year despite official
attempts to restrain it."[55] The importance of Kasravi's and Spooner's remarks lies in the fact that the symbol of Husayn's martyrdom was ever-
present in the reality of Iranians, inspiring long-lasting moods and motivations among them. A good example of this is the strong organizational
form of the Muharram rites in the Iranian bazaar.

Professional groups of bazaaris (hay'at-i senfi) played a major role in
sponsoring the Muharram ceremonies in urban centers in Iran. The various Muharram rituals in the Tehran bazaar were organized almost exclusively by members of the various groups. Allotments were made on a yearly
basis as each member tried to hold a memorial service at least once a year in
his home, usually in fulfillment of a vow. Within the group, there were also
subgroup gatherings that stressed one particular ritual. Some of these
subgroups, which met on a weekly, biweekly, or monthly basis, stressed the
holding of sermons, while others emphasized emotional outbursts and self-
flagellation.[56] In contrast with Iraq, where there did not develop an institution similar to the Iranian hay'a, the existence of such associations in Iran
reinforced the group identity and religious values of the bazaaris, drawing
them closer to the ulama. One result of that contact was the greater political effectiveness of the Muharram sermons in Iran as compared with Iraq.

The fusion between state and religion in Islam enabled the rawza-khwan
to address issues that transcended the Karbala episode. He could use the
context of 'Ashura' to stress the current socioeconomic grievances of the
population, and to mobilize people for political action. The unique features of Iranian society made it easier for the rawza-khwan in Iran to

[54] Ahmad Kasravi, al-Tashayyu' wa al-shi'a (Tehran, 1945), 88.

[55] Brian Spooner, "The Function of Religion in Persian Society," Iran 1 (1963): 91.

[56] Gustav Thaiss, "Religious Symbolism and Social Change: The Drama of Husayn"
(Ph.D. diss., Washington University, 1973), 202–4, 217, 278–81.

transform the problem of religious suffering into the problem of political evil and unjust government, and to use the Muharram sermons to generate political protest. Important mujtahids often delivered the sermons in Iran, using the occasion to address current political issues. The *rawza* sermons in Iran proved effective in mobilizing people for political action as late as the 1960s and 1970s. In 1963 they were directly connected to the major anti-government protest movement of that year. In 1978 the sermons played an important role in initiating the mass demonstrations that led eventually to the Shah's departure from Iran.[57]

The state in Iraq gained greater control over the *rawza* sermons and the public processions than did its Iranian counterpart. The measures taken by the British and successive Iraqi governments proved effective in controlling the sermons and diminishing the influence of the *rawza-khwan*. A case in point is Sayyid Salih al-Hilli (d. 1940), said to be the most effective preacher and *rawza-khwan* in Iraq in his time.[58] The British portrayed Hilli as a political agitator, and twice deported him from Iraq in the early 1920s. During Ramadan 1925, for example, when he performed as a *rawza-khwan* in 'Amara, his movements and sermons were closely watched in order to prevent him from using the occasion to engage in anti-government propaganda.[59] By 1935 the government could already use its authority effectively to control the *rawza-khwan*s of Kazimayn. Police reports reveal that when dissatisfaction with the government was loudly expressed in Kazimayn during the Muharram period that year, the custodian of the shrine instructed the *rawza-khwan*s to deliver only very brief *ta'ziyas*.[60]

In seeking to control the *rawza* sermons, the state was helped by Shi'i intellectuals and ulama who envisioned the creation of a new generation of preachers in Iraq. While they did not deny their Shi'i identity, these individuals and groups were perplexed by how much of their old rituals they should maintain and how much they should change in order to lower sectarian boundaries in Iraq. They advocated the training of well-educated sermon leaders as an alternative to the majority of preachers, who used Traditions of disputed authority as well as other means to increase their impact on their audience in the memorial services. The heated debate in

---

[57] Gustav Thaiss, "Religious Symbolism and Social Change: The Drama of Husayn," in *Scholars, Saints, and Sufis*, ed. Nikki Keddie (Berkeley, 1972), 359–60; Shaul Bakhash, "Sermons, Revolutionary Pamphleteering and Mobilisation: Iran, 1978," in *From Nationalism to Revolutionary Islam*, ed. Said Amir Arjomand (Albany, 1984), 180–82.

[58] Khalili, *Hakadha 'araftuhum*, 1:214; Khaqani, *Shu'ara' al-hilla*, 3:160–63. Hilli's status was acknowledged also by the mujtahid Muhsin al-Amin, who became an object of his strong criticism on account of Amin's position toward the Muharram rituals: *Risalat al-tanzih*, 12.

[59] Special Service Officer, 'Amara, 29 March 1925, Air 23/454; Extract from Special Service Officer, Report no. 484/6, Basra, 16 April 1925, Air 23/379.

[60] Iraq Police, Political Gazette, 11 May 1935, Air 23/590.

Najaf in the mid-1930s concerning the role of the *rawza* preacher split the Shi'i community, enabling the government to take sides in this internal conflict and to gain leverage over the sermons.[61]

Moreover, in 1935, during his second Premiership, Yasin al-Hashimi, whom Shi'i opposition groups call "the Ataturk of Iraq," attempted to prohibit the Muharram processions altogether. The government's prohibition of the public processions was cited as one of the factors behind the tribal insurrections of 1935–1936.[62] Under the monarchy, the processions lost much of their former religious fervor, a development that was reinforced by the rise of communism, which vied with religion over the influence of Shi'is in Iraq. Indeed, supporters of the Iraqi Communist Party used Shi'i mass gatherings on such occasions as *ziyarat 'ashura'* and *ziyarat al-arba'in* to spread slogans and to promote their own political cause with little hindrance from the government.[63]

The drop in the fervor of the Muharram observances in Iraq can be seen in the decline of flagellation from the 1930s.[64] It was the custom in Najaf and among other Shi'i communities in Iraq to give some contributions, mainly in the form of food or white cloth, to the group of flagellants following their performance.[65] In 1951, the British consul reported from 'Amara: "Fifteen years ago the Muharram processions . . . were properly enthusiastic with knives and chains. This last year it was quite obvious that they were greatly enjoyed by the performers who indeed performed only on a strictly cash basis."[66] The performance of flagellation only on a cash basis was an indication of the decline of the practice in Iraq as had been the case among flagellant fraternities in Christianity in late sixteenth-century Italy. When flagellation as a form of religious devotion disappeared in all but name among the Venetian *Scuola di San Rocco*, for example, this fraternity began hiring flagellants on holy religious occasions to preserve, if only symbolically, the ancient spirit of the ritual.[67]

[61] On the attempts to train a new generation of *rawza* preachers in Iraq see Ja'far al-Khalili, "Rijal al-manabir wa-wajib al-'ulama' tujahahum," *al-Hatif* 68 (2 April 1937): 3; idem, *Hakadha 'araftuhum*, 1:244–45; Muhammad Mahdi al-Asifi, *Madrasat al-najaf wa-tatawwur al-haraka al-islahiyya fi-ha* (Najaf, 1964), 132–34.

[62] Kerr to Eden, Baghdad, 22 May 1936, FO 371/20015/3062; Edmonds to Kerr, Baghdad, 2 June 1936, FO 371/20015/3560; Durra, *Hayat 'iraqi*, 25; Ahmad al-Katib, *Tajrubat al-thawra al-islamiyya fi al-'iraq* (Tehran, 1981), 138; Hasan al-'Alawi, *al-Ta'thirat al-turkiyya fi al-mashru' al-qawmi al-'arabi fi al-'iraq* (London, 1988), 122.

[63] Muhammad Mahdi al-Asifi, *Min hadith al-da'wa wa al-du'a*, 2d ed. (Najaf, 1966), 61–62, 66–67; Elizabeth Fernea, *Guests*, 218.

[64] Khalili, *Hakadha 'araftuhum*, 1:232.

[65] Sharqi, *al-Najaf al-ashraf*, 227–28.

[66] Stewart to Maitland, British Consulate, 'Amara, 12 May 1951, FO 624/201/1016/4.

[67] Christopher Black, *Italian Confraternities in the Sixteenth Century* (Cambridge, 1989), 100. For the decline of flagellant practices in Florence see Ronald Weissman, *Ritual Brotherhood in Renaissance Florence* (New York, 1982), 206–7.

By the end of the monarchy, the public Muharram observances had already lost much of their effectiveness as a political instrument. It is true that Muharram sermons voicing Shi'i grievances were still held in Iraq after 1958 as may be gathered from the poetry used in the Muharram sermons.[68] These sermons, however, did not prove as capable of generating political protest as effectively as those in Iran in the 1960s and 1970s since the Iraqi state succeeded in containing the public Muharram observances under the pretext that it was seeking to abolish superstitious beliefs and practices. Under the Ba'th, the government apparently even went so far as to portray the majority of *rawza* preachers as promoters of sectarianism, thus touching a most sensitive nerve in the relations between Sunnis and Shi'is in Iraq.[69] The Ba'th went to great lengths in its effort to prohibit the Muharram processions altogether, culminating in 1977 when the government took bold steps to suppress the traditional march of Shi'is from Najaf to Karbala on the occasion of *ziyarat al-arba'in*. Indeed, Iraqi Shi'i Islamic groups painfully acknowledge that by abolishing the public rites, the government had taken a great step toward bolstering its rule, for these rites had posed a real danger to the Sunni dominance of the state in Iraq.[70]

Yet, while Iraq's rulers succeeded in reducing the effectiveness of the Muharram rites as a political instrument, they still had to curb the major sources of income of the shrine cities based on the pilgrimage, the corpse traffic, and the flow of charities from Iran.

[68] For examples see Ibrahim Haidari, "Zur Soziologie des Schiitischen Chiliasmus: Ein Beitrag zur Erforschung des Irakischen Passionsspiels" (Ph.D. diss., Freiburg, 1975), 226–47; Kovalenko, "Le Martyre de Husayn," 220–22.

[69] Hasan al-'Alawi, *al-Shi'a wa al-dawla al-qawmiyya fi al-'iraq* (Paris, 1989), 243.

[70] Anon., *al-Haraka al-islamiyya fi al-'iraq* (Beirut, 1985), 140; Katib, *Tajrubat al-thawra*, 138, 161.

Chapter Six

PILGRIMAGE TO THE SHRINE CITIES
AND THE CULT OF THE SAINTS

THE VISITATION to the shrines of the imams is only recommended for the Shi'i believers. Unlike the pilgrimage to Mecca (the hajj, which by Islamic law is obligatory for all Muslims who are financially and physically capable of undertaking it, and should be performed in the month of Dhu al-Hijja), the visitation is not confined to any specific time of the year. There are, however, a number of special dates in the Shi'i-Islamic calendar when the visitation to one or all of the shrines of Najaf, Karbala, Kazimayn, and Samarra is particularly auspicious. Among the various shrines, those of Najaf and Karbala, where the tombs of 'Ali and his son Husayn are believed to be located, carry the highest importance.[1]

The visitation of the shrines of the imams is intended to acknowledge their authority as the leaders of the Muslim community following the death of Muhammad, and to maintain the contact and understanding ('ahd) between the Shi'i believer and his imam, who is capable of interceding with God on his behalf on the day of resurrection. Besides serving as an act of covenant renewal between the believer and the imam, the visitation is also aimed at preserving the collective Shi'i memory and group identity as distinguished from that of the Sunnis. Hence the effort in Shi'i piety to turn Karbala and Husayn's shrine to a focus of devotion for the Shi'is, which at times challenged the position of Mecca and the Ka'ba. Indeed, at various points during Muslim history, and especially in time of strife between the Safavids and the Ottomans, the visitation of Karbala substituted for the pilgrimage to Mecca.[2]

The visitation was encouraged from an early period of Shi'i history, beginning with the imams. Shi'i jurists and scholars also urged it in their works. The practice developed on a very massive scale following the establishment of Safavid Iran (1501) and the subsequent conversion of the bulk of Iranians to Shi'ism. With the collapse of the Safavid state in 1722, and

---

[1] For details see Yitzhak Nakash, "The Visitation of the Shrines of the Imams and the Shi'i Mujtahids in the Early Twentieth Century," *SI* 81 (1995): 153–64.

[2] Muhammad Rida al-Muzaffar, *'Aqa'id al-imamiyya*, 2d ed. (Cairo, 1961/2), 93; Mahmoud Ayoub, *Redemptive Suffering in Islam. A Study of the Devotional Aspects of 'Ashura' in Twelver Shi'ism* (The Hague, 1978), 181–82, 188; Musa al-Musawi, *al-Shi'a wa al-tashih: al-sira' bayn al-shi'a wa al-tashayyu'* (Cairo, 1989), 93.

the shift of the Shi'i academic center from Isfahan to Karbala and later to Najaf from the mid-eighteenth century, the visitation became closely linked to the socioeconomic development of these two cities, and boosted the power of the Shi'i mujtahids vis-à-vis the Ottoman government in Iraq. The visitation reinforced the status of Karbala and Najaf as the focus of devotion for Shi'is following the Wahhabi attacks of the two cities early in the nineteenth century. It peaked in the nineteenth century as the bulk of Iraq's tribes was converted to Shi'ism. The large scale of the visitation of the shrine cities at that time may also be attributed to the relative improvement in Ottoman-Qajar relations after their last war of 1821–1823, and the spread of beliefs among the laity that emphasized the rewards to be gained by its performance.[3]

This chapter deals first with the foreign pilgrimage to the shrine cities, demonstrating its transformation during the monarchy. In focusing later on the role of the visitation among the Iraqi Shi'is, I will illustrate that the Arab tribal attributes and values of Iraqi Shi'is were reflected in the images which they attached to the imams, as well as to other saints in Iraq.

FOREIGN PILGRIMAGE

Iranians and Indians formed the bulk of the pilgrims to the shrine cities, the annual average of the former alone in the late nineteenth century reaching one hundred thousand. Before World War I, three routes were used by these pilgrims. Those coming from northwestern Iran used the Khanaqin-Baghdad route, the main gateway for Iranian pilgrims to Iraq, while the Persian Gulf route served pilgrims from southern Iran. Indian pilgrims usually arrived by sea through Basra. The Indians originated mainly in Uttar Pradesh, the Punjab, the North West Frontier province, and Bombay. Most pilgrims ordinarily visited Kazimayn and Baghdad first. They usually stayed in Samarra for one night, and then proceeded to Karbala and Najaf.[4]

Since mass transportation and modern communication on a large scale were introduced in Iraq only following the formation of the monarchy, the pilgrimage to the shrine cities for centuries meant a long and often difficult trip. The departure of the pilgrims from their familiar place of residence and daily labor, followed by a long journey to the far distant shrines,

[3] For the attributes attached to the visitation of the imams and their shrines see Mirza al-Mahdi al-Husayn al-Khurasani, *Mu'jizat va-kiramat-i a'imma-yi athar* (Tehran, 1949); Husayn al-Buraqi al-Najafi, *al-Durra al-bahiyya fi fadl karbala' wa-turbatiha al-zakiyya* (Najaf, 1970); 'Abd al-Hujja Balaghi, *Ta'rikh-i najaf-i ashraf va-hire* (Tehran, 1949/50), 20–25.

[4] J. G. Lorimer, *Gazetteer of the Persian Gulf, 'Oman and Central Arabia*, 2 vols. in 5 pts. (Calcutta, 1908–15), 1,2:2358, and 2A:813, 818; Government of Iraq, Dept. of Health Services, Report of the Inspector-General of Health Services for 1923–24, CO 696/5; Report of the Protector of British Indian Pilgrims, 1929, CO 730/159/2.

subjected them to a "transitional experience" and to a "conflict of distance and expectation." The act of the pilgrimage meant a movement from a mundane center to a sacred periphery which suddenly became central to the individual. It reflected the commitment of the pilgrims to the "therapy of distance" by recognizing that what they wished for could not be attained in their immediate environment.[5]

But distance was there to be overcome, as the following story illustrates. On one occasion in 1919, a British officer met on the road from Hilla to Karbala a party of Indian pilgrims consisting of two men and one woman all of whom were over fifty years of age. They told the officer that they had started from Karachi eleven months earlier, and walked the entire distance to perform their obeisance at the shrine of Husayn.[6] Upon their arrival at the shrine cities, the golden minaret of the shrine, which seemed to hold out so fair a promise of welcome and rest, sharpened the effect of the "therapy of distance" for the weary pilgrims. Indeed, the shrine, as may be gathered from its description by the Shi'i mujtahid Muhammad Mahdi al-Kazimi Qazwini, had a therapeutic, oasis-like, effect: "[The] magnificent shrines . . . shield the pilgrims from the hot and cold weather, and from the rain and the windy storms of the desert."[7]

Until the beginning of the twentieth century, the shrine cities could feed on the mode of distance and expectation which many of the foreign pilgrims experienced. The cities reaped the economic fruits provided by the visitation, their major source of income. Najaf and Karbala in particular became the object of organized pilgrimages, which helped consolidate their political position vis-à-vis the Ottomans and the Qajars. The importance of the pilgrimage in boosting the economy of these cities in the nineteenth century may be appreciated from a report compiled in 1875 on the Iranian pilgrimage:

> The number of persons making the pilgrimage annually may as an average be stated as 100,000 and those may be divided into three classes, the rich, the middle class and the poor. It is calculated that the rich expend on the round journey [from Khanaqin to the shrine cities and back] from 200 to 300 tomans each, and the average expenditure of the three classes for living alone is computed at twenty tomans a head, or 2,000,000 tomans in all . . . On his return, every pilgrim however poor sets aside a certain amount of his funds to

[5] Victor Turner and Edith Turner, *Image and Pilgrimage in Christian Culture* (New York, 1978), 4, 14–15, 34–35, 36–37; Victor Turner, "The Center Out There: Pilgrim's Goal," *HR* 12 (1973): 192, 195; Peter Brown, *The Cult of the Saints, its Rise and Function in Latin Christianity* (Chicago, 1981), 86–87.

[6] Great Britain, Administration Report of the Hilla Division for the Year 1919, FO 371/6348/99.

[7] "Mas'alat al-qubur wa al-mashahid 'ind al-shi'a: munazara bayna 'alim shi'i wa-'alim sunni," *al-Manar* 28 (1927): 365.

be expended on articles of little intrinsic value . . . The total amount thus
invested may be also estimated at 2,000,000 tomans . . . Adding [to these]
250,000 tomans as an average amount of mule hire on the round journey
. . . the total amount expended by Persian pilgrims annually may be estimated
at 4,250,000 tomans equal to 1,070,000 pounds sterling.[8]

There was thus a close link between the pilgrimage and the development
of extensive marketing systems in the shrine cities. The four cities catered
to the needs of different social classes and ethnic groups, and developed
various types of recreational activities and lodging arrangements. The
main imported goods, and the produce of the cities themselves, were
geared primarily for the consumption of pilgrims. Many social and religious services were also closely connected with the pilgrim traffic. The
influx of foreign, tourist-like pilgrims provided income for such people as
khan owners, various servants, and the attendants (the *khuddam*). For
varying fees, the attendants assisted the pilgrims at every stage of their
journey at a time when pilgrimage transport arrangements were not organized on a through-ticket basis. The attendants, who were established in
the shrine cities, Baghdad, and Basra, met the pilgrims on arrival. They
conducted them to rest houses, and were responsible for making arrangements for their accommodation. The attendants also conducted pilgrims to
the shrines and recited prayers on their behalf. They usually did not receive
any commission or salary other than what they were given by the pilgrims.[9]

Among the various services offered in the shrine cities, that of temporary
marriage (*mut'a*) was described by Lady Drower, who visited Najaf around
1922. While many pilgrims used to visit the shrine cities together with their
wives, some men traveled alone either because they were not married or
because they had left their wives in their home country. On the arrival of a
single pilgrim, usually an Iranian, he was met in the khan by a tout. If the
pilgrim wished to contract a temporary marriage, the tout, for a fee, would
bring to him several suitable girls. After the pilgrim had selected a girl and
the parents' permission had been obtained, the pair were married by an
'alim, who likewise was paid for his service. The length of the marriage
varied, and could range from an hour to several months; it terminated at
the end of the period agreed upon by the contracting parties. In 1922, the
fees of the woman or her guardian were reported to be two rupees an hour,
ten rupees a day, and fifty rupees a month.[10]

[8] Thomson to Derby, 30 September 1875, FO 60/373, cited in Charles Issawi, *The Economic History of Iran, 1800–1914* (Chicago, 1971), 129.

[9] Adib al-Mulk, *Safarnama-yi adib al-mulk bi-'atabat (dalil al-za'irin) 1273 h.q.* (Tehran,
1985/6), 113–14; Hajji Pirzadeh, *Safarnama-yi hajji pirzadeh*, ed. Hafez Farman-Farmayan,
2 vols. (Tehran, 1963), 1:311, 322; Report of the Protector of British Indian Pilgrims, 1929,
CO 730/159/2.

[10] Lady E. S. Stevens Drower, *By Tigris and Euphrates* (London, 1923), 37. An earlier
account of this service is provided by Peters, who visited Najaf and Karbala in 1890: John

Before World War I, the policies of the Ottoman and the Iranian governments were a major factor affecting the pilgrimage. In the early 1730s and early 1740s Nadir Shah twice invaded Iraq. One of the important provisions of the peace treaty which Nadir concluded with the Ottomans after his second invasion was a guarantee of almost unimpeded access for Iranian pilgrims to the shrine cities. This greatly improved the welfare of the merchants, shopkeepers, and clerics that lived off the pilgrim trade.[11] But since the economy of the Baghdad province as a whole benefited from the pilgrimage, the Iranian government sometimes used this fact to exert pressures on the Ottoman authorities in Iraq to reduce the fees exacted from the Iranian pilgrims. Moreover, for several years from around 1877 the Qajars prohibited the pilgrimage of their subjects to the shrine cities. Citing the outbreak of cholera in Iraq, they diverted Iranians instead to the shrine of the eighth imam 'Ali Rida in Mashhad. The attempt to substitute that city for Najaf and Karbala failed, but the sharp drop in the number of Iranian pilgrims to the shrine cities had for several years a very unfavorable effect on Iraq's economy.[12]

This episode not only highlighted the dependence of the shrine cities on the pilgrimage as their major source of income, but their vulnerability as well. Indeed, Karbala at times experienced marked economic recessions followed by local disturbances. One such episode occurred in 1909, when, owing to the paucity of pilgrims and the slackness of trade that year, the religious students attempted to force those mujtahids who were recipients of the Oudh Bequest (see chapter 8) to distribute some of this money to them to provide for their maintenance. During World War I very few pilgrims visited the shrine cities, whose economies consequently experienced deep recessions. It is evident that Najaf suffered sharp inflation; thus, a tin of kerosine oil, which had cost five rupees before the War, sold for fifty in 1919. Conditions in Kazimayn and Samarra were no better, both being gate-cities for the majority of the pilgrims on their way to Najaf and Karbala. When during the War pilgrim traffic was sharply reduced, Kazimayn's well-being was reported to be at an extremely low ebb and many khans and houses, ordinarily inhabited by the pilgrims, lay vacant.[13]

Before World War I, Iranians accounted for about 90 percent of all the

Peters, *Nippur or Explorations and Adventures on the Euphrates*, 2d ed. (New York, 1898), 316.

[11] Juan Cole, "Shi'i Clerics in Iraq and Iran, 1722–1780: The Akhbari-Usuli Conflict Reconsidered," *IS* 18 (1985): 18; idem, *Roots of North Indian Shi'ism in Iran and Iraq: Religion and State in Awadh, 1722–1859* (Berkeley, 1988), 29–31.

[12] Meir Litvak, "The Shi'i Ulama of Najaf and Karbala, 1791–1904: A Socio-Political Analysis" (Ph.D. diss., Harvard University, 1991), 95; Lorimer, *Gazetteer*, 1,1B:1513–14; Issawi, *Economic History of Iran*, 129.

[13] Edmund Candler, "Pilgrimage to the Shrine at Najaf, Arabia," *MW* 9 (1919): 88; Administration Reports of the Baghdad Wilayat, 1917, CO 696/1; Great Britain, Naval Intelligence Division, *Iraq and the Persian Gulf*, September 1944, 536.

foreign pilgrims to Iraq; as noted above, their annual average in the late nineteenth century was one hundred thousand. In 1919 British officials in Iraq predicted that the pilgrimage from Iran would resume, if not exceed, its pre-War level; this prediction rested on the very large number of pilgrims that arrived from Iran between June and December 1919, following the renewal of the pilgrimage.[14] It soon became clear, however, that one could not foresee the number of Iranian pilgrims that might arrive in any given year. This was due mainly to the policies of the Iranian and Iraqi governments, and to economic conditions in Iran. Thus, whereas between 1905 and 1914 the annual average of pilgrims from Iran who used to cross the frontier at Khanaqin alone was 37,000, the equivalent annual figure for the years 1919–1928 dropped to 17,569 at a time when Khanaqin was still a major crossing point. This decline stands out particularly against the increase in the volume of Indian pilgrim traffic, which almost resumed its pre-War level of several thousand a year.[15]

Strained Iraqi-Iranian relations between 1921 and 1928 greatly hampered the influx of Iranian pilgrims and the economic welfare of the shrine cities. In 1923 the Iranian government imposed an embargo on the pilgrimage to Iraq, much to the detriment of the holy cities. For their part, British and Iraqi officials argued that Iraq was better off without the pilgrim traffic, as the embargo meant a decrease in Iranian influence in the shrine cities.[16] In 1924 the Shi'i Lebanese journal *al-'Irfan* reported that the embargo had caused a deep economic recession in the shrine cities. In December of that year, Reza Khan visited Iraq. In Najaf, mujtahids presented him with a petition requesting that Iranians be given permission to resume the pilgrimage to Najaf and Karbala, as the people of these two cities depended on the pilgrims for their livelihood.[17]

When the pilgrimage from Iran was renewed in the fall of 1925, its nature had been transformed. The shrine cities no longer reaped the profits of former years, and the Iranian pilgrims stayed only a few days at the shrine cities, at the end of which they hurried back to their country. The removal of the embargo resulted in the appearance of some eighteen hundred thousand pilgrims that year, drawn mainly from among the poorer

[14] Administration Report for the Shamiyya Division, 1919, CO 696/2; Office of the Civil Commissioner, Baghdad, 12 September 1919, FO 371/4151/147630; Annual Administration Report of the Health Service Dept. for 1920, CO 696/3.

[15] Report of the Inspector-General of Health Services for 1923–24, CO 696/5; Report on the Work of the Protector of British Indian Pilgrims, 1929, CO 730/159/2; Annual Administration Reports of the Dept. of Health Services for 1919–28: CO 696/3; CO 696/4; CO 696/5; CO 696/6.

[16] Intelligence Report no. 14, 9 July 1925, FO 371/10833/4813; Report on Iraq, 1920–25, CO 730/77/37753.

[17] "Al-'Iraq," *al-'Irfan* 10 (1924): 616; Special Service Officer, Baghdad, 30 December 1924, Air 23/454.

classes. Although this greatly benefited Iraqi Railways, residents of the shrine cities complained that the company had deprived them of their former profits, as the pilgrims no longer came riding on their mules or horses. Instead, the pilgrims now made a cheap round-trip excursion as quickly as possible, spending little money in Iraq. Other Iraqis complained that, whereas pilgrims formerly used to scatter money at every khan, they now made the journey to Karbala by train and thence to Najaf by taxi, stopping nowhere along the way. In many cases, the pilgrims arriving from the interior of Iran on pack animals were obliged to leave them either at Kirmanshah or Khanaqin, where they were taken care of until their owners returned. Also, the money carried by the pilgrims was scrutinized by the Iranian officials at the frontier, and each pilgrim was allowed to bring into Iraq only a minimal amount just sufficient for a brief visitation. In subsequent years, the Iranian government also restricted its pilgrims from taking with them carpets and other goods for sale in Iraq to defray the cost of the pilgrimage.[18] This hindered the custom among many Iranian pilgrims of combining the pilgrimage with retail trade in the products of their country.

Between 1919 and 1924, the British and the Iraqi government made serious efforts to regulate the pilgrimage. Passports were required by all pilgrims, fees for visas were fixed, health regulations set, quarantine stations reestablished, and the period of stay of pilgrims in Iraq was limited to two to three months.[19] Three railway sections were completed and improved between 1921 and 1923: Khanaqin-Baghdad, Basra-Baghdad, and Hindiyya-Karbala. Another section, Karbala-Jumaymu, which passed through Najaf, was added several years later. A good part of the services offered by these sections catered to the Iranian and Indian pilgrims.[20] In 1925, Iraqi Railways started selling tickets to pilgrims in Iran and India. During the years 1926–27, 1927–28, and 1928–29 the company sold 19,160, 47,259, and 75,447 cheap tickets, respectively, mainly in India. In those years, vouchers for longer periods of stay, to enable pilgrims to make several visitations, were also sold in the two countries; the numbers were

[18] Intelligence Reports nos. 23 and 24, 12 and 26 November 1925, FO 371/10833/7276 and CO 730/80/57326; Report by Her Majesty's Government to the League of Nations on the Administration of Iraq, 1925; Administration Report of the Iraq Railways for the Year Ending March 1931, CO 696/7; Report of the Protector of British Indian Pilgrims, 1929, CO 730/159/27.

[19] British Consul, Kirmanshah, to Civil Commissioner, Baghdad, 26 April 1919, FO 248/1258; The Residence, Baghdad, 16 February 1922, CO 730/20/10675. See also The Iraq Residence Law of 1923 in Reports by Her Majesty's Government to the League of Nations on the Administration of Iraq, 1925; Annual Reports of the Dept. of Health Services, 1921, 1922, and 1923–24, CO 696/4 and CO 696/5.

[20] Report by Her Majesty's High Commissioner on the Finances and Administrative Condition of Iraq for October 1920–March 1922; Report on the Administration of Iraq, The Iraq Railways, April 1922–March 1923, CO 730/57; Naval Intelligence Division, Iraq, 578.

5,322, 4,061 and 5,376, respectively. While the introduction of a faster transport system and the sale of cheap tickets attracted a large portion of the Iranian and Indian pilgrims to Iraqi railways, the services offered by the company absorbed most of the transportation budget of the pilgrims from which the local population had formerly benefited.[21]

Between 1927 and 1929 Reza Shah embarked on an attack against all "popular and obsolete" traditions in Shi'i Islam. This was part of his effort to consolidate his power in Iran, having assumed the crown in 1926. In November 1928 the Shah went to Qum, where through the use of threats, arrests, and the beating to death of two ulama, he secured *fatwa*s from the rest of the ulama prohibiting among other things the pilgrimage to the shrine cities.[22] In December, the Court Minister Timourtash revealed to the British minister in Iran that Iranian pilgrims would not, in future, be allowed to waste months in the holy cities of Iraq. He explained to the British minister that this policy was not directed against Iraq, and was implemented in the interests of Iran.[23]

New restrictions on the pilgrimage to the shrine cities, and the granting of visas to Iranians who wished to visit Iraq, were imposed by the Iranian government in 1927–1929. They were part of the overall policy that took shape in subsequent years of reducing Iran's ties with the shrine cities. The impending Iraq Nationality Law, which the Iranian government regarded as specially designed to undermine the status of the large Persian community in Iraq, was used by Iranian officials as a pretext for restricting the pilgrimage. Later in 1927, the government prohibited the travel of Iranians to Iraq, citing the outbreak of cholera at Basra, the ill-treatment of pilgrims by Iraqi customs and quarantine officials, and the high tax imposed on the pilgrims. From 1928 the Iranian government also refused to allow Iranians, who wished to make the pilgrimage to Mecca, to proceed to the Hijaz via Iraq. The result was to divert traffic from the Najaf-Medina route traditionally used by Iranian pilgrims after their visitation of the shrine cities. Many of them now had to proceed to the Hijaz through Baku, Batum, and the Caucasus, or through Istanbul, or even by boat through Bombay. Consequently, many pilgrims complained about the difficulties they experienced and the expenses they incurred throughout the journey; they argued that formerly, using the Najaf-Medina route, they had money to spend at the shrine cities, but now most of their money was spent in foreign countries *en route*.[24]

[21] Administration Report for Iraq, The Iraq Railways, 1925–26, CO 730/96/21564; Administration Reports for the Iraq Railways for the Years Ending March 1928 and 1929, CO 696/6 and CO 696/7; Administration Report of the Iraq Railways for the Year Ending March 1930, CO 696/7.
[22] Special Service Officer, Baghdad, 21 December 1928, Air 23/124.
[23] Clive to Chamberlain, No. 12, Tehran, 22 December 1928, FO 416/84.
[24] Persia, Annual Report, 1927, FO 416/113; Enclosure no. 1 in Tehran Despatch No. 132

The Iranian restrictions on the pilgrimage to the shrine cities continued almost throughout the 1930s, 1940s, and 1950s. Reinforced by the disturbances of World War II, the decrease in the Iranian pilgrimage hampered the economies of Najaf and Karbala. When British troops marched into Iran in August 1941, it was reported from 'Amara that the mujtahids in Iraq had no intention of supporting Reza Shah, for he had stopped the pilgrimage, thereby depriving them of a most lucrative source of income.[25] Following the Anglo-Soviet invasion of Iran in the same year, some Iranians hoped that the presence of British troops might help renew the pilgrimage to the shrine cities which had been restricted by the Iranian government.[26] But when the pilgrimage was renewed toward the end of World War II, the Iranian government imposed tight restrictions on foreign exchange. It is evident from the report of the British vice-consul who visited Najaf and Karbala in November 1942 that both cities suffered from a high cost of living and the cutting off of the pilgrim trade. The people whom he considered to suffer most were those whose livelihood depended on fixed revenues as received from outside and who did not own land or did not have business interests in Iraq.[27] Although during the short Premiership of Mossadeq (1951–1953) Iranian pilgrims again visited the shrine cities in significant numbers, in subsequent years the number of Iranian pilgrims apparently did not exceed a few thousand per year. The decline of the Iranian pilgrimage was a major factor in upsetting the economic development of Najaf and Karbala under the monarchy.[28]

The attempt of the Iranian government to bring pressure to bear on Iraq through restriction of the pilgrimage did not prove effective. Overall, the annual income of the Iraqi government from the pilgrimage was low.[29] As Iraq's income from the concessions and production of oil increased, whatever profit it might have gained from the pilgrim traffic dwindled as a share of its total annual income. Moreover, the main desire of the Iraqi government was to reduce the Persian and Indian presence in Iraq, and to shift the socioeconomic orientation of the shrine cities toward Baghdad. Against this, the restrictions imposed on the pilgrimage by the Iranian government

---

to His Majesty's High Commissioner Baghdad, 6 May 1927, CO 730/117/5; Clive to Chamberlain, no. 286, Tehran, 4 May 1928 and Intelligence Summary no. 16 for the Period Ending 4 August 1928, Enclosure in no. 49, FO 416/82; Intelligence Report no. 18, 29 August 1928, FO 371/13027/4495.

[25] Report from 'Amara for the Period Ending 28 August 1941, FO 838/1.

[26] From Tehran to Kermanshah, 28 September 1941, FO 371/27156/7177.

[27] Report on Najaf and Karbala by Vice-Consul Bagley, Baghdad, 22 February 1943, FO 624/33/537.

[28] From Ambassador, Baghdad, to the State Department, 10 March 1953, USNA, 787.11/3–1053; Troutbeck to Eden, 16 October 1953, FO 371/104666/1016–57.

[29] Enclosure 3 in no. 1, Memorandum on the Persian Complaints against Iraq, FO 371/12274/3908.

only helped the Iraqi government to achieve that end. The latter could now even more easily turn its attention to abolishing the old practice of destitute pilgrims who left their countries with the intention of settling in the shrine cities. The way this issue was dealt with may be seen in the case of the Indian pilgrims.

In 1929 there were estimated to be some five thousand Indians in Najaf and Karbala; only a few hundred worked as artisans and shopkeepers. The Iraqi government took several measures to cope with the problems of destitution and the pilgrims' search for employment in the shrine cities. The implications of the Iraq Residence and Nationality Laws of 1923 and 1924, and of the 1935 law prohibiting certain trades and crafts to foreigners in Iraq, were discussed in chapter 3. The introduction of the cheap return tickets that the pilgrims were required to purchase in India before their departure coincided with attempts of British and Indian officials to strongly discourage pilgrims from leaving their country without sufficient funds. From 1935, when the Iraqi government banned all public ceremonies in commemoration of 'Ashura', the important visitation of 10 Muharram (ziyarat 'ashura') lost much of its colorful character. Consequently, many Indian pilgrims were unable to perform the visitation to Karbala, Najaf, and Kazimayn in March and April that year on the occasion of 'Id al-Adha and 'Ashura'.[30] Another measure taken by the Iraqi government was to limit the maximum period of the pilgrimage to three months a year, an act which was greatly resented by the Indian Shi'is.[31] On different occasions in 1945–1946, Indians made representations to their government complaining that the three-month period fixed for the pilgrimage, usually from the first of Muharram, was much too short. They also complained about the small amount of money, food, and cloth that the pilgrims were allowed to bring into Iraq, and about the need for a visa.[32]

The measures taken by the Iraqi government affected the nature of the pilgrimage to the shrine cities. The establishment of rapid transportation between India and Iraq helped reduce the stay of Indian pilgrims in the cities; they could visit Iraq by sea and rail and return to India within three

[30] Report on the Work of the Indian Section of the British Consulate at Baghdad for 1935, Government of India, Foreign and Political Dept., NAI, file 551-G/1936.

[31] Report of the Protector of British Indian Pilgrims, 1929, CO 730/159/2; Government of India, External Dept., Proceedings nos. 1–3, 1937, NAI, file 105-N/37; Iraq, Annual Reports, 1937 and 1938, FO 371/21856/794 and FO 371/23214/932.

[32] See, for example, From President, The Isna-Ashari Federation, Bombay, to the Secretary of the Government of India, 10 December 1945; From Mohamed Ali D. Nasser, Manekia Chamber, Bombay, to N. B. Khare, Member of the Government of India, Commonwealth Relations, 14 December 1945, Government of India, External Affairs Dept., NAI, file 17 (13) M.E.; From Khan Bahadur Haji Hasanally P. Ebrahim, Vice President, Faiz-i-Panjestani (Pilgrim Institution), to the Secretary of the Government of India, Bombay, 17 May 1946, Government of India, External Affairs Dept., NAI, file 17 (13) M.E.

weeks. These measures affected the intensity of the Indian pilgrimage to the shrine cities and led to a decrease in the number of Indians in Iraq; this was evident already in the census of 1932 which put the total number of Indians in Iraq at only 2,362. The decrease of the Indian pilgrimage hampered the livelihood of the attendants, who, following the decline in the number of the Iranian pilgrims to Iraq, strongly competed over the patronage of the Indian pilgrims. Indeed, unemployment in Najaf and Karbala was rife as many of the services traditionally offered in the cities to the pilgrims were no longer required.[33]

The rise of the modern state led to the organization and bureaucratization of the pilgrimage to the shrine cities. The pilgrimage utilized modern forms of mass transportation and was subjected to the policies of the Iraqi and Iranian governments. It became shorter and more solemn in tone. This trend continued after the monarchic period and was particularly noticeable during much of the 1970s and the Iran-Iraq War of 1980–1988 when Iranian pilgrims were not allowed to visit the shrine cities. Consequently, Najaf and Karbala lost one of their main sources of income, and were no longer exposed to an intense Persian presence as had been the case in the past.

INTERNAL VISITATION

The visitation of tombs in Iraq carried important sociopolitical functions and was not confined to the shrines of the imams alone. As in other parts of the Middle East, the cult of local dead saints was prevalent in Iraq. Often it even exceeded in intensity the visitation of the shrines of the imams. It was believed that through the visitation, prayers said by the tomb, and votive offerings, the supplicants could obtain the help and intercession of the saints with God on their behalf. The manner in which the imams and other saints were identified and their attributes acknowledged was shaped by the values and composition of Iraqi Shi'i society. Like the saints in Egypt and Morocco, those in Iraq were a symbolic representation of a total order of things. While the veneration of the saints reflected the tension of people with their social reality, it also helped people to preserve their daily life and cultural identity.[34] In dealing with the visitation in Iraq I will be concerned

[33] Report of the Protector of British Indian Pilgrims, 1929, CO 730/159/2; Census of Iraq's Population, 1932, FO 406/70; Report on the Work of the Indian Section of the British Consulate at Baghdad for 1933, Government of India, Foreign and Political Dept., NAI, file 449-N/34.

[34] Michael Gilsenan, *Saint and Sufi in Modern Egypt* (Oxford, 1973), 42–43; Ernest Gellner, *Saints of the Atlas* (London, 1969), 300; Dale Eickelman, *Moroccan Islam: Tradition and Society in a Pilgrimage Center* (Austin, 1976), 10.

with four major questions: At which stage in the development of Iraq's tribes can one clearly identify their observance of the cult of saints? What light does the tribesmen's expectations of the imams, as well as their cult of other dead saints, throw on the social values and religious identity of the Iraqi Shi'is? What were the functions of the visitation of the shrines and other tombs? What impact did changes in internal visitation during the monarchy have on the position of the shrine cities and the contacts between the mujtahids and the laity?

The paucity of religious rituals among Arab nomadic societies has been noted in North Africa, Yemen, Oman, and Arabia.[35] This feature, which may be attributed in part to the fact that life in the desert generally invokes images of puritanism, is perhaps nowhere more visible than in the cult of saints. Studying the Rawala of northern Arabia, Alois Musil observed that the bedouins "know of no communication with the saints" and that "they have no saints whatsoever." In this respect Michael Meeker commented that "the north Arabian bedouin world seems sober and drab." Patricia Crone noted that bedouin religion comes across as "down-to-earth." The Arabian Bedouin did not participate in the Islamic pilgrimage to Mecca, and those of the inner desert despised the saintly graves of the peasants and disapproved of the cult of saints.[36]

Iraq's nomadic tribes shared many similarities in their life-style with their Arabian counterparts. They were not inclined to visit Najaf and Karbala on pilgrimage, nor did they attach any other religious importance to them.[37] The nomadic tribes of Iraq only faintly acknowledged 'Ali ibn Abi Talib as the fourth caliph or the first Shi'i imam, viewing him more as an ideal figure. They closely associated 'Ali with their own life in the desert, and he was known among them as the "blessed rider" (rakib al-maymun).[38]

The visitation of the shrines of the imams as well as tombs of other saints intensified from the nineteenth century as the bulk of Iraq's nomadic tribes settled down and took up agriculture. The transition of the tribes from nomadic to sedentary life resulted in a major crisis of sociopolitical organization among the tribesmen, reinforced by the fragmentation of the confederations and the decline in the authoritative status of the shaykhs. This, in turn, created a pressing need for saintly services to ease the breaking

[35] E. L. Peters, "Aspects of the Family among the Bedouin of Cyrenaica," in *Comparative Family Systems*, ed. M. F. Nimkoff (Boston, 1965), 124–25; Paul Dresch, *Tribes, Government, and History in Yemen* (Oxford, 1989), 11; Patricia Crone, "Tribes Without Saints," Paper Submitted in the Melon Seminar, 19 April 1991, Department of Near Eastern Studies, Princeton University, 2, 18, 19, 25.

[36] Alois Musil, *The Manners and Customs of the Rwala Bedouins* (New York, 1928), 417–18; Michael Meeker, *Literature and Violence in North Arabia* (Cambridge, 1979), 24; Crone, "Tribes Without Saints," 18, 19.

[37] 'Abbas al-'Azzawi, *'Asha'ir al-'iraq*, 4 vols. (Baghdad, 1937–1956), 1:398.

[38] 'Ali al-Wardi, *Dirasa fi tabi'at al-mujtama' al-'iraqi* (Baghdad, 1965), 239.

down of tribal order and to compensate for the decline in the moral and political authority of the shaykhs. Following their settlement, the tribesmen developed new contacts with Najaf and Karbala, thus gradually restructuring their identity and beginning to share the peasants' view of holy things. As has been seen in chapter 1, the fragmentation of tribal society was linked to the proliferation of the *sayyids* among Iraq's settled tribes. Fulfilling religious, social, and administrative functions within the tribes, *sayyids* often enjoyed the status of living saints among the tribespeople. The functioning of *sayyids* as living saints was supplemented by the development of the visitation of the shrines of the imams and the cult of other dead saints, our concern in this chapter.

Despite the change in their nomadic and religious status, there was still continuity of the former social and cultural values of the tribesmen and thus the Arab attributes of ideal manhood did not cease to be effective in their lives. This may be gathered from the metaphors, values, and images attached to the main characters in the folk stories of such Shi'i tribes in Iraq as the Muntafiq, the Bani Hukayyim, and the Al Fatla. Moreover, as late as the 1950s, Shi'i marsh Arabs continued to identify themselves as bedouin. Calling themselves pure Arabs, they took a fierce pride in danger and suffering, claiming superiority over villagers and townspeople. They valued lineage highly, their honor was easily offended, and they were quick to repay an insult.[39]

The emissaries who propagated Shi'ism among the tribes in Iraq portrayed the imams as possessing the Arab attributes of ideal manhood (*muruwwa*). Attempting to appeal to tribesmen who appreciated values like masculinity, courage, pride, honor, and chivalry, the emissaries dramatized the heroic stand of Husayn during the battle of Karbala and highlighted 'Ali's courage, his eloquence of speech, honesty, and simple way of life. Using poetry as well, they portrayed 'Ali as a wonder man to whom one could turn to in times of trouble:

> Call 'Ali the bearer of miracles
> [and] you will find him an aide for your wishes.[40]

The moral values of Iraq's Shi'i tribes were built into their cult of the saints. The "*minimum de religion*" with which Shi'i Islam influenced the sedentarized tribesmen was transformed in Iraq into a cult of saints, the starting point of which was the ideal manhood of the Arabs. For the Shi'i

[39] See, for example, "The Story of Maqdad, the Hero of Hilla," in *Tales from the Arab Tribes: A Collection of the Stories Told by the Arab Tribes of the Lower Euphrates*, trans. C. G. Campbell (London, 1949), 70–109; Shakir Salim, *Marsh Dwellers of the Euphrates Delta* (London, 1962), esp. 4, 7; Wilfred Thesiger, *The Marsh Arabs* (London, 1964), 93–94.

[40] "Al-Bida' wa al-khurafat wa al-taqalid wa al-'adat 'ind al-shi'a: risala min al-bahrayn," *al-Manar* 13 (1910): 308.

marsh Arabs, the imams, or the saints, were not so much intercessors for the sinners with God. They were more the protectors of property and crops, and the avengers of false oaths. These attributes of the saints gained the highest precedence among tribesmen in general in Iraq, and thus the visitation of the tombs of some local saints was shared by both Shi'i and Sunni tribesmen.[41]

Some of the tribesmen's expectations of the imams may be gathered from the accounts of Iranians, as well as Sunni ulama, who were critical in describing the visitation of Arabs to the shrines. Adib al-Mulk, who visited Iraq in 1856/7, described how Arabs asked imam Husayn to cure them from their illnesses. Visiting Karbala around 1888, the Iranian sufi Pirzadeh described the visitation of Arab tribesmen during Muharram. Pirzadeh criticized them for their view of Husayn as a wonder man able to fulfill personal wishes in this world. He recounted their requests, which included better crops, recovery from illnesses, the bearing of sons, and assistance against enemies. From Pirzadeh's account it is also evident that the religious observances of the tribesmen on the occasion of the visitation differed from those of the other ethnic groups to the extent that he considered them impure. He was particularly critical of the custom whereby men and women used to mix and enter into the inner part of Husayn's shrine together. This custom still existed early in the 1930s, and was criticized by Sunni ulama and by the Shi'i mujtahid Muhsin al-Amin, who visited Iraq in 1933.[42] The access into the inner part of the shrine where the tomb was located often carried the danger that the tomb itself, and the figure believed to be buried in the shrine, would become the focus of worship.

The loyalty of the settled tribesmen to imam 'Ali, as the Iraqi Shi'i sociologist 'Ali al-Wardi has stressed, was based on their admiration of 'Ali on account of his attributes of ideal manhood. The tribesmen did not believe in the emotional commemoration of 'Ali's death or that of Husayn, and saw in their death the object of every hero.[43] This may be gathered also from the following observation:

> The *official* [sic] teaching [of Shi'i Islam] no longer makes any appeal to the masses. They live and thrive on the memory of their saints, whose moral qualities are rarely if ever remembered, but whose feats in the battlefield form an unfailing source of conversation. What use has the cultivator for Allah?

[41] Ibid., 309; "Mas'alat al-qubur wa al-mashahid 'ind al-shi'a," 443, 596; Wardi, *Dirasa*, 236–44; 'Abdallah al-Nafisi, *Dawr al-shi'a fi tatawwur al-'iraq al-siyasi al-hadith* (Beirut, 1973), 72–76.

[42] Adib al-Mulk, *Safarnama*, 207–8; Pirzadeh, *Safarnama*, 1:352–53; "Mas'alat al-qubur wa al-mashahid 'ind al-shi'a," 443, 595–56; "al-Bida' wa al-khurafat," 309; Muhsin al-Amin, *Rihlat al-sayyid muhsin al-amin fi lubnan wa al-'iraq wa-Iran wa-misr wa al-hijaz*, 2d ed. (Beirut, 1985), 133.

[43] Wardi, *Dirasa*, 239–40.

None. That Allah may be the Merciful, the Wise, the Judge to the ninety-ninth power, is of absolutely no interest to him, and has no effect on his daily life. But the stature of 'Ali or Husayn, the way they fought, the blows they gave, the slaughter which they themselves carried out single-handed, the streams of blood which marked their passage through the hordes of the enemy, these are things that the people understand. Here are natural human personalities, exhibiting the perfection of the very qualities that they themselves possess: physical endurance and bravery in warfare . . . a steadfastness and patience in suffering, which is characteristic of all the tribesmen.[44]

This type of veneration, which stressed the physical attributes of the imams, reflected the negligible influence of Sufism and mysticism among the Shi'i rural and tribal population of Iraq. Sufism did not gain ground among Shi'is in Iraq and was recognizable more among Sunnis or the numerically marginal Shi'i extremist groups like the Shabbak of Turkish origin. Such Bektashi and Naqshbandi traces as could be found in the shrine cities early in the twentieth century were the result of Sunni Ottoman influences.[45] The limited influence of Sufism on Shi'is in Iraq stands out when compared with Iranian society, where the presence of mysticism was very strong for at least half a millennium. Among the Iranian pilgrims sufi influences played a more significant role, and thus their contact with the imams during the visitation was often of an essentially different character from that of the Arab tribesmen. The Iranians sought to lift the imams into a supernatural, divine sphere, and crossed the border between human and divine more easily than the tribesmen. Indeed, the Iranians advanced far along the road to deification of the imams, thereby demonstrating the strong mass appeal of the mystics in their society.[46]

Besides the shrines of the imams, there existed other holy sites and tombs of saints in various locations in Iraq, most notably those connected with members of the family of the imams (see appendix 2). It is related that dreams and visions led to the appearance of some of the tombs in southern Iraq, a practice which probably intensified following the settlement of the tribes and their conversion to Shi'ism. Thus, in the mid-nineteenth century a tomb attributed to Sagban, presumably a son of the sixth imam Ja'far al-Sadiq, was identified in Hindiyya. Tombs near Najaf were identified even as

[44] Thomas Lyell, *The Ins and Outs of Mesopotamia* (London, 1923), 183.

[45] Kamil Mustafa al-Shaybi, *al-Tariqa al-safawiyya wa-rawasibuha fi al-'iraq al-mu'asir* (Baghdad, 1967), 39–58; Muhammad al-Khalisi, "al-Tawa'if al-islamiyya fi al-'iraq," *Risalat al-Islam* 6 (1954): 53; 'Abbas al-'Azzawi, *Ta'rikh al-'iraq bayna ihtilalayn*, 8 vols. (Baghdad, 1935–1956), 4:152–55; Administration Reports of the Baghdad Wilayat, 1917, CO 696/1.

[46] Roy Mottahedeh, *The Mantle of the Prophet: Religion and Politics in Iran* (New York, 1985), 144; Ignaz Goldziher, "Veneration of Saints in Islam," in his *Muslim Studies*, ed. S. M. Stern, 2 vols. (London, 1966), 2:294. See also Amin, *Rihlat*, 231.

late as the first half of this century.[47] The following story sheds more light on the way in which tombs of Shi'i saints were acknowledged and developed as sites of visitation. It is said that toward the end of the 1880s, the 'alim Mirza Husayn Nuri reaffirmed that Sayyid Muhammad was a son of the tenth imam. The tomb in question, which before that date had fallen into decay, was rebuilt and was sheathed with copper. It was reported in 1917 that a family of about thirty looked after the tomb and obtained their living from the charity of the visitors.[48]

Overall, five tombs of saints carried particular importance. In the order of their eminence these were the tombs of: 'Abbas, a son of imam 'Ali and Husayn's half-brother, in Karbala; Sayyid Muhammad, a son of the tenth imam, near Balad; 'Abdallah, also a son of 'Ali, south of Qal'at Salih; 'Ali al-Sharqi, a brother of the eighth imam, in Kumayyit; and the tomb of 'Ali al-Yathribi, a son of the seventh imam, near Badra.[49] Believed to possess special attributes, these tombs were frequented by the local population, who made pledges and votive offerings there.

The tribesmen in Iraq venerated dead saints, believing them to possess superior knowledge, particularly the power to determine whether a person was lying. That saints came to function as a kind of a conscience for the settled tribesmen may be gathered from the latter's socioeconomic activities. An oath in the name of a saint played a central part in the daily interaction of Iraqi Shi'i tribesmen and between them and city dwellers. The oath gave force to both personal agreements and business transactions. The selection of the saint in whose name the oath was taken depended on the nature and importance of the contact or transaction involved. An oath in the name of 'Abbas, whose figure became the focus of the tribesmen's admiration, carried more weight among them than one in the name of the Prophet or the imams.[50] Among the tribesmen 'Abbas became known as the "Quick to Anger" (abu ra's al-harr), famed for the swiftness of his vengeance. The tribesmen believed that since the Prophet and the imams were infallible, they would not harm a person who ventured to take a false oath in their name. But 'Abbas was not infallible. An oath in his name was the most binding of all oaths, one that the marsh Arab feared to break lest some dire calamity would speedily befall him or his family. Indeed, the ceiling of the mosque of 'Abbas shows the embedded head of a

---

[47] 'Ali al-Wardi, al-Ahlam bayn al-'ilm wa al-'aqida (Baghdad, 1959), xiii-xiv.

[48] Administration Report of the Baghdad Wilayat, 1917, CO 696/1. See also Yunus Ibrahim al-Samarra'i, Ta'rikh madinat samarra', 3 vols. (Baghdad, 1968–1973), 3:119–20.

[49] Wardi, Dirasa, 241, 244–46.

[50] Nafisi, Dawr, 74–75; Fulanain, The Marsh Arab Haji Rikkan (Philadelphia, 1928), 181. For occasions during which an oath in the name of 'Abbas was taken see Thesiger, The Marsh Arabs, 29, 56.

man; it is believed to have flown off as a result of his swearing falsely in 'Abbas's name.[51]

The breaking down of tribal order helps explain the eminent position and the role that such a figure as 'Abbas came to play among the settled tribesmen. Against the decline in the political and moral authority of the shaykh, the cult of 'Abbas demonstrated the search of the tribesmen for a new father figure who would articulate authority and leadership. Seen from this perspective, the visitation of his shrine by the tribesmen meant to go to where the power was. The patron-client relationships, which were an integral part of the life of the tribes, were built into the cult of the saints in Iraq. Thus, the image attached to some saints reflected their function as patrons, protectors, and mediators, who were ever present in people's lives. In the case of 'Abbas, this was reinforced by the invention of traditions that highlighted his physical capabilities and portrayed him as the ideal cavalier. The relationship of the tribesmen with the saint, however, transcended the abrasive qualities of normal patron-client relationships, for the saint was not a tribal shaykh or a usurper. His cult by the tribesmen, to an extent like the cult of some saints in Latin Christianity as studied by Peter Brown, may be seen as a form of work or piety necessary to the welfare of their daily life. The cult of saints was adopted to enable people to articulate manageable urgent and muffled debates on the nature of power in their own world. Their search for ideal relationships with ideal figures enabled them to examine the relation between power and justice as practiced around them.[52]

In encouraging the visitation of the shrines of the imams, ulama and mujtahids in Iraq attempted to use religion to create political organization over the settled tribesmen. They sought to confirm the contact of the shrine cities with their hinterland, to stimulate religious devotion among the converted tribesmen, and to increase the sense of Shi'i solidarity and unity as a group. For many tribesmen the visitation of the shrines of the imams was a substitute for the hajj to Mecca. The tribesmen were not strict in their religious practices, rarely observing prayers or the fast of Ramadan, but they came to consider the visitation of the shrines of 'Ali, Husayn, and 'Abbas a sacred ritual. They saved money to visit these shrines, and the returned pilgrim was regarded a pious man among his fellow tribesmen.[53]

[51] Wardi, *Dirasa*, 241–42; Fulanain, *The Marsh Arab*, 182, 184–85; Drower, *By Tigris and Euphrates*, 40.

[52] Peter Brown, "The Rise and Function of the Holy Man in Late Antiquity," in his *Society and the Holy in Late Antiquity* (Berkeley, 1982), 121; idem, *The Cult*, 63.

[53] Salim, *Marsh Dwellers*, 12–13; Thesiger, *The Marsh Arabs*, 44, 82; Robert Fernea, *Shaykh and Effendi: Changing Patterns of Authority among the El Shabana of Southern Iraq* (Cambridge, Mass., 1970), 21.

The experience of a Shi'i marsh Arab, who related in the early 1920s how his visit to Karbala subsequently affected both his social position and his own self-image, is worth relating:

> We returned . . . My tribe made *hosa* [a clamorous reception], firing their rifles in the air. And in jest, because I had been to distant Karbala, one of my uncles called me Haji, which nickname clung to me although, long absent as I had been, never had I set foot in distant Mecca. Thus in later years, when I began to have dealings outside the marsh, it became clear to me that this title brought me respect and greater consideration wherever I might be; so with boldness I called myself Haji . . . *w'Allah* [by God], even I myself at times am verily persuaded that I have indeed made the pilgrimage [to Mecca].[54]

The ritual of the visitation and its collective celebration offered a joint experience vital for the maintenance of organized religion and the existing set of social networks. The visitation of the tomb of the imam gave the tribesman a sense of acceptance; he was now a Shi'i by devotion if bedouin by birth. The stress of visitation on specific dates of the year drew together the people of several nearby communities in an emotionally charged display of common purpose. Najaf and Karbala in particular used this to highlight their shrines apart as special destinations. Indeed, when the visitation peaked to extraordinary highs, the two cities could maintain a pilgrimage cultus that thrived on the experience derived from being caught up in mass celebration. This function of the visitation to Najaf and Karbala resembled the three annual visitations performed by the ancient Israelites to the Temple in Jerusalem on the occasion of Passover, Shavuot, and Sukkot; a major aim of these visitations was to strengthen the religious and social solidarity of the Jews of ancient Israel.[55]

At least one visitation, as celebrated at Najaf on the occasion of the Persian new year's day of *Nawruz*, was closely tied to the annual agricultural cycle. As such, it resembled the ancient Israelite pilgrim festival of Shavuot, which marked the end of the barley season and the beginning of the wheat harvest.[56] The Arab tribesmen did not celebrate *Nawruz* as a Persian holiday in the same way that their Persian coreligionists in Iraq did. For the tribesmen *Nawruz* symbolized the first day of spring and the beginning of a new cycle of agricultural and herding activities. This occasion removed them from their ordinary occupations; they celebrated the day by conducting horse races, wearing new clothes, and also by visiting the shrines.[57]

---

[54] Fulanain, *The Marsh Arab*, 84–85.

[55] *Encyclopaedia Judaica*, s.v. "Pilgrimage."

[56] *Encyclopaedia Judaica*, s.v. "Shavuot."

[57] Talib 'Ali al-Sharqi, *al-Najaf al-ashraf: 'adatuha wa-taqaliduha* (Najaf, 1978), 77; 'Abd al-Hadi al-Fadli, *Dalil al-najaf al-ashraf* (Najaf, 1966), 37.

Before World War I, an auspicious visitation could attract at times as many as 150,000 people to Karbala or Najaf, drawn primarily from among the rural and tribal population. This was also the case during *'Id al-Ghadir* and the *'Arafa* festival in 1918 and in 1919, respectively.[58] In subsequent years, however, the influx of the local population to the shrine cities dropped off, caused by the rise of the modern state, the large scale of migration from the Shi'i south to Baghdad, the relative population decrease of Najaf and Karbala, as well as by the increase in education and the changing values of Shi'is already under the monarchy. The drop in the influx of Shi'is to Najaf and Karbala continued after 1958.[59]

The decrease in the intensity of the visitation reinforced the traditionally strong competition between the shrine cities over the local visitors, each city trying to highlight the unique attributes of its own shrines. Thus, with the approach of the days of a visitation much effort was made by ulama in Najaf, Karbala, and Kazimayn to attract pilgrims to their own city's shrines. Stories and rumors were spread in various parts of Iraq regarding deformed pilgrims who had visited the shrines and had been supernaturally cured of their afflictions. One example of a miracle, supposedly wrought in the shrine of the imam Musa al-Kazim at Kazimayn, will suffice. Late in July 1928 a blind and aged *sayyid* was said to have entered the shrine and touched the tomb of the imam, and then suddenly to have recoiled crying out that his sight had been restored. He was at once surrounded by a large crowd, and his clothes were stripped from his back by persons eager to have fragments of his garments as relics. Three times he was clothed again with garments hastily brought from the bazaar, and each time the crowd stripped him. At last, fearing that the man might himself be harmed, the ulama removed him from the crowd and sent him home. The *sayyid* was subsequently visited by many people. He told his visitors that he had been discharged from the Baghdad hospital several months before as incurably blind. Despairing of human aid, he went to the shrine to seek divine mercy; as he touched the tomb a dazzling light struck his eyes, and he heard a voice saying: "go back! your sight is restored to you." The *sayyid* staggered back, and realizing that he could see, proclaimed the miracle to those who were standing by. Although the records of the hospital did not altogether confirm the *sayyid*'s version of his

[58] Fortnightly Report no. 20 by Civil Commissioner to Secretary of State for India, 15 September to 1 October 1918, IO L/P&S 10/732; Administration Report for the Shamiyya Division, 1919, CO 696/2; Office of the Civil Commissioner, Baghdad, 12 September 1919, FO 371/4151/147630. Celebrated on the 9th of the Muslim month of Dhu al-Hijja, the *'Arafa* festival marks the day on which the pilgrims in Mecca visit mount 'Arafat. *'Id al-Ghadir*, which falls on the 18th of the same month, is regarded by Shi'is as the day on which the Prophet Muhammad nominated 'Ali to be his successor.

[59] Sharqi, *al-Najaf al-ashraf*, 81–83.

discharge as incurable, the story of the miracle won some popular credence.[60]

The propaganda of ulama in Najaf and Karbala as manifested in 1932 illustrated how strong the competition between the cities came to be. *Ziyarat al-arba'in*, which marks the fortieth day after the death of Husayn in the battle of Karbala, was a most auspicious one among the seven annual visitations allocated to Karbala by Shi'i traditions. Some time before the visitation of 1932, Shi'is of the Euphrates were exposed to propaganda urging them to visit Najaf on the occasion of *ziyarat al-arba'in* instead of going to Karbala. It was argued that only Husayn's body was buried in Karbala whereas his head was buried in Najaf. Subsequently, the majority of the population visited Najaf that year. This was followed by the issue of circulars from Karbala urging the people to resume the visitation to that city. As is evident from the title of the circular, the importance of *ziyarat al-arba'in* was exalted to the level of a religious obligation incumbent on all Shi'i Muslims:

> You are the best nation that has been raised up for mankind.
> You enjoin the good and forbid the evil.[61]

> *Ziyarat al-arba'in* was specifically assigned to Karbala from the year in which [Husayn] had died . . . The adherence of the ulama of all the countries, particularly those of Najaf, . . . to *ziyarat al-arba'in* and their diligence in visiting Karbala was a practice maintained for over a thousand years. All the people of Najaf, distinguished and common, used to come in processions every year like all other people; save for what has occurred [this year] . . . How can one inflict [such] a *bid'a* on the *shari'a*? Why did the Shi'is replace *ziyarat al-arba'in* of Karbala and go to Najaf, which was given the visitation of *tashri'* Muharram? . . . This is a satanic trick . . . The road to Husayn's tomb will not be blocked, his shrine will not be relinquished, and his visitors will not be driven away.[62]

The drop in the number of visitors to Karbala may have been influenced by an incident during *ziyarat al-arba'in* to that city in 1929 when two groups from Kazimayn and Najaf clashed violently, reviving an older feud between the two cities. Consequently, as late as the 1970s Karbala was deprived of many pilgrims from Najaf as Najafis refrained from visiting the city after that skirmish. Moreover, many residents of the hinterland of Najaf were encouraged to limit their annual visitations of Karbala to

---

[60] Intelligence Report no. 16, 1 August 1928, FO 371/13027/4087.

[61] Koran, Surat al-'Imran: III, 110.

[62] Report by No. 7, 16 June 1932, Air 23/385. The visitation of *tashri'* Muharram was not included among those recommended by the imams. It was probably a late innovation intended to increase the socioeconomic contacts between Najaf and its hinterland.

ziyarat al-arba'in and to visit the shrine of 'Ali at Najaf on such occasions as the anniversary of the death of the Prophet Muhammad.[63]

The rise of the modern state in Iraq highlighted the political function of the visitation. In propagating the visitation of the shrines of the imams, ulama and mujtahids attempted to bolster the political status of Najaf and Karbala vis-à-vis the government in Baghdad. As has been seen in chapters 2 and 3, on various occasions ulama and mujtahids sought to use the visitation to mobilize people for political action through the use of religious symbols. This was clearly demonstrated in Ramadan 1920, when the visitation to Karbala facilitated contact and coordination between mujtahids and tribal shaykhs, and between Shi'is and Sunnis just before the revolt. With the establishment of the monarchy, however, the attempts of ulama and mujtahids to use the visitation as a lever against the government often proved unsuccessful as they lacked the support of the majority of the big tribal shaykhs. This was evident already during the Karbala Conference held on the occasion of the visitation of 15 Sha'ban 1922, just before the deportation of Mahdi al-Khalisi and the departure of other leading mujtahids to Iran. In subsequent years, the government proved capable of managing the majority of the big shaykhs and minimizing the effectiveness of the visitation as an instrument for generating anti-government opposition in Iraq.

For more than a century, the foreign pilgrimage and the internal visitation to the shrine cities bolstered the position of Shi'i Islam in Iraq. While the former reinforced the socioeconomic links of Najaf and Karbala with Iran, the latter became connected to the process of the making of Iraqi Shi'i society in establishing new socioeconomic and religious ties between the settled tribal communities and the shrine cities. The rise of the modern state reversed these trends, leading to a significant decrease in the foreign pilgrimage and internal visitation, as well as in the links of the shrine cities with their hinterland and Iran.

The unfavorable impact which this development had on the welfare of Najaf and Karbala was reinforced by the decline of the corpse traffic from Iran to the shrine cities under the monarchy.

[63] Wardi, *Dirasa*, 190–91; Sharqi, *al-Najaf al-ashraf*, 253.

Chapter Seven

THE CORPSE TRAFFIC

It is related that the commander of the faithful ['Ali] once sought solitude and went to a place on the edge of the city of Najaf for seclusion. One day while 'Ali was glancing at Najaf, he suddenly saw a man approaching from the desert, riding a camel and transporting a corpse. When the man saw 'Ali, he walked up to him and greeted him. 'Ali returned the greeting and asked the man: where are you from? The man answered: from Yemen. And what is this corpse? It is my father's corpse; I came to bury it in this land. Why did you not bury him in your own land? It is my father who ordered me to do so, and he said that [one day] there will be buried a man [in Najaf] whose intercession [with God] would be so far reaching that it would go back in time to Rabi'a and Mudar. Do you know who this man is? asked 'Ali. No said the man. 'Ali then said: by God, I am that man. Go and bury your father.[1]

THE BURIAL of corpses in holy places is well established in Judaism, Christianity, and Islam. In Judaism, for example, the slopes of the Mount of Olives have been the most sacred burial ground for centuries. Traditions relate that the prophet Zechariah is buried at the foot of the Mount; it is also believed that at the end of days the Messiah will ascend the Mount, and it will be there that Ezekiel will blow his trumpet for the resurrection of the dead.[2] According to Islamic traditions, many Muslim saints and heroes were buried near the Temple Mount or the Mount of Olives, evidently so that they too might be among the first to rise on the day of resurrection.[3]

The location of a person's grave has generally been considered a matter of importance in Islam. In late medieval Egypt, for example, people thought it essential to bury the dead as far as possible from the graves of the sinful and in close proximity to saints. Consequently, many graves were identified as tombs of saints and the areas around them became highly sought after as ground for burial.[4] An anecdote from a much later period,

---

[1] Ibrahim al-Musawi al-Zanjani, *'Aqa'id al-imamiyya al-ithna 'ashariyya*, 2d ed., 3 vols. (Beirut, 1973–1977), 2:256. The two brothers Rabi'a and Mudar ibn Nizar were Jahili figures, the latter the ancestor of the Prophet Muhammad.

[2] *Encyclopaedia Judaica*, s.v. "Mount of Olives"; *Encyclopaedia Judaica*, s.v. "Holy Places."

[3] *Encyclopaedia Judaica*, s.v. "Eschatology"; *Encyclopaedia of Islam*, 2d ed. s.v. "Kiyama."

[4] Christopher Taylor, "The Cult of the Saints in Late Medieval Egypt" (Ph.D. diss., Princeton University, 1989), 238, 241.

cited by Edward Lane, who visited Egypt during the 1820s and 1830s, again demonstrates the importance attached to the burial ground. It describes how a dead saint compelled the bearers of his corpse to take it to a particular spot. The bearers had carried the corpse to a tomb that had been prepared for it in one of Cairo's big cemeteries. On arriving at the gate of the cemetery, however, the bearers had found themselves unable to proceed farther. After several unsuccessful attempts to force the corpse through the gate, they realized that the dead saint was determined not to be buried in that cemetery, preferring a different spot.[5]

In Shi'i Islam the shrine cities emerged as the preferred burial ground for Shi'i believers, who sought to pass the interval between death and resurrection in the vicinity of their imams. The development of the practice symbolized the apprehensions of human individuals regarding the hereafter. It reflected the perception of death by Shi'i believers, and their image of the imams as capable of interceding on their behalf on the day of resurrection.

In this chapter I will first discuss the development of the practice of transferring corpses to the shrine cities, showing how it was linked to the welfare of various professionals and social groups. I will then illustrate the tension in Shi'i Islam between scripture and social custom as manifested in the controversy among mujtahids over the practice. The tension highlighted the delicate position of the reformers, who sought to change social norms and reshape Shi'i religious practices. I will finally show how the policies of the Iraqi and Iranian governments, aimed at reducing the ties of the shrine cities with Iran, affected the transfer of corpses from that country to the shrine cities.

DEVELOPMENT AND SOCIOECONOMIC FUNCTIONS

The transfer of corpses is known as *naql al-jana'iz* or *naql al-amwat*. Shi'is maintain that 'Ali ibn Abi Talib was the first Shi'i whose corpse was taken from its original grave and buried in Najaf.[6] Although subsequently Shi'is began transporting corpses to Najaf and other shrine cities, the practice developed on a very massive scale only after the establishment of Safavid Iran (1501) and the conversion of Iranians to Shi'ism. The corpse traffic gained further momentum in the nineteenth century as the bulk of Iraq's tribes was converted to Shi'ism. The four major consecrated cemeteries in the shrine cities in the order of their importance were: Wadi al-Salam at Najaf, Wadi al-Iman at Karbala, Maqabir Quraysh at Kazimayn, and al-Tarima at Samarra. Corpses of particularly distinguished or affluent

[5] Edward Lane, *An Account of the Manners and Customs of the Modern Egyptians*, 3d ed. (reprint, London, 1890), 479.

[6] 'Abd al-Husayn Ahmad al-Amini al-Najafi, *al-Ghadir fi al-kitab wa al-sunna wa al-a'dab*, 3d ed., 11 vols. (Beirut, 1967), 5:68.

figures were buried in the precincts of the shrines themselves (see appendix 3).

More than any other shrine city in Iraq, it was Najaf that emerged as the major magnet attracting the bulk of the corpse traffic. The burial grounds in Najaf came to be regarded as the most sacred by Shi'i believers. This was partly the consequence of the prevalence of beliefs among Shi'is that portrayed 'Ali as the most effective protector, aide, and intercessor on behalf of believers, both immediately after their death, when their acts were judged by the two angels Munkir and Nakir, and on the day of resurrection.[7] For example, one Shi'i Tradition relates that burial in the vicinity of 'Ali will eliminate the ordeal of the dead in the grave, and reduce the interval (barzakh) between death and resurrection. Another Tradition, attributed to the sixth imam Ja'far al-Sadiq, relates that being next to 'Ali for a day is more favorable than seven hundred years of worship.[8]

The story connected with the development of Maqabir Quraysh suggests that in its initial stages the transportation of corpses to consecrated cemeteries may have been more prevalent among the elite than the masses, who usually could not meet the high costs involved. It is related that around 767 the 'Abbasid caliph Abu Ja'far al-Mansur buried his son in a cemetery in Kazimayn, to which he gave the name Maqabir Quraysh. The cemetery thus became a place of burial for members of the family of the Prophet Muhammad (who originated from the Arab tribe of Quraysh), notably members of the 'Abbasid dynasty and those of 'Ali's family. Maqabir Quraysh increased in sanctity following the burial there of the seventh and ninth imams Musa al-Kazim and his grandson Muhammad al-Jawad in 799 and 835, respectively.[9] The data on Najaf shed further light on the custom of families of Shi'i rulers and notables to bury their dead in or near the city's shrine. By the Buyid period (945–1055), this custom seems to have been well developed. Thus, for example, the two Buyid rulers 'Adud al-Dawla and his son Sharaf al-Dawla were buried in the city in 983 and 990, respectively. A large number of rulers of other Shi'i dynasties, as well as many ministers, dignitaries, and ulama, were also buried near or around the shrine of 'Ali.[10]

With the conversion of the majority of the population of Iran to Shi'ism

[7] Ja'far al-Mahbuba, *Madi al-najaf wa-hadiruha*, 3 vols. (Najaf, 1955–1958), 1:14–15; 'Ali al-Wardi, *Dirasa fi tabi'at al-mujtama' al-'iraqi* (Baghdad, 1965), 252–53; 'Abd al-Hujja Balaghi, *Ta'rikh-i najaf-i ashraf va-hire* (Tehran, 1948/9), 171. See also Mirza Mahdi al-Husayni al-Khurasani, *Mu'jizat va-kiramat-i a'imma-yi athar* (Tehran, 1949), 21–22.

[8] Mahbuba, *Madi al-najaf*, 1:15. See also Ahmad Kasravi, *al-Tashayyu' wa al-shi'a* (Tehran, 1944/5), 94.

[9] Ja'far al-Khalili, *Mawsu'at al-'atabat al-muqaddasa, al-juz' al-awwal min qism al-kazimayn*, 10 vols. (Baghdad and Beirut, 1965–1970), 5,1:22; 'Abd al-Razzaq Kammuna al-Husayni, *Mawarid al-athaf fi nuqaba' al-ashraf*, 2 vols. (Najaf, 1968), 2:155–69.

[10] Mahbuba, *Madi al-najaf*, 1:237–48; Khalili, *al-Madkhal ila mawsu'at al-'atabat al-muqaddasa*, 1:100.

in the sixteenth century, Najaf and Karbala became the focus of devotion for larger numbers of Iranians. The increase in the proportion of Shi'is among Muslims as a result of mass conversion was a precondition to the development of the corpse traffic on a much larger scale than that which had existed prior to 1501. The transfer of corpses in caravans by professional contractors reduced costs, enabling a growing number of Iranians to meet the expenses involved in transporting their dead to the shrine cities. The transfer of corpses from Iran to the shrine cities was linked to the claims of the Safavids, and their successors the Qajars, that the Shah should be the sole protector of Shi'i affairs in Iraq. By 1573, the practice was already a factor in fueling the tension between Safavid Iran and the Ottoman Empire. As may be gathered from an Ottoman report cited by Colin Imber, fifty appointees of the Shah marched in that year with standards from the shrine of 'Abbas in Karbala to meet caravans of corpses from Iran. Upon their return to Karbala, they paraded with the corpses around the holy places of the shrine. Since at that time the Ottoman government sought to reduce tensions with Iran (because of ongoing hostilities on its western frontier), it permitted the burial of Iranians in the shrine of 'Abbas, on condition that the corpses would not be laid in the direction of Ardabil, where the Safavid order had developed.[11]

The corpse traffic increased in scale from the mid-eighteenth century as Najaf and Karbala emerged as the main Shi'i strongholds in Iraq, and the bulk of Iraq's tribes was converted to Shi'ism. The practice was closely linked to the pilgrimage and the internal visitation of the shrine cities, which, as has been shown in the previous chapter, intensified from around that time.[12] Shi'i ulama in Iraq encouraged the corpse traffic to reinforce the position of the shrine cities as the focus of devotion for Shi'i believers. Thus, the important Najafi mujtahid Shaykh Ja'far Kashif al-Ghita (d. 1812) issued a *fatwa* in which he apparently not only permitted the transportation of a whole corpse for burial in the shrine cities, but even of small parts of it.[13] The corpse traffic reached its peak in the late nineteenth century and became an integral part of a whole set of rituals, visitations, and religious practices that helped ensure the welfare of Najaf and Karbala, as well as their ties with their hinterland and other parts of the Shi'i world.

By late Ottoman time, as many as 20,000 corpses were brought annually to Najaf alone both from within and outside Iraq.[14] This figure seemed to

[11] C. H. Imber, "The Persecution of the Ottoman Shi'ites according to the Mühimme Defterleri, 1565–1585," *Isl* 56 (1979): 246–47.

[12] See also Wardi, *Dirasa*, 251.

[13] Muhammad al-Hasan al-Najafi, *Jawahir al-kalam fi sharh shara'i' al-islam*, 6th ed., 42 vols. (Najaf, 1958), 4:348; Mirza Muhammad Tunakabuni, *Qisas al-'ulama'* (Tehran, n.d.), 198.

[14] Great Britain, Administration Reports of the Shamiyya Division, 1918, Najaf, CO 696/2; Annual Administration Report on the Iraq Health Services for the Year 1921, CO 696/4.

reflect the legal as well as the high rate of illegal transfer of corpses. Official estimates also put the annual average of foreign corpses, brought primarily to Najaf from Iran, at 5,300.[15] So massive was the transfer of corpses to Najaf and Karbala from the mid-eighteenth century that much of the recently built residential areas of the two cities were on old cemeteries that sank with time.[16] Moreover, Wadi al-Salam, Najaf's main cemetery, is claimed by Shi'is to be one of the largest in the world.[17] Once inside Wadi al-Salam, Shi'i sources tell us, Shi'i visitors were strongly affected by the cemetery, for they felt as if they were looking over the great relics of the world and facing a profound silence which had engulfed both rulers and subjects. They looked upon graves newly made, graves which had sunk, those which were on the verge of sinking, and graves within graves with mounds over them.[18] It is evident from this description of Wadi al-Salam that the holy cemeteries in Shi'i Islam, like the shrines of the imams, were intended to achieve the important goal of reinforcing the collective memory of Shi'is as well as their group identity.

The increase in the number of corpses transported to the shrine cities from within Iraq in the nineteenth century may be attributed to the changing values of Iraqi tribesmen following their settlement and conversion, particularly their perception of death and eschatology. The bedouin, to cite Alois Musil, "do not know and never visit individual graves."[19] Like many of their Arabian counterparts, Iraq's nomadic tribes were not very much consumed with the hereafter, and their idea of it was quite hazy. It is also doubtful whether they had any permanent burying places as they probably buried their dead on the spot. By contrast, eschatology came to play a growing role in shaping the religious morality of the settled and converted tribesmen, and they began conceiving the burial in holy cemeteries, close to the imams, as a meritorious act which results in heavenly rewards.

The corpse traffic became an integral part of the life of Iraqi Shi'i tribesmen as may be gathered by its mention in their folktales.[20] Like the cult of

[15] Government of Iraq, Dept. of Health Services, Report of the Inspector-General of Health Services for the Year 1923–24, CO 696/5.

[16] Hasan al-Amin, "Wadis Salam," *ISE* 4 (1973): 97; Sultan Muhammad Farzand Sayf al-Dawla, *Safarnama-yi sayf al-dawla*, 2d ed. (Tehran, n.d.), 228.

[17] Muhsin 'Abd al-Sahib al-Muzaffar, "Wadi al-salam fi al-najaf: min awsa' maqabir al-'alam," *al-'Irfan* 51 (1963): 164; Amin, "Wadis Salam," 95; 'Abd al-Hadi al-Fadli, *Dalil al-najaf al-ashraf* (Najaf, 1966), 110; Khalili, *al-Madkhal*, 1:104.

[18] Amin, "Wadis Salam," 95–96; Muzaffar, "Wadi al-salam," 165–67, 285–88; Hajji Pirzadeh, *Safarnama-yi hajji pirzadeh*, ed. Hafez Farman-Farmayan, 2 vols. (Tehran, 1963), 1:327; Adib al-Mulk, *Safarnama-yi adib al-mulk bi-'atabat (dalil al-za'irin)*, 1273 h.q. (Tehran, 1985/6), 192.

[19] Alois Musil, *The Manners and Customs of the Rwala Bedouins* (New York, 1928), 418.

[20] See "The Story of the Lost Soul" as related among the Bani Hukayyim in *Tales from the Arab Tribes: A Collection of the Stories Told by the Arab Tribes of the Lower Euphrates*, trans. C. G. Campbell (London, 1949), 56–69.

the saints, the corpse traffic reflected the social order and the reliance of the tribesmen in their daily lives on a protector.[21] The image of 'Ali as the protector of the dead was very strong among Shi'i tribes and marsh dwellers in Iraq still in the first half of this century. Shakir Mustafa Salim observed that dwellers from all over the marsh region, however far, wished to be buried in the sacred grounds of Najaf. If this could not be done immediately after death, the corpse was usually buried in a local site, or near the tomb of a distinguished *sayyid* or *'alim*, or even in the closest shrine city, until the family was able to transfer it to Najaf.[22] That 'Ali came to be regarded by the converted tribesmen as the most effective intercessor with God may also be gathered from their saying: "There is no saint but 'Ali" (*maku wali ila 'ali*).[23]

One of the particular characteristics of the practice as observed by Iraqi Shi'i tribesmen was their collective effort in transferring corpses to the shrine cities. Assisting one's family in transporting their dead was a major obligation of Shi'i tribal clans, and all members were expected to abide by it. The clan assisted the family of the deceased either by contributing to the collection of a sufficient sum of money to transfer the corpse to Najaf, or by offering food on behalf of the family to those who came to offer their condolences. When the family decided to follow the usual custom and transfer the corpse itself, the clan was divided into three sections, each bearing the expenses for one of the three-day mourning ceremonies that preceded the transfer. During the ceremonies other clans who maintained a friendly relationship with the deceased or his family also offered gifts. At times, even the budget of municipalities in Shi'i districts included a certain amount of money set aside for the purpose of transporting corpses to the shrine cities.[24]

The different class attributes of Iraqi Shi'i society were evident in the ways in which they buried their dead. Tribes, cities, and families had separate grounds set aside for their use in Wadi al-Salam. A burial in the portico of the shrine of Najaf, in the chambers of the courtyard, or in its grounds was considered most auspicious; these places of burial were reserved for important mujtahids and for affluent people whose relatives could afford it. Among families of well-to-do ulama there was a strong tendency to bury their dead either in particular grounds within Wadi al-Salam, or in or near their own houses. Special cellars or catacombs (*saradib*) were built for that purpose. This custom developed in keeping with the will of the dead, the desire of members of the family to be in the

[21] Wardi, *Dirasa*, 253–54.

[22] S. M. Salim, *Marsh Dwellers of the Euphrates Delta* (London, 1962), 13.

[23] Thomas Lyell, *The Ins and Outs of Mesopotamia* (London, 1923), 97.

[24] Salim, *Marsh Dwellers*, 46; Talib 'Ali al-Sharqi, *'Ayn al-tamr* (Najaf, 1969), 135; Wardi, *Dirasa*, 252; 'Abd al-'Aziz al-Qassab, *Min dhikrayati* (Beirut, 1962), 87.

company of one another after their death, and in order to save their graves from being effaced or demolished.[25]

Lady Drower, who visited Najaf in 1922, was somewhat disappointed at the size of the cemeteries in the city given the fact that thousands of corpses were brought there annually for interment: "One wonders, not at the size of these cemeteries, but at their smallness. They are not bigger than would be justified by the size of the town if only its own dead were buried in them. I was told that there are ten thousand graves in Najaf, never more and never less, in spite of the annual import of corpses. What is the explanation of this strange phenomenon?"[26] At least part of the explanation was given by Hasan al-Amin and Muhsin 'Abd al-Sahib al-Muzaffar. They explained that because of the unique composition of the soil in Wadi al-Salam, the rocks and soil around the grave would hold for only a short period of time before collapsing; this in turn would cause the cavity containing the corpse to sink down and disappear.[27]

The Ottomans imposed taxes both on the importation of corpses and on the transfer of corpses of Ottoman Shi'i subjects to the shrine cities; in the case of the latter the fees were on a lower scale. Late in the nineteenth century the cost of transporting a corpse of an Iranian subject from Kirmanshah to Karbala, for example, was as high as 1.35 Turkish gold lira, about one English pound. This rate also reflected the fees collected by the Ottoman consulate at Kirmanshah for the issue of a pass for the importation of the corpse, and by the sanitary officials at Khanaqin where it was later inspected.[28] As shown in appendix 3, the Ottoman government levied a tax (dafniya or turabiyya) on the burial of corpses in the main cemeteries of the shrine cities and in the precincts of the shrines. A fixed tariff that varied according to the sanctity of the site, the annual average income from this tax amounted to 7,700 Turkish liras, about £6,930.[29]

Both within and outside the shrine cities there were groups whose livelihood depended on the number of corpses transported for burial annually, particularly to Najaf and Karbala. Ottoman sanitary regulations stipulated the burial of foreign corpses for at least three years before they could be brought into Iraq. There were, therefore, professionals near the border posts between Iran and Iraq whose task was to dry moist corpses so that they could

---

[25] Amin, "Wadis Salam," 96–97; Muzaffar, "Wadi al-salam," 613–15; Talib 'Ali al-Sharqi, al-Najaf al-ashraf: 'adatuha wa-taqaliduha (Najaf, 1978), 128–34. A detailed list of burial grounds of families of ulama in Najaf may be found in Fadli, Dalil al-najaf, 111–17.

[26] Lady E. S. Stevens Drower, By Tigris and Euphrates (London, 1923), 29.

[27] Amin, "Wadis Salam," 96; Muzaffar, "Wadi al-salam," 608.

[28] J. G. Lorimer, Gazetteer of the Persian Gulf, 'Oman and Central Arabia, 2 vols. in 5 pts. (Calcutta, 1908–15), 1,2:2361–62.

[29] Lorimer, Gazetteer, 2A:859–60; Administration Report of the Baghdad Wilayat for 1918, Karbala and Najaf, CO 696/1.

pass the inspection of the Ottoman health officials. At the same time, the lucrative income from the corpse traffic resulted in the development of a brisk illegal transfer of corpses, which was intended to avoid the fees imposed by the Ottoman authorities and the inspection of the health officials.[30]

The welfare of the contractors and carriers who transported the corpses in caravans from Iran to the shrine cities was also influenced by the scale of the traffic. The contractors, who used to collect corpses in various locations in Iran, were paid for their services by those Iranians who could not transport their dead to the shrine cities themselves. It may be that some contractors were given commissions by those dwellers in the shrine cities, whose livelihood depended on this trade, to make sure that they would not bury the corpses somewhere along the way. In the mid-nineteenth century, when such a caravan arrived at Najaf, the corpses were left outside the walls while usually the leader of the caravan attempted to negotiate for the burial place. Often, several days could be spent on these preliminaries before the Ottomans in a later period fixed the tariffs. From the accounts of travelers in Iraq it is evident that caravans of mules, loaded with up to six corpses each, were a common site in khans and along the routes leading to Najaf and Karbala in the nineteenth and early twentieth centuries. The corpses, or the remaining bones, were usually transported in long, narrow wooden boxes covered with felt.[31]

Within the cities, the livelihood of shroud makers, grave diggers, tomb builders, servants in the shrines, as well as ulama and students was also closely connected to the corpse traffic.[32] The newly arrived corpse was washed, wrapped in a shroud and taken for burial accompanied by hired mourners and ulama who chanted Koranic verses. The servants of the shrines apparently used to circulate with corpses of important figures within the shrine before burial, an act which was considered meritorious for the dead, and for which the servants were well paid.[33] Students were paid for trimming the light and for reciting prayers over the graves of the dead whose families had sent money for that purpose. The money was

[30] Hibat al-Din al-Shahrastani, "Hal yajuz naql al-jana'iz 'ala al-awjuh al-sha'i'a," al-'Ilm 2 (1911): 116, 120–21.

[31] William Loftus, Travels and Researches in Chaldaea and Susiana (London, 1857), 54–55; John Ussher, A Journey from London to Persepolis (London, 1865), 439, 459–60, 481–82; H. Cowper, Through Turkish Arabia: A Journal from the Mediterranean to Bombay by the Euphrates and Tigris Valleys and the Persian Gulf (London, 1894; reprint, 1987), 371–72; John Peters, Nippur or Explorations and Adventures on the Euphrates, 2d ed. (New York, 1898), 324–25; Madame Jane Dieulafoy, La Perse la Chaldée et la Susiane (Paris, 1887), 611–12; Drower, By Tigris, 25.

[32] Wardi, Dirasa, 251; 'Abdallah al-Nafisi, Dawr al-shi'a fi tatawwur al-'iraq al-siyasi al-hadith (Beirut, 1973), 77.

[33] Drower, By Tigris, 30; Tunakabuni, Qisas al-'ulama', 187.

usually entrusted to the custodian of the shrine for disbursement. It was reported in 1918 that there were as many as two thousand readers of prayers in Najaf recruited from among the student population there. Each usually looked after three tombs for a monthly fee of five rupees per tomb.[34]

By late Ottoman times, corpses were being transported to the shrine cities on a massive scale, both legally and illegally. At that time, rapid transportation systems and regulations for the dignified transportation of corpses were not yet in existence. Strict sanitary measures that would prevent the spread of epidemics were hardly observed by the carriers. Against this, Shi'i mujtahids were engaged in a debate over the moral and legal aspects of the practice and its desirability.

THE RELIGIOUS CREED VERSUS THE SOCIAL ORDER

The discussion of *naql al-jana'iz* in Shi'i jurisprudence usually centers around two major issues. The first concentrates on the transfer of a corpse, whether already buried or not, for burial in non-holy ground. The second focuses on the transfer of a corpse, whether before or after its initial burial, to holy ground like that near the shrines of the imams. It is the second issue that concerns us here.

Sunni and Shi'i ulama addressed themselves to the question of transfer of corpses for burial in holy sites at least from the tenth century. The discussions focused on the legal aspects of the practice and the restrictions governing it.[35] As may be gathered from nineteenth-century discussions, the increase in the scale of the corpse traffic at that time resulted in new complexities arising from the massive transfer of corpses or their parts to the shrine cities. The increase in scale in the nineteenth century triggered Sunni-Shi'i polemics over the legal, moral, and sanitary aspects of the practice as well as its prevalence among Shi'is in particular.[36] Thus, for example, the chronicler of the Sunni Ottoman governor Da'ud Pasha attacked early in the nineteenth century one of the practices associated with *naql al-jana'iz*. He claimed that some of the residents of Karbala owned big catacombs or tanks (*saharij*) and charged money for burial inside them. When the catacombs became full, the owners used to sell the corpses to the

---

[34] Administration Report of the Baghdad Wilayat, 1918, Najaf, CO 696/1.

[35] An overview of the position of the four Sunni schools may be found in 'Abd al-Rahman al-Jaziri, *Kitab al-fiqh 'ala al-madhahib al-arba'a*, 2d ed., 4 vols. (Cairo, 1964), 1:537. Two representative classical Shi'i discussions of *naql al-jana'iz* are Abu Ja'far Muhammad al-Tusi, *al-Mabsut fi fiqh al-imamiyya*, 8 vols. (Tehran, 1967), 1:187–88; Muhammad ibn Mansur ibn Ahmad ibn Idris al-Hilli, *Kitab al-sara'ir*, 2d ed., 2 vols. (Qum, 1989), 1:170.

[36] Najafi, *Jawahir al-kalam*, 4:348; Amini, *al-Ghadir*, 5:66.

local bathhouse, where they were burnt, probably to generate hot water.[37] The debate among Shi'i mujtahids early in the twentieth century reflected the impact of the Islamic modernists, who sought to increase the role of the Koran in daily life and to reduce religious differences between Sunnis and Shi'is.[38] As has been seen in chapter 2, the restoration of the Turkish Constitution in 1908 led to a relative increase in the freedom of publication in the Ottoman Empire. The new freedom of expression enabled Shi'i mujtahids to discuss the corpse traffic in the form of articles published in Shi'i journals that appeared in Lebanon and Iraq around that time (al-'Irfan in Sidon in 1909 and al-'Ilm in Najaf in 1910), reaching a wider audience than the treatises written by their predecessors.

In July and August 1911 Hibat al-Din al-Shahrastani published a sharp criticism of *naql al-jana'iz*.[39] His attack on the custom as observed by the laity did not go unanswered. It activated a debate, notably between 'Abd al-Husayn Sharaf al-Din of Jabal 'Amil and Shahrastani, and led to the issue of legal opinions by two of the most prominent Shi'i mujtahids of the time, Muhammad Kazim Khurasani and 'Abdallah Mazandarani.[40]

Shahrastani's point of departure was that the laity, the majority of the believers, performed rituals and practices immoderately; they ignored the legal limits imposed by the mujtahids and did not grasp the harmful effect of these practices on society. One of these practices was *naql al-jana'iz*, and Shahrastani announced that it was his intention to warn of the abuse of the practice by the laity and to present the legal facts regarding its permissibility.[41] He asserted that Islam in its original form did not permit the transfer of corpses from one place to another and questioned the authenticity of Traditions that maintained that the corpses of distinguished Ko-

---

[37] 'Uthman ibn Sanad al-Basri al-Wa'ili, *Mukhtasar kitab matali' al-su'ud bi-tayyib akhbar al-wali da'ud*, ed. Amin al-Hilwani (Cairo, 1951/2), 75.

[38] See especially "al-Bida' wa al-khurafat wa al-taqalid wa al-'adat 'ind al-shi'a: risala min al-bahrayn," *al-Manar* 13 (1910): 311.

[39] Hibat al-Din al-Shahrastani, "al-Mawta yastaghithuna," and "Hal yajuz," *al-'Ilm* 2 (1911): 50–57, 112–21. These may have been, in whole or in part, a reproduction of a short treatise published by Shahrastani earlier that year: *Tahrim naql al-jana'iz* (Baghdad, al-Adab, 1911). For Shahrastani's position concerning the practice later in the twentieth century see "Nabsh al-qubur wa-naql al-mawta," *al-Murshid* 3 (1928), 71.

[40] 'Abd al-Husayn Sharaf al-Din al-Musawi, "al-Shahrastani wa-naql al-amwat," *al-'Irfan* 3 (1911): 897–902, 977–84; Hibat al-Din al-Shahrastani, "Naql al-amwat wa al-sayyid al-musawi," *al-'Irfan* 4 (1912): 108–18. For the *fatwas* see "Tahrim naql al-jana'iz," *al-'Irfan* 3 (1911): 914–16. The following two treatises were not available to me: 'Abd al-Husayn Sharaf al-Din al-Musawi, *Bughyat al-fa'iz fi naql al-jana'iz*; Sayyid Sadiq Al al-Sayyid Radi, *al-Hujja al-baligha li al-shi'a fi jawaz naql al-mawta fi al-shari'a*, 1911/12. For a short discussion of the 1911 controversy over *naql al-jana'iz* see Werner Ende, "Eine Schiitische Kontroverse über *Naql al-Ğana'iz*," ZDMG, Suppl. 4 (Wiesbaden, 1980), 217–18.

[41] Shahrastani, "al-Mawta," 50; "Hal yajuz," 112–13; "Naql al-amwat," 108–9.

ranic figures like Adam, Jacob, and Joseph were transferred for burial at Najaf (in the case of Adam) and at the Temple in Jerusalem (in the case of the latter two). Citing other Traditions, he attempted to prove that the Prophet prohibited the transfer of the corpses of his warrior followers to Medina, ordering their burial at the battleground. Shahrastani pointed out that imam 'Ali also prohibited the practice, warning the Muslims not to follow the Jewish custom of transferring corpses to the Temple.[42]

Shahrastani argued that it was only from the tenth century that Shi'i ulama had begun permitting the transfer of corpses to the shrines of the imams, the first being Ibn Babawayh, who relied on weak Traditions. Citing Muhammad Baqir Majlisi, Shahrastani attempted to show that there was no consensus among the Shi'i jurists over the various aspects of the practice. He highlighted the restrictions imposed on the transfer by prominent Shi'i jurists, notably al-Shaykh al-Mufid, Muhammad ibn al-Hasan al-Tusi, Ibn Idris, Ibn Hamza, and al-Shahid al-Awwal. Shahrastani explained that the practice must be subject to three major conditions: First, it should conform with the will of the dead; second, the transfer should not lead to the disgrace of the corpse, the dishonor of the dead, or the violation of Islamic code of burial; and third, it should not harm society or the environment.[43]

Furious with the disgraceful manner in which most of the corpses were transferred, and with the harmful consequences to the environment, Shahrastani made an emotional appeal to the Shi'i community: "Until when O my coreligionists, shall we continue to commit these forbidden [acts], displaying them under the mantle of worship and obedience? God has fixed boundaries to his decrees. Do not go beyond them for whoever goes beyond the boundaries fixed by God will be in hell." Shahrastani argued that the laity chose to emulate those mujtahids, who, out of fear of them, permitted the practice, thereby ruling against their own conscience. Ignoring the limits imposed by the mujtahids, the laity transferred their dead without distinction, disgraced the latter's honor, and harmed the environment by spreading epidemics.[44]

Shahrastani pointed to two widespread customs among the laity, neither of which, he asserted, was sanctioned by Islamic law. The first was the temporary deposit (*amana*) of the dead, for example in a cool cellar (*sir-dab*), sometimes for years, until the corpse could be transferred to the shrine cities for burial; this delay, he explained, deprived the dead of a legal burial and often led to the disgrace of the corpse. A second custom was the transfer of the corpse in stages from one shrine to another until it finally reached the one most highly sought after, that of 'Ali at Najaf. Shahrastani

[42] Shahrastani, "al-Mawta," 51–52, 54–55; "Hal yajuz," 114.
[43] Shahrastani, "al-Mawta," 50, 52–53, 56; "Naql al-amwat," 117–18.
[44] Shahrastani, "al-Mawta," 50–51, 53–54.

argued that once a corpse was buried in a holy place where the spirit of the dead could enjoy the blessing of the place, there was no need to transfer it further.[45]

Attempting to alert people, Shahrastani demonstrated how in many cases corpses were disgraced by carriers who depended on this trade for their livelihood, or by health officials who had to determine whether the corpses were dry enough to be admitted to Iraq, or even by family members who transported their dead themselves.[46] He told, for example, the story of a renowned *sayyid* and *'alim* of Behbahan. After the *sayyid*'s death, his son decided to take his father's corpse for burial at Najaf. Consequently, a large number of people in the community of Behbahan among which the *sayyid* had lived sent with the son many of their own dead relatives to be buried next to the distinguished *sayyid*; they hoped that this would enable their dead to reach heaven more easily. Whenever the son passed through a village or a town, residents added more corpses. By the time the son had reached Basra there were already some four hundred corpses in his charge. The corpses, however, never reached Najaf, for a fire that broke out near Basra where the son was encamping incinerated them all.[47]

Shahrastani maintained that no jurist would have permitted the transfer of corpses when this disgraced the honor of the dead or harmed the environment. He considered this a humiliation both to the Shi'i community and to the shari'a. Against this, he even wondered whether one should put an end to the practice altogether even in cases that involved a relatively short transfer like that from Kufa to Najaf.[48] In advocating a sweeping abolition of the practice, Shahrastani broke ranks with the legal opinions of such classical Shi'i jurists as Muhammad ibn al-Hasan al-Tusi (d. 1067) and even Ibn Idris (d. 1202). Both Tusi and Ibn Idris recommended the transfer of corpses which had not been initially buried to the shrine cities. While the former reluctantly also permitted the transfer of corpses after they had already been buried, the latter prohibited this type of transfer and considered it a *bid'a*.[49]

The response to Shahrastani's criticism was blunt. Sharaf al-Din reproached him for failing to distinguish between the various categories of *naql al-jana'iz* and charged that it was evident from Shahrastani's discussion that the latter sought to prohibit the practice altogether, thereby taking a stand against the consensus of the mujtahids. Sharaf al-Din went so far as to suggest that in doing so Shahrastani had disapproved of the

[45] Ibid., 50, 54, 56–57.
[46] Shahrastani, "Hal yajuz," 115–21. For this point see also Kasravi, al-Tashayyu' wa al-shi'a, 95.
[47] Shahrastani, "Hal yajuz," 116–17.
[48] Shahrastani, "al-Mawta," 51.
[49] Tusi, al-Mabsut, 1:187; Ibn Idris, al-Sara'ir, 1:170.

Muslim way of life, contenting himself only with Western values as capable of reforming Islam.[50] So strong were these charges that Shahrastani later had to clarify his position. He explained that his criticism of *naql al-jana'iz* was confined to immoderate acts on the part of the laity and to those cases that led to the disgrace of the honor of the dead and harmed the environment.[51]

In comparison with the opinions of Tusi and Ibn Idris, Sharaf al-Din's discussion of *naql al-jana'iz* may be regarded as most permissive, in sanctioning various forms of transferring corpses to the shrine cities. His position also demonstrates the extent to which the social order could shape the legal arguments of a mujtahid in modern times. Sharaf al-Din maintained that the transfer of a corpse to holy ground before it had been already buried was recommended by all Muslim jurists. This type of transfer, he argued, was common in Islam, and none of the Sunni ulama denounced it. He brought examples of both Koranic figures, as well as of Shi'i and Sunni ulama and kings, whose corpses were transferred to holy places. He asserted that this type of transfer was observed by all Muslims throughout Islamic history, and that this should be taken as proof of its desirability. Responding to Shahrastani's criticism of the custom of the laity to transfer their dead from one holy place to another, Najaf being their ultimate destination, Sharaf al-Din argued that burial in the vicinity of 'Ali's tomb in Najaf was the most auspicious. He cited a Tradition whereby seventy thousand from among those buried there will be eligible to enter heaven without first being subject to any judgement or accounting for their acts in this world. It was on account of such Traditions, he maintained, that believers transferred their dead, even from other shrines, to the shrine of 'Ali.[52]

Sharaf al-Din argued that, overall, many Shi'i and Sunni ulama permitted the transfer of a corpse to holy ground even after it had been buried, provided that this did not result in desecration of the grave or the dishonor of the dead. He pointed out that Sunni ulama at times even allowed the transfer of corpses for burial in non-holy ground, an act regarded by both Shi'i and Sunni Islam as either reprehensible or forbidden, depending on the circumstances. This, Sharaf al-Din maintained, was evident in many instances, most notably in the case of Muhammad 'Abduh, whose corpse was transferred from Alexandria to Cairo. Sharaf al-Din pointed to the prevalence of the custom in Judaism, and to the fact that the Christians did not denounce it either. He argued that the Muslims, who observed this practice in compliance with the shari'a and the ruling of prophets, saints, and ulama, should not be embarrassed by its criticism by other commu-

[50] Sharaf al-Din, "al-Shahrastani," 897, 902, 981; "Tahrim," 914–15.
[51] Shahrastani, "Naql al-amwat," 111–14.
[52] Sharaf al-Din, "al-Shahrastani," 897–902, 983.

nities that likewise observed it. He asserted that throughout his long stay in Najaf, corpses were transported to the town in coffins, which ensured the honor of the dead and protected the environment from the spread of diseases. For Sharaf al-Din, the transfer of a corpse to the shrine of the imam symbolized the glorification of the dead; it was the highest act of care and reverence which a son could show toward his deceased parent.[53]

The controversy over *naql al-jana'iz* highlighted the tension over the extent of compromise between the Shi'i Islamic legal, moral, and ethical codes, and the social order. This may be gathered also from the *fatwa*s of Khurasani and Mazandarani. They permitted the practice provided that certain conditions were met, most notably that the deceased had ordered it in his will, and that the transfer did not disgrace the honor of the dead or harm society.[54] In calling for an end to the corpse traffic, Shahrastani not only stood against the motivation of the laity, but also broke ranks with Shi'i classical treatments of *naql al-jana'iz*, which permitted the practice under certain conditions. Consequently, some portrayed Shahrastani as an infidel and an atheist, and his life was endangered. His magazine *al-'Ilm* was closed late in 1911 even before the debate was over and he was forced to leave Najaf and Iraq. He spent two years in India, then made a pilgrimage to Mecca before settling in Karbala.[55] Moreover, his position and future in the Shi'i hierarchy suffered a major setback. Shi'i sources relate that on account of the criticism of *naql al-jana'iz*, and his overall attempt to reform other Shi'i religious practices, Shahrastani lost the good prospect that he had of becoming a leading mujtahid.[56]

THE STATE AND THE CORPSE TRAFFIC

When Shahrastani published his criticism he was, no doubt, attuned to the efforts of the Iranian and Ottoman governments, encouraged by European states, to increase the sanitary conditions and to control both the pilgrim and the corpse traffic. As early as 1869, the Shah's chief physician suggested in a letter addressed to Nasir al-Din Shah that either the corpse traffic should be discontinued, or that adequate sanitary measures should be adopted to reduce the spread of epidemics caused by the practice.[57] During the Shah's visit to Iraq in 1870, he met the Ottoman governor

[53] Ibid., 902, 977–80, 983.
[54] "Tahrim," 915–16. Subsequent mujtahids also permitted the practice provided that it did not disgrace the honor of the dead: Khalili, *al-Madkhal*, 1:104n; and see the *fatwa*s of Abu al-Qasim Khu'i, *Manhaj al-salihin*, 10th ed., 10 vols. (Beirut, n.d.), 1:96.
[55] Muhammad Salih al-Kazimi, *Ahsan al-athar fi man adraknahu fi al-qarn al-rabi' 'ashara* (Baghdad, 1933), 44.
[56] Ja'far al-Khalili, *Hakadha 'araftuhum*, 2 vols. (Baghdad, 1963–1968), 2:196–97, 199, 203, 205; Hasan al-Amin, "al-Sayyid hibat al-din al-shahrastani," *al-'Irfan* 58 (1970): 501.
[57] Thomson to Clarendon, Tehran, no. 50, 3 September 1869, FO 60/320.

Midhat Pasha, who raised the issue of sanitary problems which the transfer of moist corpses from Iran to the shrine cities created in Iraq. Although the Shah promised to permit in the future only the transfer of dry corpses to Iraq after they had been buried in Iran for at least one year, the practice did not stop and a large number of corpses continued to be smuggled into the country.[58] The recommendations of the International Sanitary Conferences, held in the late nineteenth and early twentieth centuries, led to the introduction of quarantines and lazarets at major points in the Persian Gulf. Established also in Khanaqin, Qasr-i Shirin, and Basra, they were intended to increase the Ottoman and Iranian states' sanitary control of the pilgrim and corpse traffic.[59]

Yet, effective measures to control the corpse traffic, and to curtail the high rate of corpse smuggling that developed mainly as a result of the restrictions on the transfer of moist corpses, were introduced only following the British occupation of Iraq and the subsequent formation of the monarchy. The Ottoman system for detecting moist corpses was not effective, and was reported to exist mainly for the purpose of gaining revenues. A new system of inspection was introduced in November 1918. Under its provisions, all dry foreign corpses had to be brought first to a special mortuary in Baghdad, where they were inspected before their transfer to Najaf or Karbala was permitted. During the winter months, permission was given for the immediate transfer of moist corpses in sealed coffins from Baghdad to the shrine cities. In all other cases, the corpse had to be buried in a local cemetery for at least three months before its transfer.[60] In 1921 the system was reorganized, and the local traffic was entrusted to agents appointed by the district governors. The move was intended to control the large number of corpses brought to Najaf mainly from the Basra district, the Euphrates, Nasiriyya, and Suq al-Shuyukh. This coincided with a refinement of the system of inspection and classification of foreign corpses. Also, for the first time, Iraqi Railways accepted corpses for transit to the shrine cities, thereby undermining the livelihood of the traditional carriers.[61]

[58] Sadiq al-Damluji, Midhat pasha (Baghdad, 1953), 45–46; 'Abbas al-'Azzawi, Ta'rikh al-'iraq bayna ihtilalayn, 8 vols. (Baghdad, 1935–1956), 7:245.

[59] Lorimer, Gazetteer, 1,2:2517–55; International Sanitary Convention, Paris, 3 December 1903, IO L/P&S 10/123 and 10/124; The Proceedings and Conclusions of the International Sanitary Conference, Paris, 17 January 1912, FO 368/778/12895; Sessions of the Tehran Sanitary Council, 5 January 1915, IO L/P&S 10/284; International Sanitary Conference, Paris, 21 June 1926, FO 371/12655/2691. See also Anja Pistor-Hatam, "Pilger, Pest und Cholera: Die Wallfahrt zu den Heiligen Stätten im Irak als Gesundheitspolitisches Problem im 19. Jahrhundert," WI 31 (1991): 228–45.

[60] Annual Administration Report of the Health Services for the Year 1920, CO 696/3.

[61] Annual Administration Report on the Iraq Health Services for the Year 1921, and Annual Report of the Baghdad Health Services Department for the Year 1921, CO 696/4.

By 1924, an efficient system of sanitary inspection was already in operation in Iraq. It was evident, however, that far more corpses were still being buried at Najaf and Karbala than could be accounted for by the permits issued at the quarantine stations and by the records of the local civil surgeons. To deal with the considerable amount of corpse smuggling, the Corpse Traffic Law was passed at the end of 1924. The Director of Public Health, subject to the Minister of Interior, was now in charge of prescribing the form of transit and issuing burial permits. The law also provided for the examination of corpses at the border of Iraq by quarantine officials, and for the issue of transit passes, which were later checked by quarantine officials at the place of burial itself. Prior to the implementation of this law, foreign corpses once in Iraq could be transferred to the shrine cities as local corpses free from transit fees and official interference. The new law, by which special transit passes for local corpses were also required, rendered it difficult for corpses to be buried in the shrine cities without the proper documents or payment of transit fees. The implementation of the law proved effective, and by 1926 the bulk of the corpse traffic was already under government control.[62] The law of 1924, and the appendix added to it in 1943, remained in force for forty-three years. It was replaced by the Corpse Traffic Law of 1967, which stipulated that Iraqi officials in foreign countries should be present during the procedures connected with the transfer of corpses to Iraq.[63]

Like much of the income from the foreign pilgrimage to the shrine cities, the burial dues were also increasingly absorbed by the state. In the late Ottoman period, the burial dues were set for the benefit of the Ottoman *Awqaf* Department. In the period immediately preceding the British occupation, perhaps even earlier, the Ottoman *Awqaf* Department used to farm out the dues on burials in the Shi'i cemeteries and shrines to local merchants for specific periods of time. The merchants, or their agents, traveled to cities and villages in Iran to collect corpses and then transferred them to the shrine cities. It is known that in 1914 a Jewish merchant of Baghdad gained the concession for a period of three years, paying 13,000 Turkish liras, or about £11,700, for it.[64] Despite its profit from the burial dues, the Ottoman *Awqaf* Department made only small allowances for the lighting and cleaning of the Shi'i shrines and mosques. It also fixed the salaries of the

[62] Government of Iraq, Dept. of Health Services, Report of the Inspector-General of Health Services for the Year 1923–24, CO 696/5; Report by Her Majesty's Government to the League of Nations on the Administration of Iraq, 1925; Government of Iraq, Dept. of Health Services, Report of the Inspector-General of Health Services for the Years 1925 and 1926, CO 696/6; Report by Her Majesty's Government to the League of Nations on the Administration of Iraq, 1926.

[63] Kamil al-Samarra'i, *al-Waqf: tasfiyatuhu wa al-qawanin al-khassa bi-hi* (Baghdad, 1968), 187–91.

[64] Nafisi, *Dawr*, 78.

Shiʻi functionaries there at a much lower rate than in Sunni mosques.[65] In 1917 the British reversed this policy for a while by diverting the income from the dues on burial to the Shiʻi shrines and mosques.[66] With the formation of the monarchy, the income from the burial dues came under the control of the Iraqi Ministry of *Awqaf*. In 1923, the Ministry farmed out the burial dues for three years to a Sunni merchant of Baghdad, who paid 80,000 rupees, or about £5,333, for the concession.[67] In 1927, the Ministry assumed direct control over the income from the burial dues through the enforcement of the Corpse Fee Law, which was approved by the Iraqi government that same year.[68] In 1929, the Ministry was converted into a Directorate General. It was attached to the Iraqi Prime Minister's office, which controlled both Sunni and Shiʻi *waqf* funds.[69]

The transfer of corpses, notably to Najaf, continued throughout the monarchy at an estimated annual average rate of about 17,500.[70] It is evident, however, that foreign corpses were no longer brought into Iraq in significant numbers. It was reported in late 1924 that the Tehran ulama had decided to issue a decree forbidding the transfer of corpses from Iran to the shrine cities. They argued that the rise in the burial fees at Karbala did not benefit Islam but the British.[71] Moreover, following his capture of the throne, Reza Shah sought to abolish the time-honored custom of sending corpses to the shrine cities. In 1928 the Shah forced ulama at Qum to issue *fatwa*s forbidding the transfer, and his Court Minister Timourtash revealed to the British minister in Iran the intention of the Iranian government to put an end to the corpse traffic altogether.[72] The application of this policy, coupled with the attempt of Reza Shah to enhance the religious status of Mashhad, resulted in subsequent years in a gradual shift of the Iranian corpse traffic from Najaf and Karbala to Mashhad and Qum. The decrease in the intensity of the corpse traffic from Iran to Iraq was evident by 1928–1930, when the number of foreign corpses had decreased to 2,194, 2,443, and 1,891, respectively, as compared with 4,124 and 5,104

[65] Review of the Civil Administration of the Occupied Territories of Iraq, 1914–1918, FO 371/4148/34799; Fortnightly Report no. 1 to Secretary of State for India, 1–15 November 1917, FO 248/1207.

[66] Fortnightly Report, Ibid.; Agha Najafi Quchani, *Siyahat-i sharq ya zindeginama va-safarnama-yi agha najafi quchani* (Mashhad, 1972), 577.

[67] Intelligence Report no. 20, 2 October 1924, CO 730/62/48225.

[68] For the law and the burial tariffs see Report on the Work of the Protector of British Indian Pilgrims, 1929, Appendix C (2), CO 730/159/2.

[69] Report by her Majesty's Government to the League of Nations on the Administration of Iraq, 1929.

[70] Fadli, *Dalil al-najaf*, 110.

[71] Intelligence Report no. 20, 2 October 1924, CO 730/62/48225.

[72] Special Service Officer, Baghdad, 21 December 1928, Air 23/124; Clive to Chamberlain, no. 12, Tehran, 22 December 1928, FO 416/84.

in 1925–1926.[73] The number of corpses transferred from India was also very low as only affluent Indian Shiʻi families could afford to transport their dead to the shrine cities. Their annual figure, when given, was usually around ten.[74] The scale of the Iranian and Indian corpse traffic decreased further in the period after 1958, and the traffic was confined mainly to the transportation of corpses within Iraq.

With the rise of the modern state, the decline of the corpse traffic from Iran was closely linked to the transformation of the foreign pilgrimage to the shrine cities. In both cases, important religious practices that, for centuries, cut across geographic and national borders were subjected to the policies of the Iranian and Iraqi governments. The reduction of the ties of Najaf and Karbala with Iran hindered their welfare. The blow to the socioeconomic position of these two cities will become further apparent in the next chapter, in dealing with Shiʻi money.

[73] Government of Iraq, Dept. of Health Services, Report of the Inspector-General of the Health Services for the Years 1925 and 1926, CO 696/6; Reports by Her Majesty's Government to the League of Nations on the Administration of Iraq, 1926–1930. I was unable to obtain data on the 1930s and 1940s. The health reports of Iraq in the 1950s do not give specific figures on the number of foreign corpses transported annually to the shrine cities.

[74] Report on the Work of the Protector of British Indian Pilgrims, 1929, CO 730/159/2; Reports on the Work of the Indian Section of the British Consulate at Baghdad for the Years 1933 and 1934, Government of India, Foreign and Political Department, NAI, files 449-N/34 and 598-G/1935.

PART FOUR

The Decline of Financial and Intellectual Institutions

Chapter Eight

SHI'I MONEY AND THE SHRINE CITIES

IN 1918 a British report estimated that a good administration of Najaf's receipts of charities and endowments from Iran might produce an annual income of almost one million pounds.[1] This estimate uncovered one of the major factors of both the strength of the shrine cities and their vulnerability, lacking as they did viable sources of income within Iraq. Until the British occupation of Iraq, Najaf and Karbala in particular could take advantage of the country's position as a frontier and feed on being the centers of Shi'i scholarship. At that time, mujtahids and other religious groups in the shrine cities benefited from diverse contributions and bequests often made directly to them by Shi'i rulers, followers, and ulama-agents, notably in Iran and in India.

The flow of foreign money to the shrine cities had major consequences on their political orientation and socioeconomic organization. The shrine cities developed an economy based on charities and payments for religious services, and on the income from the pilgrimage and the corpse traffic. This money consolidated in particular the status of the Persian mujtahids, who enjoyed contributions from followers in Iran. It also fostered structures of patronage, affected the position of the supreme mujtahid, and enhanced the power of the mujtahids vis-à-vis the Iranian and Ottoman governments. With the rise of the modern state, however, the inability of Najaf and Karbala to attract money from within Iraq to compensate for their loss of foreign revenues was a major factor in their socioeconomic decline.

Besides the tax of *zakat*, which was one of the religious duties of Muslims and was to be paid directly by Shi'i believers to the poor in their localities, there were as many as seven other types of religious payments made by Shi'is to the mujtahids and the custodians of the shrines.[2] These may be roughly divided into three categories. The first category included two types of charity incumbent on all Shi'i believers and paid directly to their mujtahids. The first type was the share of the imam (*sahm al-imam*), which is half of the fifth (*khums*) of a believer's net income, gained in modern times mainly from business transactions.[3] The second type (*radd al-mazalim*)

---

[1] Great Britain, Administration Reports, Najaf, 1918, CO 696/1.

[2] On *zakat* see Norman Calder, "Zakat in Imami Shi'i Jurisprudence, from the Tenth to the Sixteenth Century A.D.," *BSOAS* 44 (1981): 468–80.

[3] On the fifth see Abdulaziz Sachedina, "*Al-Khums*: The Fifth in the Imami Shi'i Legal System," *JNES* 39 (1980): 275–89; Norman Calder, "Khums in Imami Shi'i Jurisprudence, from the Tenth to the Sixteenth Century A.D.," *BSOAS* 45 (1982): 39–47.

was a fee which Shiʻis remitted to their mujtahids as an absolution payment for oppressive wrongdoing; this included the acceptance of government employment, which for a strict Shiʻi was unlawful.[4] The second category of payments was composed of three types of charity of a voluntary nature, also sent directly to mujtahids. The first type (*haqq al-wasiya*) was one-third paid to mujtahids from the heritable property of deceased Shiʻi believers; it was usually dedicated for a certain specified purpose, the mujtahid acting as the trustee. The second type (*sawm wa-salat*) was a fee paid by Shiʻi believers to mujtahids who were expected to arrange with a third party to observe prayers and fasting on behalf of the former's deceased relatives for periods that varied according to the amount paid. The annual fee which Shiʻis paid early in the twentieth century for these services was negotiable, ranging anywhere from three to six Turkish pounds, or four rials *majidi*, or three to four tomans.[5] The third type of voluntary charity was money vowed to leading mujtahids in return for recovery from sickness or extrication from danger. Under the third category there were two types of contributions, usually paid directly to the custodians of the shrines. The first was a charity dedicated for the distribution of water to the poor in Najaf, the annual amount of which was reported in 1918 to be around £6,000. Though not incumbent on Shiʻi believers, this charity was highly recommended since its aim was to preserve the memory of imam Husayn's suffering from thirst during the days that immediately preceded his death. The second type of contribution was money intended for lighting the shrines of the imams and for the upkeep of tombs of affluent believers buried in the holy cemeteries of Najaf and Karbala. It was estimated in 1918 that the annual income of the shrine of Najaf alone from that source was about £10,000.[6]

The flow of various charitable money to the shrine cities was due in great part to the conscientious effort of Shiʻi mujtahids to reconstruct and expand their economic base in Iraq. The roots of this development go back to the mid-eighteenth century.

THE BUILDING OF AN ECONOMIC BASE

During the Safavid period, the income of many scholarly families in Iran depended heavily on government land grants and emoluments in Iran. The

[4] Said Amir Arjomand, *The Shadow of God and the Hidden Imam: Religion, Political Order, and Societal Change in Shiʻite Iran from the Beginning to 1890*, 2d ed. (Chicago, 1987), 231; Administration Reports, Najaf, 1918, CO 696/1.

[5] Agha Najafi Quchani, *Siyahat-i sharq ya zindeginama va-safarnama-yi agha najafi quchani* (Mashhad, 1972), 433, 538–39. In the late nineteenth and early twentieth centuries, the Turkish gold pound was equal to about eighteen shillings under the official exchange rate. In cash transactions the Turkish pound was usually equal to 5.4 silver rials *majidi*. The toman, the Iranian gold coin, was equal to about four rials.

[6] Administration Reports, Najaf, 1918, CO 696/1.

close relationship between Shi'i religious leaders and the state was disrupted in the eighteenth century in the period of insecurity and flux which followed the breakdown of central power in Iran. As has been seen in chapter 1, the Sunni-Afghan capture of Isfahan in 1722, as well as the attempts of Nadir Shah (1736–1747) to promote Sunni-Shi'i rapprochement and to expropriate many of the endowments supporting the Shi'i clergy, displaced hundreds of families of ulama, many of whom fled to Iraq during 1722–1763. The center of Shi'i scholarship thus moved from Isfahan to Karbala and later to Najaf.

Unable to look to the government in Iran for material support, mujtahids and ulama had to restructure their socioeconomic bases. In Iraq, the effort of the mujtahids to generate new sources of income manifested itself in their drive to convert the tribesmen to Shi'ism, which among other things was intended to create a body of local potential contributors. The effort of the mujtahids to achieve relative financial independence coincided with the revival of the Usuli school of thought. Against the breakdown of central power in Iran and the geographical dislocation of many clerical families, the Shi'i Akhbari and Usuli schools of thought struggled not only over the definition of the sources of law that may be used for juridical decision-making, but also over the functions of the mujtahid. When many Iranian ulama came to Iraq during 1722–1763, the Akhbari school was dominant in the shrine cities. Yet, by the end of the 1770s, the Usuli school had already managed to reassert itself in the shrine cities. In subsequent years, Usuli ideas also regained dominance in India and in other parts of the Shi'i world.[7]

The Usuli victory greatly enhanced the juristic authority of the Shi'i mujtahids. It provided a legal justification for the diversion of money from the laity directly to the mujtahids. While the Akhbaris discredited the claim of the mujtahids to the *khums*, the Usulis asserted that the mujtahids, as representatives of the hidden imam, could fulfill some of his functions, among them the collection of half of the *khums*. This Usuli position manifested itself in the act of the influential Najafi mujtahid Shaykh Ja'far Kashif al-Ghita, who made the gesture of putting the share of the imam at the Shah's disposal for the duration of the Perso-Russian War of 1810–1813, thus indicating the claim of the mujtahids for this religious tax. During his visits to Iran Kashif al-Ghita personally collected *khums* and *radd mazalim*, and he was also said to consider anyone who withheld the payment of *khums* as a rebel against the imam and his representative the mujtahid. The collection of the religious taxes by the mujtahids had sustained the Usuli movement and constituted the economic basis of their

---

[7] Juan Cole, "Shi'i Clerics in Iraq and Iran, 1722–1780: The Akhbari-Usuli Conflict Reconsidered," *IS* 18 (1985): 13, 15, 19–20, 23–26; idem, *Roots of North Indian Shi'ism in Iran and Iraq: Religion and State in Awadh, 1722–1859* (Berkeley, 1988), 33–34.

religious and scholarly activity.[8] Indeed, the works of twentieth-century mujtahids clearly state that during the occultation of the imam, the *khums* is to be paid to the righteous mujtahid, the representative of the hidden imam. The mujtahid was to divide it into two parts: the *sahm* or *hissat al-imam* and the *sahm al-sadat*. Whereas the first portion was to be used for the financing of religious activities, the second was to be set aside for the privilege of the *sayyids*.[9]

In the late 1840s Shaykh Murtada al-Ansari (d. 1864), who resided in Najaf, was acknowledged as the supreme Shi'i mujtahid. This centralization of the Shi'i leadership coincided with the expansion of the economic basis of the senior mujtahids in the shrine cities. By the mid-1850s it had already become customary to pay the *khums* directly to the grand mujtahids in the shrine cities.[10] Ansari gained enormous financial support from merchants, landowners, and the Qajar government. At one stage in the late 1850s, it was estimated that 200,000 tomans were received annually by Ansari as religious taxes, a sizeable figure given the Qajar's government total annual revenue of about 3 million tomans around that time.[11] In subsequent years, the residence of the supreme mujtahid, or the existence of a number of recognized grand mujtahids, in the shrine cities was an important factor for the flow of Iranian and Indian money to Iraq. The grand mujtahids in Iraq enjoyed a higher ranking than their counterparts in Iran on account of their scholarship and teaching qualities. Overshadowed by the former throughout the nineteenth century, many mujtahids and ulama in Iran performed the role of agents for the leaders in the shrine cities.

The sharp increase in the number of mujtahids in the shrine cities from the second half of the nineteenth century intensified their competition over new sources of income which could finance their activity in Iraq. In the first four decades of the nineteenth century the total number of recognized mujtahids was said to be less than a dozen.[12] By the early twentieth century there were already in Najaf and Karbala alone some forty-one persons whom the British political resident in Baghdad recognized as either first-, second-, or third-class mujtahids. Moreover, from petitions sent to the resident during 1902–1903 it is evident that there were in Najaf and

[8] Arjomand, *The Shadow*, 230–31.

[9] Muhammad al-Husayn Kashif al-Ghita, *Asl al-shi'a wa-usuluha* (Beirut, n.d.), 129; Muhsin ibn Mahdi al-Tabataba'i al-Hakim, *Mustamsak al-'urwa al-wuthqa*, 12 vols. (Najaf, 1961), 9:504–5, 507–9.

[10] Ann Lambton, "A Reconsideration of the Position of the *Marja' al-Taqlid* and the Religious Institution," *SI* 20 (1964): 132.

[11] Abbas Amanat, "In Between the Madrasa and the Marketplace: The Designation of Clerical Leadership in Modern Shi'ism," in *Authority and Political Culture in Shi'ism*, ed. Said Amir Arjomand (Albany, N.Y., 1988), 112.

[12] Arjomand, *The Shadow*, 245.

Karbala no less than two thousand and two hundred persons, respectively, claiming to hold certificates as mujtahids.[13]

Although the number of individuals claiming to hold a certificate as mujtahids was probably far in excess of the number recognized as such, the large number of claimants may be seen as an indication of the increase in both the number of mujtahids in the shrine cities as well as their competition over sources of income. The growing number of senior mujtahids who vied for the leadership increased the role that money and the laity played in the emergence of the leader. In theory, only the attributes of knowledge, probity, and piety were to be taken to determine the relative superiority of one mujtahid over another. These prerequisites, however, were somewhat subjective ideals open to arbitrary interpretation. Since there were no institutional authorities such as the church or the state to verify these prerequisites or to designate their possessors, the mandate of the laity was extremely important in determining the status of mujtahids.[14] Indeed, the follower became the ultimate arbiter, deciding upon and presenting his loyalty to the mujtahid of his choice. This entrusted the former with considerable room to maneuver; he could shift from one mujtahid to another to obtain favorable opinions, and direct religious dues to his chosen recipient. A mutual dependency was created between the mujtahid and his followers. At times, even more than the qualities of scholarship and piety, it was a mujtahid's success in attracting the support of a large number of contributors that gained him the leadership.

More than any other body of contributors, it was the bazaar in Iran that from the late nineteenth century affected the designation of a senior mujtahid as the sole head and enabled certain mujtahids in the shrine cities to enjoy access to large financial resources. While bazaaris probably contributed money to mujtahids in Iraq even before the nineteenth century, one cannot really point to the formation of a clear alliance between the two groups before the late 1880s. The relatively late date of the alliance was due primarily to the fact that until then the bazaar financed much of government activity in Iran both in the urban and rural areas. The Iranian government maintained close cooperation with the big merchants; it gave them almost complete freedom in their economic activities, making no attempt to interfere with their economic enterprises. In return, by custom the merchants had to give a share of their profits to the ruling class, namely, the Shah, members of the court, and to high officials in the central and the provincial administration. Many members of the elite thereby became the silent partners of powerful wholesale merchants. When in need of

[13] J. G. Lorimer, *Gazetteer of the Persian Gulf, 'Oman and Central Arabia*, 2 vols. in 5 pts. (Calcutta, 1908–15), 1,2:2364; Meir Litvak, "The Shi'i Ulama of Najaf and Karbala, 1791–1904: A Socio-Political Analysis" (Ph.D. diss., Harvard University, 1991), 354.

[14] Amanat, "In Between," 98; Lorimer, *Gazetteer*, 1,2:2364.

money, the elite did not hesitate to borrow from merchants and moneylenders, who also assumed the role of investment bankers and conducted the bulk of the money transactions in Iran. This relationship between the government and the big merchants was disrupted from the late 1880s. While the government faced growing fiscal difficulties, the merchants were not prepared to increase their scope of assistance and credit. Failing to increase its income from other sources within Iran, the government encouraged an expansion in the activities of foreign trading firms in the country at the expense of the local large-scale merchants, who, in turn, grew resentful of the privileges granted to the foreign traders.[15]

In March 1890 a fifty-year monopoly over the production of tobacco and its domestic and foreign trade was granted by the government to a British subject. The 1891–92 Tobacco Revolt that ensued symbolized the alliance that matured between powerful bazaaris in Iran and senior mujtahids in the shrine cities. This found its expression in the role played by the leading mujtahid Muhammad Hasan Shirazi (d. 1895) whose fame throughout the 1880s surpassed any other mujtahid. He came from a family of minor clerics from Shiraz which had long-established links with the bazaaris of southern Iran. His mercantile background and bazaari connection put Shirazi in an advantageous position in vying for the religious leadership, enjoying as he did the support of both Iranian and Indian merchants. The Tobacco Concession was a direct threat to the prosperity of Shirazi's major financiers, notably, the merchants of Fars, Isfahan, and Tabriz. Their pressures on Shirazi were a major factor in his decision to cast off his prudence and to side with his constituency against the Qajar government's sale of the concession to foreigners.[16]

The interdependency that began to mark the relations between the bazaaris and senior mujtahids in the shrine cities reinforced the strong orientation of the latter toward Iran. The bazaar emerged as the major source of credit for senior mujtahids in Iraq while the latter became both the superior authority for arbitration between bazaaris and mujtahids in Iran, as well as a counterpoise against the government. The interdependency of the mujtahids and the bazaaris was bolstered by the conflicts between their interests and those of the state. As the Constitutional period demonstrated, powerful mujtahids and bazaaris demanded a greater say in shaping national policy in Iran, seeking to introduce a legal framework that would define the limits of the government and reduce foreign encroachment.[17]

[15] Amanat, "In Between," 100–102, 116, 123; Gad Gilbar, "The Big Merchants (*tujjar*) and the Persian Constitutional Revolution of 1906," *AAS* 11 (1977): 282–84, 288; Shaul Bakhash, "Iran," *AHR* 96 (1991): 1485–86.

[16] Amanat, "In Between," 116–17, 119.

[17] *Encyclopaedia Iranica*, s.v. "Bazaar"; Guity Nashat, "From Bazaar to Market: Foreign Trade and Economic Development in Nineteenth-Century Iran," *IS* 14 (1981): 77–78.

Yet, the dependency of the mujtahids on foreign contributions ultimately proved ruinous for the autonomy of the Shi'i religious hierarchy in Iraq as well as for the economies of Najaf and Karbala. This will be demonstrated in the next two sections.

THE OUDH BEQUEST

The emergence in the eighteenth century of the Shi'i state of Awadh (or Oudh) in north India (1720–1856) proved lucrative for the shrine cities. Between 1780 and 1844, rulers, ministers, and other notables of Oudh remitted more than one million rupees for philanthropic purposes, economic projects, and religious functions in the shrine cities. The Indian money helped expand the economic basis of those Persian mujtahids in Najaf and Karbala who enjoyed the Oudh connection. The Arab families, most notably the Kashif al-Ghita, failed to gain control over the Indian money because of the preference of the mujtahids in Lucknow to work with Persian mujtahids with whom they shared common origin and culture. Offering higher stipends and distributing charities, these Persian mujtahids could attract more students and followers than the Arab mujtahids and shore up their position in the shrine cities.[18] Indian contributions also financed the building of the Hindiyya canal, which brought water to Najaf. As was shown in chapter 1, the ecological changes caused by the construction of the canal led to the attraction of Arab tribes to the area near Najaf, exposing them to Shi'i propaganda. Indian money still continued to reach the shrine cities long after the state of Oudh had been annexed by the British in 1856.

In 1825, during a period of financial constraints occasioned by a war in Burma, the British Governor General of India accepted a ten-million-rupee loan from Ghazi al-Din Haydar, the King of Oudh. The character of the loan was perpetual: The principal was never to be repaid, and the interest, fixed at 5 percent per annum, was to be applied by the government of India in perpetuity to specified objects. Among the beneficiaries from the interest were four women: Nawwab Mubarak Mahal, Sultan Maryam Begam, Mumtaz Mahal, and Sarfaraz Mahal (the first two being wives of the King), were to be paid a monthly allowance of 10,000, 2,500, 1,100, and 1,000 rupees, respectively. Other allowances amounting altogether to Rs.929 a month were assigned to servants and dependents of Sarfaraz Mahal.

The agreement stipulated that upon the death of the four women, one-third of their allowance would be paid to whomever they appointed in their wills, the remaining two-thirds being delivered to the mujtahids residing in Najaf and Karbala for distribution among "deserving persons." In case of

---

[18] Juan Cole, "'Indian Money' and the Shi'i Shrine Cities of Iraq, 1786–1850," *MES* 22 (1986): 463–65, 468–69, 472, 476; Litvak, "Shi'i Ulama," 205.

intestacy, the mujtahids were to receive the entire allowance. If any of the assignees connected with Sarfaraz Mahal also died without heirs, their entire allowance was to be allotted to the Najaf and Karbala benefactions as well. The funds thus provided for disbursement in Najaf and Karbala came to be known as the Oudh Bequest. The maximum annual amount that the two cities could gain from this source was Rs.186,148, about £15,512 under the official exchange rate in the mid-nineteenth century, when one British pound was equal to about ten rupees.[19]

Money under the Oudh Bequest first reached Najaf and Karbala around 1850, after the death of Maryam Begam and Sultan Mahal. The welfare of Shi'i residents and mujtahids in the shrine cities thus became tied to the payments of interest resulting from the expansion of British commercial enterprise and political involvement in India. In the absence of data on the annual revenue of Najaf and Karbala from Iran it is difficult to determine what the volume of Oudh Bequest funds was in relation to Iranian contributions. Nonetheless, an idea about the magnitude of the Oudh Bequest may be gathered from its comparison with the estimated annual revenue of the supreme mujtahid Murtada al-Ansari. By the late 1850s the annual amount received in Najaf and Karbala from the Oudh Bequest was around Rs.120,000, or about £10,000. The annual volume of the Oudh Bequest was thus greater than Ansari's annual revenue from religious taxes, which, as has been seen in the previous section, was estimated at one point to be 200,000 tomans, or around £9,000.[20]

The examination of the Oudh Bequest over a period of a century between 1850 and 1953 sheds light on the relative position of classes and ethnic groups in Najaf and Karbala, as well as the relations between mujtahids, ulama, and students. It also illustrates how the status and welfare of religious groups was linked to their ability to draw on Oudh Bequest funds. On another level, the Oudh Bequest is a good case study for demonstrating the complexity of British strategy vis-à-vis Shi'i affairs as well as the different priorities of British officials in Iraq, Iran, and India who sought to use the Bequest in accordance with their own preferences and local considerations. The development of the Oudh Bequest from 1902 also uncovers Britain's growing involvement and influence in Iraq in the twentieth century. Finally, the rise of the modern state and the tight control of the Bequest by the Indian government elucidate how the decline in the flow of charities undermined the welfare of various religious groups in Najaf and Karbala under the monarchy.

For some time until 1852 the two most senior mujtahids at Karbala and

---

[19] Lorimer, *Gazetteer*, 1,1B:1409–11, 1483.

[20] Under the average exchange rate between 1851 and 1864 (when Ansari died), one pound was equal to about 22.1 and 22.5 tomans, respectively: Charles Issawi, *The Economic History of Iran, 1800–1914* (Chicago, 1971), 343.

Najaf drew on the British Bombay treasury for the Oudh Bequest money through their agents in India. Whereas Sayyid 'Ali Naqi al-Tabataba'i was the recipient in Karbala, Muhammad Hasan al-Najafi (d. July 1850) and his successor Murtada al-Ansari, were Tabataba'i's counterparts in Najaf. From October 1852 the Oudh Bequest was made payable through the British political agent in Iraq, who was given a judicious supervision over the expenditure of the money. In May 1854, following communications between the political agent and Ansari and Tabataba'i, it was decided to use the funds to provide for the individual claims of the mujtahids, and for various religious and charitable purposes in the two shrine cities. It is hard to determine for exactly how long Ansari received funds under the Oudh Bequest. Ansari probably did not deal directly with the distribution of the money, delegating this function to Shaykh Mahdi Kashif al-Ghita. Sometime between 1857 and 1860 Ansari himself apparently withdrew his association with the Oudh Bequest altogether.[21]

A significant change with respect to the destination of the funds was introduced around 1860. In contradiction with the original agreement which stipulated that the money was to be received and distributed by the mujtahids of Najaf and Karbala alone, a third (about Rs.40,000) was set aside annually for the benefit of poor Indian residents at Najaf, Karbala, and Kazimayn. A separate "Indian fund" was thus created. This was due not only to a misinterpretation of the original agreement, but also to the great influence of the Nawwab Iqbal al-Dawla, a nephew of King Ghazi al-Din Haydar. Residing at Kazimayn until his death in 1887, the Nawwab became actively involved in the administration of the Oudh Bequest, and hence Indian residents, pilgrims, and students in the shrine cities benefited greatly. Until 1903 when the "Indian fund" was abolished, the money available through the fund attracted many Indians to Iraq, leading to a steady increase in their number in the shrine cities.[22]

Between 1860 and 1903, the remaining two-thirds of the Oudh Bequest were shared exclusively by two mujtahids, one in Najaf, the other in Karbala; they were chosen by the British political agent or resident at Baghdad. Although attempts were probably made to select the mujtahids according to their relative popular support and preeminence in legal matters, several senior mujtahids thus selected, notably Agha Hasan Najmabadi, apparently refused to accept the money.[23] In Najaf, Sayyid 'Ali Bahr al-'Ulum, an Iranian by origin who became an Ottoman subject, was made the Oudh Bequest mujtahid distributor sometime between 1858 and 1860. After the latter's death in 1881, he was replaced by another family member, Muhammad Bahr al-'Ulum, who held the post until 1903. 'Ali Bahr al-'Ulum's

[21] Lorimer, *Gazetteer*, 1,1B:1413–14; Litvak, "Shi'i Ulama," 313.

[22] Lorimer, *Gazetteer*, 1,1B:1478–80, 1599.

[23] Isma'il Ra'in, *Huquq-i begiran-i englis dar iran* (Tehran, 1968), 102.

counterpart in Karbala until 1872 was Sayyid 'Ali Naqi al-Tabataba'i, who held Iranian nationality. Following his death, the post was conferred on his brother Abu al-Qasim al-Tabataba'i. When the latter died in 1891, he was replaced by his son Muhammad Baqir, who held the post until 1903.[24] Thus, for more than forty years, the post of the Oudh Bequest mujtahid distributor was held exclusively by the Bahr al-'Ulum and the Tabataba'i families.

Protests against the misuse of the money by the mujtahids were made occasionally by rival mujtahids, other residents of Najaf and Karbala, and even by the Persian and Ottoman governments. In 1883 it was alleged that the money was appropriated mainly for the enrichment of the mujtahid distributors and the support of their relatives and friends, the poor gaining little from it. In 1889 it was found that Abu al-Qasim al-Tabataba'i was deeply in debt and that he, or his sons, had borrowed from the money changer of the British Residency on the security of the Oudh Bequest payments due to him. In 1891, Muhammad Bahr al-'Ulum was reported to have borrowed funds at Najaf on the strength of his connection with the Oudh Bequest. Moreover, by 1902, the proceeds of the Bequest were no longer paid directly to the two mujtahid distributors but to the Jewish money changer of the Residency, Eliahu Ezekiel Danus. The latter produced only periodically a receipt from each of the mujtahids for half the amount, keeping part or all of the other half for himself as the interest payments of the mujtahids on account of their debt to him.[25]

The system by which one-third of the money was set aside for the "Indian fund" and the rest was allotted to the two mujtahid distributors remained in force until 1903. Despite the lack of legal basis for its existence, the serious financial irregularities in its administration, and even the objection of the government of India to its function, the "Indian fund" remained practically intact. With respect to the mujtahid distributors, the government did not approve any measure that would prescribe the ultimate distribution of the money received by the two mujtahids. Against this, random attempts by the British political agents or residents at Baghdad to induce the mujtahids to prepare lists of actual payees, to submit regular accounts to Baghdad, and to establish small committees of supervision over the distribution of the money did not prove effective.[26]

Between 1902 and 1904 the question of the administration of the Oudh Bequest was raised energetically by Major Newmarch, the newly appointed British resident at Baghdad. The "Indian fund" was abolished by May 1903. Gaining the approval of the government of India, Newmarch also ended the monopolies of the Bahr al-'Ulum and the Tabataba'i families.

[24] Lorimer, *Gazetteer*, 1,1B:1481–84, 1598–99.
[25] Ibid., 1601, 1605, 1610; Litvak, "Shi'i Ulama," 331–32, 345.
[26] Lorimer, *Gazetteer*, 1,1B:1601–8, 1611–12.

During 1902–1903 Newmarch prepared a list of mujtahids resident in Najaf and Karbala. He secured the approval of the government for the principle that in the future the power to make the final appointments and removals of the mujtahid distributors would remain in the hands of the resident. This was explained as necessary in order to prevent the formation of a Persian clique that would totally exclude Indian and Arab mujtahids from the receipts of the Oudh Bequest.[27] The reorganization of the Oudh Bequest ended the concentration of large sums of money and power in the hands of only two mujtahids and their families. Newmarch offered fourteen shares, valued at either Rs.500 or Rs.1,500 a month, to the mujtahids of the highest repute. Although he could not persuade the five most senior mujtahids in Najaf and Karbala to receive shares under the Oudh Bequest, a number of other very respectable mujtahids did accept shares and became mujtahid distributors. By May 1903 Newmarch had already distributed Oudh Bequest funds among fourteen mujtahids in Najaf and Karbala, seven in each city.[28] A year later, there were ten mujtahid distributors in each city, all equally sharing the revenues of the Oudh Bequest and each individual gaining Rs.500 a month.[29] Under the new system the Persian mujtahids remained the main beneficiaries. Indeed, among the mujtahid distributors there was only one Arab mujtahid, Muhammad Hasan al-Jawahiri, who held Iranian nationality. The selection of a large number of Persian mujtahid distributors was an indication of the dominance of the Shi'i religious hierarchy in Karbala and Najaf by Persians early in the twentieth century.

The 1902–1904 reorganization of the Oudh Bequest reflected the growing British political involvement in Iraq and Iran. Subsequently, British officials sought to use the Bequest as a patronage resource in Iraq and to

[27] Ibid., 1613–14.

[28] Muhammad Baqir al-Tabataba'i and Muhammad Bahr al-'Ulum were each given Rs.1,500 monthly, while the other twelve received a monthly share of Rs.500. The six mujtahids at Karbala, besides Tabataba'i, were: Sayyid Hashim Qazwini, Shaykh Husayn Mazandarani, Sayyid Ja'far al-Tabataba'i, Shaykh 'Ali Yazdi, Sayyid Murtada Husayn Hindi, and Sayyid Sibta Husayn (Ja'far al-Tabataba'i was apparently replaced in June 1903, and Mirza Fadlallah Mazandarani and Sayyid Hasan Kashmiri were probably added in July). The six mujtahids at Najaf, besides Bahr al-'Ulum, were: Muhammad Kazim Khurasani, Shaykh 'Abdallah Mazandarani, Shaykh Muhammad Hasan al-Jawahiri, Mulla 'Ali Nahavandi, Sayyid Muhammad Hindi, and Sayyid 'Abd al-Hasan Ja'isi Lucknawi. Lorimer, *Gazetteer*, 1,1B:1612–14; Litvak, "Shi'i Ulama," 347–48, 350–51.

[29] In Karbala, Muhammad Baqir al-Tabataba'i lost his place among the mujtahid-distributors for at least one year. The new shareholders in that city were: Shaykh Husayn ibn Zayn al-'Abidin Mazandarani, Sayyid Muhammad Kashani, Sayyid 'Ali Tunaqabuni, and Sayyid Muhammad Baqir Behbahani. In Najaf, the position of Muhammad Bahr al-'Ulum was further reduced, his share being matched with the other mujtahid distributors. The new recipients were: Shaykh al-Shari'a Isfahani, Sayyid Abu al-Qasim Ishkawari, and Akhund Mulla 'Ali Khunsari. Newmarch to Dane, Baghdad, 30 May 1904, IO L/P&S 10/77.

gain greater leverage over Iranian affairs as well. The beginning of British attempts to use the Oudh Bequest to influence Shi'i affairs in Iraq may be gathered from the fact that among the twenty mujtahid distributors in 1904 there were no less than five Indians, whose selection was intended to offset Persian dominance and to establish new structures of patronage in Najaf and Karbala. This is also evident from Newmarch's own remark, which suggests that he himself clearly envisaged the creation of a new generation of mujtahids more prone to British influence: "The present mujtahids of the Oudh Bequest are gradually getting more important, the older . . . mujtahids are dying off, and the time cannot be far distant when our payees will themselves be the leaders, and under my proposed . . . system . . . the creators of mujtahids in the future."[30]

British attempts to use the Bequest to influence affairs in Iran were evident during the Iranian Constitutional Revolution of 1905 in which several leading mujtahids in Iraq played a leading role. Noting that nearly all the mujtahid distributors kept the money for themselves and their families, investing it mainly in real estate,[31] Sir Arthur Hardinge, the British minister in Iran, sought to utilize the influence of some of these mujtahids to prevent riots and disturbances and to obstruct Russian policies in Iran. Hardinge's strong advocacy of using the Bequest to influence Iranian affairs apparently created some tension between him and Newmarch, who was probably worried that a too pronounced political handling of the Oudh Bequest would ultimately backfire against the British, particularly in Iraq. In 1905, Hardinge suggested to Newmarch the names of two protégés in Iran, with the result that one of the mujtahid distributors, Muhammad Baqir al-Tabataba'i, was induced to make a monthly allowance to the two.[32]

By 1908, it was already commonly held in the shrine cities that most of the Oudh Bequest funds were paid to the Persian mujtahids since the British were contemplating the takeover of Iran and therefore thought that the influence of the mujtahids would prove useful.[33] Among the mujtahids a line was drawn between the majority, who were willing to accept shares under the Oudh Bequest, and those who declined the offers of the British resident. At stake was the acceptance of funds derived from interest on a loan and the direct involvement of the mujtahid distributors with the

[30] Newmarch to Secretary to the Government of India, Baghdad, 15 June 1905, IO L/P&S 10/77.
[31] Ibid.; Wilson to the Secretary to the Government of India, Baghdad, 29–30 August 1919, FO 371/4198/167721.
[32] Lorimer, *Gazetteer*, 1,1B:1615–16; Sir Arthur Hardinge, *A Diplomatist in the East* (London, 1928), 323–24; Litvak, "Shi'i Ulama," 358–59.
[33] Political Diary for the Week Ending 11 February 1908, FO 195/2274/122–18. See also Ra'in, *Huquq-i begiran-i englis*, 97–100, 104–6, 109–10.

growing British ambitions in Iraq and Iran. As early as 1907, Mirza Khalil and Kazim Yazdi advocated a change in the system and made explicit statements that the whole revenue of the Oudh Bequest should be disbursed among the poor. In 1908, Yazdi and Muhammad Ismaʻil al-Sadr declined a share under the Oudh Bequest. Pointing to the act of Ansari, who used to distribute the entire Oudh Bequest money among the poor, Yazdi reiterated that the funds should be distributed by the mujtahids for the benefit of the poor. To the contrary, many of the mujtahid distributors adopted a different position. Their view was articulated in 1909 by Muhammad Kazim Khurasani, who maintained that the mujtahid distributors were free to spend the money as they saw fit, being responsible to God alone. To an extent, this position reflected the overall decrease in the income of several Persian mujtahids who at that time found it difficult to raise funds in Iran after the bazaaris no longer needed them as a lever against the Shah.[34] In view of this, many mujtahid distributors were reluctant to give up any part of their income derived from the Oudh Bequest.

The financial magnitude of the Oudh Bequest did not escape the notice of other major Shiʻi players and interest groups in the shrine cities. The struggle over the receipts of the Oudh Bequest not only sharpened the different class and ethnic attributes of the various groups, but also demonstrated the power of the student population in the shrine cities. As will be shown in the next chapter, student-mujtahid relations experienced major tensions in 1908–1910, resulting from the latter's reduction of student allowances and supply of bread. The decline in the welfare of students was largely the result of the decrease in the flow of money from Iran, the slack trade and paucity of pilgrims, as well as the high prices in the shrine cities following the Iranian Constitutional Revolution and the attempt of the Young Turks to undermine the power of the madrasa and the position of students and mujtahids in the shrine cities. Against this, Shiʻi public opinion in Najaf and Karbala was reported to be unanimous in condemning the mujtahid distributors, who, with only very few exceptions, kept the money entirely in their own families.[35]

In October 1909, Colonel Ramsay, Newmarch's successor, reported that the Persian students at Karbala and Najaf were determined to get as much as possible out of all the available charity funds in the two cities. They sent petitions to Ramsay asking him to have a certain amount of the Oudh Bequest set aside from the share of each mujtahid distributor for the exclu-

[34] Ramsay to Dane, Baghdad, 20 December 1907, IO L/P&S 10/77; Ramsay to Butler, Baghdad, 20 October 1909, FO 371/1244/34634; Lorimer to McMahon, Baghdad, 11 August 1911, FO 195/2368/690–34; Political Diary for the Week Ending 2 June 1908, FO 195/2274/484–50.

[35] Extract from Summary of Events in Turkish Iraq during December 1909 and January 1910, FO 371/1244/34634.

sive use of the students. On several occasions, students also exerted pressures on the mujtahids. In one case an Indian mujtahid distributor, Mawlavi Sayyid Murtada Husayn of Karbala, even took the unusual step of complaining to the British resident. The mujtahid wrote that he received threatening messages after he had declined the demand of Persian students to give them Rs.150 a month from his share of the Oudh Bequest.[36] So strong was the power of the Persian students at Karbala that in April 1910 they were the dominant force behind the decision of seven mujtahid distributors to waive two-fifths of their share and give it to charities and to the support of the students. In taking this move, the seven hoped that they would be left free to enjoy the remaining three-fifths without future annoyance.[37]

In the three years that preceded the reform of 1912, the activity of Indians in the shrine cities reflected the attempt of this group to secure the major share of the Oudh Bequest for their own benefit. In January 1909 a large number of Indian residents of Karbala and Najaf sent a petition to Ramsay. They complained against the established system of distribution, arguing that Indians in the shrine cities were the only suitable people to profit from money that originated in India. The petitioners maintained that the abolition of the "Indian fund" in 1903 was ruinous to the Indian population in the shrine cities. They considered the Oudh Bequest a charity fund, the receipts of which had to be distributed in full by the mujtahids. Pointing out that Yazdi and Sadr refused to accept shares under the Oudh Bequest, this being considered a form of personal salary, the petitioners asserted that in the past Ansari and Shirazi used to distribute whatever funds they had received for charities among deserving people. The petitioners suggested the appointment of three reliable mujtahids, an Arab, an Indian, and a Persian, each paid Rs.300 per month to carry on the work of distribution.[38]

Lacking the power of the Persian mujtahids and students, the Indians attempted to bypass the former by using their status as British subjects. On several occasions individuals and associations in India objected to the idea that the mujtahid distributors be allowed to retain any part of their Oudh Bequest share. It was suggested that the mujtahids should be required to entrust their entire shares to committees of distribution. Working under the management of the resident at Baghdad, the Indians sought to reduce the power of the mujtahids by turning the committees into a powerful body that would supervise the disbursement of the funds among poor Indian residents and pilgrims. In March 1911, public opinion in Lucknow was

---

[36] Ramsay to Butler, Baghdad, 20 October 1909, FO 371/1244/34634.

[37] Lorimer to Butler, Baghdad, 11 April 1910, FO 371/1244/34634.

[38] Ramsay to the Secretary to the Government of India, Baghdad, 17 February 1909, FO 371/1244/34634.

reported to be unanimous in holding that the Oudh Bequest was essentially a charitable fund and that the mujtahids were merely distributors. Senior mujtahids in India requested that a standing committee in Lucknow should be consulted as to the selection and removal of the mujtahid distributors and on other issues of importance.[39]

Although the suggestions made by the Indian petitioners were rejected by the government of India, the idea of reducing the power of the mujtahid distributors appealed to the British residents in Iraq since this could further increase British influence among the religious classes in Najaf and Karbala. In this connection, the residents, notably Ramsay and his successor Lorimer, considered the "importation" of mujtahids from India to Iraq and the formation of distribution committees a most effective lever. Late in 1908 Sayyid Ahmad 'Allama Hindi, son of the most senior mujtahid at Lucknow, wrote to Ramsay. The Sayyid proposed the use of at least some of the money for the building of a hospital for the poor at Karbala, suggesting that he himself was willing to take responsibility for the work. Ramsay recognized the potential advantages of such a move and recommended to the government that a senior mujtahid of Lucknow would be gradually given increasing power over the distribution of the money. Gaining the approval of the government, Ramsay wrote back to Sayyid Ahmad, promising to assist him in introducing a more satisfactory system for disbursing the Oudh Bequest funds in Najaf and Karbala if the Sayyid became a resident of either city. He wrote that there was no legal obstacle in the 1825 agreement to prevent the British resident at Baghdad from selecting resident mujtahids whose views were in sympathy with the resident's. Ramsay promised Sayyid Ahmad the first share to become vacant, adding that if the Sayyid's efforts met with success, it might be possible to increase his share in the future.[40] In 1912 Sayyid Ahmad did indeed move to Najaf and became a mujtahid distributor.

Between 1909 and 1911 both Ramsay and Lorimer attempted to persuade the government of India to place more power in the hands of the British resident at Baghdad, seeking to turn the Bequest into a leverage for influencing Shi'i affairs primarily in Iraq. Ramsay stated that in the future it would become very difficult to find senior mujtahids who would be willing to accept a share under the Oudh Bequest. He stressed that if it were realized among the mujtahids that the British resident had the power to give more than one share to one mujtahid, the resident could then acknowl-

[39] Sayyid Ahmad 'Allama Hindi to Foreign Secretary to the Government of India, Lucknow, 6 May 1910, and Chief Secretary to the Government of the United Provinces to the Secretary to the Government of India, Allahabad, 18 March 1911, FO 371/1244/34634.

[40] Sayyid Ahmad 'Allama Hindi to British-Consul General of Baghdad, 28 December 1908, FO 371/1244/34634; Ramsay to the Secretary to the Government of India, and Ramsay to Sayyid Ahmad 'Allama Hindi, Baghdad, 13 February 1909, FO 371/1244/34634.

edge the position of the actual leading mujtahids by giving them two or more shares. This opinion was reinforced by Lorimer, who maintained that the fact that the greater and the smaller in reputation among the mujtahid distributors enjoyed equal allowances was one of the major faults of the system as it was then established. He considered it essential that the resident should retain the power to confer and withdraw shares without reference to the government. Fearing that the seven mujtahid distributors at Karbala who waived two-fifths of their shares might be worked upon by others and induced to repent of what they had done, Lorimer urged the government to act without delay in order to introduce a new system of distribution. The proper administration of the Bequest, he stressed, would increase the British moral and political reputation in Iraq, Iran, and India.[41]

In August 1911, before a final decision was reached by the government of India, Lorimer took the initiative. He formulated a new scheme for the distribution of the funds and forwarded it to India. His suggestions gained the approval of the government in January 1912. Based on a new reading of the 1825 agreement, it was accepted that the entire Oudh Bequest funds should be paid only to the resident mujtahids of Najaf and Karbala and that direct payment of any part of the money to any other person would be contrary to the terms of the agreement. This, however, left two issues still unresolved. First, should payment be made to all the mujtahids of Najaf and Karbala or only to some of them? Second, who might be included under the expression "deserving persons" among whom the money was to be disbursed?

Lorimer argued that, left unsupervised, even the best available mujtahids could not be trusted as distributors. He maintained that if the matter were left to popular opinion in Najaf and Karbala, there would not be a single Indian mujtahid among the shareholders. An Indian mujtahid, he explained, may be all very well at Lucknow, but in Najaf or Karbala he would appear servile in the presence of the aloof and all-powerful Persian hierarchy. Only a few individuals in Najaf and Karbala, Lorimer wrote, could be taken to be undisputed mujtahids; the claim of the great majority to the title of experts in religious law and jurisprudence was doubtful and the only test of their genuineness was a vague and divided popular opinion. He therefore suggested that the money should be given only to mujtahids who were willing to distribute a share of their receipts of Oudh Bequest funds; they would be selected by the representative of the government of India.

[41] Ramsay to Butler, Baghdad, 20 October 1909; Lorimer to Butler, Baghdad, 11 April 1910; Lorimer to the Secretary to the Government of India, Baghdad, 3 September 1910, FO 371/1244/34634; Memorandum by S.B.A. Patterson, 3 August 1911, and Lorimer to Clarke, Baghdad, 29 January 1911, Government of India, Foreign and Political Dept., NAI, Proceedings nos. 7–33, June 1912.

Lorimer's scheme stipulated that every present and future mujtahid distributor would be required, as a condition of his becoming or remaining a distributor, to disburse a proportion of his share through public committees to "deserving persons." In 1912 Lorimer fixed the amount at half of the share of each mujtahid distributor, suggesting that if the system worked well, the proportion disbursed through the committees might be gradually increased. He also maintained that in future the number of mujtahid distributors as well as their respective shares should be flexible, depending entirely upon circumstances. Lorimer stressed that the Oudh Bequest was a stream capable of vivifying thousands of people in Najaf and Karbala. He maintained that the expression "deserving persons" did not necessarily mean the poor. Sometimes, he argued, even a mujtahid himself could be treated as a deserving person entitled to some remuneration from the Bequest. He concluded that an impartial distribution of the money could best be achieved by the formation of two public committees, one in each city, working under the supervision of the resident at Baghdad. Headed by the British vice-consul at Karbala (who was of Indian origin), each committee was to consist of seven other people appointed by the resident.[42]

Thus, from 1912 the British resident in Iraq was given the power to acknowledge individuals as mujtahids with respect to the receipt of Oudh Bequest funds. The selection of the mujtahid distributors by the resident did not involve the most senior recognized mujtahids of the day as this, Lorimer maintained, could result in a "considerable danger of a rebuff." Instead, the status of the Indian mujtahids was inflated by the British resident, who could appoint several of them as mujtahid distributors in no proportion to their actual standing in the religious hierarchy of the shrine cities. The resident was also given direct control over the committees as he could sway their decisions whenever he deemed it necessary. Finally, the wide interpretation of the expression "deserving persons" enabled the resident to gain influence over a greater number of mujtahids, ulama, and students in Najaf and Karbala.

The new scheme alarmed the Ottoman authorities, who considered it as likely to increase British influence in Iraq. During much of the nineteenth century the Ottomans apparently did not perceive the Oudh Bequest as a British instrument capable of undermining their own influence over Shi'i affairs in Iraq.[43] By contrast, British growing interests in Iraq, as well as their reorganizations of the Oudh Bequest in the twentieth century, led the Ottomans to believe that the British were seeking to use the Bequest to influence Shi'i affairs in the country. Consequently, some difficulties hung over the workings of Lorimer's new system in 1912. The authorities at-

---

[42] Lorimer to McMahon, Baghdad, 11 August 1911, FO 195/2368/690–34.

[43] Litvak, "Shi'i Ulama," 328–29.

tempted to dismantle the committees. Ottoman subjects, notably Arabs, were prohibited from sitting on the committees at Karbala and Najaf, and the Persian consul at Baghdad was asked to put pressure on the Persian members to submit their resignations. By 1913, however, following the return of the Committee of Union and Progress to power in Istanbul, official interference with the working of the committees decreased. While the local authorities still did not allow Arabs to receive any relief directly from the committees, this could not prevent Lorimer from implementing the new scheme.[44]

When asked to confirm their acceptance of the new system and give it their support, only seven mujtahids, of whom three were Indians, expressed their willingness to accept the changes. Hence, Lorimer first started working with this group, while reserving the shares of the other mujtahid distributors who declined to cooperate. In June 1912 he wrote to the government of India saying that it might be necessary to fall back temporarily on the exclusive agency of Indian mujtahids; he suggested that suitable mujtahid candidates should be selected in India for the possibility that they might be sent to Iraq on short notice. The same month, he also suspended the senior mujtahid Husayn Mazandarani, who expressed strong dissatisfaction with the new scheme and with the resident's unwillingness to pay him his arrears from 1910. In August 1912 Lorimer added a new Indian mujtahid in Najaf, Sayyid Ahmad 'Allama Hindi. By November 1913, there were already fourteen mujtahid distributors working under the terms of the new scheme, of whom no less than five were Indians; they all had to sign receipts for an amount double what they actually received since one-half of their share was set aside for distribution as charity through public committees.[45]

By the eve of World War I, the British had been able to greatly reduce the status and influence enjoyed by the former senior mujtahid distributors. More second- and third-class mujtahids were vying for a share under the Oudh Bequest; indeed, the growing number of applicants for future vacancies enabled the British resident to prepare a confidential waiting list of acceptable candidates. It was reported that all applicants were considered, and that their credentials were carefully examined and weighed. The inclusion or exclusion of names was done after consultation between the British

[44] Extracts from Events in Turkish Iraq for May and June 1912, IO L/P&S 10/77; Lorimer to McMahon, Baghdad, 12 August 1912, FO 371/1522/50561; Lorimer to Wood, Baghdad, 15 November 1913, IO L/P&S 10/77.

[45] The seven mujtahid distributors in Karbala were: Sayyid 'Ali Tunaqabuni, Sayyid Muhammad Baqir Behbahani, Shaykh Hadi Isfahani, Sayyid Muhammad Kashani, Sayyid Murtada Husayn (Indian), Sayyid Qalb-i Mahdi (Indian), and Sayyid Ibn Hasan (Indian). The other seven in Najaf were: Shaykh al-Shari'a Isfahani, Shaykh Muhammad Hasan al-Jawahiri, Shaykh Mahdi Asadallah, Shaykh Mahmud Agha, Sayyid Ja'far Bahr al-'Ulum, Shaykh Muhammad Mahdi Kashmiri (Indian), and Sayyid 'Allama Ahmad (Indian).

resident in Baghdad and his vice-consul in Karbala. The welfare of mujtahids, ulama, students, and other residents of Najaf and Karbala was
increasingly influenced by the amount of support that they could gain
directly from the committees. Particularly in Najaf, the share of the students was reported to be the highest among the recipients. Overall, however, the greatest part of the money disbursed before the War still went to
charity. Free bread was occasionally distributed to the poor in Najaf and
Karbala. Money was also disbursed among Indian pilgrims and some was
used for the repatriation of Indians in Iraq. In both cities, only a few Arabs
benefited from the Bequest, and thus it was mostly Persians and Indians
who enjoyed the money. At three distributions in 1912–1913, a total of
4,372 people received money under the Oudh Bequest. Persians constituted almost 76 percent of the recipients, collecting 74 percent of the total
money disbursed.[46] The last distribution under the Oudh Bequest before
the War took place in April 1914.

In March 1915, even before the occupation of Iraq was completed, the
government of India had decided that it would be of political value to
continue as long as possible with payments to all the recognized mujtahid
distributors of the pre-War period, regardless of their attitude toward the
British since the outbreak of the War. Sayyid Husayn Kashani was probably
the first to be given money during the War on account of arrears due to his
father Muhammad. This reportedly led to satisfactory results, as the son
later rendered good services in propaganda work. Following the occupation of Nasiriyya in August 1915, the route to Najaf and Karbala through
the Euphrates became fairly safe. Money in the form of commercial drafts
was sent occasionally to mujtahid distributors and committee members.
Up to March 1917, the total amount distributed during the War was
around Rs.119,015 out of the Rs.365,979 due to the Oudh Bequest fund
from April 1914.[47]

The occupation of Iraq enabled the British to gain greater influence over
the structure of power and the religious hierarchy in Karbala and Najaf.
The first regular distribution under British occupation took place in Karbala in November 1917. By that time six of the seven pre-War mujtahid
distributors had either died or moved away from the city, and it was decided not to appoint new ones. Only Sayyid Qalb-i Mahdi remained in
Karbala and was given his share under the Oudh Bequest. Three senior
mujtahids, Husayn Mazandarani, Muhammad Sadiq al-Tabataba'i, and
'Abd al-Husayn al-Tabataba'i, were given donations on a temporary basis;

[46] Extract from Reports on Turkish Iraq for June 1912, IO L/P&S 10/77; Lorimer to
McMahon, Baghdad, 28 August 1912, FO 371/1522/50561; Lorimer to Wood, Baghdad, 15
November 1913, IO L/P&S 10/77.
[47] Wilson to the Secretary to the Government of India, Baghdad, 29 August 1918, FO
371/4198/3746.

the former received the highest amount on account of his relatively senior position in Karbala. The distribution process was placed under tighter British control and the head of each quarter was instructed to prepare lists of the poor in his quarter. Allowance cards were issued, and the amount disbursed was determined according to the merits of each applicant. A register was also prepared containing the names and thumb impressions of all cardholders. White cards were issued to those who were permanently in need of support, like the disabled or the aged, while colored cards were issued to people who were found in need of temporary support, but who were likely to be able to earn their living after the War was over. In several distributions in Karbala between November 1917 and April 1919 the poor received between 52 and 64 percent of the amount distributed. Junior mujtahids, ulama, and students formed the second largest group in Karbala to gain support under the Oudh Bequest. In November 1917 the 133 people in this group were divided by the committee of distribution into four classes. The first three were composed of junior mujtahids and ulama, sixty altogether, while the fourth class included seventy-three students. Sums of one hundred, seventy, forty, and twenty-five rupees were apportioned to each individual in the first, second, third, and fourth class, respectively. Between November 1917 and April 1919 the religious classes in Karbala received between 13 and 19 percent of the amount distributed in the city.[48]

In Najaf, with the exception of Sayyid Ahmad, who returned to India, and Muhammad Hasan al-Jawahiri, who died in 1917, all the other pre-War mujtahid distributors still remained and were given shares under the Oudh Bequest in 1918.[49] Shaykh al-Shari'a Isfahani was given an additional sum along with his share on account of his high standing among the mujtahid distributors. Isfahani became the supreme mujtahid in August 1920 following the death of Mirza Muhammad Taqi Shirazi; he enjoyed this rank for four months until his death in December. The card system was introduced in March 1918, and later extended to include students as well. A list of mujtahids, ulama, and students who were given Oudh Bequest funds was prepared too, which included 492 people. There were thirty first-class and fifty second-class mujtahids and ulama. Given the large student population in Najaf (estimated at that time at about 6,000), only 412 could be included in the list of recipients of Oudh Bequest funds in March 1918. By the next distribution in September 1918, the number of the religious classes in Najaf who received funds under the Oudh Bequest further increased, reaching 515. Among the first-class recipients was

[48] Ibid.; Wilson to Grant, Baghdad, 14 November 1918, and Wilson to the Secretary to the Government of India, Baghdad, 1 July 1919, FO 248/1250.

[49] Jawahiri's share was received by his son Hasan. Shaykh Mahdi Kashmiri died in January 1920.

Muhammad Husayn Kashif al-Ghita, who would rise as the most prominent Arab mujtahid under the monarchy. The religious classes emerged as
the largest group to benefit from the Oudh Bequest in Najaf. Whereas in
the distribution of September 1918 they received only 30 percent of the
total amount distributed as compared with the 46 percent received by the
poor, in February 1919 the religious classes already received 46 percent of
the total amount distributed, the poor receiving only 24 percent.[50]

The British thus became the direct benefactors of mujtahids, ulama, and
students in Najaf and Karbala, interfering with the autonomy of the religious hierarchy and the status of groups and individuals. Traditional structures of patronage were gradually eroded as students received money directly from the distribution staff. Indeed, the list prepared in Karbala in
1917 drew objections from Husayn Mazandarani and 'Abd al-Husayn al-
Tabataba'i. The former complained that certain persons who deserved to
be placed in the second class were actually categorized in the third or fourth
and vice versa; he also claimed that certain deserving students were left out
of the list altogether. Mazandarani's students complained as well, asserting
that they had not been paid in accordance with their real status.[51]

With the introduction of the card system the pre-War committee members were no longer necessary. The new system enabled the British to
maintain a good record of the recipients; all that was required in order to
identify an individual was to compare his name and thumb impression as it
appeared on his card with the list of deserving recipients. At that time
British officers in Iraq also felt that while the mujtahid distributors still had
their use, the filling of vacant posts in the future should be given serious
consideration. It was highly improbable that the grand mujtahids would
accept such a post since they regarded the Oudh Bequest funds as government pay. Most of the pre-War mujtahid distributors, it was also argued,
assumed the title of mujtahid only on account of their official appointment
as Oudh Bequest distributors.[52]

Against this, a new scheme was sent for the approval of the government
of India in August 1919. One of the most significant proposals advocated
by its writers was to increase the weight of Arab Shi'is among the mujtahid
distributors. This proposal was an indication of the new reality created in
Iraq following the occupation and the attempt of British officials to enhance the position of Arab Shi'is at the expense of Persians and Indians.

[50] Wilson to the Secretary to the Government of India, Baghdad, 29 August 1918, FO
371/4198/3756; Wilson to Grant, Baghdad, 14 November 1918, and Wilson to the Secretary
to the Government of India, Baghdad, 1 July 1919, FO 248/1250.

[51] Wilson to the Secretary to the Government of India, Baghdad, 1 July 1919, FO
248/1250; Wilson to the Secretary to the Government of India, Baghdad, 29 August 1918,
FO 371/4198/3756.

[52] Administration Reports, 1918, Najaf, CO 696/1.

The writers proposed that the government should retain control over the Oudh Bequest through one central committee. The committee would be composed of five ex-officio members: the Civil Commissioner (President) as well as four other British officers. The role of non-government individuals was to be gradually reduced. The idea was to continue the shares and salaries of the pre-War mujtahids and committee members until they died or were relieved of their posts for one reason or another. Aware that the terms of the 1825 agreement stipulated that mujtahids should be the actual distributors of the money, the writers suggested that in the future three mujtahid distributors in both Najaf and Karbala would take part in the distribution. Their appointment, where possible, should be according to ethnic criteria, so that the three would comprise a Persian, an Arab, and an Indian. These mujtahids would have to accept that they were only a medium of distribution, and that the proceeds of the Oudh Bequest were to be impartially distributed to those for whom the money was intended. The attempt of British officials to use the Oudh Bequest as an effective instrument to influence the structure of power in the shrine cities may be gathered from their advocacy that the religious classes should continue to have precedence over other groups and charitable objects. Moreover, with a view to making the largest possible sums available for distribution among students and Shi'i Arabs, the writers suggested reducing support to Indians and cutting the monthly share of future appointed mujtahid distributors to Rs.300 each.[53] The 1919 scheme was accepted in principle by the government of India, and many of the propositions put forward were implemented during the mandatory period.

Whereas in 1913 there were altogether fourteen mujtahid distributors and fourteen committee members in Najaf and Karbala (five and six of each of these groups, respectively, being Indians), by 1931 their number had decreased significantly. Only two mujtahid distributors and seven committee members remained. There was one Indian mujtahid in Karbala, Sayyid Mustafa Kashmiri, who was appointed in March 1931 following the death of Qalb-i Mahdi. There was also one Persian mujtahid distributor left in Najaf. Each received a monthly share of Rs.350. The committee in Karbala included three members (a Persian, an Arab, and an Indian), whereas the one in Najaf was composed of four (two Persians, an Arab, and an Indian). Throughout the Mandate, the main recipients were mujtahids, ulama, and students, divided into three classes in that order. It was reported in 1929 that the maximum annual grant of the religious group under the first class was 100 and 160 rupees in Karbala and Najaf, respectively. The Persians and Arabs were the main beneficiaries among the

[53] Wilson to the Secretary to the Government of India, Baghdad, 29–30 August 1919, FO 371/4198/167721.

religious group. They gained the highest grants under the Oudh Bequest, the bulk of the Indians and the non-clerical poor receiving only small sums.[54]

Until 1929, the head clerk of the British Residency in Baghdad acted as the supervisor of the Oudh Bequest. The distribution took place four times a year in Najaf and Karbala in the head clerk's presence, the High Commission staff and the remaining members of the two committees in each town acting as the actual distributors. Following the death of the British head clerk in 1929, the protector of Indian pilgrims, who was attached to the secretariat of the High Commissioner, took over the supervision of the Bequest. In 1931, as the Mandate was drawing to an end, it was also agreed that the government of India should be more involved in any future changes in the Oudh Bequest.[55]

From 1933, as part of the increase in power sharing between the British and Indians in India, the Oudh Bequest was placed under more direct control of the government of India. The Indian consul attached to the British consulate in Iraq assumed the duty of supervising the Oudh Bequest. While accepting that money under the Oudh Bequest should be set aside primarily for the benefit of the religious classes, the consul introduced new restrictions aimed at limiting the allocation of funds. In 1933, perhaps under British influence in Iraq or even because of a request by the Iraqi government itself, it was decided that no grant would be made to any person who took part in political agitation of any kind. Under this ruling, the important Arab mujtahid Muhammad Husayn Kashif al-Ghita was removed that same year from the list of recipients on account of his anti-government actions in Iraq. This was followed by another ruling, which prohibited members of the same family from receiving separate allowances. In 1934 the committee of distribution in Karbala was suspended on the grounds that two members opposed the attempt to administer the Bequest as a religious fund. A new committee was formed in 1935 and placed under the control of the Indian consul. It included only three people: Sayyid Mustafa Kashmiri (an Indian mujtahid), Shaykh Muhammad Khatib (an Arab mujtahid), and Shaykh Muhammad 'Ali (a Persian member).[56]

In April 1938, as a consequence of a new distribution of power in India,

[54] Report on the Work of the Protector of British Indian Pilgrims, 1929, CO 730/159/2; Hewett to Howell, Baghdad, 9 July 1931, IO L/P&S 12/2847.

[55] Secretariat of the High Commissioner for Iraq to the Secretary to the Government of India, Baghdad, 12 and 29 August 1930, FO 369/2269/8912 and CO 730/159/2; Hewett to Howell, Baghdad, 9 July 1931, IO L/P&S 12/2847.

[56] Reports on the Work of the Indian Section at the British Consulate at Baghdad for 1933, 1934, and 1935, Government of India, Foreign and Political Dept., NAI, files 449-N/1934, 598-G/1935, and 551-G/1936.

the control of the Oudh Bequest was transferred from the Foreign and Political Department of the government of India to the provincial government of Uttar Pradesh where the Bequest had originated. The latter government was perhaps at the time favorably disposed to the transfer of the Oudh Bequest distribution arrangements to the All India Shi'a Conference (AISC). The Oudh Bequest subsequently received greater attention from Shi'i public opinion in India. Between 1938 and 1946, Indian Shi'is made strong representations to their government to the effect that the Bequest should be administered by Indian mujtahids in Najaf and Karbala. In 1939 Shi'is in Lucknow and Radauli demanded that the Indian supervisor of the Oudh Bequest should be removed and a mujtahid be appointed in his stead, and that as much as two-thirds of the funds be set aside for the benefit of Indians in Iraq. It was also demanded in 1938, 1939, and 1946 that the full amount of the Oudh Bequest (Rs.186,000) be made available for distribution annually, and that past arrears at the rate of Rs.66,000 per year (probably kept by the government of India) should be paid as soon as possible.[57] These demands were rejected by the government of India, and the attempt by the AISC to gain control over the Oudh Bequest did not succeed.

In 1951 the Indian Legation in Baghdad took control over the administration of the Bequest. Subsequently, the Oudh Bequest lost much of its importance as a source of income for the religious classes in Najaf and Karbala. From 1953, money under the Oudh Bequest was distributed only from Baghdad by the staff of the Indian Embassy. The committees of distribution in Najaf and Karbala were abolished and mujtahids were no longer active in the process of supervision or distribution of the money. The secretary at the Embassy consulted a mujtahid only if a doubt existed with regard to particular applicants. Moreover, under the new system the number of recipients was sharply reduced from 3,200 to only 450 in 1953.[58] It seems that the allocation of funds under the Oudh Bequest in Iraq was gradually brought to a standstill, the Indian government thus defaulting on its interest payments of the Bequest. The Oudh Bequest, which for more than a century had been a constant stream, no longer served as a source of relief for thousands of residents, students, ulama, and mujtahids in Najaf and Karbala and they had to look for alternative sources of income.

[57] British Consulate to the Secretary to the Government of India, Baghdad, 24 February 1939, and K. B. Bhatia, Deputy Secretary, Government of the United Provinces to the Secretary to the Government of India, Lucknow, 5 July 1939, Government of India, External Dept., NAI, Proceedings nos. 1–8, 1939, file 983-G; Resolutions nos. 22 and 32 passed by the AISC at Patna, 29–31 December 1938, and at Masulipatam (Madras), 27–29 December 1946, Government of India, External Affairs Dept., NAI, file T/53/99132/19.

[58] In 1954, the number of recipients increased somewhat to 477. For the administration of the Oudh Bequest between 1951 and 1954 see Government of India, External Affairs Dept., NAI, file T/53/99132/19.

As will be shown in the next section, the disruption of the flow of charitable funds from Iran following the rise of the modern state, and the lack of close interaction between the Shi'i economic and religious sectors in Iraq, were two other major factors in reinforcing the economic decline of Najaf and Karbala.

THE CONSEQUENCES OF DEPENDENCY ON FOREIGN FUNDS

The inability of the mujtahids to develop viable financial sources within Iraq may be attributed in large part to the nature of government and society in that country as distinguished from Iran. In Qajar Iran, the Shi'i hierarchy and the state maintained cooperative relations until the rift between the two under Muhammad Shah (1834–1848) in the middle of the nineteenth century. The state used Shi'i religion as a source of legitimacy while allowing the mujtahids to keep their own spheres of control. On their part, the mujtahids sanctioned the legitimacy of the Shah and recognized the state on a de facto basis. Thus, Fath 'Ali Shah (1797–1834) enhanced the position of mujtahids and ulama in order to rally clerical and public support behind the monarchy. He channeled resources for the support of religious activities and education, for the building of mosques, and for the embellishment of shrines.[59] Even after the rift between the state and the religious hierarchy, which was reinforced by the Tobacco Revolt, Muzaffar al-Din Shah (1896–1907) still made annual grants of 3,000 and 2,500 tomans, respectively, to the custodians of the shrines in Karbala and Najaf, thereby seeking to gain patronage over Shi'i religious affairs. He was also said to be a follower of the prominent mujtahid Fadil Sharabiyani (d. 1904) of Najaf.[60]

In Iraq, as has been seen in chapter 3, both the Sunni Ottoman government and the monarchy perceived the presence of the Shi'i mujtahids and the sizeable Persian community as a Trojan horse in the country, the power and influence of which had to be curtailed. Unlike the Qajars, the Ottoman authorities in the nineteenth century and the Iraqi monarchy only rarely attempted to gain the cooperation of the Persian mujtahids through "silence money" or state support of Shi'i religious activities. Moreover, successive governments in modern Iraq sought to sever the economic links of the shrine cities with Iran and to shift their orientation toward Baghdad. In seeking to reduce the ties between Iraqi and Iranian Shi'is, Iraq's rulers benefited greatly from Reza Shah's policies. During the latter's rule (1925–

[59] Abdul-Hadi Hairi, "The Legitimacy of the Late Qajar Rule as Viewed by the Shi'i Religious Leaders," *MES* 24 (1988): 272, 275–76; Abbas Amanat, *Resurrection and Renewal: The Making of the Babi Movement in Iran, 1844–1850* (Ithaca, 1989), 20, 25, 411; Arjomand, *The Shadow*, 218, 248.

[60] Lorimer, *Gazetteer*, 1,2:2357; Quchani, *Siyahat-i sharq*, 334.

1941), he attempted to divert the flow of Iranian charitable funds from Karbala and Najaf to Mashhad. Consequently, the amount of money which the mujtahids in Iran gained increased at the expense of their counterparts in Iraq. The unfavorable effects of the Shah's policy on the economy of Najaf and Karbala were noticeable already in November 1927. It was reported that Iranians no longer sent money to Najaf for the support of the lesser ulama there, the number of whom was estimated to be more than five thousand. In addition, Iranians apparently stopped sending the third as derived from the heritable property of deceased Shiʻi believers. Although the blame was placed on Reza Shah, there was also a very strong feeling in Najaf against the Iranian mujtahids for not standing against the Shah's actions, thus leaving so many of their own kin destitute.[61] In 1933 the protector of Indian pilgrims reported that unemployment was rife in Najaf and Karbala and that charity funds were insufficient to meet the demands placed upon them, especially after the "severe falling off in the contributions which at one time reached Iraq from Persia."[62]

Even after his emergence as the supreme mujtahid around 1942, Abu al-Hasan Isfahani, who resided in Najaf, apparently found it difficult to attract large funds from Iran. Although it is said that Isfahani's annual budget was between ID550,000 and ID600,000, Shiʻi sources acknowledge that both before World War II and afterward the religious leadership (marjaʻiyya) in Iraq "suffered from the weakness of its Iranian wing," since Reza Shah banned the sending of khums to Iraq.[63] One consequence of this policy was the growing economic base as well as the importance of mujtahids and religious centers like Qum and Mashhad in Iran. This manifested itself with the emergence of Husayn Burujirdi of Qum as the supreme mujtahid following Isfahani's death in 1946. The shift in the religious headship from Iraq to Iran further undermined the economy of Najaf and Karbala as the Najafi mujtahids were faced with a growing competition with their Iranian counterparts. From the 1950s, only a few individual mujtahids in Najaf, most notably Muhsin al-Hakim (d. 1970) and Abu al-Qasim Khuʼi (d. 1992), still enjoyed contributions from either the bazaar in Iran or rich Shiʻis in Kuwait.[64] Often, however, a large part of these funds could not be kept in Iraq, let alone used freely to finance Shiʻi religious or

[61] Extract from Special Service Officer, 25 November 1927, Baghdad's Report no. I/Bd/35, Air 23/379.

[62] Report on the Work of the Indian Section of the British Consulate at Baghdad for the Year 1933, Government of India, Foreign and Political Dept., NAI, file 449-N/1934.

[63] Anon., al-Imam al-sayyid abu al-hasan (Najaf, 1946/7), 60; Muhammad ʻAli Jaʻfar al-Tamimi, Mashhad al-imam aw madinat al-najaf, 2 vols. (Najaf, 1954), 2:23; Ahmad al-Katib, Tajrubat al-thawra al-islamiyya fi al-ʻiraq (Tehran, 1981), 103. When it was introduced into circulation in 1932, one Iraqi dinar equaled one British pound.

[64] For the Iraqi Shiʻi-Kuwaiti connection see ʻIsam al-Khafaji, al-Dawla wa al-tatawwur al-raʼsmali fi al-ʻiraq, 1968–1978 (Cairo, 1983), 112n.

anti-government activity in the shrine cities or elsewhere in the country. Thus, for example, when following the Ba'th execution of Muhammad Baqir al-Sadr in 1980 Khu'i asked to leave Iraq, his personal funds as well as religious funds in his care (the latter said to amount to ID780,000 or about $2 million) were confiscated from Rafidayn Bank.[65] These developments diminished the ability of mujtahids in modern Iraq to act as grand patrons and benefactors, and eroded their clientele connections with the lesser ulama, the students, and the *sayyids*.

On the social level, the overall lack of a community of interest between the Shi'i religious and commercial classes in Iraq stands out when compared with Iran, where religion has been closely interwoven with the daily life of ordinary Iranian Shi'i believers. In Iran, the active involvement of ordinary Shi'is in shaping religious activity lasted through the Pahlavi period and has been most noticeable in the relations between ulama and bazaaris in that country for well over a century. The bazaar in Iran was always overwhelmingly mainstream Muslim, and only a minority of merchants were Christians or Jews. Ulama and bazaaris shared considerable similarities in lifestyle and values, and viewed the government as only quasi-legitimate. The bazaar and Shi'i Islam in Iran acted to give each other shape and substance. The sociocultural milieu of the bazaar and its immediate environs provided most of the financial and moral support for the clergymen in Iran. For its part, Shi'i Islam affected the operations of the marketplace in Iran. It shaped the social activity of the bazaaris, giving direction to their conduct and holding them to religion. Particularly in the Tehran bazaar, religion acted as a basic common denominator which created cross-cutting ties and a bond among bazaaris of different professional groups.[66]

The religious schooling of bazaaris promoted traditional conservative values, which enabled the bazaar to emerge as a major bulwark of Shi'i Islam in Iran. Many bazaaris conducted their business within the framework and morality of Islamic economics. This strong sense of morality in the Tehran bazaar centered around the Islamic obligation of "enjoining the good and forbidding the evil." The bazaaris differentiated between a person who follows religion in word and deed and one who assumes a pious exterior for public appearance only.[67] As Roy Mottahedeh put it: "To be

[65] Joyce Wiley, *The Islamic Movement of Iraqi Shias* (Boulder, 1992), 57.

[66] Ahmad Ashraf, "The Roots of Emerging Dual Class Structure in Nineteenth-Century Iran," *IS* 14 (1981): 16; *Encyclopaedia Iranica*, s.v. "Bazaar"; Howard Rotblat, "Social Organization and Development in an Iranian Provincial Bazaar," *EDCC* 23 (1975): 298; Gustav Thaiss, "The Bazaar as a Case Study of Religion and Social Change," in *Iran Faces the Seventies*, ed. Ehsan Yar-Shatar (New York, 1971), 193.

[67] Gustav Thaiss, "Religious Symbolism and Social Change: The Drama of Husayn" (Ph.D. diss., Washington University, 1973), 26, 52, 158–59. See also Michael Bonine, "Shops and Shopkeepers: Dynamics of an Iranian Provincial Bazaar," in *Modern Iran: The Dialectics*

successful, especially in commercial dealings in the long term, a Muslim bazaar merchant needed the capital of good reputation as much as he needed material capital."[68] There were thus pressures within the bazaar in Iran to exhibit modesty and piety in one's daily life, to observe Shiʿi rituals, and to support religious structures and activity. As has been pointed out in chapter 5, the Iranian bazaar was not merely the center of commercial activity but also a major location of places of worship and religious gathering. The main vehicle which helped solidify socioreligious cohesion among the bazaaris was the small religious gathering or association (*jalsat*, known in the twentieth century as *hay'at*). These gatherings have been the most indigenous expression of bazaar life in Iran. In their capacity as preachers and prayer leaders, ulama also participated in these gatherings, and thus the relationship between religion and urban economic life gained a solid material foundation.[69]

In contrast with their Iranian coreligionists, the Shiʿi Arab population of Iraq did not channel significant funds to the mujtahids in the shrine cities. Members of the rural communities of the south, the bulk of the Iraqi Shiʿi population under the monarchy, contributed money mainly for the maintenance of the *sayyid*s who lived among them. So strong was the influence of some of these *sayyid*s among the settled tribesmen that the latter considered them as saints and took oaths in their name. The central position of the *sayyid*s among the rural communities of southern Iraq enabled them to vie with the mujtahids and the latter's agents in the competition for the small resources of these communities, attracting a great deal of these resources for their own benefit.[70] A much stronger competition over funds existed between the mujtahids on the one hand, and the custodians and servants of the shrines on the other. With the arrival of an affluent pilgrim to the shrine cities, he would usually proceed straight to the shrine, where the custodian and servants would try to persuade him to make his contribution to the shrine.

Moreover, unlike the Iranian bazaaris, the Arab Shiʿi mercantile class in Iraq made only very few contributions to the mujtahids even after they began playing an important role in the commercial activity of the country from the early 1950s. Until the 1950s, the financial capacity of the Iraqi Shiʿi merchants was not a very solid one. This stemmed less from the

---

of Continuity and Change, ed. Michael Bonine and Nikki Keddie (Albany, N.Y., 1981), 235; Rotblat, "Social Organization," 299–300.

[68] Roy Mottahedeh, *The Mantle of the Prophet: Religion and Politics in Iran* (New York, 1985), 346.

[69] *Encyclopaedia Iranica*, s.v. "Bazaar"; Thaiss, "Bazaar," 190, 202; Joanna de Groot, "Mullas and Merchants: The Basis of Religious Politics in Nineteenth Century Iran," *Mashriq* 2 (1983): 14.

[70] Shakir Mustafa Salim, *Marsh Dwellers of the Euphrates Delta* (London, 1962), 62–64.

presence of the Sunni government in the major urban centers of the country like Baghdad and Basra than it did from the nature of Iraq's trade; this was based on a transit trade controlled by non-Arabs. In addition, the major commercial activity in the country was dominated by Jewish merchants. Thus, early in the twentieth century, the Jews were reported to have literally monopolized much of the trade of Baghdad and Basra, thereby preventing both Muslims and Christians from competing.[71] The Jews continued to play a dominant role in Iraq's commercial activity even after the formation of the monarchy, particularly in Baghdad. In 1938–1939, 10 out of the total of 25 first-class members of the Baghdad chamber of commerce were Jewish. At the same time, 215 (or about 43 percent) of the 498 who formed the entire membership of the chamber were likewise Jewish. Also, 35 of the 39 registered moneylenders and traditional bankers of Baghdad in 1936 were Jewish.[72] So dominant was the role of the Jewish community in the economic life of Baghdad during the monarchy that they also affected the socioreligious activity of the Shi'i mercantile community in Baghdad and Kazimayn. Visiting Kazimayn in 1934/5, the Lebanese Shi'i mujtahid Muhsin al-Amin noted the practice of the Shi'i merchants of Baghdad of visiting the shrines of the imams at Kazimayn on a Saturday instead of a Friday, although the latter was the preferable day for the weekly visitation of the shrine. He explained that the business activity of the Shi'i merchants depended on the services of the Jewish merchants and brokers who dominated Baghdad's trade; hence, like the Jewish merchants, the Shi'is had to take their weekly day off on Saturday.[73]

The vacuum created in the commercial activity of Iraq following the exodus of the Jews in the late 1940s and early 1950s was largely filled by the Arab Shi'i mercantile class. By the mid-1950s, the latter dominated the cloth and wheat markets of Baghdad. They also played a dominant role in flour milling in Baghdad and the middle Euphrates region on account of their strong foothold in the grain trade of central and southern Iraq. The Baghdad chamber of commerce came under their control; whereas in 1935 the Shi'is held only two of the eighteen seats on the chamber's administrative committee, by 1957 they occupied fourteen of the eighteen seats.[74] Nonetheless, in contrast with the bazaaris in Iran, the Shi'i merchants in Iraq did not constitute the financial backbone of the Shi'i religious estab-

---

[71] Great Britain, Admiralty, *A Handbook of Mesopotamia*, 4 vols., London, 1916–1917, 1:77; Elie Kedourie, "The Jews of Baghdad in 1910," *MES* 7 (1971): 358. See also Hanna Batatu, *The Old Social Classes and the Revolutionary Movements in Iraq*, 2d ed. (Princeton, N.J., 1982), 225, 232–33, 247.

[72] Batatu, *The Old Social Classes*, 244–46, 250.

[73] Muhsin al-Amin, *Rihlat al-sayyid muhsin al-amin fi lubnan wa al-'iraq wa-iran wa-misr wa al-hijaz*, 2d ed. (Beirut, 1985), 134.

[74] Batatu, *The Old Social Classes*, 271–72.

lishment in their country. Likewise, the bazaar in Iraq did not emerge as a stronghold of political protest. This may be attributed in great part to the lack of a traditionally close interaction and shared values between the Shiʻi religious and commercial sectors in Iraq.

The conflicting interests of the Shiʻi commercial and religious groups in Iraq surfaced on two major occasions, discussed in chapters 2 and 3, respectively. In the 1919 plebiscite the majority of the Shiʻi Arab commercial classes in Baghdad, Kazimayn, and Najaf expressed a desire for continued British rule in Iraq. This stood in contradiction to the opinion of the supreme Persian mujtahid Mirza Muhammad Taqi Shirazi, who advocated the establishment of an Islamic government free from foreign control. Later on, in 1923, the deportation of Mahdi al-Khalisi and the subsequent departure of the senior Persian mujtahids to Iran was followed by the attempt of important Shiʻi merchants to demonstrate their loyalty to the state. This found its clearest expression in the position of Muhsin al-Shallash, who throughout the 1920s was the richest merchant and major financier of Najaf; he veered in the direction to which his commercial interests urged him, rendering many useful services to the British.[75]

The reluctance of the Shiʻi commercial classes in Iraq to channel funds for the support of religious activity as well as the poor was strongly criticized by a number of Iraqi Shiʻis. The tensions over this issue surfaced in Najaf as early as 1936. This may be gathered from an article by the famous Iraqi Shiʻi literary figure Jaʻfar al-Khalili; it was written against the background of a high unemployment rate in the city in the mid-1930s, exacerbated by the decline in the pilgrimage and the flow of foreign charities. Khalili was alarmed by what he considered the collapse of the gentle fabric that held Najafi society together. He lamented the lack of charitable associations, hospitals, and other welfare services in Najaf, pointing a blaming finger at the rich. The mujtahid Muhammad al-Kazimi Qazwini also directed his criticism toward rich Shiʻis, who according to Qazwini, declined to give *khums* and *zakat* and neglected other religious obligations. Shiʻi opposition groups asserted that the merchants had opted to lead a comfortable life, withdrawing themselves from political matters and pursuing a non-rebellious attitude. In doing so, it was explained, they helped preserve the power of the Sunni government.[76] The inability of Iraq's Shiʻi Islamic opposition groups to mobilize the merchants and turn them into one of the social bases of their movement against the government was evident after 1958. The difficulties facing the opposition reflected the search of Iraqi Shiʻi merchants for individual mobility and accommodation with the state,

[75] Ibid., 292.

[76] Jaʻfar al-Khalili, "Allahumma ihriqhum bi-narika," *al-Hatif* 38 (3 July 1936): 1; Muhammad al-Kazimi al-Qazwini, *al-Islam wa-waqiʻ al-muslim al-muʻasir* (Najaf, 1961/2), 111–14; Katib, *Tajrubat al-thawra*, 238–39.

as well as the Ba'th policy of the "carrot and the stick," which succeeded in detaching the important Shi'i Shurja market in Baghdad from the effective influence of the Shi'i ulama.[77]

Another major difference in the interaction between religion and economy in Iraq and Iran has been the existence of diverse Shi'i endowments and bequests in Iran on the one hand and the lack of significant Shi'i *waqf* property in Iraq on the other. Both the Safavids and the Qajars established endowments to sustain Shi'i Islam in their country. The support of the Iranian private economic sector for religion manifested itself in the rich *awqaf* attached to religious schools, shrines, and mosques as well as in those devoted to various Muharram observances in Iran. The shrine of imam Rida in Mashhad was reported in both the nineteenth and twentieth centuries to be very well endowed, its *awqaf* situated in different parts of Iran. In 1890 it was estimated that the income from the lands attached to the shrine amounted to sixty thousand tomans; this constituted one of the largest clerical incomes in Iran during the Qajar period. The endowments of the shrine were enough to support its servants, whose livelihood did not depend on the charity of the visitors nor, at least until the mid-1930s, on government salaries. In Yazd in the twentieth century *waqf* constituted almost one-fourth of bazaar property. The hinterland of Yazd also contained considerable *waqf* for the city. In many of the villages there were gardens, agricultural land, and shares of water from irrigation canals which had been turned into *waqf* for the benefit of religious structures in Yazd. Moreover, as late as the mid-1960s the *awqaf* properties of the religious schools in Iran were sufficient to support the students there.[78] Iran's Pahlavi rulers were not fully successful in absorbing the proceeds of the *awqaf* or changing the purpose for which they had been originally devoted. The state's supervision of the *awqaf*, to cite Lambton, was "of the most perfunctory kind." And when under Muhammad Reza Shah the state tightened its control over the religious deeds, Fischer was informed that people stopped making endowments and made more contributions directly to their mujtahids.[79]

In contrast, the bulk of *waqf* property in Iraq was Sunni and under tight

[77] Khafaji, *al-Dawla*, 111–12, 181–82; 'Abd al-Karim al-Uzri, *Mushkilat al-hukm fi al-'iraq* (London, 1991), 249–50, 275–78; Fadil al-Barrak, *al-Madaris al-yahudiyya wa al-iraniyya fi al-'iraq: dirasa muqarina* (Baghdad, 1984), 147–58; Wiley, *The Islamic Movement*, 94–96.

[78] Ann Lambton, *Landlord and Peasant in Persia*, 2d ed. (Oxford, 1969), 233–35; idem, "A Reconsideration," 132; Bonine, "Shops," 235; idem, "Islam and Commerce: Waqf and the Bazaar of Yazd, Iran," *Erdkunde* 41 (1987): 187–89, 194; Hamid Algar, *Religion and State in Iran, 1785–1906: The Role of the Ulama in the Qajar Period* (Berkeley, 1969), 14; Amin, *Rihlat*, 219–22.

[79] Lambton, *Landlord*, 236; Michael Fischer, *Iran: From Religious Dispute to Revolution* (Cambridge, Mass., 1980), 117.

government control. Thus, it was reported in 1918 that "practically none of the land in Karbala district is *waqf*" and that only "a small income is derived from properties, khans and shops in the town."[80] The welfare of servants of the shrines in the shrine cities depended on the money they received from pilgrims well into the late 1940s, when the Iraqi government fixed their salaries. Clearly, the *waqf* funds of Karbala were insufficient to provide for the upkeep of the mosques and other religious structures in that city. This was also the case in Najaf, Kufa, Hilla, and other densely populated Shi'i areas.[81]

A number of reasons may be adduced for the lack of significant Shi'i *waqf* property in Iraq. Najaf and Karbala emerged as the two strongholds of Shi'ism only from the mid-eighteenth century following the Afghan occupation of Isfahan and the subsequent migration of Persian ulama to Iraq. Unlike Iran where the population became Shi'i already from the sixteenth century, the Shi'is did not constitute the majority of Iraq's population before the settlement and conversion of the bulk of the nomadic tribes in the nineteenth century. It may very well be that the domination of the Iraqi countryside by the tribes until the nineteenth century, as well as the large contributions from Iran and India in this century, did not encourage the mujtahids of the shrine cities to push hard for the establishment of sizeable Shi'i *waqf* property in Iraq. There was perhaps also a calculated attempt on the part of the mujtahids to let Shi'i property escape the control of the Ottoman government. The mujtahids' fear that Shi'i *waqf* property might fall into the control of the Sunni authorities became real in 1838, when the Ottoman government established the *Awqaf* Department as part of the *Tanzimat* reforms. Alarmed by this development, the mujtahids made repeated appeals to the British agent in Baghdad; they asserted that Ottoman control of Shi'i *awqaf* would lead to the suppression of Shi'ism. Realizing the unfavorable impact that such a move would have on Ottoman-Iranian relations, the Ottomans eventually settled for an indirect control over the shrines. The only significant Shi'i *waqf* in Iraq was the fees levied on the burial of Shi'is in the holy cemeteries of the shrine cities, absorbed by the Ottoman *Awqaf* Department.[82]

With the formation of the monarchy, the Iraqi government increased its control over Shi'i charities and *waqf* property. In 1929 the *Awqaf* Directorate was placed under the Prime Minister's office. The tight government control over Shi'i *waqf* may be gathered from Shi'i accounts. As early as

---

[80] Administration Reports for 1918, Karbala, CO 696/1.

[81] Administration Report of the Baghdad Wilayat, 1917, and Administration Reports for 1918, Najaf, CO 696/1; Administration Report of the Hilla Division for 1919, FO 371/5080/13054.

[82] Litvak, "Shi'i Ulama," 98, 143–44; Administration Reports of the Shamiyya Division and Najaf, 1918, CO 696/1 and CO 696/2.

1931 during a discussion in the Iraqi parliament over the *Awqaf* General
Budget Law for 1931–32, a Shi'i member protested against the insufficient
allocation of *waqf* funds to Najaf and Karbala and against the government's neglect of these two cities. He pointed to the uncompleted work of
the gilding and repair of the dome of Husayn's shrine in Karbala, for which
money had been contributed by a certain Indian in 1921. A number of
years later, the mujtahid Muhammad al-Khalisi even went so far as to
claim that the government not only controlled Shi'i *waqf*, but also set the
entire revenue from endowments in Iraq for the benefit of the Sunnis
alone.[83]

While the dependence of the religious classes in Najaf and Karbala on
funds from outside Iraq enhanced their local autonomy in the nineteenth
century, the lack of a solid source of income within the country hindered
their welfare in the twentieth century. The unfavorable consequences of the
mujtahids' lack of a strong financial basis within Iraq were nowhere more
apparent than in the decline of the Shi'i madrasa in the twentieth century.

[83] Review of the Civil Administration of the Occupied Territories of Iraq, 1914–1918, FO
371/5081/13898; Report by Her Majesty's Government to the League of Nations on the
Administration of Iraq, 1929; Intelligence Report no. 9, 29 April 1931, IO L/P&S 10/1313.
For Khalisi's accusations see Mahmud al-Mallah, *al-Wahda al-islamiyya bayn al-akhdh wa
al-radd* (Baghdad, 1951), 45.

Chapter Nine

THE SHI'I MADRASA IN IRAQ

ALTHOUGH the madrasa was probably long in the making, this Muslim institution of higher learning made its explicit appearance only in the second half of the eleventh century. The development of this institution gained impetus during the period of the Seljuq vizier Nizam al-Mulk, who established a number of madrasas, the most famous of which was the Nizamiyya of Baghdad, opened in 1067. The madrasa embodied three major aspects of Muslim education and religious life: the mosque as the center for religious instruction and preaching of sermons, the mosque-khan complex which served as a lodging for out-of-town students, and the library which was adjacent to mosques and to academies of higher learning. Founded on substantial charitable trusts, the madrasa was intended to give its students, who often boarded there, an education in Islamic law and jurisprudence under the supervision of paid teachers. The uniqueness of the madrasa lay in its restrictive character. The nature of the mosque enabled people of the various Islamic legal schools and sects to gain relatively easy access to it. In contrast, the endowment deeds of the madrasa enabled the founder to retain a degree of control over the administration of the institution, its curriculum, and the teaching positions. The founder-patron of the madrasa could thus establish an institution of learning for the benefit of only one legal school or sect, thereby excluding from the madrasa teachers and students of other schools or sects.[1]

The emergence of the madrasa reflected in part the Sunni-Shi'i rivalry for political and intellectual supremacy during the tenth and eleventh centuries. Fatimid rule of Egypt (969–1171) and Buyid control of a large area of Iraq (945–1055) led to the establishment of state-sponsored Shi'i institutions of learning. In Cairo, al-Azhar mosque and the academy of learning (*Dar al-'Ilm*) were most prominent. In Baghdad, while the academy of learning (also known as *Dar al-'Ilm*) was not entirely Shi'i, it was nonetheless staffed with a large number of Shi'i personnel. Against the spread of Shi'ism, Sunnis regarded the madrasa as an effective institution capable of

---

[1] *Encyclopaedia of Islam*, 2d ed. s.v. "Madrasa"; George Makdisi, *The Rise of Colleges* (Edinburgh, 1981), 31–32; idem, "Muslim Institutions of Learning in Eleventh-Century Baghdad," *BSOAS* 24 (1961): 14–16, 37–40, 49; idem, "Madrasa and University in the Middle Ages," *SI* 32 (1970): 259; A. L. Tibawi, "Origin and Character of *Al-Madrasa*," *BSOAS* 25 (1962): 227, 236.

strengthening Sunni Islamic law. This concept found embodiment in the Nizamiyya, the establishment of which caused a setback to the position of Shi'ism in Baghdad. The Shafi'i school gained preference in the Nizamiyya, the curriculum of which laid stress on training Sunni preachers, probably as a countermeasure against Shi'i propaganda.[2]

The Seljuq occupation of Baghdad was followed by strong sectarian strife. The house of the prominent Shi'i scholar Abu Ja'far Muhammad al-Tusi was raided and his great library was plundered and burned. Unable to continue teaching in Baghdad, Tusi in 1056 moved to Najaf, where he later established the first Shi'i madrasa; it was said to have been attended by some three hundred students.[3] Until the sixteenth century, however, Shi'i learning in southern Iraq remained precarious in the absence of Shi'i dynasties. Shi'i madrasas were built in Iraq in large numbers only after the rise of the Safavids in Iran in 1501. The transformation of Iran into a Shi'i state, and the growing Iranian interest in the shrine cities (including two brief periods of Safavid rule over Iraq), greatly benefited the shrine cities, although their status as the leading Shi'i centers of study was somewhat overshadowed by the importance of Isfahan as the largest center of learning. It was only from the mid-eighteenth century that the shrine cities in Iraq emerged as the focal point of Shi'i scholarship. Following the Afghan occupation of Isfahan in 1722 and the subsequent collapse of the Safavid state, a large number of ulama migrated from Iran to the shrine cities. The major Shi'i centers of learning in Iran declined in the eighteenth century, and the center of scholarship shifted to Karbala and then to Najaf.

If for many Shi'is Karbala symbolized the focus of devotion, Najaf emerged in modern times as the leading academic center. Indeed, contemporary Shi'i scholars of the madrasas of Najaf consider themselves to be the successors of Tusi through a continuous line of teachers stretching from the eleventh to the twentieth century.[4] Retaining the leading status was by no means easy. By the late eighteenth century Najaf had twice lost its leading role within Iraq when the Shi'i center of learning shifted first to Hilla (from

[2] A. S. Tritton, *Materials on Muslim Education in the Middle Ages* (London, 1957), 103; Muhammad Amin, *al-Awqaf wa al-hayat al-ijtima'iyya fi misr, 963–1517* (Cairo, 1970), 233–34; John Pedersen, "Some Aspects of the History of the Madrasa," *IC* 3 (1929): 530–32, 535; A. L. Tibawi, "Muslim Education in the Golden Age of the Caliphate," *IC* 28 (1954): 429, 435–37; idem, "Origin and Character," 235; Makdisi, "Muslim Institutions," 7–8; Gary Leiser, "Notes on the Madrasa in Medieval Islamic Society," *MW* 76 (1986): 18; H. Laoust, "Les Agitations Religieuses à Baghdad aux IV et V Siecles de l'Hegire," in *Islamic Civilisation, 950–1150,* ed. D. S. Richard (Oxford, 1973), 178–79.

[3] Ja'far al-Khalili, *Mawsu'at al-'atabat al-muqaddasa, qism al-najaf,* 10 vols. (Baghdad and Beirut, 1965–1970), 2,2:28–35; Hasan al-Amin, "an-Najaf," *ISE* 4 (1973): 82; Naji Wada'a, *Lamahat min ta'rikh al-najaf al-ashraf* (Najaf, 1973), 243.

[4] Roy Mottahedeh, *The Mantle of the Prophet: Religion and Politics in Iran* (New York, 1985), 91–92.

the early thirteenth to the late fifteenth century), and then to Karbala (from around 1737 until 1797).[5] Najaf began to recover during the time of the mujtahids Muhammad Mahdi Bahr al-'Ulum (d. 1797) and Shaykh Ja'far Kashif al-Ghita (d. 1812). It regained the leadership firmly after the death of the mujtahid Muhammad Sharif Mazandarani (d. 1830/31) of Karbala and the Ottoman occupation of the latter city in 1843. Although following the migration of the grand mujtahid Muhammad Hasan Shirazi from Najaf to Samarra (1875–1895) the status of the latter city increased in importance, Najaf still did not lose its supremacy as the leading Shi'i academic center and managed to retain this status until the first half of the twentieth century.[6]

Many factors were at work in determining the rise and decline of the Shi'i centers of learning. The fluctuations reflected changes in water supply and security, developments within the Shi'i legal system and jurisprudence, the place of residence of the preeminent mujtahid, the flow of funds and students, and the policies of both Sunni and Shi'i governments. Because of the unsteady nature of these factors, and the constant competition of Shi'i academic centers for supremacy, no place was immune to loss of importance, or even a complete decline as the case of Samarra demonstrates. Following Shirazi's migration from Najaf to Samarra in 1875, the latter grew from a very small shrine city into a prosperous center of learning. Many pilgrims flocked to the city, which experienced an economic boom. Shirazi enjoyed a large number of contributions and attracted many students. The status of his madrasa, which rested on Shirazi's reputation, challenged the fame of some of the madrasas of the larger and more established academic center of Najaf. Yet within a year following Shirazi's death in 1895, his large circle of students dissolved as most of them left Samarra for Najaf and Karbala. The decline of Samarra from that time was reinforced by the sharp drop in charities and pilgrims. By the early twentieth century, the city's economy was almost at a standstill. In 1933 there were barely forty students left in the city, and their portion of bread depended on the charity of a single Azarbayjani merchant.[7]

Like Samarra, Najaf's fortunes changed, and it eventually lost its status

[5] Khalili, *Mawsu'a*, 2,2:52–53, 72–74; 'Abd al-Hadi al-Fadli, *Dalil al-najaf al-ashraf* (Najaf, 1965/6), 40–43; Nur al-Din al-Shahrudi, *Ta'rikh al-haraka al-'ilmiyya fi karbala'* (Beirut, 1990), 128–34; Hasan al-Amin, "an-Najaf," 84.

[6] Muhammad Hasan al-Najafi, *Jawahir al-kalam fi sharh shara'i' al-islam*, 6th ed., 42 vols. (Najaf, 1958), 1:8–9; Khalili, *Mawsu'a*, 2,2:78–82; Fadli, *Dalil al-najaf*, 48; Meir Litvak, "The Shi'i Ulama of Najaf and Karbala, 1791–1904: A Socio-Political Analysis" (Ph.D. diss., Harvard, 1991), 85–86, 135, 209–10, 273.

[7] Muhammad Mahdi Kubba, *Mudhakkirati fi samim al-ahdath, 1917–1958* (Beirut, 1965), 9–15; Muhsin al-Amin, *Rihlat al-sayyid muhsin al-amin fi lubnan wa al-'iraq wa-iran wa-misr wa al-hijaz*, 2d ed. (Beirut, 1985), 126; Yunus Ibrahim al-Samarra'i, *Ta'rikh madinat samarra'*, 3 vols. (Baghdad, 1968–1971), 2:174.

as the major Shi'i academic center, which shifted back to Iran in the second half of the twentieth century. As will be seen, Najaf succumbed to religious, socioeconomic, and political developments in Iraq and Iran which led to its decline and the rise of Qum.

FEATURES AND FUNCTIONS

Political and socioeconomic conditions in the nineteenth century were on the whole conducive to the general prosperity of Najaf and its rise as the center of Shi'i learning. Unlike Karbala, Najaf was saved from the Wahhabi sack. It also did not experience the same serious Ottoman pressures as Karbala did. Responding to the Wahhabi challenge, prominent Najafi mujtahids beginning with Mahdi Bahr al-'Ulum and Ja'far Kashif al-Ghita strove to bolster the position of Najaf and to increase the propagation of Shi'i Islam both within and outside Iraq. The last of the Ottoman-Iranian wars ended in 1823 with the first treaty of Erzurum. The relative stability which this brought to the Iraqi frontier was reinforced by the fact that until the late nineteenth century large parts of the Shi'i Islamic world escaped major European pressures or occupation. This facilitated the flow of large amounts of private and government funds from Iran, India, and elsewhere to the shrine cities in general and to Najaf in particular. The completion around 1803 of the Hindiyya Canal assured a more regular supply of water to Najaf. The great improvement in the city's water supply enabled Najaf to sustain dynamic academic activity as many new madrasas were built to accommodate the large number of students who flocked to the city to study with the leading mujtahids of the day. Finally, Najaf's prestige in the Shi'i Arab world was also derived from its status as a center of literary activity, an image reinforced by the revival of Arabic poetry and prose in neighboring Hilla in the late nineteenth century.[8]

Shi'i sources put the number of students at Najaf in the late nineteenth and early twentieth centuris between ten and fifteen thousand. A British report on Najaf compiled in 1918 provides a more conservative estimate, putting their number at some six thousand.[9] Since, as will be seen below, during the decade that preceded 1918 there was already a serious drop in the number of students, it is likely that there were as many as eight thou-

---

[8] Najafi, *Jawahir al-kalam*, 1:9–12; 'Abbas 'Ali, *al-Imam sharaf al-din: huzmat daw' 'ala tariq al-fikr al-imami* (Najaf, 1968), 99; Yusuf Karkush al-Hilli, *Ta'rikh al-hilla*, 2 vols. (Najaf, 1965), 2:134.

[9] 'Ali al-Wardi, *Lamahat ijtima'iyya min ta'rikh al-'iraq al-hadith*, 6 vols. (Baghdad, 1969–1978), 3:79; Hajji Pirzadeh, *Safarnama-yi hajji pirzadeh*, ed. Hafez Farman-Farmayan, 2 vols. (Tehran, 1963), 1:333; Muhammad al-Hashimi al-Baghdadi, "Laysa al-azhar akbar jami'a islamiyya," *al-Muqtataf* 53 (1918): 597; Great Britain, Administration Reports for 1918, Najaf, CO 696/1.

sand in Najaf at the turn of the century. The largest group were Iranians, who formed about a third of the student population in 1918. Azarbayjanis, Indians, and Arabs from Lebanon, the Persian Gulf, and Iraq constituted the other major groups. There were about twenty functioning madrasas at Najaf in 1918, all residential, the largest of which had accommodated five hundred students. Among these, the oldest institution was said to be the *Madrasat al-Sadr*, built around 1824 by Muhammad Husayn Khan Isfahani, one of the viziers of Fath 'Ali Shah.[10] The location of some of these madrasas was at the actual site of older madrasas, whose buildings were repaired by nineteenth- and twentieth-century mujtahids who established their own institutions there. Usually named after their founders, the madrasas were in essence boarding houses, built to accommodate single students, at times of specific ethnic or regional origin. Married students and their dependents lived in private housing in the city.

The madrasas were an integral part of the socioeconomic life of Najaf; the welfare of students and city dwellers was closely tied together. If we are to accept the figure of eight thousand students at the turn of the century, this number represented some 27 percent of Najaf's permanent population, estimated at thirty thousand in 1908. The welfare of local merchants depended on goods and services provided to the students. The madrasas generated a large payroll and employed various servants and attendants. At the same time, the staff of these institutions offered various legal and consultative services to the city's population. Students also catered to the needs of pilgrims and provided various religious services, thereby gaining extra income to supplement their allowances.

One of the most striking features connected with the establishment and maintenance of the nineteenth- and early twentieth-century madrasas of Najaf was their lack of solid local *waqf* property. As has been pointed out in the previous chapter, this stood in contrast with the rich endowments supporting Iranian Shi'i madrasas in Qum and Mashhad. The lack of viable local *waqf* property in Najaf had its root in the scarcity of Iraqi benefactors, the bulk of the contributors being Iranians and Bukharis. Many of the founders of Najaf's madrasas were foreign merchants, officials of the Qajar government, viziers of the Bukhari sultan, or even mujtahids who enjoyed large private contributions and could thus establish their own madrasas.[11] The Bukhari-Najafi connection is particularly intriguing since the Sultanate of Bukhara was known to adhere to the Sunni creed. It seems that the Bukhari contributors were Shi'i slaves who had been captured

[10] Administration Reports for 1918, Najaf, CO 696/1; Khalili, *Mawsu'a*, 2,2:135–36; Ibrahim al-Musawi al-Zanjani, *'Aqa'id al-imamiyya al-ithna 'ashariyya*, 2d ed., 3 vols. (Beirut, 1973–1977), 3:245.

[11] See the list of madrasas, founders, and sources of income in Khalili, *Mawsu'a*, 2,2:132–69. See also Fadli, *Dalil al-najaf*, 75.

during raids in Iran (mainly in Khurasan), and who later became high-ranking officials in the Sultanate. The Najafi mujtahids Kazim Khurasani and Kazim Yazdi benefited most from the contributions of these Bukhari officials, who financed the establishment of no less than five madrasas in Najaf between the late nineteenth and early twentieth century.[12] Before the rise of modern Iraq, Pahlavi Iran, and the Soviet Union (into which the Sultanate of Bukhara was incorporated as part of the Republic of Uzbekistan), when foreign money could flow relatively easily to the shrine cities, this worked to the advantage of Najaf. Indeed, in contrast with Sunni madrasas where after the death of the founder, and sometimes even before, control of the institution fell into the hands of the state, Shi'i mujtahids had often no problem gaining actual control of the madrasa following the founder's death, if they were not themselves the original founders.[13]

The power of the madrasas of Najaf, Shi'i sources assert, lay in the success of the institutions in retaining their independent Islamic identity over a period of thirteen centuries. Unlike the famous Egyptian madrasa of al-Azhar or any other Sunni madrasa, those of Najaf did not lose their political and financial independence. Rejecting government funds, they relied on private contributions and religious taxes, which assured the financial and political independence of the madrasas as well as their intellectual freedom.[14] This freedom found embodiment in the activity of the prominent mujtahids. Not subject to government control, they acted as great patrons operating outside the autonomy of the Ottoman state. Those who succeeded in controlling the teaching circles of Najaf and establishing a network of student-disciples mainly in Iran, India, and Lebanon rose to prominence within the religious hierarchy. They dispensed money among *sayyids* and the poor, and sponsored elementary health and social services. They administered their own madrasas, appointed drill masters, provided support for the students, issued certificates for graduates, gave legal opinions in response to queries addressed to them, and received delegations from various parts of the Shi'i world.[15]

By establishing their own madrasas in Iraq, families of mujtahids bol-

---

[12] Khalili, *Mawsu'a*, 2,2:145, 146, 150–55; Araz Muhammad Sarli, *Turkistan dar ta'rikh* (Tehran, 1985/6), 58, 80–84; Hélène Carrére d'Encausse, *Réforme et Révolution chez les Musulmans de l'Empire Russe, Bukhara 1867–1924* (Paris, 1966), 52–53.

[13] On Sunni Islam in general see Makdisi, "Muslim Institutions," 16; Tibawi, "Origin and Character," 232.

[14] Muhammad Mahdi al-Asifi, *Madrasat al-najaf wa-tatawwur al-haraka al-islahiyya fi-ha* (Najaf, 1964), 14–17; Fadli, *Dalil al-najaf*, 75.

[15] Asifi, *Madrasat al-najaf*, 16, 53–54; Anon., *al-Imam al-sayyid abu al-hasan* (Najaf, 1946/7), 63; Ja'far al-Mahbuba, *Madi al-najaf wa-hadiruha*, 3 vols. (Najaf, 1955–1958), 1:380–82; Abbas Amanat, "In Between the Madrasa and the Marketplace: The Designation of Clerical Leadership in Modern Shi'ism," in *Authority and Political Culture in Shi'ism*, ed. Said Amir Arjomand (Albany, N.Y., 1988), 103, 106–7, 116–17.

stered their status within the religious hierarchy. The control of the madrasa by family members also assured a low level of bureaucratization of this institution, and enabled Shi'i mujtahids to enhance their position vis-à-vis the Ottoman and the Qajar governments. One such example is the *Madrasat al-Mu'tamid* of the Kashif al-Ghita family, the building of which was made possible by a nineteenth-century contribution by the Iranian vizier 'Abbasquli Khan, while the actual control of the institution was in the hands of the family.[16] This unique feature of the Shi'i madrasas in Iraq, whereby the mujtahids succeeded in removing this institution from the realm of the Ottoman state even as late as the nineteenth century, differed radically from Mamluk Egypt, for example, where the Sunni madrasas were integrated into the state's bureaucratic structure. Indeed, in Mamluk Egypt most madrasas were established by local sultans and emirs, and the Mamluk elite retained actual control of that country's institutions of higher learning.[17]

Modern Najafi sources stressed the continuous renewal of Islamic thinking in the city's madrasas, the intellectual stimulation and exchange between mujtahids and students, and the freedom which the latter enjoyed. They maintained that even in the twentieth century students did not have to pass periodic examinations. The students came to the madrasa for the sake of study and to acquire expertise in religious law. They did not pursue a degree, a government position, or material reward. For graduation, they were expected to master the latest developments in Shi'i Imami thinking and religious law. Because of the more open attitude of Shi'i Islam toward the process of producing legal opinion (*ijtihad*), the graduates of the Shi'i madrasa were allegedly more capable of applying Islamic law in daily life than their Sunni counterparts.[18]

In reality, study in the madrasa meant a long experience of endurance. Students ranged in age from twenty to sixty. Some stayed at the madrasa for as long as thirty or forty years, relying on a small allowance, a daily ration of bread, and free accommodation. Lecture halls did not exist, a feature which reflected the informal organization of studies. Relations of patronage between mujtahids and students were a central feature of academic life in Najaf. Students were disciples of a particular mujtahid and relied on him for their monthly allowance. They also needed their mujtahid's attention and goodwill in order to obtain a room in the madrasa. Moreover, their professional career depended on the certificate of *ijtihad* which they received directly from their teacher, not from the madrasa itself. Teaching was organized in the form of study circles (*halaqat*), centered

[16] Khalili, *Mawsu'a*, 2,2:138.

[17] Jonathan Berkey, *The Transmission of Knowledge in Medieval Cairo* (Princeton, N.J., 1992), 12.

[18] Khalili, *Mawsu'a*, 2,2:91; Asifi, *Madrasat al-najaf*, 11–12, 18–26.

around individual mujtahids. It took place either in the spacious court-yards of the mosques and the shrine of imam 'Ali or in the teacher's house. The students would sit on the floor around the teacher, or next to the pulpit from which he sometimes used to deliver his lesson. Some mujtahids con-trolled an entire complex of introductory, intermediate, and advanced levels of courses, thereby expanding their patronage and network of stu-dents. Indeed, it is said that several hundred students used to attend the lectures of famous mujtahids like Murtada al-Ansari and Kazim Khurasani. When the mujtahid died, his study circle dissolved; some of the senior disciples would try to set up their own circles, others would join the circle of another senior mujtahid, and still others would return home.[19]

Teaching itself was divided into three stages. In the first stage (al-muqaddamat), which lasted three to five years, one or more students would choose a teacher, usually a more advanced student, to be their instructor. Their studies focused on Arabic grammar, syntax, prose, and logic. Stu-dents could also add theology, Arabic literature, and mathematics to their curricula. The second stage (al-sutuh) emphasized the study of rational jurisprudence and the principles of jurisprudential inference, interpreta-tion of the Koran and Traditions, and religious philosophy. Students were again free to choose their own teacher, with whom they decided on the books to be read. This stage usually lasted three to six years. The first two stages were the most exhausting levels of study, classes being conducted in the form of small sessions. The criteria for establishing students' progress were their regular attendance of classes and their devotion to their studies. Attrition was high, and thus only a few students reached the final stage. Studies at the third level (bahth al-kharij) were more collective in nature, and not structured around any particular book. Usually a large number of students, and even some mujtahids, would gather to hear the lectures of one of the prominent mujtahids on either the principles of jurisprudence or practical jurisprudence. The mujtahid would usually pose a problem, com-ment on it, touch upon the opinion of different Muslim schools, and finally give his own opinion. Students could debate the legal points and challenge the mujtahid, thereby building their self-confidence and skill at disputa-tion. Having spent some fifteen to twenty-five years at the madrasa, suc-cessful students obtained a certificate from their mujtahid qualifying them to pass judgment in religious legal matters. Students thus built their careers on the reputation of their mujtahid-teacher.[20]

The madrasas of Najaf not only trained experts in religious law but also produced a generation of Iraqi literary figures who acquired at least part of

[19] Litvak, "Shi'i Ulama," 54, 70–74; Khalili, Mawsu'a, 2,2:107–10; Fadli, Dalil al-najaf, 70; Hasan al-Amin, "an-Najaf," 86; Asifi, Madrasat al-najaf, 25.
[20] Khalili, Mawsu'a, 2,2:91, 92–100; Mahbuba, Madi al-najaf, 1:379–80; Fadli, Dalil al-najaf, 53–69; Asifi, Madrasat al-Najaf, 7–13; Hasan al-Amin, "an-Najaf," 84–86.

their education in the madrasa. Indeed, Muhammad Rida al-Shabibi, Muhammad Mahdi al-Jawahiri, and 'Ali al-Sharqi, to name but a few, became major literary figures in twentieth-century Iraq. The combination of a pilgrimage center and a university town offered Najaf's students great opportunities for religious and literary stimulation. The madrasas were repositories of religious ideas and ideologies, and centers of literary activity. The pilgrims brought news to Najaf, and the city itself had a large number of libraries. There were weekly meetings at which ulama responded to queries on issues relating to literature, jurisprudence, Koranic commentary, tradition, and philosophy. Early in the twentieth century, the mujtahid Muhammad Husayn Na'ini was said to have introduced a new type of intellectual activity, the forums for producing legal opinions (*majalis al-istifta'*). Several junior mujtahids and teachers in the madrasa, led by one of the prominent mujtahids, would hold a discussion and give a legal opinion in response to queries that had reached the latter from various parts of the Shi'i world. The participants, who gathered the legal and jurisprudential data on which the senior mujtahid would base his reply, thus participated in a collective process of *ijtihad*.[21]

One type of activity played a particularly important role in Najafi life until the rise of the modern state. Frequent sessions (*majalis* or *dawawin*) were held in which educational, literary, and sociopolitical activities were fused. The "soul of Najaf," these sessions were said to date from the city's early history and to reflect its true spirit and aspirations. The sessions were often held in the houses of those religious figures who also enjoyed social esteem in Najaf. Some of the famous sessions early in the twentieth century were those of Shaykh Jawad al-Jawahiri, 'Abd al-Rida al-Shaykh Radi, Shaykh 'Abd al-Karim al-Jaza'iri, and Sayyid Muhammad 'Ali Bahr al-'Ulum. In these sessions, which were also held in the courtyards of the shrine or the city's mosques, students and ulama debated religious, literary, and social issues. Often an alternative to the Ottoman state courts, these sessions provided a mechanism for conflict resolution among members of Najafi society. It is also related that the strategies that were formulated in these sessions laid the basis for political action in such episodes as Najaf's 1918 revolt and the 1920 revolt in Iraq.[22]

Thus, Najaf was not only the Shi'i center of learning and intellectual activity but also a base for dissemination of Shi'i ideas and political action. The existence of some twenty institutions in one city made it extremely difficult for the Ottoman government to exercise effective control over their religious and political activities. Preachers and sermon leaders who origi-

[21] Asifi, *Madrasat al-najaf*, 26–39, 58.

[22] Ja'far al-Khalili, *Hakadha 'araftuhum*, 2 vols. (Baghdad, 1963–1968), 1:313–18, 369–70. A detailed list of the *majalis* of various Najafi families may be found in Haydar al-Marjani, *al-Najaf al-ashraf qadiman wa-hadithan* (Baghdad, 1986), 101–81.

nated from the madrasa propagated Shi'ism both within and outside Iraq. Najaf's self-image as one of the leading Islamic academic centers prompted it to take a stand vis-à-vis governments and sociopolitical issues in the Islamic world. Indeed, Najafis considered it essential for their city to play an active role in Islamic affairs so that it would not lose its centrality.[23]

By the twentieth century, the power of mujtahids and students in the city posed a serious challenge to the Qajar and Ottoman governments, as well as to the growing British interests in Iraq and Iran. Najaf became a major player in Iranian politics, a development which culminated during the Constitutional Revolution. As has been seen in chapter 2, the city emerged as a force attempting to lead a jihad movement against the growing European penetration of Muslim territories, and it played a dominant role in instigating the 1920 revolt in Iraq.

SIGNS OF DECLINE

The clear signs of the beginning of decline of the Shi'i madrasa in Iraq may be traced to the period of the Iranian Constitutional Revolution, when Najaf seemed to be at its height. The affairs of the Revolution strained student-mujtahid relations. The divisions between supporters and opponents of the Revolution on the one hand, and people's backing of different factions in the National Assembly on the other, pulled students and mujtahids apart. Iranian students acted as emissaries of the liberal group and pressed those mujtahids who supported the Revolution to back this group, whose members were drawn primarily from the intelligentsia and pushed for extensive reforms. But the mujtahids (led by Kazim Khurasani) were willing to support the Assembly only to the extent that they considered it an institution capable of checking the Shah's actions and the process of legislation. Indeed, the Supplementary Fundamental Laws which were formulated by the delegates to the Assembly stipulated that a supreme committee of five mujtahids was to scrutinize the bills introduced into parliament to ensure that no law contradicted the shari'a. Within the Assembly, the mujtahids had their own preference and gave their support to the moderate group, which was headed by the bazaaris, the major financiers of the mujtahids.[24]

The sharp drop in the number of pilgrims and in charitable income from Iran during the Revolution further strained student-mujtahid relations. The decrease in pilgrimage may have been a result of the disturbances in

---

[23] Asifi, *Madrasat al-najaf*, 79.

[24] Ramsay to Cecil, Baghdad, 18 March 1907, FO 195/2242/169; Political Diary for the Week Ending 5 October 1907, FO 195/2243/867–111; Political Diary for the Week Ending 14 September 1908, FO 195/2275/830–94; Ervand Abrahamian, *Iran Between Two Revolutions*, 2d ed. (Princeton, N.J., 1983), 90.

Iran; perhaps it also reflected Ottoman attempts (in the period before the Young Turk Revolution in the summer of 1908) to bear pressures on those mujtahids who emerged as major players in Iranian national affairs. By undermining the welfare of residents in the shrine cities, the Ottomans could use the residents' dissatisfaction to reduce the power of those mujtahids. The decline in the income from charities starting in 1908 was mainly a consequence of the decrease in private contributions to the mujtahids after the bazaaris apparently felt that they no longer needed the mujtahids as a counterpoise to the Shah.[25] In January 1908, the British resident in Baghdad reported that political events in Najaf had taken a "curious turn." Reacting to the drop in pilgrimage and in the flow of charity on which many students depended for their living, the shopkeepers of the city no longer agreed to give food to the students on credit. The latter turned to the prominent mujtahid Khurasani and begged him to arrange with the shopkeepers the renewal of their lines of credit. Khurasani rejected the students' request and replied that he had no intention of intervening with the shopkeepers. The attitude of this prominent mujtahid further distanced him from his students.[26]

The welfare of students deteriorated further when some prominent mujtahids, who no longer enjoyed large contributions from the bazaar in Iran, stopped paying them their allowances. Their major sources of income cut, students began leaving the shrine cities in large numbers, while others came close to declaring a revolt against the mujtahids. By March 1908 some two hundred students left, and five hundred others reportedly decided to give up their studies and return to Iran. Muhammad Hasan Muhsin, a Shi'i of Indian origin who acted as the British vice-consul at Karbala, wrote that although the mujtahids received large amounts of money during the first two years of the Revolution, they stopped paying the students. The latter's grievances were directed mainly against Khurasani, whose sons were accused of spending public money in purchasing over a hundred pieces of property which they registered in their own name. It was alleged that until around December 1907 Khurasani used to distribute bread to the students, giving each one an allotment according to the size of his family. Subsequently, however, due to the drop in his revenues from bazaari contributions from Iran, he stopped this distribution, reducing many students to starvation. The students demanded that the mujtahids,

[25] Political Diary for the Week Ending 2 June 1908, FO 195/2274/484–50; Selim Deringil, "The Struggle against Shi'ism in Hamidian Iraq: A Study in Ottoman Counter-Propaganda," WI 30 (1990): 56.
[26] Political Diary for the Week Ending 7 January 1908, FO 195/2274/30–3. On the difficult condition of students during 1908–1909 see also Agha Najafi Quchani, Siyahat-i sharq ya zindeginama va-safarnama-yi agha najafi quchani (Mashhad, 1972), esp. 296, 314–16.

who were the recipients of religious funds, should prove to the public that they disposed of what they received in accordance with the law by establishing a treasury (*Bayt al-Mal*). Students, *sayyids*, and mujtahids would then get their share of the funds from the treasury through public distribution, as was the case in the early period of Islam.[27]

The refusal of some mujtahids to renew the allowances, and the diminishing funds in the shrine cities, reinforced class, regional, and ethnic divisions among the students. *Sayyids*, Turks, Iranians, and Indians each formed their own society in an attempt to compel the mujtahids to distribute allowances according to class and ethnic criteria. Different student groups competed with one another over money, claiming that it should be distributed according to geographical origin. Thus, some four hundred Rashti students demanded that Khurasani assign a charity of two hundred Turkish pounds a month, made by the Rashti donor Mushir al-Saltana, to their own exclusive use. As has been seen in the previous chapter, students at Karbala also sought to force the mujtahids to disperse some of their Oudh Bequest funds, while Indian students petitioned the British consul urging that Oudh Bequest money be given only to Indians. Noting these strained student-mujtahid relations, the British vice-consul at Karbala concluded in his report that if the mujtahids continued in their course, the importance of Najaf as the Shi'i center of learning would greatly decline.[28]

Conditions in the madrasa deteriorated further before and during World War I as the Ottomans increased their pressures on this institution, seeking to hinder its independence. Alarmed by the active involvement of mujtahids and students in politics, and by the growing presence of Persians in the shrine cities, the Ottomans sought to reduce the power of the madrasa, which they considered to be at its paramount during the Constitutional period. Early in November 1910, the governor of Karbala received an order from Istanbul that all schools in his jurisdiction, the establishment of which had not been authorized by the government, should be closed at once. The order included both the madrasas and the secular schools established in Karbala by Iranian societies during the Revolution. It stipulated that the schools be reopened only after permission was obtained from Istanbul. On 16 November, the heads of all the madrasas of Najaf were notified that they had to obtain a sanction for the continuation of their institution from Istanbul within ten days; otherwise the government would take possession of their madrasa and manage it itself. The prospects that the Ottomans might control the madrasas and their *waqf* revenues caused a panic among mujtahids and students in Najaf and Karbala. The promi-

[27] From British Vice-Consul to British Consul General, Karbala, 27 March 1908, FO 195/2274/266–31.

[28] Ibid. See also Political Diary for the Week Ending 22 June 1908, FO 195/2274/340–60; Political Diary for the Week Ending 30 August 1909, FO 195/2309/929–106.

nent mujtahid Kazim Yazdi was even reported to have considered emigration from Najaf to Muhammara in Iran before the government eventually reversed its decision.[29]

The Ottoman attitude toward the madrasas was part of its overall policy aimed at reducing the presence and influence of Persians in the shrine cities. Prior to the restoration of the Turkish Constitution in 1908, the Ottoman government recognized the special status of the large number of Persians in the shrine cities, and had accorded them some privileges, the most prized being exemption from taxes and military conscription. But the doctrine of equality advocated by the Committee of Union and Progress following the rise of the Young Turks to power meant the scaling down of privileges that had been granted to non-Ottoman subjects.[30] Persians in the shrine cities were subsequently registered as liable for service in the Ottoman army. The entire Persian community was ordered to pay an income tax (*tamattu‘*) and a tax in lieu of four days' forced labor per annum (*'amaliyya mukallafa*). With the introduction of a new burial tax, the burial of foreign subjects resident in Karbala and Najaf was no longer exempted from taxation. The Ottomans also dissolved the Persian political and literary societies in the shrine cities, and closed the newspaper *Najaf*, edited by Persians. Seen from the perspective of the Persian students, these measures not only meant the loss of their privileges and immunities, but also the undesired possibility of becoming Turkish subjects. In the course of only two days in November 1910, sixteen large boats carrying students and their dependents left Kufa, the river port of Najaf, for Basra and thence Iran. At that time, the mujtahid Mirza Muhammad Taqi Shirazi of Samarra was also considering emigrating to Iran with some of his students. During World War I some Persians were compelled to join the Ottoman forces. The pilgrimage and the corpse traffic were almost at a standstill, and very little money reached the shrine cities. The Ottomans also seized large amounts of money and valuables from the shrines of Najaf and Karbala. More students gave up their studies and returned to their countries of origin.[31]

The madrasa not only did not recover following the formation of the monarchy in Iraq, but lost much of its remaining power. A secular state-controlled school system was established, and Iraqi Sunni politicians and educators like Sati‘ al-Husri who stressed Pan-Arabism were inimical to

[29] Summary of Events in Turkish Iraq for the Month of November 1910, FO 195/2341/1085–67.

[30] Review of the Civil Administration of the Occupied Territories of Iraq, 1914–1918, FO 371/4148/34799.

[31] Summaries of Events in Turkish Iraq for the Months of June and December 1910, January, March, and June 1911, FO 195/2339/562–28; FO 195/2367/33–1; FO 195/2367/T-2; FO 195/2368/312–21; FO 195/2368/575–26; Lorimer to Lowther, Baghdad, 1 April 1911, FO 195/2368/283–18; Yate to Gray, 7 May 1915, FO 371/2430; "Laysa al-azhar akbar jami‘a islamiyya," 597.

the existence of schools of sectarian character, let alone madrasas dominated by Persian mujtahids and students. In seeking to undermine the
status of the madrasa among Iraqi Shi'is, the government pursued several
strategies. The position of Minister of Education was almost exclusively
reserved for Shi'i politicians in order to promote state-controlled education
in the Shi'i regions and discredit the mujtahids' claims that the state dis-
criminated against Shi'is in education.[32] The government encouraged the
publication of Shi'i magazines in which Shi'i contributors discussed the
benefits of modern education. One such journal was *al-Murshid*, which
was issued in Baghdad for four years starting from 1925, and in which
Hibat al-Din al-Shahrastani, himself a former Minister of Education,
played a major contributing role.[33] Moreover, those mujtahids who objected to secular and girls' education also found themselves under the attack
of prominent Iraqi Shi'i intellectuals and literary figures, notably, Muhammad Mahdi al-Jawahiri and Ja'far al-Khalili.[34]

In an effort to train religious functionaries loyal to the new state, the
government in 1924 opened a faculty of religious studies in Baghdad
(*Jami'at Al al-Bayt*), the curriculum of which combined courses in Sunni
and Shi'i jurisprudence as well as modern sciences. King Faysal was one of
the major figures pushing for this institution, which he considered capable
of reducing sectarian boundaries in Iraq. Yet the palace and the government, as well as the Ministry of Education and the *Awqaf* Directorate,
struggled for control of the school, its curriculum, and endowments. The
faculty was eventually closed by the Premier Nuri Sa'id in 1930, but this
project, as will be seen later in this chapter, inspired Iraqi Shi'i intellectuals
to push for the establishment of a new madrasa in Najaf to compensate for
the loss of this institutional link between Shi'is and the state.[35]

Although the curricula of the Shi'i madrasas in Iraq were not dictated by
the modern state (as was the case with the famous institution of al-Azhar,

[32] Wardi, *Lamahat*, 6:122, 124–25; idem, *Wu"az al-salatin* (Baghdad, 1954), 398–99;
Muhammad al-Kazimi al-Qazwini, *al-Islam wa-waqi' al-muslim al-mu'asir* (Najaf, 1961/2),
28–30; Abbas Kelidar, "The Shi'i Imami Community and Politics in the Arab East," *MES* 19
(1983): 12.

[33] See, for example, "al-Islam wa al-'ilm," *al-Murshid* 2 (1927): 289–92; "bi-Ma tasluh
halatuna al-ijtima'iyya?" *al-Murshid* 2 (1927): 234–35, 313, 352; "al-'Ilm wa al-din," *al-
Murshid* 3 (1928): 92; "al-Sha'b wa al-'ilm," *al-Murshid* 3 (1928): 99; "al-'Ilm wa al-jahl,"
al-Murshid 3 (1928): 143; "Bayn al-'ilm wa al-din," *al-Murshid* 3 (1928): 221–24, 269–74.

[34] 'Abd al-Sahib al-Musawi, *Harakat al-shi'r fi al-najaf al-ashraf wa-atwaruhu khilal al-
qarn al-rabi' 'ashara al-hijri: dirasa naqdiyya* (Beirut, 1988), 134–36.

[35] On *Jami'at Al al-Bayt* see Sati' al-Husri, *Mudhakkirati fi al-'iraq, 1921–1941*, 2 vols.
(Beirut, 1967–1968), 1:419–20, 431; Husayn al-Dujayli, *al-Ta'lim al-'ali fi al-'iraq*
(Baghdad, 1963), 10, 12, 19–21, 39–40, 45–46, 49, 57; 'Abd al-Hamid al-Rashudi and
Khalid Muhammad Isma'il, eds., *Maqalat fahmi al-mudarris* (Baghdad, 1970), 19, 316;
Yusuf 'Izz al-Din, *Fahmi al-mudarris: min ruwwad al-fikr al-'arabi al-hadith* (Baghdad,
1970), 168–69, 178, 210.

the curriculum of which has been revised repeatedly since the nineteenth century by successive Egyptian governments), the traditional madrasas of Najaf lost much of their former economic power, and the prominent Persian mujtahids withdrew from overt politics after their exodus to Iran in 1923. The institution no longer maintained its image among Arab Shiʻis as the center of Arabic intellectual and literary activity. And by the end of the monarchy, Najaf also came closer to losing its status in the Shiʻi world as the center of religious learning, challenged by the steady rise of Qum in Iran.

The problems facing the madrasa under the monarchy are echoed in a number of sources. The richest is the Najafi literary journal *al-Hatif*, edited by Jaʻfar al-Khalili, which provides indispensable insight into life in the madrasa during the twentieth century, and from which the following discussion is mostly drawn. Under the monarchy some of the madrasas of Najaf lost their material independence and became dependent on government funds. During the 1920 revolt the grand mujtahid Shaykh al-Shariʻa Isfahani struggled to protect the academic activity in the madrasas by distributing bread to the students of the city.[36] In subsequent years mujtahids in Iraq found it increasingly difficult to maintain the prosperity of their madrasas and to provide for students' material needs. Some Shiʻis attributed the decline in the amount of contributions to the donors' realization that their money was not properly managed and spent by the mujtahid recipients in Najaf. It was argued that mujtahids misused the funds that they had received. They neglected their obligation to support the poor and the orphans, did not build enough madrasas, and did not provide sufficient material support for the students. In order to regain the donors' trust, it was suggested that each madrasa should maintain a budget which would list annual income and expenditure, and that a committee headed by an accountant would audit the funds received by each mujtahid who administered such an institution.[37]

The mismanagement of funds by mujtahids was not, however, the major factor for the economic decline of the madrasas. It has been seen in previous chapters how the policies of both the Iraqi and the Iranian governments resulted in the decrease of foreign pilgrimage and corpse traffic, and in the flow of charities to the shrine cities. This seriously hindered the prosperity of the madrasas and the extra income of the students, who increasingly had to rely for their income on state funds. From the 1920s students became the main recipients of Oudh Bequest money, which was

[36] Wardi, *Lamahat*, 5,2:78.

[37] Jaʻfar al-Khalili, "al-Islah al-dini: kayfa yajib an tunfaq al-amwal," *al-Hatif* 57 (11 December 1936): 3; ʻAli al-Zayn, "Bawadir al-islah fi jamiʻat al-najaf aw nahdat kashif al-ghitaʼ," *al-ʻIrfan* 29 (1939): 180, 183. See also idem, "Awdaʻ al-madaris al-diniyya fi al-najaf," *al-ʻIrfan* 58 (1970): 311–12.

first under British and later Indian government control. The Iraqi government supervised the main Shi'i *waqf* funds derived from burial fees and also sought to tie the *waqf* property of the madrasas to the *Awqaf* Directorate.[38] Although by 1958 the government probably still had not gained full control of Shi'i *waqf*, whatever free *waqf* property remained was not sufficient by itself to assure the prosperity of the madrasas and the welfare of students. As may be gathered from a memorandum written by King Faysal, the acute financial condition of the Shi'i madrasas also stemmed from the fact that the Sunni ulama in Iraq gained more income from the *awqaf* property controlled by the government than did their Shi'i counterparts.[39]

Both the British, through their control of the Oudh Bequest, and the Iraqi government emerged as direct benefactors of mujtahids and students. They exercised leverage over the two groups, thereby dismantling traditional mujtahid-student structures of patronage. In 1927 Muhammad Husayn Kashif al-Ghita, the most prominent Arab Shi'i mujtahid in Iraq, circulated a draft of a manifesto among several other mujtahids which listed Shi'i grievances and asked for their comments. The demands as drafted by Kashif al-Ghita included the establishment of a government theological college in Najaf and the allocation of a portion of the *awqaf* revenues for the benefit of the religious students in the shrine cities.[40] As has been seen in chapter 4, Kashif al-Ghita made similar demands during the 1935 revolt in which he played an important role. In a document sent to King Ghazi and the Prime Minister Yasin al-Hashimi, Kashif al-Ghita demanded the renewal of Shi'i religious freedom, recognition of the madrasa as an institution of higher learning, and the allocation of funds from *waqf* property for the benefit of the madrasas and other Shi'i Islamic institutions. The demands of Kashif al-Ghita in 1927 and 1935 reflected not only the serious financial difficulties of this important mujtahid but also his recognition that the Baghdad government was the power in control of the allocation of resources in Iraq. Just how dependent on government aid some madrasas had become by 1953 may be gathered from Kashif al-Ghita's conversation with the British ambassador to Iraq. Kashif al-Ghita complained that the contributions which Shi'is and tribal shaykhs made to the mujtahids decreased markedly under the monarchy, and that the Ministry of Education and the *Awqaf* Directorate sent only a small grant-in-aid once a year, which was barely enough to meet the expenses of one or two months.[41]

[38] Asifi, *Madrasat al-najaf*, 16–17.

[39] 'Abd al-Razzaq al-Hasani, *Ta'rikh al-wizarat al-'iraqiyya*, 2d and 3d eds., 10 vols. (Sidon, 1953–1965), 3:291.

[40] Iraq Police, Abstract of Intelligence no. 49, 3 December 1927, NAI, file 7/15/3.

[41] Muhammad al-Husayn Kashif al-Ghita, *Muhawarat al-imam al-muslih kashif al-ghita' al-shaykh muhammad al-husayn ma'a al-safirayn al-baritani wa al-amiriki fi baghdad*, 4th

Although the number of madrasas in Najaf probably remained almost the same until the mid-1950s, as may be gathered from Mahbuba's account of the history of Najaf which lists twenty-one madrasas, there was a drastic decline in the number of students. In December 1957 there were only 1,954 students in Najaf, a figure which represents a sharp drop from the city's estimated 8,000 students at the turn of the century.[42] Under the monarchy, restrictions and delays in granting visas to Iranian theological students who wished to study in Najaf were not uncommon.[43] Many mujtahids no longer had sufficient funds to properly feed students and to provide for their clothes and pocket money. The welfare of the Iraqi students, a minority of about 17 percent among the entire student body population of Najaf in 1957, was particularly bad. Some of them had to earn their living outside Najaf and to seek employment from merchants and landowners during the crop seasons. There were complaints about protectionism and discrimination with regard to the allocation of allowances by mujtahids within the madrasas. The system whereby money was distributed to students according to criteria of ethnic identity or geographic region, in keeping with the origin of the funds, hindered Iraqis the most since their own countrymen did not channel sufficient resources for their upkeep.[44]

The problems of the Iraqi students were reinforced by their low ratio among the various groups of students, and the existence of madrasas for specific ethnic, regional, and national groups. In Karbala, where the students were predominantly Persians, Arabs formed only a very small fraction of the student population. Adib al-Mulk, who visited Karbala in 1857, recounted that of the four madrasas in that city, one was attended by Indian students and the other by Turks.[45] In Najaf, the *Madrasat al-Irawani* (built 1889) was geared for Turkish students, the *Madrasat al-Badkuba'i* (built 1907) for Bukharis and students from Baku, and the *Madrasat al-'Amiliyyin* (built 1957/8) mainly for Lebanese from Jabal 'Amil.[46] In the absence of a madrasa geared specifically for Iraqis, the latter were in a disadvantaged position when compared with the foreign students.

---

ed. (Najaf, 1954), 15–16; cf. Troutbeck to Eden, Baghdad, 16 October 1953, FO 371/104666/1016–57.

[42] Mahbuba, *Madi al-najaf*, 1:125–46; Fadil Jamali, "The Theological Colleges of Najaf," *MW* 50 (1960): 15.

[43] Edmonds to Cornwallis, Baghdad, 20 January 1945, FO 624/72/323.

[44] Jamali, "The Theological Colleges," 22; Khalili, "al-Islah al-dini: kayfa yajib an tunfaq al-amwal," 3; Muhammad Hasan al-Suri, "Hayat al-talib fi al-najaf," *al-'Irfan* 25 (1936): 235; 'Abd al-Sahib al-Dujayli, "Tullab al-dirasa al-diniyya (II)," *al-Hatif* 62 (5 February 1937): 6.

[45] Adib al-Mulk, *Safarnama-yi adib al-mulk bi-'atabat (dalil al-za'irin)*, 1273 h.q. (Tehran, 1985), 158.

[46] Khalili, *Mawsu'a*, 2,2:141, 150, 157.

The development of the government school system posed another challenge to those Iraqi students who attended the traditional madrasas. Comparing themselves to their colleagues in the government schools, many felt disadvantaged and sensed that they were sacrificing the most precious years of their lives in vain. Since they did not become familiar with the new developments in science, the gaps were growing between them and other segments of Iraqi society. Staying in the madrasa undermined their chances of gaining any major government grant, and graduation only rarely promised a respectable independent income that would enable the new mujtahid to maintain his freedom of speech and action.[47] These challenges not only posed new dilemmas to the students, but also sharpened the pedagogical and psychological problems which they experienced in the madrasa. The most commonly cited were: the lack of close supervision of student progress, the narrow focus of the curricula and preoccupation with grammatical problems in the first stage of study, the gap between mujtahids and students, the lack of skilled teachers, and the loneliness of academic life. There were also irregularities and long intervals in the studies due to the many religious holidays and other interruptions.[48] The quality of education and moral values in the madrasa deteriorated, and Shi'is felt that this institution, and indeed Najaf, which used to be the center of learning, had lost their viability and centrality, and were not capable of preparing the new generations of Shi'is for modern life.[49]

During the 1920s and 1930s many Iraqi students left the madrasas in search of opportunities for social mobility. Some became teachers in the government school system, while others sought various government positions. Students in the Shi'i madrasas in Iraq thus reacted in the same fashion as their Egyptian counterparts, who, from the period of Muhammad 'Ali, began deserting al-Azhar, which was losing its position as the major source of recruitment for teaching and governmental posts.[50] So massive was the number of students who left the madrasas of Najaf in those years that one city dweller lamented that the Hindi mosque, which in the

---

[47] Salman al-Safwani, "Mushkila ana waqt 'ilajiha," al-'Itidal 4 (1936): 22–24; Zayn, "Awda' al-madaris," 317.

[48] S. N., "Nazra fi al-madaris al-diniyya," al-'Irfan 1 (1909): 588, 590; Suri, "Hayat al-talib," 236–37; 'Abd al-Sahib al-Dujayli, "Tullab al-dirasa al-diniyya (I)," al-Hatif 61 (29 January 1937): 6–7; 'Abd al-Zahra al-Saghir, "Li-madha dakhaltu madrasat muntada al-nashr," al-Hatif 162 (7 April 1939): 14; Muhammad 'Ali Nasir, "al-Dirasa al-diniyya fi al-najaf al-ashraf," al-'Irfan 38 (1951): 982–85; Zayn, "Awda' al-madaris," 308.

[49] Husayn Muruwwa, "Sarkha jari'a hawla al-islah al-dini," al-Hatif 58 (8 January 1937): 6; Muhammad 'Ali al-Balaghi, "al-Dirasa fi al-najaf," al-'Itidal 5 (1946): 323–24.

[50] Sa'id Isma'il 'Ali, al-Azhar 'ala masrah al-siyasa al-misriyya: dirasa fi tatawwur al-'alaqa bayn al-tarbiya wa al-siyasa (Cairo, 1974), 163–64; P. J. Vatikiotis, The History of Egypt, 3d ed. (London, 1985), 300.

past had been a center of teaching and literary activity in the form of *majalis* and *halaqat*, stood almost empty. It was feared that the madrasas would eventually have to close their doors for lack of students.[51]

A clear sign of decline of the madrasas of Najaf, as seen by Arab Shiʿis, was the lack of a charismatic mujtahid who could lead the Shiʿi community in Iraq. For a long period after the death of Mirza Muhammad Taqi Shirazi and Shaykh al-Shariʿa Isfahani, in August and December 1920, respectively, there was no one recognized preeminent mujtahid in the Shiʿi world. In addition to this, Shiʿis pointed out that in the past mujtahids had derived their power from the laity. The grand mujtahid assumed the role of the leader of the Shiʿi community, and shaped its development. The decline in the quality of the mujtahids turned relations between the mujtahids and the laity upside down, and the latter became the driving force behind the mujtahids. Consequently, the madrasa as an institution, and the mujtahids as leaders of the community, lost their status and influence among the Iraqi Shiʿi masses, proving also unable to protect their own position vis-à-vis the state.[52]

Another major reason for the decline of the madrasa, as seen by Iraqi Shiʿis, stemmed from the long process starting in the mid-eighteenth century in which Najaf lost its strong Arab identity. It was pointed out that until that time Najafi society and culture were Arab. The influx of Persian ulama and students to the city was a mixed blessing. Najaf's fame as the center of learning grew as the network of ulama who graduated from Najaf spread in countries like Iran and India. Its economy prospered and the city became a leading center of political activity, as demonstrated during the Iranian Constitutional Revolution. Yet, whereas until the mid-eighteenth century Arabic was the only language used in the madrasa, in subsequent years this was no longer the case since the Arabs were only a minority within the student population.[53]

The setback to the position of Arabic had a tremendous impact on Najafi society and culture. There were differences in the grammar books used by Arab and non-Arab students, the latter using less comprehensive works. Many Persians, Azarbayjanis, Afghans, Indians, and other non-Arab students did not manage to command or speak Arabic well enough, and relied on their teacher's translations of the Arabic material during the first two stages of study. Consequently, students who reached their final stage of

[51] Zayd, "Badirat al-islah al-dini fa-madha waraʾuha?," *al-Hatif* 61 (29 January 1937): 4; Safwani, "Mushkila," 22; Muhsin al-Amin, *Rihlat*, 106.

[52] Anon., *al-Haraka al-islamiyya fi al-ʿiraq* (Beirut, 1985), 46; ʿAbd al-Mahdi Matar, "Ma huwa al-islah wa-man huwa al-muslih," *al-Hatif* 426 (16 August 1946): 1; ʿAbd al-Karim Thabit, "Khatira fi al-islah," *al-Hatif* 456 (16 May 1947): 3.

[53] ʿAli al-Sharqi, "al-Hala al-ʿilmiyya wa al-haraka al-fikriyya fi al-najaf," *Lughat al-ʿArab* 4 (1926): 327; Jaʿfar al-Mahbuba, "Sayr al-ʿilm fi al-najaf," *al-ʿirfan* 21 (1931): 500; idem, *Madi al-najaf*, 1:380–81.

study still needed clarifications of Arabic terms in languages other than Arabic.[54] Iraqi Shi'is asserted that unlike intellectual activity at al-Azhar, which was molded by the local culture and trends in modern Egypt, activity at Najaf became less influenced by the city's indigenous Arab environment and instead was dominated by a Persian spirit. The strong Persian presence in the madrasa distanced Najaf from Baghdad, thereby hindering the potential social and intellectual exchange between Sunnis and Shi'is in Iraq. Foreign linguistic elements penetrated into the Arabic dialect of Najaf, and the method of study became patterned after the Persian. As the majority of students and ulama came to be of non-Arab origin, people in the madrasa were no longer intensively engaged in the study of Arabic language, literature, history, philosophy, and hadith, confining themselves to religious studies alone. Najaf consequently produced relatively few works in Arabic.[55]

Iraqi and Lebanese Shi'is felt that as a result of the madrasa's loss of much of its former Arab spirit, Najaf lost its status as a major center of intellectual and literary activity in the Arab world. The madrasa did not influence the style of modern Arabic language in the twentieth century, nor did it make lexical contributions as did the Carmelite journal *Lughat al-'Arab*, which was issued in Baghdad from 1911. In the twentieth century the madrasa did not produce great literary figures who could direct the intellectual and mental development of their society, as individuals like 'Abd al-Husayn al-Hilli, Muhammad Rida al-Shabibi, Muhammad Mahdi al-Jawahiri, 'Ali al-Sharqi, and others had done in the past. Indeed, Arab Shi'is pointed to what they considered to be the gap in quality between the previous generations and those of the twentieth century. They felt that the madrasas of Najaf could no longer influence modern trends in Arabic literature and prose, let alone lead a renewal in these fields, something which was yielded to new literary figures who graduated from the government school system.[56]

The decline of Najaf was contrasted by the rise of Qum in the twentieth century as the leading Shi'i religious center, at least as far as Iranians were

[54] 'Iraqi, "Kutub al-qira'a wa-tariqat al-tadris 'ind al-shi'a fi al-'iraq," *Lughat al-'Arab* 2 (1913): 442; Khalili, *Mawsu'a*, 2,2:100; Dujayli, "Tullab al-dirasa al-diniyya (I)," 6; Hasan al-Amin, *al-Sayyid muhsin al-amin: siratuhu bi-qalamihi wa-aqlam akharin* (Sidon, 1957), 51.

[55] Sharqi, "al-Hala al-'ilmiyya," 326–27, 231–32.

[56] Ja'far al-Khalili, "Rukud al-adab fi al-najaf," *al-Hatif* 384 (13 July 1945): 1–2, and 385 (27 July 1945): 1; Nasir, "al-Dirasa al-diniyya," 983; Zayn, "Awda' al-madaris," 315; Muhammad Husayn Fadlallah, "Hadith 'an mushkilat al-adab al-najafi: min muhadarat al-majma' al-thaqafi li-muntada al-nashr fi al-najaf al-ashraf," *al-'Irfan* 43 (1956): 824–26; Muhammad Jawad Mughniyya, *Min dha wa-dhak* (Beirut, 1979), 128–29. See also Jaroslav Stetkevych, *The Modern Arabic Literary Language: Lexical and Stylistic Developments* (Chicago, 1970), 13n.

concerned. The deportation of Mahdi al-Khalisi and the exodus of the prominent mujtahids from Iraq to Iran in 1923, as discussed in chapter 3, dealt a major blow to the political power and esteem of the religious establishment in Iraq. In addition, a monthly allowance of up to Rs.10,000, which was formerly paid out by Na'ini and Isfahani to defray the expenses of the religious students in Najaf, ceased following the mujtahids' departure to Iran.[57] At that time Qum was just beginning to become an important clerical center under the leadership of Shaykh 'Abd al-Karim Ha'iri, who had moved to that city from Arak in Iran in 1920. Ha'iri needed students in order to assert his own position in the religious hierarchy and establish Qum as a center of study.[58] Around December 1923, while the mujtahids of Iraq were still in Qum, letters were sent from that city to the shrine cities in Iraq inviting students to proceed to Qum and to continue their studies there under the same benefits they had enjoyed in Najaf, Karbala, and Kazimayn. While there is no evidence that Ha'iri himself supported this act, there were some other ulama in Iran who sought to enhance the position of Qum vis-à-vis Najaf and might have initiated these letters. On his part, too, Mahdi al-Khalisi was reported to have written to his brother that Qum "is now to be considered the religious educational center of the Shi'i world."[59] The rise of Qum was also made possible by the diversion of Iranian funds to that city, as well as to Mashhad, at the expense of Najaf and Karbala, a policy instigated by Reza Shah from the late 1920s.

Qum's position was bolstered further in 1946 with the shift of the Shi'i religious leadership from Najaf to Qum following the death of Abu al-Hasan Isfahani and the emergence of Husayn Burujirdi as the sole *marja' al-taqlid*. Until his death in 1961 Burujirdi, through his agent Shaykh Nasrallah Khalkhali, emerged as a major patron and financier of the Shi'i madrasas in Iraq, building two new madrasas in Najaf. Besides his distribution of funds among the ulama, Burujirdi had also spent some ID6,000 (equal to about $16,800 at the exchange rate of the late 1950s) per month in Najaf, Karbala, and Samarra for bread and monthly allowances for some five hundred students.[60] Thus, for fourteen years between 1947 and 1961 the moving figure behind Shi'i academic activity in the madrasas of Iraq was the grand mujtahid based in Iran. This eroded the status of

[57] Report to Special Officer 1, 24 January 1924, Air 23/453.
[58] Abdul-Hadi Hairi, *Shi'ism and Constitutionalism in Iran* (Leiden, 1977), 135; Shahrough Akhavi, *Religion and Politics in Contemporary Iran: Clergy-State Relations in the Pahlavi Period* (Albany, N.Y., 1980), 27–28.
[59] Intelligence Report no. 24, 15 December 1923, FO 371/10097/291.
[60] Khalili, *Mawsu'a*, 2,2:151, 155–57, 159; Jamali, "The Theological Colleges," 17; "Alf tunn hinta ila al-najaf wa-karbala'," *al-Hatif* 479 (2 January 1948): 8; Shahrudi, *Ta'rikh*, 201–3.

prominent mujtahids in Iraq while causing a setback to the fame of their madrasas. It is said that from the second half of the twentieth century many graduates of the madrasas of Qum rose to prominence within the Shi'i religious hierarchy without studying in Najaf for any period of time as had previously been the case.[61] The number of students in Qum, which may have been about 1,000 around 1937 when Ha'iri died, increased to over 5,000 during Burujirdi's time.[62] This increase is all the more significant when compared to the sharp drop of Najaf's student population from 8,000 early in the twentieth century to 1,954 in 1957. The number of students in Najaf decreased further under the Ba'th and particularly after the Iranian Islamic Revolution of 1978–79. The city's madrasas not only experienced severe pressures by the Iraqi government, but a growing competition with those of Qum. Just how intense the competition between Najaf and Qum came to be in the 1980s may be gathered from reports alleging that a son of the former grand Najafi mujtahid Muhsin al-Hakim rejected a call by Ruhallah Khumayni to move the Shi'i seminary of Najaf to Qum.[63] It is said that by 1985 the total number of students, mujtahids, and religious functionaries in Najaf dropped to less than 150. The deportations and flow of ulama and students from Najaf to Qum, coinciding with the strong competition between the two cities, led to augmenting the latter's academic status at the expense of Najaf.[64]

Unlike the madrasas of Najaf, which had no impact on Iraqi education in the Sunni government school system, those of Qum and Mashhad did influence Iranian educational life. Indeed, even the mnemonic, text-centered style of Iranian secular education had its roots in the Iranian madrasa system.[65] There was also a major difference in the impact of the madrasa on religious life in the two countries. Unlike mujtahids in Iran whose power and esteem stemmed from the laity, most of their counterparts in the Shi'i religious centers in Iraq lost their status and influence among the Iraqi Shi'i mass. Qumi preachers and sermon leaders proved more effective in mobilizing Shi'is for political action in their country than their Najafi counterparts. The number of preachers and ulama per capita in Iraq was by far smaller than in Iran.[66] In part, this was a result of the

[61] Ahmad al-Katib, *Tajrubat al-thawra al-islamiyya fi al-'iraq* (Tehran, 1981), 172; Salih al-Shahrastani, "Jami'at qumm wa al-sayyid al-burujirdi," *al-'Irfan* 56 (1968): 755–56.

[62] Mottahedeh, *The Mantle of the Prophet*, 236.

[63] Christine Helms, *Iraq: Eastern Flank of the Arab World* (Washington, D.C., 1984), 161.

[64] Fadil al-Barrak, *al-Madaris al-yahudiyya wa al-iraniyya fi al-'iraq: dirasa muqarina* (Baghdad, 1984), esp. 106–7; Anon., *al-Haraka al-islamiyya*, 133; Akhavi, *Religion*, 131–32; Michael Fischer, *Iran: From Religious Dispute to Revolution* (Cambridge, Mass., 1980), 78.

[65] Mottahedeh, *The Mantle of the Prophet*, 237.

[66] Hanna Batatu, "Shi'i Organizations in Iraq: al-Da'wah al-Islamiyyah and al-

small number of Iraqi Shi'i students (and their relative old age) who attended the madrasas. It also reflected the declining number of Iraqi preachers that the madrasas of Najaf produced under the monarchy, who could not meet the growing Shi'i population in the cities and rural areas of Iraq.

Moreover, there was a fundamental difference in attitude toward the practice of preaching in Najaf and Karbala as opposed to Qum and Mashhad in Iran. In the two Iraqi cities, the prominent mujtahids and teachers in the madrasas distanced themselves from preaching, an activity which they considered detrimental to a mujtahid's academic standing. Against the aloofness of their Iraqi counterparts, the Iranian mujtahids were very conscious about the need to train preachers, considering this profession an art in itself. Indeed, prominent mujtahids in Qum and Mashhad, as well as students at all stages of their study, were said to be very actively engaged in preaching, thereby reaching out to the Iranian masses and increasing their contacts with the laity. Shi'i Islam in Iraq, on the contrary, lost much of its potential influence over Iraqi Shi'is as well as its power vis-à-vis the state because of the attitude of the mujtahids in Iraq toward preaching and the inability of the madrasas of Najaf to produce a new generation of Iraqi preachers.[67]

Qum seems to have gradually gained an advantage over Najaf in the field of publications as well. The importance of the Shi'i center of learning depended on its ability to maintain a large volume of religious publications, which served to propagate Shi'i Islam on the international level. In the 1950s Najaf experienced a drop in the volume of publications, which may have been the cumulative result of diminishing financial resources, intellectual stagnation, government restrictions, and the spread of Communism, which competed with religion for the allegiance of the Shi'i masses in Iraq in those years. Najaf did not adopt modern dissemination techniques, the quality of its publications deteriorated, and it did not give enough attention to the importance of sending delegations abroad. Najaf, in short, turned inward and became introverted.[68] Qum, on the other hand, enjoyed an increased reputation during and after Burujirdi's period. Institutions and presses for the propagation of Shi'ism were established in the city, and journals and letter-answering in different languages were

---

Mujahidin," in *Shi'ism and Social Protest*, ed. Juan Cole and Nikki Keddie (New Haven, 1986), 193.

[67] Katib, *Tajrubat al-thawra*, 173; Anon., *al-Haraka al-islamiyya*, 196–97; al-Lajna al-thaqafiyya li-madrasat al-imam amir al-mu'minin al-'ilmiyya, *al-Qadiyya al-'iraqiyya min khilal mawqif al-imam al-shirazi* (Mashhad, 1981), 35; Muhammad Mahdi al-Asifi, *Min hadith al-da'wa wa al-du'at*, 2d ed. (Najaf, 1966), 5–8, 17.

[68] Asifi, *Madrasat al-najaf*, 54, 110; Mughniyya, *Min dha wa-dhak*, 128–29.

produced. Qum consequently encroached on Najaf's reputation at the international level.[69]

The rise of Qum in the twentieth century should also be examined in the context of the era of the modern nation-state, which led to a growing polarization of the Shi'i world. Ethnic and local identities, of course, were important components in student life even before the twentieth century. Madrasas were built according to these criteria at least from the time of Shah 'Abbas I (d. 1629). Thus, the founder of the Fazil Khan madrasa in Mashhad is said to have left a provision that Indians should be refused admission as students because they are "void of truth," that Mazandaranis should be excluded because they are "quarrelsome," and that Arabs should not be admitted because they are "dirty."[70] Madrasas in Najaf were also built for specific ethnic groups, and, in the case of the *Madrasat al-Irawani*, which accommodated mainly Turkish students, clearly because of ethnic tensions. Indeed, it became quite common to speak in Najaf of the Madrasa of the Qazwinis, that of the Turks, or that of the Indians.[71]

With the creation of the Arab states and modern Iran in the twentieth century, the barriers between Shi'i Arabs and Iranians grew higher than in the past. The rise of Iraq, and the establishment of clearer border lines between that country and Iran, put an end to the former frontier status of Najaf and Karbala. Consequently, Iranian students and mujtahids could no longer migrate to the shrine cities as freely as their predecessors had. Qum attracted mainly Iranians and Azarbayjanis, who formerly used to compose the bulk of Najaf's student population. Arab Shi'is, however, continued to go to Najaf despite its declining fame and the relatively better economic conditions offered to students in Qum. Arabic and Persian began to play a greater role in fostering the differences between Arab Shi'is and Iranians. During and after Burujirdi's time, the major Shi'i legal works and biographies in Arabic were translated into Persian, thereby reducing the need for Iranian students to consult the original Arabic. The mujtahid Muhsin al-Amin (d. 1952) remarked sadly that, whereas in the past some of the greatest mujtahids were Persians who had a command of Arabic and wrote extensively in that language, this was no longer the case in the twentieth century, when prominent Iranian mujtahids had difficulties in communicating in Arabic.[72] Indeed, one of the very few Arab students who did study in Qum during Burujirdi's period complained that Arabic was

[69] On publications and translations in Qum during and after Burujirdi's period see Shahrastani, "Jami'at qumm," 745–47; Fischer, *Iran*, 84, 91–92.

[70] James Fraser, *Narrative of a Journey into Khorasan in the Years 1821 and 1822* (London, 1840), 457.

[71] Khalili, *Mawsu'a*, 2,2:141; Sharqi, "al-Hala al-'ilmiyya," 329.

[72] Muhsin al-Amin, *Ma'adin al-jawahir wa-nuzhat al-khawatir*, 2 vols. (Beirut, 1981), 1:42.

used only for reading texts in classes, and that it was a "dead" language among the Iranian students. Those very few Arabs who lived in Qum had to comply with sociocultural customs foreign to them, and were not well integrated into the local society.[73]

A New Iraqi Shiʻi Madrasa

The future of the madrasas of Najaf was the subject of much debate among Iraqi and other Arab Shiʻis after the establishment of the monarchy. The importance of the debate as manifested mainly in *al-Hatif* from the mid-1930s goes far beyond the insight which it provides into the problems facing the madrasa. It reveals several trends within the Shiʻi religious establishment in Iraq. It introduces us to a core of Iraqi and Arab Shiʻi intellectuals, notably, Jaʻfar al-Khalili, Husayn Muruwwa, Muhammad Sharara, Muhammad Hasan Suri, and Safa Khulusi, who had a clear sense of purpose. It also sheds light on the wider social issues with which educated Shiʻis were concerned, and it uncovers the direction of political development pursued by Iraqi Shiʻis under the monarchy. Moreover, the movement for reforming the madrasas of Najaf reflected the greater and more effective pressures of the state on Shiʻi Islam and society in Iraq in the first half of the twentieth century when compared with Iran. The reform movement was an indication of both the powerful challenge which modern education and Sunni state policies posed to the traditional madrasa in Iraq, as well as the feelings of ulama and mujtahids that they were rapidly losing contact with the young generations of Iraqi Shiʻis. By contrast, the big movement for reform of the religious hierarchy and the madrasa in Iran surfaced only in 1961. This relatively late date may be seen as an indication that the pressures of the state on the religious establishment in Iran, and the mujtahids' recognition of their degree of isolation, were not strong or alarming enough to generate a large-scale Iranian reform movement before the second half of the twentieth century.[74]

Shiʻis often pointed to the existence of a bitter struggle between two opposing groups within Najafi society. On the one hand there were the radical modernists, who sought to completely detach present-day life from the past, and on the other the extreme conservatives, who insisted on preserving life as it had been during the time of their predecessors. The problem of Shiʻi intellectuals and members of the religious establishment who sought to move cautiously and adapt Shiʻi society, Islam, and the

[73] ʻIsa ʻAbd al-Hamid al-Khaqani, "al-Majmaʻ al-ʻarabi fi qumm," *al-ʻIrfan* 50 (1963): 660, 663, 674.

[74] On the reform movement in Iran in which Murtada Mutahhari was a moving figure see Ann Lambton, "A Reconsideration of the Position of the *Marjaʻ al-Taqlid* and the Religious Institution," *SI* 20 (1964), esp. 118–19, 131–34; Fischer, *Iran*, 85; Akhavi, *Religion*, 119.

madrasa to the new reality in Iraq was how to find a third way between these two opposing trends.[75] Within the religious circles there were some individuals who acknowledged as early as 1925 the need to reform the madrasa, citing the growing polarization between the religious circles and young secular Shi'is. The dominant figures in the group were said to be Muhammad Jawad al-Hichami, Muhammad Husayn al-Muzaffar, and Sayyid 'Ali Bahr al-'Ulum. Very few in number, the members of this group could not freely express their opinion in public. By 1935 there were said to be already some two hundred individuals who advocated reform in religious education. Yet this was still not enough to bring about a change in the traditional madrasa system, both because these individuals lacked a clear blueprint, and because many members within the madrasa were too conservative, refusing any major change in curricula and teaching methods.[76] There were only a few mujtahids, most notably Muhammad Husayn Kashif al-Ghita, who did introduce some changes in their own individual institutions, but this could not revive the vitality and appeal which the old madrasa had lost.[77]

By the mid-1930s, many Arab Shi'is in Iraq had concluded that it would be unrealistic to attempt to change the old madrasa. Realizing also that this institution was unable to provide solutions to their own specific sociopolitical and religious problems, they began pursuing a more modest course. Their focus shifted from the old madrasa to the establishment of a new type of religious school geared for the needs of Iraqi Shi'i society. The school was to be an alternative both to the old madrasa and to the secular government school system. It was to have a different financial organization from the old madrasa. The curriculum would combine the study of religion and modern sciences. The teachers would be paid a monthly salary, the students would enjoy fair treatment from the teaching staff as well as proper allowances, and there would also be periodic examinations to measure student progress. Attention would not be given to quantity but to the quality of the graduating students. Shi'is hoped that the school would produce a new generation of mujtahids and preachers whose skills would reflect the specific needs of Iraqi Shi'i society. The new mujtahids would be of wide religious education, in full command of Arabic, and capable of

---

[75] See, for example, Muhammad Sharara, "al-Qadim wa al-hadith," al-Hatif 32 (22 May 1936): 1–2, and 33 (29 May 1936): 1–2; Asifi, Madrasat al-najaf, 125.

[76] Asifi, Madrasat al-najaf, 112–16.

[77] On the changes which Kashif al-Ghita introduced into his madrasa in the late 1930s see Khalili, Hakadha 'araftuhum, 1:245; Muhammad Sharara, "Daw' jadid yaruffu shu'a'uhu fi jaww al-madrasa al-diniyya," al-Hatif 140 (30 September 1938): 3–5; 'Abd al-Hamid al-Saghir, "Nizam al-tadris al-dini al-hadith," al-Hatif 156 (24 February 1939): 11–12; idem, "Mu'assasat kashif al-ghita' wa-atharuha fi al-nahda al-'ilmiyya," al-Hatif 173 (30 June 1939): 22.

providing solutions to the complex issues of the day. Indeed, their qualifications were to reflect a new attitude toward the field of *ijtihad*.[78]

Those Shi'i intellectuals who pushed for the establishment of such a school in Najaf envisaged an Islamic institution, the character of which would be Arab. They pointed to the reforms introduced at al-Azhar by Egyptians like Muhammad 'Abduh and Sa'd Zaghlul, asserting that the Egyptian madrasa did not lose its Islamic identity as a result of these reforms. On the contrary, it was able to produce better graduates, to send delegations abroad, to counteract missionary activity, and to propagate Islam as far away as China.[79] In choosing al-Azhar as their model for successful reform, Iraqi Shi'is demonstrated both their strong orientation toward the Arab world and their realization that, like al-Azhar, the new Shi'i religious school in Iraq would inevitably be linked to the state. The advocacy of a school geared for the specific needs of Arab Shi'is in Iraq may be seen also as an act of protest of Iraqi Shi'is against Persian dominance of the study circles in Najaf.

The intellectuals who advocated the establishment of a new school felt, however, that this institution could succeed only if it was sanctioned by the leading mujtahids. They themselves could only help by attempting to create a more favorable climate for reforms in Najaf through articles and public lectures. It was suggested that a body of high-ranking mujtahids would administer the new madrasa and the schools affiliated with it. This body was to be assisted by various committees which would supervise the progress of reform, administer the sources of income, and stimulate Shi'i publications and propaganda. Those who pushed for this new institution urged the most prominent mujtahids, Abu al-Hasan Isfahani and Muhammad Husayn Kashif al-Ghita, to lead the reform movement, stressing that it was a socioreligious and national obligation of the mujtahids. They presented the proposed reform as aimed at reviving the fame of the madrasa, improving the quality of the religious establishment, and reestablishing

---

[78] Asifi, *Madrasat al-najaf*, 116–19; "al-Kalima al-qayyima allati alqaha ma'ali al-'allama hibat al-din fi muntada al-nashr," *al-Hatif* 58 (8 January 1937): 4–5; Ja'far al-Khalili, "al-Islah al-dini wa-wajib al-hay'a al-'ilmiyya," *al-Hatif* 58 (8 January 1937): 3; Muhammad Jamal al-Hashimi, "al-Islah al-dini wa-mawqif al-'ulama wa-muntada al-nashr minhu," *al-Hatif* 60 (22 January 1937): 8; Husayn Muruwwa, "al-Ijtihad haql khasib muntij yaqdi 'alayhi al-wad' al-dini al-hadir," *al-Hatif* 59 (15 January 1937): 5; idem, "Wal-takun min-kum umma yad'una ila al-khayr," *al-Hatif* 60 (22 January 1937): 5; idem, "Zahira ruhiyya: ma huwa al-islah alladhi nad'u ilayhi," *al-Hatif* 65 (5 March 1937): 3; idem, "al-Khasb alladhi huwa ghayat al-qaht," *al-Hatif* 76 (4 June 1937): 4; 'Abd al-Zahra al-Saghir, "Li-madha dakhaltu madrasat muntada al-nashr," *al-Hatif* 162 (7 April 1939): 14.

[79] Husayn Muruwwa, "Li-yasma' shuyukhuna kayfa yantaqiduna al-azhar," *al-Hatif* 72 (30 April 1937): 4–5; Muhammad Jawad Khidr, "Faqid al-islah al-'allama al-shaykh 'abd al-rida'," *al-Hatif* 92 (1 October 1937): 6–7.

Islam as a competitive force among other religions. They warned that the gap between the mujtahids and the laity was growing, and urged the mujtahids to preach and publish articles themselves in order to publicly demonstrate their approval of the reform movement. The choice which they posed to the mujtahids was phrased in terms similar to those used by 'Abduh in Egypt when he attempted to press the ulama of al-Azhar to adopt reforms in the Egyptian madrasa in the late nineteenth century: either you conduct a true and comprehensive reform, or this institution will die.[80]

The foundation for the new Shi'i madrasa, which became known as *Muntada al-Nashr*, was laid in 1935. With the approval of the Iraqi Ministry of Interior, a religious society bearing the same name was established in Najaf in May of the same year. The society became the governing body of the *Muntada*. Its members were drawn from Najaf's Arab religious circles. The mujtahid Muhammad Rida al-Muzaffar, who was among the dominant figures in the society, was the founder of the school.[81] After a hesitant start, the *Muntada* began operating regularly from 1939. By 1958 it had a faculty of jurisprudence and an affiliated elementary school. The *Muntada*'s affiliated high school was opened in 1961. All three were recognized by the Iraqi Ministry of Education. In the mid-1960s its elementary school had some 300 students, and the high school and the faculty were attended by 250 and 200 students, respectively. The curriculum of the faculty of jurisprudence was simpler and clearer than that offered by the traditional madrasa. In order to achieve this, Muzaffar edited two new textbooks on logic and the principles of jurisprudence, which were based on his own lectures in the *Muntada*. Classes in the faculty included Imami Shi'i and comparative jurisprudence, the principles of jurisprudence, Koranic commentary, tradition, Arabic grammar and syntax, Arabic literature, Islamic and modern history, philosophy, logic, pedagogy and methods of teaching, psychology, sociology, and English. The duration of study was four years,

[80] Muhammad Sharara, "Al-Mawqif yahtaj ila qiyada: hazima mukhlisa fa-ayna hiya?," *al-Hatif* 62 (5 February 1937): 4–5; 'Amer, "Madha sa-takun al-'aqiba," *al-Hatif* 63 (12 February 1937): 8; Anon., "Jabal Yahwi: marfu'a ila maqam al-za'im al-dini al-akbar al-hujja al-sayyid abi al-hasan," *al-Hatif* 63 (12 February 1937): 4–5; Husayn Muruwwa, "Kalima sariha ila maqam al-za'im al-muslih al-kabir al-imam kashif al-ghita'," *al-Hatif* 64 (19 February 1937): 4–5; idem, "Hal yahmil muntada al-nashr risalat al-islah al-manshud?," *al-Hatif* 111 (25 February 1938): 3; Ja'far al-Khalili, "Kayfa tatawahhad al-kalima wa-kayfa tattafiq al-ara'," *al-Hatif* 64 (19 February 1937): 3; Mirza Naji, "Hawla al-da'wa ila al-islah al-dini," *al-Hatif* 67 (19 March 1937): 6, 8. On 'Abduh's attempts to reform the curriculum and administration of al-Azhar see 'Ali, *al-Azhar*, 219–34; Vatikiotis, *Egypt*, 194.

[81] For the full list see "Muntada al-nashr fi al-najaf," *al-Hatif* 6 (7 June 1935): 4; Khalili, *Hakadha 'araftuhum*, 2:22. On the reorganization of the governing body in 1944 see "Intikhab majlis idarat muntada al-nashr," *al-Hatif* 386 (31 March, 1944): 6.

and graduates received a B.A. in Arabic language and Islamic studies, which was equivalent to the degrees offered by other institutions of higher learning in Iraq.[82]

The expectations of Iraqi Shi'is from the *Muntada* were high. Intellectuals regarded its establishment as the first step in the revival of learning and Arabic literature in Najaf, the creation of a new and broadly educated generation of Shi'i religious experts, and the social reform of Iraqi Shi'i society.[83] Those within the religious circles that became closely associated with the *Muntada* also expected that the school would train effective and more educated preachers. The role of the *Muntada* was thus twofold. On one level, it aimed to narrow the gap between secular state-controlled education and the old madrasa, and to link the development of Shi'i society to the modern mainstream of life in Iraq. On another, the school was intended to bring the religious and secular components of Iraqi Shi'i society closer.

The first goal seemed to have been achieved more successfully, although at the cost of placing much of Iraqi Shi'i religious education under the control of the state. The *Muntada*'s establishment was authorized by the Ministry of Interior and its curricula approved by the Ministry of Education. In authorizing the *Muntada*, the government perhaps sought to establish it in part as a substitute to *Jami'at Al al-Bayt* in Baghdad, which had been closed by Nuri Sa'id in 1930. The very small *waqf* property of the *Muntada*, and its difficulties in raising sufficient funds from Iraqi Shi'i individuals, obliged it to rely also on grants from the Ministry of Education.[84] The teaching staff was composed of Ph.D. holders from Iraqi institutions of higher learning, who taught psychology, sociology, literature, and English, as well as recognized mujtahids, who taught the Islamic sciences. The appointment of all teachers was subject to approval by the Ministry of Education.[85] Some graduates of the *Muntada* became teachers of Arabic language and literature or Islamic religion in the government's high school system. Others like Sayyid Muhammad Bahr al-'Ulum continued their studies in Islamic sciences and obtained their M.A. degrees from Baghdad University. And still others pursued their M.A. studies at Cairo

[82] Khalili, *Mawsu'a*, 2,2:182–85; "Hawla muntada al-nashr: ajwibat al-shaykh ahmad al-wa'ili," *al-'Irfan* 49 (1962): 468; Fadli, *Dalil al-najaf*, 76–77; Wada'a, *Lamahat*, 82; Asifi, *Madrasat al-najaf*, 117, 120–21, 126–30; Muhammad Rida al-Muzaffar, *The Faith of Shi'a Islam* (London, 1983), 83–86.

[83] Muhammad Jawad Khidr, "Muntada al-nashr wa al-islah al-dini," *al-Hatif* 59 (15 January 1937): 6; idem, "Ittijahat haditha fi nuzum al-dirasa al-diniyya," *al-Hatif* 148 (30 December 1938): 7.

[84] "Hawla muntada al-nashr," 469; Khidr, "Muntada al-nashr," 6; idem, "Ittijahat haditha," 7.

[85] "Hawla muntada al-nashr," 468.

University.[86] The Muntada's ideas concerning modernity were "laudable from every point of view," according to the British vice-consul who visited the school in 1942. He thought that the school deserved the highest encouragement, and suggested that a wealthy Indian Shi'i pilgrim might be given to understand that a generous gift by him to the Muntada would be welcomed by the British government.[87]

In authorizing the establishment of the Muntada and controlling its affairs, the Iraqi government gained a new generation of Shi'i teachers and religious functionaries loyal to the state. It was able to further erode the status of the old madrasa among Shi'is in Iraq by creating the Muntada as an alternative to that institution. Thus, for example, the government could appoint Shi'i religious functionaries only from among the graduates of the Muntada, thereby isolating the members and graduates of the old madrasas. The Iraqi government's move in approving the establishment of the Muntada may usefully be compared to Sa'd Zaghlul's founding of a new state-controlled school of Shari'a judges (Madrasat al-Qada' al-Shar'i) in Egypt in 1907. This school was said to be Zaghlul's most dramatic move as Minister of Education between 1906 and 1910, aimed at training judges under the supervision of his Ministry. The school's budget was under Zaghlul's control, and its curriculum approved by the Ministry of Education. Conservative Azharites strongly objected to the new school, fearing that it would further reduce the job opportunities of al-Azhar graduates, who competed with holders of state school certificates in the religious-judiciary field, and that it would eventually eliminate al-Azhar altogether.[88] Whereas in Egypt the new school was later incorporated into al-Azhar (which itself was subjected to greater government control from 1952 under a cabinet ministry for al-Azhar affairs), the Muntada has remained to this day separate from the old Shi'i madrasa in Iraq and under government control since its inception.

The Muntada did not become a focal point linking the religious and secular segments of Iraqi Shi'i society. Muzaffar's attempt around 1943 to establish a faculty for preaching and guidance generated strong opposition in Najaf, particularly among many traditional preachers, who apparently still controlled some of the pulpits.[89] Although the school succeeded nonetheless in training some preachers, their small number was not enough to

---

[86] Khalili, Hakadha 'araftuhum, 2:25; idem, Mawsu'a, 2,2:184–85. And see the biography of Husayn Bahr al-'Ulum, who was also a graduate of the Muntada: Yusuf 'Izz al-Din, Shu'ara' al-'iraq fi al-qarn al-'ishrin (Baghdad, 1969), 342.

[87] Report of Vice-Consul Bagley on Visit to Karbala and Najaf in November 1942, British Consulate, Baghdad, 22 February 1943, FO 624/33/537.

[88] Vatikiotis, Egypt, 257, 300; 'Ali, al-Azhar, 264–76.

[89] Asifi, Madrasat al-najaf, 132–34; Khalili, Hakadha 'araftuhum, 2:159.

improve the per capita ratio between preachers and laymen in Iraq.[90] The school issued two journals, *al-Badhra* and *al-Najaf*, but they apparently did not enjoy a wide circulation.[91] The institution had difficulties in gaining sufficient funds from Iraqi Shi'i donors. The general reluctance of Iraqi Shi'is to channel funds in support of religion in their country was reinforced by the fact that many members of the Shi'i religious establishment in Najaf did not recognize the *Muntada* as a true madrasa, and discouraged pious Shi'is from contributing money to the school. Subsequently, the most prominent mujtahid, Abu al-Hasan Isfahani, had to issue a *fatwa* in 1942 to explain that the *Muntada* was a religious school, and that it was permissible to support it.[92]

The *Muntada* was an indigenous Iraqi Shi'i religious school, the ethnic Arab composition of its teachers and students reflecting that of their society. In a state that strongly advocated Pan-Arabism, only a Shi'i religious school of Arab character had any chance of operating within the state's domain. Indeed, the school's importance lay in that it provided an institutional link between Shi'i religion and the Sunni state in Iraq. The *Muntada* produced government officials as well as some members of the Iraqi Shi'i opposition groups, most notably the *Da'wa* which gained strength in the late 1960s and the 1970s.[93] As such, the *Muntada* did not differ much from al-Azhar, from which emerged both state employees and members of Egyptian Islamic opposition groups. The mujtahids associated with the *Muntada*, and its graduates, did not have a chance to be recognized as true mujtahids within the universal Shi'i religious hierarchy. The teaching level of jurisprudence in the *Muntada* apparently was not advanced enough, and the training techniques did not include thorough debates (*mujadala* or *majalis al-jadal*) among the prospective mujtahids aimed at assessing their scholarship and establishing their prestige, as was the case in the traditional madrasa. At the same time, the *Muntada* was regarded as too closely associated with the state. Even Muzaffar, who was himself a qualified mujtahid by the time the *Muntada* was established, was said to have lost his chance to compete over the religious leadership because of his teaching techniques and close association with this institution.[94]

The *Muntada* was established at a clear cost, but one which Iraqi Shi'is were willing to pay in order to give their society a better chance to become integrated into the modern state of Iraq.

[90] The important preachers trained by the *Muntada* are listed in Khalili, *Hakadha 'araftuhum*, 2:25.

[91] Asifi, *Madrasat al-najaf*, 136.

[92] "Ra'y ayatullah fi jam'iyyat muntada al-nashr," *al-Hatif* 313 (15 October 1942): 7. See also 'Abdallah al-Fayyad, *al-Thawra al-'iraqiyya al-kubra sanat 1920* (Baghdad, 1963), 90.

[93] Anon., *al-Haraka al-islamiyya*, 134.

[94] Khalili, *Hakadha 'araftuhum*, 2:23.

Conclusion

THE RISE of Najaf and Karbala as the two strongholds of Shi'ism reflected the shift of the Shi'i academic center from Iran to Iraq in the mid-eighteenth century, the frontier nature of the latter country, the incomplete Mamluk and later Ottoman domination of the countryside, as well as the Ottoman-Iranian rivalry over the control of Shi'i affairs in Iraq. The arrival of a large number of Persian religious families in Najaf and Karbala had a tremendous impact on the composition of Iraqi Shi'i society, as well as on the position and organization of Shi'i Islam in Iraq. The Shi'i religious hierarchy in Najaf and Karbala came under the control of Persian mujtahids, who attracted the bulk of student followers and charitable income from Iran and India. The two cities, most notably Najaf, enjoyed a semi-autonomous status. In their capacity as centers of pilgrimage and learning, as well as desert market-towns, Najaf and Karbala functioned as the major socioeconomic centers in southern Iraq, thus vying with the local government for influence over the tribes.

The conversion of the bulk of Iraq's nomadic tribes to Shi'ism mainly during the nineteenth century invigorated the development of a Shi'i polity in southern Iraq. The conversion gained momentum from 1831, following the Ottoman attempt to settle the tribes and to increase agricultural production and tax revenue. As in other parts of the Middle East, government control in Iraq became more effective in the nineteenth century, and the area of cultivation increased when nomadic tribes settled down and took up agriculture. But what really set Iraq apart from other territories was the fact that the disruption of the balance between nomadic and settled tribes altered the ratio of Sunnis to Shi'is in the country. The tribes settled in the area near Najaf and Karbala simply because it was there that sufficient water for agricultural activity could be found. And as changes in tribal attitudes and organization occurred, individual groups restructured their identity and developed new contacts with the cities in the area to which they had become attached, notably, Najaf and Karbala.

In seeking to bolster the position of Shi'i Islam in Iraq, ulama and mujtahids succeeded in converting those tribes whose former political and socioeconomic organization had been broken during the transition from nomadic life to agriculture. The introduction of Shi'i rituals and religious practices, as well as Shi'i law, into the settled tribal communities served as a vehicle through which the mujtahids attempted to unify the tribes and create a political entity in southern Iraq. Shi'i rituals and religious practices came to be part of the cultural life and folklore of the settled Arab tribes, shaping the religious identity of the tribesmen. While the rituals and religious practices reinforced the interaction between Najaf and Karbala and the settled tribes, Shi'i law was intended to establish socioeconomic foundations for daily activities and principles for the religious observances of the converted tribesmen. The proliferation of *sayyids* among the settled tribes not only offset the fragmentation of tribal society, but also provided a human mechanism to weld the converted tribes together. On another level, the interaction between *sayyid* families and tribal shaykhs marked the appearance of Shi'i notables, *a'yan*, in southern Iraq during the nineteenth century. The growing bonds between the two groups found clear embodiment in intermarriage between daughters of tribal shaykhs and members of *sayyid* families, most notably the Bahr al-'Ulum and the Qazwinis. At the top of the social ladder stood the big tribal shaykhs and the grand mujtahids, who constituted the elite of the Shi'i regional polity which evolved in southern Iraq.

The swiftness of the process of formation of Iraqi Shi'i society in the nineteenth century suggests that one cannot make a clear-cut distinction in social and cultural values between the bulk of Arab Shi'is and Sunnis in Iraq on the eve of the formation of the monarchy. While Shi'ism was blended with Iraqi tribalism, it did not preempt the former social and cultural values of the converted Arab tribesmen. The limits of conversion of the tribes to Shi'ism were evident in the fact that Shi'i law did not replace tribal custom, and in the way that Shi'i rituals reflected the durability of Arab social values among Iraqi Shi'is well into the twentieth century. Indeed, Iraq's Arab Shi'is shared common cultural characteristics with Arab Sunnis, which could be translated into unified action as manifested in the 1920 revolt.

In pushing during the 1919 plebiscite and the 1920 revolt for the nomination of a king whose actions would be controlled by a national assembly, the prominent mujtahid Mirza Muhammad Taqi Shirazi sought to implement in Iraq a political theory which laid down principles for the mujtahids' own representation in politics. The desire of Shi'i mujtahids to shape the politics of the nascent Iraqi state was a major factor in driving Shirazi to cooperate with the Sharifians and to take a leading role in the 1920 revolt. But the mujtahids' plan to use the revolt to oust the British and to dominate Iraqi national affairs backfired. And in subsequent years, Iraq's Sunni rulers were inimical to the existence of a highly autonomous and politically active Shi'i religious establishment in the country. Indeed, the major conflict between the Shi'i mujtahids and the Sunni government in the early 1920s stemmed from the clash between the process of Shi'i state formation and the establishment of the Iraqi Sunni monarchy.

The British occupation of Iraq and the subsequent formation of the monarchy created new realities in the country. The development of the

CONCLUSION   271

state apparatus and of political institutions during the mandatory period
enabled the Sunni Arab minority to gain precedence in the new state vis-
à-vis other sectarian and ethnic groups. Pan-Arabism became the major
nationalist trend in Iraq, and government policies undermined the position
of Persians in the country. In reacting to the rise of the modern state, Shi'is
sought to increase the scope of their participation in Iraqi politics and to
accommodate their Iraqi Shi'i identity within the framework of the state.
The Shi'i attempt to gain access to key political positions in the state has
been, however, a major factor in feeding the tension between Shi'is and
Sunnis in modern Iraq.

Against the emergence of Baghdad as the dominant center in the new
state, Najaf and Karbala declined in importance and failed to mobilize
Shi'is for political action. Successive Sunni governments succeeded in splitting the pre-monarchic Shi'i elite. While the big tribal shaykhs emerged as
players in Iraqi politics, the mujtahids were isolated as the state sought to
establish clear boundaries between religion and politics. A strong Shi'i
religious establishment did not emerge in modern Iraq. Unlike the Iranian
ulama, who managed to retain their status as part of the traditional power
elite and played a dominant role in Iranian affairs under the Pahlavis, their
Shi'i counterparts in Iraq were much less able to shape national politics.
Indeed, the state succeeded in eradicating much of the power of the Shi'i
mujtahids in Iraq. It controlled Shi'i institutions like the madrasa and *waqf*
property, and it restricted the Muharram observances, thereby reducing
their effectiveness as a political instrument.

In highlighting the differences between Iraqi and Iranian Shi'ism, this
study has attempted to demonstrate that it is the interaction between culture, society, and economy, as well as government policies, which determined the distinct characters of Iraqi and Iranian Shi'ism. The nature of
rituals in Iraq and Iran was a reflection of the distinct socioethnic composition and cultural attributes of Iraqi and Iranian Shi'i society. The Arab
tribal origin of the bulk of the Iraqi Shi'is found embodiment in the Muharram observances and the images attached to the imams and saints.
Whereas the commemoration of 'Ashura' and the cult of the saints among
Iranian Shi'is focused on elements of martyrdom and future rewards, the
stress in these practices in Iraq was on the Arab ideal of manhood, that is,
the worldly attributes of masculinity, honor, and bravery, which appealed
to the Iraqi Shi'is. Indeed, these attributes, as believed to be exemplified in
the battle of Karbala, played a major role in shaping the distinct nature of
the commemoration of 'Ashura' in Iraq and its symbolic meaning for the
Iraqi Shi'is.

The organizational form of Shi'i Islam in Iraq and Iran reflected the
different types of interaction between religion, society, and economy in the
two countries. In contrast to the clergy in Iran, whose madrasas relied on

rich endowments, their Shiʻi counterparts in Iraq suffered from the lack of viable sources of income within the country. And in contrast to the interdependence between religious and commercial life in Iran, close links did not develop between the Shiʻi religious and economic sectors in Iraq. Whereas Iranian bazaaris expressed their group identity and community of interest with the clergy in channeling funds for the support of religion in their country, Iraqi Shiʻi merchants were on the whole unwilling to support religious activity and structures in their country as their class identity surpassed their sectarian allegiance. The bonds between the urban merchants and the clergy in Iran persisted through the Pahlavi period despite the attempt of the state to reduce the power of religion in the country. The close interaction between Shiʻi religion, society, and economy in Iran, and the lack of such a feature in Iraq, helps explain why the political development of Iranian and Iraqi Shiʻis has taken such different courses in the twentieth century.

The rise of the modern state not only had its impact on the relative position of Shiʻi Islam in Iraq and Iran, but led to a growing polarization of the Shiʻi world in the twentieth century. These trends intensified following the Iranian Islamic Revolution. For more than a century, the pilgrimage and the corpse traffic, as well as the flow of foreign charities, helped bolster the position of Najaf and Karbala as the major centers of Shiʻism and influenced their strong orientation toward Iran. By contrast, the policies of successive Iraqi governments and of Iran's Pahlavi rulers eroded the long-established socioeconomic links of the shrine cities with Iran. The decrease in the scale of the pilgrimage and the corpse traffic from Iran, and the attempts of the Pahlavis to divert Iranian resources from Najaf and Karbala to Mashhad and Qum, were a major factor in the decline of Shiʻi Islam in Iraq and its rise in Iran. These developments were nowhere more apparent than in the shift of the Shiʻi religious headship from Iraq back to Iran in 1946, and in the sharp decrease in the student population of Najaf as compared with Qum. Najaf lost its position as the major Shiʻi academic center in the second half of the twentieth century, at least as far as Iranians were concerned. The growing distinction between the Shiʻi Arab world and the Iranian one was evident in the fact that unlike Najaf, which in the past had attracted diverse ethnic groups, Qum emerged as a much more homogenous center of learning, with the bulk of its student population drawn from within Iran. Perhaps this development symbolizes the extent to which Shiʻi Islam has been reshaped by the rise of the nation-state, as well as the Islamic Republic of Iran, in the twentieth century.

THE GULF WAR AND ITS AFTERMATH

ON 17 JANUARY 1991, U.S. and allied forces began striking Baghdad and other targets in Iraq and Kuwait with waves of air attacks. The Gulf War for the liberation of Kuwait thus began. This War, which the Iraqi leader Saddam Husayn predicted would be the "the mother of all battles," has had a lasting impact on Shi'is and their Sunni government, further diminishing the position of Shi'i Islam in Iraq. The themes that unfolded during the War and its aftermath are connected in one way or another to the central issues discussed in this book. The assessment attempted here of some of these themes—however inadequate for lack of sufficient sources and time perspective—is intended to sharpen the three basic questions with which I have dealt in the course of this book: Who are the Iraqi Shi'is? What is the nature of Shi'ism in Iraq? and How did the policies of the modern state influence the position of Shi'i Islam in Iraq?

While showing a remarkable, and in many ways even frightening, persistence in defying the devastating air strikes designed to force his troops out of Kuwait, Saddam also labored to gain legitimacy and the support of Iraq's Shi'i population before, during, and after the War. He used Arab tribal and Shi'i symbols, and he appealed to the concept of Iraq's honor. The old and already well-recognized posters of Saddam in which he appears dressed as a tribal shaykh were spread in central locations throughout Iraq. Some of Iraq's scud missiles launched against Israel and Saudi Arabia were known even before the Gulf War by the names 'Abbas and Husayn, two of the most venerated saints among Iraqi Shi'is. It is perhaps not a coincidence that one type of these modified missiles—the one with the longest potential range—was named after 'Abbas, who is famous among Shi'is in Iraq for the swiftness of his vengeance and the dire calamity which he was believed to be capable of causing. On several occasions Saddam was shown in public firing his pistol into the air in celebration of what he attempted to portray as Iraqi victories, as early in November 1992 when Iraqis were called to celebrate the news of U.S. President George Bush's election defeat. "Bush fell a long time ago when he decided to bomb Baghdad," Saddam said to a cheering crowd, firing his pistol in an act which symbolized a kind of a traditional Iraqi tribal celebration (the *hosa*). Saddam's mention of Baghdad's heroic stand against the allied air strikes was not a coincidence either, for in doing so he attempted to invoke the glory of this famous Islamic city and stimulate Iraqi patriotism. Indeed,

Saddam repeatedly stressed that Iraq's honor was too important to be surrendered to the dictates of the allied coalition. The War obliged Saddam to appeal to the basic components of identity of Iraq's Shi'i population, and he chose to focus on the elements of tribalism, Arabism, Iraqi Shi'ism, and the loyalty of the Shi'is to the Iraqi state. I will return to some of these points later in the discussion.

In its origin the insurrection of March 1991 was spontaneous and disorganized, but its spread in the Shi'i south and later in the Kurdish north was stimulated to a degree by foreign countries as well as by Iraqi opposition groups in exile. One of the earliest reported incidents which preceded the Shi'i insurrection is traced by the media to 10 February. On that day, a crowd of Iraqis in the predominantly Shi'i town of Diwaniyya, 110 miles south of Baghdad, protested Saddam Husayn's refusal to relinquish Kuwait. Shouting anti-Saddam and anti-Ba'th slogans, the protesters killed ten officials of the ruling Ba'th party. Five days later, U.S. President George Bush made his first explicit call for the Iraqis to topple Saddam. He suggested that if the Iraqi military and people wanted to stop the bloodshed, they should "take matters into their own hands" and overthrow their leader. "There will be no cessation of hostilities, there will be no pause, there will be no cease-fire," Bush told reporters. On 24 February, after the Iraqi leader ignored the U.S. President's deadline for beginning Iraqi withdrawal from Kuwait, allied troops launched a ground offensive, and within days drove the Iraqi army out of Kuwait and occupied a large area of southern Iraq.

The starting of the ground operations signaled a turning point in the Gulf War, shifting the focus of attention from Kuwait to Iraq, where civil commotion and anti-government unrest was growing. By the beginning of March civil unrest had already spread from Basra to a string of other predominantly Shi'i towns in the south, most notably 'Amara, Nasiriyya, and Kut. At this point, however, the insurrection was still by and large spontaneous. Iran was just beginning to show a clear interest in promoting unrest in Iraq, and there was no evidence that civil unrest in the south was coordinated by one local leader or even stimulated by the weak and divided Iraqi Shi'i opposition outside Iraq. On 7 March, a few days after the insurgency was reported to have taken root in the holy shrine cities of Najaf and Karbala as protesters poured into the streets, the Iraqi government acknowledged for the first time that it was facing an internal revolt. In the days ahead, as the restive Kurds in northern Iraq joined the revolt, Najaf and Karbala as well as other Shi'i towns in the south became battlegrounds. Dozens of Ba'thi officials and suspected collaborators were executed by the rebels, often without a trial. Iran, the U.S. administration, and some of its Arab allies, as well as the Iraqi opposition groups in exile now threw in their weight, each seeking to use the growing disorder in Iraq to achieve its own goals.

By the middle of March, Iran had already embarked on a methodical campaign to undermine the position of Saddam Husayn, after Iranian President Hashemi Rafsanjani had denounced the Iraqi leader on 8 March and called on him to resign. While the Iranian media waged a propaganda war against Saddam and his government, Kuwaiti and other allied officials asserted that Iraqi rebels were getting humanitarian and military aid as well as moral support from Iran. The Iranian campaign, officials claimed, was intended to replace Saddam with a friendly Shi'i Muslim government. The U.S. position was somewhat ambiguous. While President Bush called on the Iraqi people to rebel against their leader, reports in the media suggested that the dominant assessment among U.S. intelligence officials was that neither the Shi'is in the south nor the Kurds in the north could carry off a successful rebellion against the authority of Saddam Husayn and the tradition of Sunni control of Iraq which it represents. The perception was that the military was the most likely Iraqi institution that could act to save Iraq from "centrifugal disintegration" and challenge Saddam's claim to rule after his disastrous adventure in Kuwait. Indeed, both during the insurrection and for a long period afterward the Bush administration and some of its Arab coalition allies continued to hope for a palace coup in which "a nice Sunni general will finally get fed up and remove Saddam." While Iraqi rebels were fighting army units equipped with superior fire-arms and helicopter gunships, the opposition in exile, which included several Islamic and secular Shi'i groups, attempted to get its act together and provide direction to the revolt and an alternative leadership to Ba'th rule in Iraq. On 13 March heads of Iraqi opposition groups announced in Beirut their agreement to set up a joint leadership to intensify the struggle to topple the government of Saddam Husayn. They also stated that they had reached an agreement on general elections after the overthrow of the Iraqi government, and on an elected assembly whose members would draft a new constitution for Iraq defining its future government system. A few days later in Damascus, opposition leaders announced that they were pre-paring to establish a council inside Iraq to pave the way for a national unity government in case Saddam Husayn was overthrown. The skepticism which Western diplomats and experts on the Iraqi opposition expressed as to how long the movement would hold together was not unfounded, for, as will be seen below, within less than a month Saddam Husayn was able to split the Shi'is from the Kurds.

It took army units loyal to Saddam only a few weeks to isolate the centers of resistance, crush the Shi'i and Kurdish insurrections, and regain control of virtually all cities and towns in southern Iraq. When Iraqi army units were carrying out mopping-up operations in the Shi'i south, the U.S., Iran, and some leaders of the Iraqi opposition groups began to tone down their expectations for a quick overthrow of the government of Saddam Husayn. On 26 March U.S. officials ruled out action to aid Iraqi rebels, citing President Bush's fear that Iraq might splinter. The U.S. adopted a "hands-off" policy, and the military publicized its plan to start the withdrawal of American troops from southern Iraq. Meanwhile, some Iraqi Shi'i rebels who managed to escape to the U.S.-controlled area in southern Iraq began assessing the consequences of the Gulf War and their insurrection against Saddam. One rebel told a reporter of *The New York Times*: "Bush said that we should rebel against Saddam. We rebelled against Saddam, but where is Bush? Where is he? Kuwait is destroyed by Saddam," the rebel said, "Iraq is destroyed by the allied forces. But Saddam is still in his chair." In Iran, Tehran radio accused the U.S. and other countries of a double standard and indifference to the plight of Iraqi civilians. And as the Iraqi army began focusing on sealing the border with Iran, Muhammad Baqir al-Hakim, the leader of one Iraqi Shi'i opposition group, conceded that the rebellion had lost ground, brushing aside reports that Iran had trained and armed some thirty thousand Iraqi Shi'is loyal to him. Whatever Shi'i anti-government fighting continued in Iraq in the months ahead took the form of guerrilla warfare confined mainly to the marsh areas.

Like the 1920 revolt in Iraq, the insurrection of March 1991 will become an important event in shaping the national identity of Iraqi Shi'is and their collective memory as the stories and episodes connected with the insurrection are transmitted to younger generations. Yet unlike the organized 1920 revolt, in which Shi'i mujtahids played a leading role and Muhammad Taqi Shirazi sought to establish an Islamic government in Iraq, the 1991 insurrection is likely to be remembered as a spontaneous one. On various occasions Iraqi Shi'i refugees cited the expulsion of thousands of Shi'is to Iran during the Iran-Iraq War of 1980–1988, and the desire to get rid of Saddam and his government, as major factors in their motivation to rebel. Unlike the attacks of organized Kurdish units on Iraqi army positions in the north, the Shi'i rebels in the south were disorganized and lacked a blueprint or well-defined Islamic ideological goals prior to the insurrection. It was only after rebels in Najaf appeared to be consolidating their control of the city that the grand mujtahid Abu al-Qasim Khu'i issued a communiqué in which he sanctioned the establishment of a "Supreme Committee" of nine people under whose leadership Shi'is were called to preserve Iraq's security and to stabilize public, religious, and social affairs. While the content of this communiqué as published by Shi'i sources as well as by Middle East Watch suggests that Khu'i sanctioned some form of a Shi'i governing body in Iraq, there is no evidence that he envisioned the establishment of either an Islamic government along the lines advocated by

Shirazi in 1920 or a government led by the jurist (*wilayat al-faqih*) as advocated by Ruhallah Khumayni and implemented in the Islamic Republic of Iran after 1978.

Indeed, the 1991 insurrection in southern Iraq differed greatly from the 1978–79 Iranian Revolution in which the Ayatollahs played a significant leading role, and where much of the action against the Shah took place in the capital. The Iraqi Shi'i rebels lacked a clear religious leadership that would inspire and coordinate the insurrection in the south. And in spite of reported discontent and protests in the capital, the Baghdadis on the whole did not join the insurrection. In 1991 Iran played a role in making propaganda and it provided weapons to some Iraqi rebel groups, particularly to the Badr Brigade organized by the Supreme Islamic Council headed by Muhammad Baqir al-Hakim. The Brigade was composed of Iraqi Shi'is recruited from among refugees expelled to Iran by the Ba'th in the late 1970s and early 1980s, and it appears that several thousand of them entered Iraq a few days after the insurrection had started. In training and arming these refugees, Iran demonstrated the continuity of its traditional aspirations to gain leverage over Iraq by influencing Shi'i affairs in the country. Yet more than two years after the War, it seems that if Iran really tried to shape the ideological direction of the insurrection, this attempt did not lead anywhere.

The Gulf War and its aftermath also highlighted the different political aspirations of Shi'is and Kurds in Iraq. Unlike the Shi'is, whose primary identity came to be Iraqi following the establishment of the monarchy in 1921, the Kurds still constitute a distinct ethnic and national group, and they tend to act like one. I attempted to demonstrate in chapter 4 that one of the major sources of tension between Shi'is and successive Sunni governments in modern Iraq stemmed not from the desire of Shi'is to separate from the state, but rather from their demand for political power and representation in the government in proportion to their weight among the population. This basic Shi'i political goal surfaced during 1991–92 when time and again Iraqi Shi'i rebels and opposition members stressed that the revolt was not directed against the Iraqi state but against Saddam personally. In contrast with Iraqi Shi'i political goals, the Kurds on the whole continued to express a desire for autonomy. Although on several occasions during and after the War Iraqi opposition groups attempted to present a united front, the Kurdish aspiration to self-rule and autonomy remained strong, and was reinforced to a degree by the creation of the "safe haven" and the establishment of what has been described as a "de facto Kurdish state" in northern Iraq. In May 1992 Kurds in northern Iraq elected a legislature and its 105 members were sworn in the following June. Erbil was established as the state's capital. The new Kurdish government appointed a police force, school administration, and a bureaucracy responsible for levying taxes, collecting garbage, and delivering mail. The Gulf War thus acted to reinforce the distinct culture and tradition of the Kurds in Iraq, as well as their dream for a homeland. No such developments took place among the Shiʻis.

The different political aspirations of the Shiʻis and the Kurds played into the hands of Saddam Husayn in his struggle for survival. The Iraqi leader split the two groups, pursuing policies of divide and rule as well as the carrot and the stick. Saddam not only ruthlessly crushed the Shiʻi insurrection in the south, but succeeded in blocking it from spreading to the Shiʻi slums of Baghdad. On 21 March 1991 he forced the leading mujtahid Khuʼi to praise the Iraqi leader on national television and to appeal to his Shiʻi followers to end their insurrection. At the same time, Saddam reshuffled his cabinet on 23 March and nominated Saʻdun Hamadi (a Shiʻi from Karbala) as Prime Minister, thus signaling his willingness to give the Shiʻis a greater say in politics; a few months later, however, the Iraqi leader already felt confident enough to remove Hamadi from his position. In July Saddam added a new aspect to his effort to pacify the Shiʻis and gain legitimacy. The Iraqi President was seen on nightly television shows holding meetings with delegations of prominent Shiʻis and tribal leaders from the south of the country. In one of these sessions Saddam recalled how imam Husayn rode to his death at the hand of his Sunni foes in Karbala in the year 680. Husayn was not defeated, the Iraqi President explained, because he became a martyr. Some watching Iraqis said that Saddam Husayn's implication was that Iraq and its President were martyred, not defeated by the American-led coalition that drove Iraqi forces out of Kuwait. While working to reconsolidate his rule in Iraq, Saddam labored to divide the Iraqi opposition groups so as to prevent effective national unity against him. He therefore invited Jalal Talabani to discuss Kurdish demands for self-rule, announcing on 24 April 1991 that an agreement in principle had been reached on a new measure of autonomy for Kurdistan. Saddam thus played with a degree of success on the different political aspirations of the Shiʻis and the Kurds: greater political participation in the case of the Shiʻis and a desire for autonomy in the case of the Kurds.

In many respects Saddam seems much stronger today than he was right after the War, and he is determined to further reduce the position of Karbala and Najaf as the two Shiʻi strongholds in Iraq. While Saddam was probably not surprised by Kurdish desire for self-rule, his violent response to the Shiʻi insurrection suggests that he perhaps felt betrayed by the Iraqi Shiʻis, particularly after many had demonstrated their loyalty to the Iraqi state in fighting their Iranian coreligionists in the course of the Iran-Iraq War. In March 1991 Iraqi troops loyal to Saddam shelled Shiʻi rebels in shrines and mosques in Karbala and Najaf, pounding the two cities with artillery and tank fire. Iraqi Shiʻi refugees who escaped to the U.S. army—

run camp of Safwan on the Iraqi-Kuwaiti border told American soldiers of the extremely brutal methods which the Iraqi government had used to put down the resistance in the south, and one refugee from Najaf testified that some army tanks had the slogan "No more Shi'is after today" painted on them. In late April Western correspondents on an Iraqi government sponsored visit to Karbala, which holds the shrines of Husayn and his half-brother 'Abbas, observed that for five hundred yards in every direction around the two shrines the destruction was reminiscent of London at the height of the German blitz in World War II.

The policies of the Iraqi government in the aftermath of the Gulf War have further curtailed religious activity in Karbala and Najaf, and undermined the fabric of Shi'i culture and society in Iraq. The government decided to raze much of Karbala and rebuild it. Although by May 1992 most of the damage to the shrines had already been repaired, the bazaars around them were not rebuilt. "The project for widening and developing the area around the holy shrines" is bound to transform much of the architecture and many of the bazaars of Karbala, the appearance of which had reflected Persian influences. The setback to the position of Shi'i Islam in Najaf may be gathered from a report to the United Nations Human Rights Commission by Max van der Stoel, a former Dutch Foreign Minister, who visited Najaf in January 1992. Stoel noted that several acres in the famous Shi'i holy cemetery of Wadi al-Salam had been demolished and that a highway was under construction over graves, an act which seemed to be one of deliberate desecration on the part of the government. Stoel wrote that libraries containing manuscripts which constituted part of the Islamic tradition were deliberately destroyed. He estimated that whereas there were a few thousand students and clergymen in Najaf in 1970, by the time of the Gulf War, their number had dwindled to eight hundred. After the insurrection of March 1991, these remaining students disappeared. The destruction of libraries, as well as the flight and arrest of religious students and ulama, is likely to further reduce the importance of those few Shi'i madrasas that may still be functioning today in Najaf to the advantage of those of Qum in Iran.

While the violent way in which army units loyal to Saddam destroyed large sections of Karbala and Najaf provides a glimpse of the extent of his anger against the Shi'is, it is the Iraqi leader's grand project of diverting the Euphrates River that deserves particular attention at this time. In chapter 1 I demonstrated the ecological changes and social consequences caused by the construction of the Hindiyya canal in the nineteenth century. The Hindiyya, which left the Euphrates at Musayyib, a few miles above Karbala, was intended to bring water to Najaf. Its construction led to the diversion of the Euphrates and encouraged tribal settlement in the area close to Karbala and Najaf, facilitating the conversion of many of Iraq's

Arab tribesmen to Shi'ism. Today, Saddam Husayn is attempting to achieve
the exact opposite, that is, to reduce contact between the two cities and the
Shi'i rural population. The most powerful symbol of Iraq's determination
to rebuild itself after the War is the "Third River" (known also as The
Saddam River Irrigation Project), the digging of which has been described
by the United Nations human rights monitor for Iraq as "the environmen-
tal crime of the century." The river, actually a canal, will flow 350 miles
from Mahmudiyya (above Musayyib) to the Persian Gulf. The canal is
intended to defeat the international sanctions by increasing the cultivated
area of Iraq from the summer of 1993. Some experts suspect that the canal
is also intended to help the Iraqi army gain easier access to the south by
draining marshlands that are home to Shi'i guerrilla fighters. Indeed, U.S.
satellite photographs taken in March 1993 reportedly show that one-third
of the vast 'Amara marsh was then dry and that much of the Hawr Huwayza,
which straddles the border with Iran, was being steadily drained. While it
is too early to assess the full implications of the "Third River," its construction has already transformed the unique way of life of the Shi'i marsh
Arabs. It is also likely that in the long run the hydraulic and ecological
changes caused by the "Third River" will reduce the water supply of the
hinterlands of Najaf and Karbala, where some of Iraq's best rice fields are
located. Eventually, this development may lead to large population shifts as
Shi'i cultivators will be forced to move to other fertile areas in Iraq farther
away from Najaf and Karbala. The "Third River" thus has the potential of
further undermining the position of the two cities as the strongholds of
Shi'i Islam in Iraq.

What may the future bring to the Iraqi Shi'is? Perhaps in part because he
was seeking a boost during an election year, President Bush asked Britain
and France in August 1992 to support air action to protect Shi'is in southern Iraq. A "no fly" zone for Iraqi planes was declared below the 32d
parallel, covering the area from Najaf southward including the marshes.
The establishment of the zone coincided with reports in the media that U.S.
administration officials and policymakers had come to realize that "the
Shi'is are Iraqis first, not separatists." This moment of revelation reflected
what officials described as "a better understanding of who the Shi'is in
southern Iraq really are: a persecuted people and not necessarily the precursors of a radical Islamic state that would align itself with Iran." The
much-publicized turnabout in attitude toward the Iraqi Shi'is poses new
challenges not only to the U.S. and its allies, but to people in Iraq as well as
to the opposition groups in exile. Does this development reflect merely a
shift in tactics for undermining Saddam Husayn, or does it also signal a
genuine willingness on the part of the U.S. and its allies to reconsider long-
established policy assumptions regarding the nature of government in Iraq
which may end Sunni minority rule in the country? The task of dealing

with this difficult question and its complex potential ramifications was left to the new U.S. administration led by President Bill Clinton. As these lines were being written, the U.S. and its allies, including Saudi Arabia and Kuwait, did not demonstrate any real willingness to adopt radical changes in past concepts vis-à-vis the nature of government in Iraq. And senior Clinton administration officials began talking about Saddam Husayn as a sort of "low-grade headache" with which they would have to live for a long time, finding relief occasionally through diplomacy and occasionally through force. In the long run, whatever the new policies of the U.S. and its allies may be, their calculations will be influenced by developments in Iraq as well as by the actions of the various Iraqi opposition groups.

In this respect, it is still difficult to assess the impact of the War on the various components of Iraqi Shi'i identity and to predict the long-term sociopolitical consequences of the sectarian strife and animosities which the War fostered between Iraqi Shi'is and Sunnis. Moreover, it is unclear how the Iraqi bourgeoisie will react in the long run to such acts as the Ba'th government execution of some forty Baghdadi merchants in July 1992, on accusations of profiteering, and whether this class—including its Sunni members—will unequivocally join ranks with other groups in opposition to Saddam Husayn. It is equally unclear whether there has begun to develop any grassroots leadership following the War that can gain the recognition of the majority of the different groups and classes that constitute Iraqi society.

The responsibility for Iraq's destiny lies mainly with its people. And today, Iraqis within the country and in exile are facing their most challenging test yet: demonstrating persuasively that a new credible Iraqi leadership can emerge, a leadership which could be an alternative to the Ba'th and which could oversee the transition of Iraq into a federated state that would accommodate the diverse interests of Arab Shi'is and Sunnis, as well as those of the Kurds.

Princeton, N.J.
October 1993

Appendix 1

THE CONSTITUTION OF THE BURAQ
QUARTER OF NAJAF

. . . WE [the inhabitants of the Buraq quarter] write this document in order to secure unity and cohesion amongst ourselves . . . We have assembled ourselves and become united and of one blood, and follow one another should anything happen to our quarter from other quarters. We will rise together against an outsider who is not from [amongst] us, whether the result be to our advantage or to our disadvantage, and the conditions of our union are as follows:

1. If an outsider is killed, the murderer has to pay five liras, and the remainder of the blood money to be paid by the whole tribe.
2. If anybody from our union is killed, half of the *fasil* [blood money] is for the murdered man's family, and half for the union.
3. If anyone kills anybody from his own tribe, and the tribe has no responsible head, the murderer must leave the place for seven years, and anybody who helps him is also to be dismissed for the same period. The *fasil* is thirty liras in gold, . . . the *farshah* [his mattress], five liras, and ten silk garments. One-third is to be given to the union, and two-thirds to the relatives, payable in two installments.
4. One who wounds anyone from his own tribe, and the wound results in bleeding, has to pay one lira.
5. One who aims at his friend with his rifle, without firing, is to surrender his rifle.
6. One who wounds another, and the wound results in his illness, has to pay five liras, surrender his weapon, and leave the town for a short period; and whatever extra is paid, one-third of it will be given to our commander, Kadhim Subbi, and two-thirds to the union.
7. Should harm befall one of us who steals, robs, loots, or fornicates, we are not only not responsible, but also not his friends.
8. If any one of us is arrested for our doings by the government, or imprisoned, all his expenses will be paid by us.

The above is for all of us. We are united with Kadhim, whether he is in the town or not, and on this condition we all put our signatures, and we all agree to it, and God is our witness.

Source: Great Britain, Administration Reports, 1918, Najaf, CO 696/1.

Appendix 2

IMPORTANT SHI'I SHRINES, TOMBS, AND HOLY SITES IN IRAQ

KARBALA: the shrines of imam Husayn and his half-brother 'Abbas. Also in that city is the Khaymagah, which marks the site of Husayn's tent before the battle of Karbala. About four miles outside the city stand the tombs of Hurr ibn Yazid al-Riyahi (a military commander sent by Ibn Ziyad to intercept Husayn but who defected to the latter's camp) and 'Awn ibn 'Abdallah ibn Ja'far, who were among his party in the battle.

NAJAF: the shrine of imam 'Ali ibn Abi Talib. There are also several holy sites within the city.

KAZIMAYN: the shrines of Musa al-Kazim and his grandson Muhammad al-Jawad, the seventh and ninth imams.

SAMARRA: the shrines of 'Ali ibn Muhammad al-Hadi and his son Hasan al-'Askari, as well as the hiding site of Muhammad al-Mahdi, the tenth, eleventh, and twelfth imams, respectively.

KUFA: Kufa mosque where 'Ali was mortally wounded, and the Sahla mosque. Also in that city are the tombs of Muslim ibn 'Aqil (Husayn's cousin and his emissary to Kufa), and that of Hani ibn 'Urwa, who harbored Muslim ibn 'Aqil.

HILLA: around that city are the tombs of the sons of Muslim ibn 'Aqil, that of his brother (and son-in-law of imam 'Ali) Muhammad, as well as those of Hamza and Jasim, a son and grandson, respectively, of the seventh imam.

BALAD: near that city is the tomb of Sayyid Muhammad, a son of the tenth imam.

QAL'AT SALIH: near that town is the tomb of 'Abdallah, a son of the imam 'Ali.

MUSAYYIB: the tombs of Sayyid Ibrahim and Abu al-Qasim, sons of the seventh and eleventh imams, respectively.

TUWAYRIJ: the tombs of Ibn al-Hasan and Banat al-Hasan (children of the eleventh imam), and the tomb of Ibn Hamza, a grandchild of the seventh imam. The tombs of Banat al-Hasan became the focus of devotion for women mainly in the Najaf area.

KUMAYYIT: tomb of 'Ali al-Sharqi, a brother of the eighth imam 'Ali al-Rida.

BADRA: near that town is the tomb of 'Ali al-Yathribi, a son of the seventh imam.

SALMAN PAK: tombs of Salman al-Farisi, Jabir ibn 'Abdallah al-Ansari, and Hudhayfa ibn al-Yaman. The three were followers of the Prophet Muhammad and faithful to the Shi'i cause.

BAGHDAD: the tombs of the four representatives of the twelfth imam (*al-nuwwab al-arba'a*).

Sources: Report of the Protector of British Indian Pilgrims, 1929, CO 730/159/2, Appendix A; J. G. Lorimer, *Gazetteer of the Persian Gulf, 'Oman and Central Arabia*, 2 vols. in 5 pts. (Calcutta, 1908–15), 1,2:2356–57; Admiralty War Staff, Intelligence Division, *A Hand-*

book of Mesopotamia, 4 vols., London, 1916–1917, 1:84; 'Abbas al-Qummi, *Mafatih al-Jinan* (Beirut, 1992); 'Abd al-Razzaq Kammuna al-Husayni, *Mashahid al-'itra al-tahira wa-a'yan al-sahaba wa al-tabi'in* (Najaf, 1968); 'Ali al-Wardi, *Dirasa fi tabi'at al-mujtama' al-'iraqi* (Baghdad, 1965), 241; Ja'far al-Mahbuba, *Madi al-najaf wa-hadiruha*, 3 vols. (Najaf, 1955–1958), 1:94–98; 'Abd al-Hadi al-Fadli, *Dalil al-najaf al-ashraf* (Najaf, 1966), 118–19; Yunus Ibrahim al-Samarra'i, *Ta'rikh madinat samarra'*, 3 vols. (Baghdad, 1968–1973), 3:117–39.

Appendix 3

SHI'I HOLY BURIAL SITES

Shrine City	Location of Burial	Amount Charged for Interment (in Turkish gold piasters)
Najaf	Al-Riwaq	5,000
	Iwan al-Dhahab	2,500
	Hujrat al-Sahn	250
	Ard al-Sahn	200
	Wadi al-Salam	50
Karbala	Al-Riwaq	500
	Iwan al-Dhahab	150
	Hujrat al-Sahn	100
	Wadi al-Iman	30
Kazimayn	Al-Riwaq	200
	Iwan al-Dhahab	100
	Hujrat al-Sahn	21
	Ard al-Sahn	21
	Maqabir Quraysh	—
Samarra	Al-Riwaq	70
	Hujrat al-Sahn	40
	Ard al-Sahn	40
	Al-Tarima	40

Source: J. G. Lorimer, *Gazetteer of the Persian Gulf, 'Oman and Central Arabia*, 2 vols. in 5 pts. (Calcutta, 1908–15), 1,2:2362–63. Maqabir Quraysh is not included in Lorimer's list.

Note: 125 Turkish gold piasters were equal to about one English gold pound. *Al-Riwaq* here means the portico of the shrine, *Iwan al-Dhahab* is the golden vestibule, *Hujrat al-Sahn* are the chambers in the courtyard, and *Ard al-Sahn* refers to the ground of the courtyard.

BIBLIOGRAPHY

ARCHIVAL MATERIAL

Great Britain, Public Record Office

Air 23: (Overseas Commands, 1922–1932).
CO 696: (Iraq: Sessional Reports, 1917–1931).
CO 730: (Iraq, 1921–1932: The main source for the Mandate period).
FO 195: (Baghdad, Foreign Office, 1905–1911).
FO 248: (Persia and Mesopotamia affairs, 1918–1941).
FO 371: (Political correspondence between Baghdad, Tehran, and London, as well as interdepartmental correspondence on Iraq, 1910–1958).
FO 406: (Confidential Prints, Eastern Affairs: Reports on Iraq, 1911–1943).
FO 416: (Persia, 1905–1941).
FO 624: (Baghdad Embassy, 1933–1954. The pre-1933 records are in the National Archives in New Delhi, under BHCF).
FO 838: ('Amara Consulate: Reports on the political situation in 'Amara, 1941–1951).

Great Britain, India Office Library

Letters, Political and Secret: L/P&S 10 (1914–1921), L/P&S 11, and L/P&S 12 (1932–1941).

National Archives of India, New Delhi

Baghdad High Commission File, 1918–1933 (including the complete series of the *Weekly Abstracts of Police Intelligence*).
Government of India: Foreign and Political Department, 1911–1936, and External Affairs Department, 1937–1958.

The U.S. National Archives, Washington, D.C.

Records of the Department of State Relating to Internal Affairs of Iraq, 1930–1944: Decimal File 890G.
Confidential U.S. State Department Central Files: Iraq, 1945–1949, Internal Affairs: Decimal File 890G.
Confidential U.S. State Department Central Files: Iraq, 1950–1954, Internal Affairs: Decimal File 787.
Confidential U.S. State Department Central Files: Iraq, 1955–1959, Internal Affairs: Decimal File 787.

PRIVATE PAPERS

C. J. Edmonds Papers, St. Antony's College, Oxford University.

290 BIBLIOGRAPHY

Official Publications

Great Britain

Cmd. 1061. *Review of the Civil Administration of Mesopotamia, 1914–1920.* Compiled by G. L. Bell, 1920.

Colonial Office. *Reports by Her Majesty's Government to the League of Nations on the Administration of Iraq, 1925–1932.*

Colonial Office. *Reports on the Administration of Iraq for the Years 1918- 1925.*

Great Britain, Admiralty. *A Handbook of Mesopotamia.* London, 1916- /17. 4 vols.

Great Britain, Foreign Office, Historical Section. *Mesopotamia.* London, 1920.

Great Britain, Office of the Civil Commissioner. *The Arab of Mesopotamia.* Basra, 1917.

Lorimer, J. G. *Gazetteer of the Persian Gulf, 'Oman and Central Arabia.* Calcutta, 1908–1915. 2 vols. in 5 pts.

Naval Intelligence Division. *Iraq and the Persian Gulf.* Geographical Handbook Series. London, 1944.

Iraq

Iraq. Principal Bureau of Statistics. *Statistical Abstract 1947.* Baghdad, 1947.

Iraq-Census. *Mudiriyyat al-nufus al-'amma, ihsa' al-sukkan li-sanat 1947.* Baghdad, 1954. 3 vols.

Iraq-Census. *Mudiriyyat al-nufus al-'amma, al-majmu'a al-ihsa'iyya li-tasjil 'am 1957.* Baghdad, 1961. 1 vol. in 7 pts.

Mutasarrifiyyat liwa' Karbala'. *Dalil al-'atabat.* Baghdad, 1967.

Al-Waqa'i' al-'iraqiyya (The Iraqi Gazetteer). Baghdad, 1921–present.

Dissertations

Abuel-Haj, Samira Ali. "Class Conflict and Political Revolution in Iraq: The Socio-Economic Origins of the 1958 Revolution." University of California, Los Angeles, 1987.

Fattah, Hala Mundhir. "The Development of the Regional Market of Iraq and the Gulf, 1800–1900." University of California, Los Angeles, 1986.

Azeez, M. M. "Geographical Aspects of Rural Migration from 'Amara Province, Iraq, 1955–1964." Durham University, 1968.

Haidari, Ibrahim. "Zur Soziologie des Schiitischen Chiliasmus: Ein Beitrag zur Erforschung des Irakischen Passionsspiels." Klaus Schwarz Verlag. Freiburg im Breisgau, 1975.

Haider, Saleh. "Land Problems of Iraq." University of London, LSE, 1942.

Hamel, John Thomas. "Ja'far al-Khalili and the Modern Iraqi Story." University of Michigan, 1972.

Kovalenko, Anatoly. "Le Martyre de Husayn dans la Poésie Populaire d'Iraq." Université de Genève, 1979.

Litvak, Meir. "The Shi'i Ulama of Najaf and Karbala, 1791–1904: A Socio-Political Analysis." Harvard University, 1991.

Lokiec, Liora. "Iraqi Politics, 1931–1941." University of London, LSE, 1988.

Najar, Basil Naim. "The Dynamics of Rural-Urban Migration and Assimilation in Iraq." Wayne State University, 1976.

Nakash, Yitzhak. "Shi'ism and National Identity in Iraq, 1908–1958." Princeton University, 1992.

Pool, David. "The Politics of Patronage: Elites and Social Structure in Iraq." Princeton University, 1972.

Thaiss, Gustav. "Religious Symbolism and Social Change: The Drama of Husayn." Washington University, 1973.

JOURNALS

Al-Hatif: Najaf and Baghdad, 1935–1952.

Al-'Ilm: Najaf, 1910–1911.

Al-'Irfan: Sidon, 1909–present.

Al-I'tidal: Najaf, 1932–1936.

Lughat al-'Arab: Baghdad, 1911–1913.

Al-Manar: Cairo, 1898–1936.

Al-Murshid: Baghdad, 1925–1929.

PUBLISHED WORKS IN ARABIC AND PERSIAN

'Abd al-Darraji, 'Abd al-Razzaq. *Ja'far abu al-timman wa-dawruhu fi al-haraka al-wataniyya fi al-'iraq*. Baghdad, 1978.

Adib al-Mulk. *Safarnama-yi adib al-mulk bi-'atabat (dalil al-za'irin), 1273 h.q.* Tehran, 1985.

Agha Buzurg Tihrani, Muhammad Muhsin. *Al-Dhari'a ila tasanif al-shi'a*. Tehran and Najaf, 1936–1986. 26 vols.

———. *Hadiyat al-razi ila al-imam al-mujaddid al-shirazi*. Tehran, 1984.

———. *Tabaqat a'lam al-shi'a*. Najaf and Beirut, 1954–1971. 5 vols.

'Alawi, Hasan. *Al-Shi'a wa al-dawla al-qawmiyya fi al-'Iraq*. Paris, 1989.

———. *Al-Ta'thirat al-turkiyya fi al-mashru' al-qawmi fi al-'iraq*. London, 1988.

'Alawi, Muhammad Mahdi. *Hibat al-din al-shahrastani*. Baghdad, 1930.

Amin, Hasan. *Al-Sayyid muhsin al-amin: siratuhu bi-qalamihi wa-aqlam akharin*. Sidon, 1957.

Amin, Muhsin. *A'yan al-shi'a*. Beirut, 1960–1963. 56 vols.

———. *Al-Husun al-mani'a fi radd ma awradahu sahib al-manar fi haqq al-shi'a*. Damascus, 1909.

———. *Lawa'ij al-ashjan fi maqtal al-imam abi 'abdallah al-husayn ibn 'ali ibn abi talib 'alayhim al-salam*. Sidon, 1934/5.

———. *Al-Majalis al-saniyya fi manaqib wa-masa'ib al-'itra al-nabawiyya*. Damascus, 1954. 5 vols.

———. *Min balad ila balad: rihlat fi al-sharq wa al-gharb*. Beirut, 1974.

———. *Rihlat al-sayyid muhsin al-amin fi lubnan wa al-'iraq wa-Iran wa-misr wa al-hijaz*. 2d ed. Beirut, 1985.

———. *Al-Shi'a bayn al-haqa'iq wa al-awham*. Beirut, 1975.

———. *Al-Tanzih li-a'mal al-shabih*. Sidon, 1928.

Amini, 'Abd al-Husayn. *Shuhada' al-fadila*. Najaf, 1936.

Amini, Muhammad Hadi. *Rijal al-fikr wa al-adab fi al-najaf khilal alf 'am*. Najaf, 1964.

Anon. *Al-Haraka al-islamiyya fi al-'iraq*. Beirut, 1985.

Anon. "Al-Hawza al-'ilmiyya fi al-najaf: ma'alimuha wa-harakatuha al-islahiyya, 1920–1980." A review article of an M.A. thesis by 'Ali Ahmad Kazim al-Bahaduli. *Al-Bilad* 73 (14 March 1992): 48.

Anon. *Al-Imam al-sayyid abu al-hasan*. Najaf, 1946/7.

Anon. *Al-Imam al-shaykh muhammad taqi al-shirazi yushakkil al-hukuma al-islamiyya fi al-'iraq*. Tehran, 1983.

Asadi, Hasan. *Thawrat al-najaf*. Baghdad, 1974/5.

Asifi, Muhammad Mahdi. *Madrasat al-najaf wa-tatawwur al-haraka al-islahiyya fi-ha*. Najaf, 1964.

———. *Min hadith al-da'wa wa al-du'at*. 2d ed. Najaf, 1966.

'Awwad, Kurkis. *Mu'jam al-mu'allifin al-'iraqiyyin fi al-qarn al-tasi' 'ashara wa al-'ishrin, 1800–1969*. Baghdad, 1969. 3 vols.

'Azzawi, 'Abbas. *'Asha'ir al-'iraq*. Baghdad, 1937–1956. 4 vols.

———. *Ta'rikh al-'iraq bayna ihtilalayn*. Baghdad, 1935–1956. 8 vols.

Bahrani, Husayn ibn Muhammad. *Al-Fawadih al-husayniyya wa al-qawadih al-bayyiniyya*. 2d ed. Najaf, n.d.

Bahrani, Muhammad 'Ali. *Ma'tam al-husayn*. Najaf, n.d.

Balaghi, 'Abd al-Hujja. *Ta'rikh-i najaf-i ashraf va-hire*. Tehran, 1948/9.

Barrak, Fadil. *Al-Madaris al-yahudiyya wa al-iraniyya fi al-'iraq: dirasa muqarina*. Baghdad, 1984.

Basir, Muhammad Mahdi. *Nahdat al-'iraq al-adabiyya fi al-qarn al-tasi' 'ashara*. Baghdad, 1946.

———. *Ta'rikh al-qadiyya al-'iraqiyya*. Baghdad, 1924. 2 vols.

Basri al-Wa'ili, 'Uthman ibn Sanad. *Mukhtasar kitab matali' al-su'ud bi-tayyib akhbar al-wali da'ud*. Cairo, 1951/2.

Bayati, 'Ala' al-Din Jasim. *Al-Rashidiyya: dirasa antrobolojiyya ijtima'iyya*. Najaf, 1971.

Bazirgan, 'Ali. *Al-Waqa'i' al-haqiqiyya fi al-thawra al-'iraqiyya*. Baghdad, 1954.

Buraqi, Husayn ibn Ahmad. *Al-Durra al-bahiyya fi fadl karbala'*. Najaf, 1970.

Dalwi, Nisrin Mahmud Hamza. *Al-Jughrafiya al-ijtima'iyya li-madinat al-kazimiyya al-kubra*. Baghdad, 1975.

Damluji, Sadiq. *Midhat pasha*. Baghdad, 1953.

Dujayli, 'Abd al-Karim. *Al-Jawahiri sha'ir al-'arabiyya*. Najaf, 1972.

Dujayli, 'Abd al-Sahib. *Al-Shu'ubiyya wa-adwaruha al-ta'rikhiyya fi al-'alam al-'arabi*. Najaf, 1960.

Dujayli, Husayn. *Al-Ta'lim al-'ali fi al-'iraq*. Baghdad, 1963.

Durra, Mahmud. *Hayat 'iraqi min wara' al-bawwaba al-sawda'*. Cairo, 1976.

Fadli, Hadi. *Dalil al-najaf al-ashraf*. Najaf, 1966.

Fahmi, Ahmad. *Taqrir hawla al-'iraq*. Baghdad, 1926.

Fakiki, 'Abd al-Hadi. *Al-Shu'ubiyya wa al-qawmiyya al-'arabiyya*. Beirut, 1961.

Fayyad, 'Abdallah. *Al-Thawra al-'iraqiyya al-kubra*. Baghdad, 1963.

Fir'awn, Fariq al-Muzhir. *Al-Haqa'iq al-nasi'a fi al-thawra al-'iraqiyya sanat 1920 wa-nata'ijuha*. Baghdad, 1952.

———. *Al-Qada' al-'asha'iri*. Baghdad, 1941.

Ha'iri, Muhammad 'Ali. *Al-Mashahid al-musharrafa wa al-wahhabiyyun*. Najaf, 1926/7.

Hasani, 'Abd al-Razzaq. *Al-'Iraq fi dawrai al-ihtilal wa al-intidab*. Sidon, 1935.

———. *Ta'rikh al-'iraq al-siyasi al-hadith*. Sidon, 1946.

———. *Ta'rikh al-wizarat al-'iraqiyya*. 2d and 3d eds. Sidon, 1953–1965. 10 vols.

———. *Al-Thawra al-'iraqiyya al-kubra*. Sidon, 1952.

———. *Al-Usul al-rasmiyya li-ta'rikh al-wizarat al-'iraqiyya*. Sidon, 1964.

Hasu, Nizar Tawfiq Sultan. *Al-Sira' 'ala al-sulta fi al-'iraq al-malaki*. Baghdad, 1984.

Haydari, Ibrahim Fasih. *Kitab 'unwan al-majd fi bayan ahwal baghdad wa al-basra wa-najd*. Baghdad, n.d.

Hilali, 'Abd al-Razzaq. *Al-Hijra min al-rif ila al-mudun fi al-'iraq*. Baghdad, 1958.

———. *Ta'rikh al-ta'lim fi al-'iraq fi al-'ahd al-'uthmani, 1638–1917*. Baghdad, 1959.

Hilli, 'Abd al-Husayn. *Al-Naqd al-nazih li-risalat al-tanzih*. Najaf, 1928/9.

Hilli, Yusuf Karkush. *Ta'rikh al-hilla*. Najaf, 1965. 2 vols.

Husayni, 'Abd al-Razzaq Kammuna. *Mashahid al-'itra al-tahira wa-a'yan al-sahaba wa al-tabi'in*. Najaf, 1968. 2 vols.

———. *Mawarid al-athaf fi nuqaba' al-ashraf*. Najaf, 1968. 2 vols.

Husri, Sati'. *Mudhakkirati fi al-'iraq*. Beirut, 1967–1968. 2 vols.

'Izz al-Din, Yusuf. *Shu'ara' al-'iraq fi al-qarn al-'ishrin*. Baghdad, 1969.

Jamil, Husayn. *Al-Afkar al-siyasiyya li al-ahzab al-'iraqiyya fi 'ahd al-intidab, 1922–1932*. Baghdad, 1985.

———. *Al-Hayat al-siyasiyya fi al-'iraq, 1925–1947*. Baghdad, 1983.

Jamil, Mekki. *Al-Badw wa al-qaba'il al-rahhala fi al-'iraq*. Baghdad, 1956.

Jawahiri, Sharif. *Muthir al-ahzan fi ahwal al-a'imma al-ithna 'ashara*. Najaf, 1966.

Kashi, 'Abd al-Wahhab. *Ma'sat al-husayn bayn al-sa'il wa al-mujib*. Beirut, 1973.

Kashif al-Ghita, 'Abd al-Rida. *Al-Anwar al-husayniyya wa al-sha'a'ir al-islamiyya*. Bombay, 1928/9. 2 pts.

Kashif al-Ghita, Muhammad al-Husayn. *Al-Ayat al-bayyinat fi qam' al-bida' wa al-dalalat*. Najaf, 1927.

———. *Al-Din wa al-islam aw al-da'wa al-islamiyya*. 2d ed. Sidon, 1912/3. 2 vols.

———. *Muhawarat al-imam al-muslih kashif al-ghita' al-shaykh muhammad al-husayn ma'a al-safirayn al-baritani wa al-amiriki fi baghdad*. 4th ed. Najaf, 1954.

Kasravi, Ahmad. *Al-tashayyu' wa al-shi'a*. Tehran, 1945.

Katib, Ahmad ibn Husayn. *Tajrubat al-thawra al-islamiyya fi al-'iraq, 1920–1980*. Tehran, 1980.

Kazimi, Muhammad Mahdi al-Musawi al-Isfahani. *Mu'jam al-qubur*. Baghdad, 1939.

Khafaji, 'Isam. *Al-Dawla wa al-tatawwur al-ra'smali fi al-'iraq, 1968–1978*. Cairo, 1983.

Khalili, Ja'far. *Hakadha 'araftuhum*. Baghdad, 1963–1968. 2 vols.

———. *Mawsu'at al-'atabat al-muqaddasa*. Baghdad and Beirut, 1965–1970. 10 vols.

Khalisi, Muhammad ibn Mahdi. *Al-'Uruba fi dar al-bawar fa-hal min munqidh: muqayasa bayn al-ghabir wa al-hadir wa-nazra ila al-mustaqbal*. Mashhad, n.d.

Khaqani, 'Ali. *Funun al-adab al-sha'bi*. Baghdad, 1962–1968. 8 vols.

———. *Shu'ara' al-ghari aw al-najafiyyat*. 2d ed. Qum, 1988. 12 vols.

———. *Shu'ara' al-hilla aw al-babiliyyat*. Baghdad, 1951–1953. 5 vols.

Khurasani, Mirza Mahdi al-Husayn. *Mu'jizat va-kiramat-i a'imma-yi athar*. Tehran, 1949.

Kilidar, 'Abd al-'Imad. *Ta'rikh karbala'*. Baghdad, 1949.

Kirkukli, Rasul. *Dawhat al-wuzara' fi ta'rikh waqa'i' baghdad al-zawra'*. Beirut and Baghdad, n.d.

Kubba, Muhammad Mahdi. *Mudhakkirati fi samim al-ahdath, 1918–1958*. Beirut, 1965.

Al-Lajna al-thaqafiyya li-madrasat al-imam amir al-mu'minin al-'ilmiyya. *Al-Qadiyya al-'iraqiyya min khilal mawqif al-imam al-shirazi*. Mashhad, 1981.

Mahallati, Dhabihallah. *Ma'athir al-kubara' fi ta'rikh samarra'*. Najaf and Tehran, 1948–1949. 3 vols.

Mahbuba, Ja'far Baqir. *Madi al-najaf wa-hadiruha*. Najaf, 1955–1958. 3 vols.

Mallah, Mahmud. *Al-Ara' al-sahiha li-bina' qawmiyya sahiha*. Baghdad, n.d.

———. *Ta'rikhuna al-qawmi bayn al-salb wa al-'ijab*. Baghdad, 1956.

———. *Al-Wahda al-islamiyya bayn al-akhdh wa al-radd*. Baghdad, 1951.

Marjani, Haydar. *Al-Najaf al-ashraf qadiman wa-hadithan*. Baghdad, 1986.

Mudarrisi, Murtaza. *Ta'rikh-i ravabit-i iran va-'iraq*. Tehran, 1973.

Mughniyya, Muhammad Jawad. *Al-Islam ma'a al-hayat*. Beirut, 1961.

———. *Ma'a 'ulama' al-najaf al-ashraf*. Beirut and Baghdad, 1962.

———. *Al-Majalis al-husayniyya*. Beirut, n.d.

———. *Min dha wa-dhak*. Beirut, 1979.

———. *Al-Shi'a fi al-mizan*. Beirut, n.d.

Muqarram, 'Abd al-Razzaq al-Musawi. *Al-'Abbas ibn al-imam amir al-mu'minin 'ali ibn abi talib*. Najaf, n.d.

———. *Maqtal al-husayn aw hadith karbala'*. Najaf, 1956.

Musawi, 'Abd al-Husayn Sharaf al-Din. *Al-Majalis al-fakhira fi ma'athim al-'itra al-tahira*. Najaf, 1967.

Musawi, 'Abd al-Sahib. *Harakat al-shi'r fi al-najaf al-ashraf wa-atwaruhu khilal al-qarn al-rabi' al-'ashara al-hijri: dirasa muqarina*. Beirut, 1988.

Musawi, Musa. *Al-Shi'a wa al-tashih: al-sira' bayn al-shi'a wa al-tashayyu'*. Cairo, 1989.

Muzaffar, 'Abd al-'Ali ibn Muhammad Hasan. *Al-Islam wa al-tatawwur al-ijtima'i*. Najaf, 1964.

Muzaffar, Muhammad Rida. *'Aqa'id al-imamiyya*. 2d ed. Cairo, 1961/2.

Nadwani, 'Abd al-Karim. *Ta'rikh al-'amara wa-'asha'iriha*. Baghdad, 1961.

Nadhmi, Wamidh Jamal 'Umar. *Al-Judhur al-siyasiyya wa al-fikriyya wa al-ijtima'iyya li al-haraka al-qawmiyya al-'arabiyya (al-istiqlaliyya) fi al-'iraq*. Beirut, 1984.

———. "Shi'at al-'iraq wa-qadiyat al-qawmiyya al-'arabiyya: al-dawr al-ta'rikhi qubayl al-istiqlal." *al-Mustaqbal al-'Arabi* 41 (1982): 74–100.

Nafisi, 'Abdallah Fahd. *Dawr al-shi'a fi tatawwur al-'iraq al-siyasi al-hadith*. Beirut, 1973.

Na'ini, Mirza Muhammad Husayn. *Tanbih al-umma wa-tanzih al-milla*. 3d ed. Tehran, 1955.

Nasir, Sattar Jabir. *Hawamish 'ala kitab 'ali al-wardi*. Baghdad, 1978.

Nawwar, 'Abd al-'Aziz Sulayman. *Ta'rikh al-'iraq al-hadith min nihayat hukm da'ud pasha ila nihayat hukm midhat pasha*. Cairo, 1968.

Pirzadeh, Hajji Muhammad 'Ali. *Safarnama-yi hajji pirzadeh*. Edited by Hafez Farman-Farmayan. Tehran, 1963. 2 vols.

Qassab, 'Abd al-'Aziz. *Min dhikrayati*. Beirut, 1962.

Qazwini, Mahdi. *Ansab al-qaba'il al-'iraqiyya*. Najaf, 1956/7.

Qazwini, Muhammad Hasan. *Al-Barahin al-jaliya fi raf' tashkikat al-wahhabiyya*. Najaf, 1927/8.

Qazwini, Muhammad al-Kazimi. *Al-Islam wa-waqi' al-muslim al-mu'asir*. Najaf, 1961/2.

Quchani, Agha Najafi. *Siyahat-i sharq ya zindeginama va-safarnama-yi agha najafi quchani*. Mashhad, 1972.

Qummi, 'Abbas. *Mafatih al-jinan*. Beirut, 1992.

Rahimi, 'Abd al-Halim. *Ta'rikh al-haraka al-islamiyya fi al-'iraq: al-judhur al-fikriyya wa al-waqi' al-ta'rikhi, 1900–1924*. Beirut, 1985.

Sa'idi, Hamud. *Dirasat 'an 'asha'ir al-'iraq: al-khaza'il*. Najaf, 1974.

Sa'di, Riyad Ibrahim. *Al-Hijra al-dakhiliyya li al-sukkan fi al-'iraq, 1947–1965*. Baghdad, 1976.

Salim, Shakir Mustafa. *Al-Chibayyish*. Baghdad, 1957. 2 vols.

Samarra'i, Kamil. *Al-Waqf: tasfiyatuhu wa al-qawanin al-khassa bi-hi*. Baghdad, 1968.

Samarra'i, Yunus Ibrahim. *Ta'rikh 'asha'ir samarra'*. Baghdad, 1961.

———. *Ta'rikh madinat samarra'*. Baghdad, 1968–1973. 3 vols.

Sarkis, Ya'qub. *Mabahith 'iraqiyya*. Baghdad, 1948–1981. 3 vols.

Sayf al-Dawla, Sultan Muhammad Farzand. *Safarnama-yi sayf al-dawla*. 2d ed. Tehran, n.d.

Shahrastani, Muhammad 'Ali Hibat al-Din al-Hasani. *Al-Dala'il wa al-masa'il*. Najaf, 1926.

Shahrudi, Nur al-Din. *Ta'rikh al-haraka al-'ilmiyya fi karbala'*. Beirut, 1990.

Shams al-Din, Muhammad 'Ali. *Al-Islah al-hadi: nazra fi fikr wa-suluk al-mujtahid al-sayyid muhsin al-amin al-husayni al-'amili*. Beirut, 1985.

Shams al-Din, Muhammad Mahdi. *Thawrat al-husayn fi al-wujdan al-sha'bi*. Beirut, 1980.

Sharqi, 'Ali. *Al-Ahlam*. Baghdad, 1963.

Sharqi, Talib 'Ali. *'Ayn al-tamr*. Najaf, 1969.

———. *Al-Najaf al-ashraf: 'adatuha wa-taqaliduha*. Najaf, 1978.

Suwaydi, Tawfiq. *Mudhakkirati: nisf qarn min ta'rikh al-'iraq wa al-qadiya al-'arabiyya*. Beirut, 1969.

Tahir, 'Abd al-Jalil. *Al-'Asha'ir al-'iraqiyya*. Beirut, 1972.

Tamimi, Muhammad 'Ali Ja'far. *Mashhad al-imam aw madinat al-Najaf*. Najaf, 1954. 2 vols.

Tu'ma, 'Abd al-Husayn al-Kilidar. *Bughyat al-nubala' fi ta'rikh karbala'*. Baghdad, 1966.

Tu'ma, 'Abd al-Jawad al-Kilidar. *Ta'rikh karbala' wa-ha'ir al-husayn 'alayhi al-salam*. 2d ed. Najaf, 1967.

Tu'ma, Salman Hadi. *Turath karbala'*. Karbala, 1964.

Tunakabuni, Mirza Muhammad. *Qisas al-'ulama'*. Tehran, n.d.

'Uraym, 'Abd al-Jabbar. *Al-Qaba'il al-rahhal fi al-'iraq*. Baghdad, 1965.

Uzri, 'Abd al-Karim. *Mushkilat al-hukm fi al-'iraq*. London, 1991.

———. *Ta'rikh fi dhikrayat al-'iraq, 1930–1958*. Beirut, 1982.

Wada'a, Naji. *Lamahat min ta'rikh al-najaf*. Najaf, 1973.

Wahhab, 'Abd al-Razzaq. *Karbala' fi al-ta'rikh*. Baghdad, 1935.

Wa'ili, Ahmad. *Hawiyat al-tashayyu'*. Beirut, 1980.

Wa'ili, Ibrahim. *Al-Shi'r al-siyasi al-'iraqi fi al-qarn al-tasi' 'ashara*. Baghdad, 1961.

———. *Thawrat al-'ishrin fi al-shi'r al-'iraqi*. Baghdad, 1968.

Wa'iz, Ra'uf. *Al-Ittijahat al-wataniyya fi al-shi'r al-'iraqi al-hadith, 1914–1941*. Baghdad, 1974.

Wardi, 'Ali. *Al-Ahlam bayn al-'ilm wa al-'aqida*. Baghdad, 1959.

———. *Dirasa fi tabi'at al-mujtama' al-'iraqi*. Baghdad, 1965.

———. *Lamahat 'ijtima'iyya min ta'rikh al-'iraq al-hadith*. Baghdad, 1969–1978. 6 vols.

———. *Wu"az al-salatin*. Baghdad, 1954.

Zanjani, Ibrahim al-Musawi. *'Aqa'id al-imamiyya al-ithna 'ashariyya*. 2d ed. Beirut, 1973–1977. 3 vols.

PUBLISHED WORKS IN OTHER LANGUAGES

Abrahamian, Ervand. *Iran Between Two Revolutions*. 2d ed. Princeton, 1983.

Adams, Doris G. *Iraq's People and Resources*. Berkeley, 1958.

Akhavi, Shahrough. *Religion and Politics in Contemporary Iran: Clergy-State Relations in the Pahlavi Period*. Albany, 1980.

Algar, Hamid. *Religion and State in Iran, 1758–1906: The Role of the Ulama in the Qajar Period*. Berkeley, 1969.

Amanat, Abbas. "In Between the Madrasa and the Marketplace: The Designation of Clerical Leadership in Modern Shi'ism." In *Authority and Political Culture in Shi'ism*, edited by Said Amir Arjomand, 98–132. New York, 1988.

Amin, Hasan. *Islamic Shi'ite Encyclopedia*. Beirut, 1973. 4 vols.

Arjomand, Said Amir. *The Shadow of God and the Hidden Imam: Religion, Political Order, and Societal Change in Shi'ite Iran from the Beginning to 1890*. 2d ed. Chicago, 1987.

———. *The Turban For the Crown: The Islamic Revolution in Iran*. Oxford, 1988.

Atiyya, Ghassan. *Iraq, 1908–1921: A Socio-Political Study*. Beirut, 1973.

Axelgard, Frederick. *A New Iraq? The Gulf War and Implications for U.S. Policy*. The Washington Papers/133. New York, 1988.

Ayoub, Mahmoud. *Redemptive Suffering in Islam: A Study of the Devotional Aspects of 'Ashura' in Twelver Shi'ism*. The Hague, 1978.

Aziz, T. M. "The Role of Muhammad Baqir al-Sadr in Shi'i Political Activism in Iraq from 1958 to 1980." *International Journal of Middle East Studies* 25 (1993): 207–22.

Baali, Fuad. *The Relation of the People to the Land in Southern Iraq*. Gainesville, 1966.

————. "Social Factors in Iraqi Rural-Urban Migration." *American Journal of Economics and Society* 25 (1966): 359–64.

Bakhash, Shaul. *The Reign of the Ayatollahs: Iran and the Islamic Revolution.* New York, 1984.

————. "Iran." *The American Historical Review* 96 (1991): 1479–96.

Baram, Amatzia. "From Radicalism to Radical Pragmatism: The Shi'ite Fundamentalist Opposition Movements of Iraq." In *Islamic Fundamentalisms and the Gulf Crisis,* edited by James Piscatori, 28–51. Chicago, 1991.

————. "The Radical Shi'ite Opposition Movements in Iraq." In *Religious Radicalism and Politics in the Middle East,* edited by Emmanuel Sivan and Menachem Friedman, 95–125. New York, 1990.

————. "The Ruling Political Elite in Ba'thi Iraq, 1968–1986: The Changing Features of a Collective Profile." *International Journal of Middle East Studies* 21 (1989): 447–93.

Batatu, Hanna. *The Old Social Classes and the Revolutionary Movements in Iraq.* 2d ed. Princeton, 1982.

————. "Class Analysis and Iraqi Society." *Peuples Medit* 8 (1979): 101–16.

————. "Iraq's Shi'a, Their Political Role, and the Processes of their Integration into Society." In *The Islamic Impulse,* edited by Barbara Stowasser, 204–13. London, 1987.

————. "Iraq's Underground Shi'a Movements: Characteristics, Causes and Prospects." *Middle East Journal* 35 (1981): 578–94.

————. "Shi'i Organizations in Iraq: al-Da'wah al-Islamiyah and al-Mujahidin." In *Shi'ism and Social Protest,* edited by Juan Cole and Nikki Keddie, 179–200. New Haven, 1986.

Bengio, Ofra. "Shi'is and Politics in Ba'thi Iraq." *Middle Eastern Studies* 21 (1985): 1–14.

————. "Ha-Shi'im be-'Iraq bi-Tzvat ha-Dat ve ha-Medina." In *Protest and Revolution in Shi'i Islam* (hebrew), edited by Martin Kramer, 60–88. Tel-Aviv, 1985.

Berque, Jacques. "Hier à Naǧaf et Karbala." *Arabica* 9 (1962): 325–42.

Blunt, Lady Anne. *Bedouin Tribes of the Euphrates.* New York, 1879.

Buxton, P. A. and V.H.W. Dowson. "The Marsh Arabs of Lower Mesopotamia." *Indian Antiquary* 50 (1921): 289–97.

Campbell, C. G., ed. and trans. *Tales from the Arab Tribes: A Collection of the Stories Told by the Arab Tribes of the Lower Euphrates.* London, 1949.

Chapple, Joe Mitchel. *To Baghdad and Back.* Boston, 1928.

Chelkowski, Peter, ed. *Ta'ziyeh: Ritual and Drama in Iran.* New York, 1979.

Cleveland, William. *The Making of an Arab Nationalist: Ottomanism and Arabism in the Life of Sati' al-Husri.* Princeton, 1971.

Cole, Juan. *Roots of North Indian Shi'ism in Iran and Iraq: Religion and State in Awadh, 1722–1859.* Berkeley, 1988.

————. "Indian Money and the Holy Shrines of Iraq." *Middle Eastern Studies* 22 (1986): 461–80.

————. "Shi'i Clerics in Iraq and Iran, 1722–1780: The Akhbari-Usuli Conflict Reconsidered." *Iranian Studies* 28 (1985): 3–33.

Cole, Juan and Moojan Momen. "Mafia, Mob and Shiism in Iraq: The Rebellion of Ottoman Karbala, 1824–1843." *Past and Present* 112 (1986): 112–43.

Cowper, H. *Through Turkish Arabia: A Journey from the Mediterranean to Bombay by the Euphrates and Tigris Valleys and the Persian Gulf*. London, 1894, reprint 1987.

Dann, Uriel. *Iraq Under Qassem: A Political History, 1958–1963*. New York, 1969.

De Groot, Joanna. "Mullas and Merchants: The Basis of Religious Politics in Nineteenth Century Iran." *Mashriq* 2 (1983): 11–36.

Deringil, Selim. "Legitimacy Structures in the Ottoman State: The Reign of Abdülhamid II (1876–1909)." *International Journal of Middle East Studies* 23 (1991): 345–59.

———. "The Struggle Against Shi'ism in Hamidian Iraq: A Study in Ottoman Counter-Propaganda." *Die Welt des Islams* 30 (1990): 45–62.

Dieulafoy, Jane Madame. *La Perse, la Chaldée, et la Susiane*. Paris, 1887.

Donaldson, Dwight. *The Shi'ite Religion: A History of Islam in Persia and Iraq*. London, 1933.

Dowson, Sir Ernest. *An Inquiry into Land Tenure and Related Questions*. Letchworth, 1931.

Drower, E. S. Stevens Lady. *By Tigris and Euphrates*. London, 1923.

———. "Marsh People of South Iraq." *Journal of the Royal Central Asian Society* 34 (1947): 83–90.

Enayat, Hamid. *Modern Islamic Political Thought*. Austin, 1982.

Ende, Werner. "Ehe auf Zeit (*mut'a*) in der Innerislamischen Diskussion der Gegenwart." *Die Welt des Islams* 20 (1980): 1–43.

———. "Eine Schiitische Kontroverse über *Naql al-Ğana'iz*." *Zeitschrift der Deutschen Morgenländischen Gesellschaft*, suppl. 4 (Wiesbaden, 1980), 217–18.

———. "Erfolg und Scheitern eines schiitischen Modernisten: Muhammad ibn Muhammad Mahdi al-Halisi." In *Gottes ist der Orient Gottes ist der Okzident*, 120–30. Cologne, 1991.

———. "The Flagellation of Muharram and the Shi'ite 'Ulama'." *Der Islam* 55 (1978): 19–36.

———. "Iraq in World War I: The Turks, the Germans and the Shi'ite Mujtahids' Call for Jihad." In *Proceedings of the Ninth Congress of Union Européenne des Arabisants et Islamisants, Amsterdam, 1978*, edited by R. Peters, 57–71. Leiden, 1981.

Farouk-Sluglett, Marion and Peter Sluglett. *Iraq Since 1958: From Revolution to Dictatorship*. London, 1987.

———. "The Historiography of Modern Iraq." *The American Historical Review* 96 (1991): 1408–21.

———. "Some Reflections on the Present State of Sunni/Shi'i Relations in Iraq." *Bulletin of the British Society for Middle Eastern Studies* 5 (1978): 79–87.

———. "The Transformation of Land and Rural Social Structure in Central and Southern Iraq, 1870–1958." *International Journal of Middle East Studies* 15 (1983): 491–505.

Fernea, Elizabeth. *Guests of the Sheik: An Anthropology of an Iraqi Village*. 2d ed. New York, 1969.

Fernea, Robert. *Shaykh and Effendi: Changing Patterns of Authority among the El-Shabana of Southern Iraq.* Cambridge, Mass., 1970.

Fernea, Robert, and Wm. Roger Louis, eds. *The Iraqi Revolution of 1958: The Old Social Classes Revisited.* London, 1991.

Fischer, Michael. *Iran: From Religious Dispute to Revolution.* Cambridge, Mass., 1980.

Fraser, James Baillie. *Travels in Koordistan and Mesopotamia with Sketches of the Character and Manners of the Koordish and Arab Tribes.* London, 1840.

———. *Narrative of a Journey into Khorasan in the Years 1821 and 1822.* London, 1825.

Fulanain. *The Marsh Arab Haji Rikkan.* Philadelphia, 1928.

Garthwaite, Gene. *Khans and Shahs: A Documentary Analysis of the Bakhtiyari in Iran.* Cambridge, 1983.

Gotlieb, Yosef. "Sectarianism and the Iraqi State." In *Religion and Politics in the Middle East,* edited by Michael Curtis, 153–61. Boulder, 1981.

Haim, Sylvia G. "Shi'ite Clerics and Politics: Some Recent Tendencies." *Israel Oriental Studies* 10 (1980): 165–72.

Hairi, Abdul-Hadi. *Shi'ism and Constitutionalism in Iran.* Leiden, 1977.

———. "The Legitimacy of the Early Qajar Rule as Viewed by the Shi'i Religious Leaders." *Middle Eastern Studies* 24 (1988): 271–86.

———. "Why Did the *Ulama* Participate in the Persian Constitutional Revolution of 1905–1909?" *Die Welt des Islams* 17 (1976–77): 327–39.

Haj, Samira. "The Problems of Tribalism: The Case of Nineteenth-Century Iraqi History." *Social History* 16 (1991): 45–58.

Harris, George. *Iraq: Its People, its Society, its Culture.* New Haven, 1958.

Hasan, M. S. "Growth and Structure of Iraq's Population, 1867–1947." *Bulletin of the Oxford University, Institute of Economics and Statistics* 20 (1958): 339–52.

Heine, Peter, ed. *Al-Rafidayn, Jahrbuch zu Geschichte und Kultur des Modernen Iraq* 1 (Würzburg, 1991): 9–90; 2 (Würzburg, 1993): 5–110.

———. "Ross ohne Reiter: Überlegungen zu den Ta'ziya-Feiern der Schiiten des Iraq." *Zeitschrift für Missionswissenschaft und Religionswissenschaft* 63 (1979): 25–33.

———. "Traditionelle Formen und Stadt Nadjaf/Iraq." *Zeitschrift für Missionswissenschaft und Religionswissenschaft* 74 (1990): 204–18.

Helms, Christine. *Iraq: Eastern Flank of the Arab World.* Washington, D.C., 1984.

Imber, C. H. "The Persecution of the Ottoman Shi'ites according to the Mühimme Defterleri 1565–1585." *Der Islam* 56 (1979): 245–73.

Ireland, Philip. *Iraq: A Study in Political Development.* New York, 1938, reprint 1970.

Jamali, Fadil. "The Theological Colleges of Najaf." *The Moslem World* 59 (1960): 15–22.

Jwaideh, Albertine. "Aspects of Land Tenure and Social Change in Lower Iraq during Late Ottoman Times." In *Land Tenure and Social Transformation in the Middle East,* edited by Tarif Khalidi, 333–56. Beirut, 1984.

———. "Midhat Pasha and the Land System of Lower Iraq." In *St. Antony's Papers: Middle Eastern Affairs* 3, edited by Albert Hourani, 106–36. London, 1963.

Keddie, Nikki. *Iran: Religion, Politics and Society*. London, 1980.

———. *Religion and Rebellion in Iran: The Tobacco Protest of 1891–1892*. London, 1966.

———. "The Origins of the Religious-Radical Alliance in Iran." *Past and Present* 34 (1966): 70–80.

———. "The Roots of the Ulama's Power in Modern Iran." *Studia Islamica* 29 (1969): 31–53.

Kedourie, Elie. *The Chatham House Version and Other Middle Eastern Studies*. London, 1970.

———. *England and the Middle East: The Vital Years, 1914–1921*. London, 1956.

———. "Anti-Shiism in Iraq under the Monarchy." *Middle Eastern Studies* 24 (1988): 249–53.

———. "Continuity and Change in Modern Iraqi History." *Asian Affairs* 62 (1975): 140–46.

———. "The Iraqi Shiʻis and Their Fate." In *Shiʻism, Resistance and Revolution*, edited by Martin Kramer, 135–57. Boulder, 1987.

———. "Réflexion sur l'Histoire du Royaume d'Irak, 1921–1958." *Orient* 11 (1959): 55–77.

———. "The Shiite Issue in Iraqi Politics, 1941." *Middle Eastern Studies* 24 (1988): 495–500.

Kelidar, Abbas. *Iraq: the Search for Stability*. London, 1975.

———, ed. *The Integration of Modern Iraq*. London, 1979.

———. "The Shii Imami Community and Politics in the Arab East." *Middle Eastern Studies* 19 (1983): 3–16.

Khadduri, Majid. *Independent Iraq, 1932–1958*. Oxford, 1961.

———. *Republican Iraq: A Study in Iraqi Politics since the Revolution of 1958*. London, 1969.

Khalil, Samir. *The Monument: Art, Vulgarity and Responsibility in Iraq*. Berkeley, 1991.

———. *Republic of Fear: The Inside Story of Saddam's Iraq*. Berkeley, 1989, New York reprint, 1990.

Lambton, Ann. *Landlord and Peasant in Persia*. Oxford, 1969.

———. *Qajar Persia*. London, 1987.

———. "A Reconsideration of the Position of the *Marjaʻ al-Taqlid* and the Religious Institution." *Studia Islamica* 20 (1964): 115–35.

———. "Social Change in Persia in the Nineteenth Century." *Asian and African Studies* 15 (1981): 123–48.

Loftus, William Kennett. *Travels and Researches in Chaldaea and Susiana*. London, 1857.

Longrigg, Stephen. *Four Centuries of Modern Iraq*. Oxford, 1925, Beirut reprint, 1968.

———. *Iraq, 1900 to 1950*. Oxford, 1953.

Luizard, Pierre-Jean. *La Formation de l'Irak Contemporain: Le Rôle Politique des Uléma Chiites à la Fin de la Domination Ottomane et au Moment de la Construction de l'Etat Irakien*. Paris, 1991.

———. "La Construction de l'Etat et la Defaite des Ulamas Chiites en Irak: Mythe

National et Verites Historiques." In *Etudes Politique du Monde Arabe*, edited by Jean Claude Vatin, 117–49. Dossier du CEDEJ, Cairo, 1991.

Lyell, Thomas. *The Ins and Outs of Mesopotamia*. London, 1923.

Makiya, Kanan. *Cruelty and Silence: War, Tyranny, Uprising and the Arab World*. New York, 1993.

Mallat, Chibli. *The Renewal of Islamic Law: Muhammad Baqer as-Sadr, Najaf and the Shi'i International*. Cambridge, 1993.

———. "Iraq." In *The Politics of Islamic Revivalism*, edited by Shireen Hunter, 71–87. Bloomington, 1988.

———. "Religious Militancy in Contemporary Iraq: Muhammad Baqer as-Sadr and the Sunni-Shia Paradigm." *Third World Quarterly* 10 (1988): 699–729.

Marr, Phebe. *The Modern History of Iraq*. New York, 1985.

Martin, Pierre. "Les Chi'ites d'Irak: Une Majorité Dominée à la Recherche de son Destin." *Peuples Méditerranéens* 40 (1987): 127–69.

———. "Le Clergé Chiite en Irak Hier et Aujourd'hui." *Maghreb Machrek* 115 (1987): 29–52.

Un Mèsopotamien. "Le Programme des Études ches les Chiites et Principalment ches ceux de Nedjef." *Revue du Monde Musulman* 23 (1913): 268–79.

Momen, Moojan. *An Introduction To Shi'i Islam*. New Haven, 1985.

Mottahedeh, Roy. *The Mantle of the Prophet*. New York, 1985.

Musil, Alois. *The Middle Euphrates: A Topographical Itinerary*. New York, 1927.

Nakash, Yitzhak. "An Attempt to Trace the Origin of the Rituals of *'Ashura'*." *Die Welt des Islams* 33 (1993): 161–81.

———. "The Conversion of Iraq's Tribes to Shi'ism." *International Journal of Middle East Studies* 26 (1994): 443–63.

———. "The Visitation of the Shrines of the Imams and the Shi'i Mujtahids in the Early Twentieth Century." *Studia Islamica* 81 (1995): 153–64.

Nieuwenhuis, Tom. *Politics and Society in Early Modern Iraq: Mamluk Pashas, Tribal Shaykhs and Local Rule between 1802 and 1831*. The Hague, 1982.

Peters, John Punnett. *Nippur or Explorations and Adventures on the Euphrates*. 2d ed. New York, 1898.

Phillips, Doris G. "Rural Migration in Iraq." *Economic Development and Cultural Change* 7 (1959): 405–21.

Pinault, David. *The Shiites: Ritual and Popular Piety in a Muslim Community*. New York, 1992.

Pistor-Hatam, Anja. "Pilger, Pest und Cholera: Die Wallfahrt zu den Heiligen Stätten im Irak als Gesundheitspolitisches Problem im 19. Jahrhundert." *Die Welt des Islams* 31 (1991): 228–45.

Sachedina, 'Abd al-'Aziz. *The Just Ruler (al-Sultan al-'adil) in Shi'ite Islam*. Oxford, 1988.

Salim, Shakir Mustafa. *Marsh Dwellers of the Euphrates*. London, 1962.

———. "Traditional Stratification among the Marsh Dwellers." In *Peoples and Cultures of the Middle East*, edited by Ailon Shiloh, 205–15. New York, 1969.

Shikara, Ahmad. *Iraqi Politics, 1921–1941: The Interaction Between Domestic Politics and Foreign Policy*. London, 1987.

Simon, Reeva. *Iraq Between the Two World Wars: The Creation and Implementation of a Nationalist Ideology*. New York, 1986.

Sluglett, Peter. *Britain in Iraq, 1914–1932*. London, 1976.

Spooner, B. J. "The Function of Religion in Persian Society." *Iran* 1 (1963): 83–95.

Tabataba'i, Hossein Modarressi. *An Introduction to Shi'i Law: A Bibliographical Study*. London, 1984.

Tarbush, Mohammad. *The Role of the Military in Politics: A Case Study of Iraq to 1941*. London, 1982.

Teixeira, Pedro. *The Travels of Pedro Teixeira*. Translated by William Sinclair. London, 1802.

Thaiss, Gustav. "The Bazaar as a Case Study of Religion and Social Change." In *Iran Faces the Seventies*, edited by E. Yar-shater, 189–216. New York, 1971.

———. "Religious Symbolism and Social Change: The Drama of Husayn." In *Scholars, Saints, and Sufis*, edited by Nikki Keddie, 349–66. Berkeley, 1972.

Thesiger, Wilfred. *The Marsh Arabs*. London, 1964.

Ussher, John. *A Journey from London to Persepolis*. London, 1865.

Vinogradov, Amal. "The 1920 Revolt in Iraq Reconsidered: The Role of Tribes in National Politics." *International Journal of Middle East Studies* 3 (1972): 123–39.

Westphal-Hellbusch Sigrid, and Heinz Westphal. *Die Ma'dan: Kultur und Geschichte der Marschenbewohner im Süd-Iraq*. Berlin, 1962.

Wiley, Joyce. *The Islamic Movement of Iraqi Shi'as*. Boulder, 1992.

Wilson, A. T. *Loyalties: Mesopotamia, 1914–1917*. London, 1930.

———. *Mesopotamia, 1917–1920: A Clash of Loyalties*. London, 1931.

Young, Gavin. *Return to the Marshes: Life with the Marsh Arabs of Iraq*. London, 1977.

Zubaida, Sami. *Islam, the People, and the State*. London, 1989.

INDEX